Fiduciary Law and Responsible Investing

This book is about fiduciary law's influence on the financial economy's environmental performance, focusing on how the law affects responsible investing and considering possible legal reforms to shift financial markets closer towards sustainability. Fiduciary law governs how trustees, fund managers or other custodians administer the investment portfolios owned by beneficiaries. Written for a diverse audience, not just legal scholars, the book examines in a multi-jurisdictional context an array of philosophical, institutional and economic issues that have shaped the movement for responsible investing and its legal framework. Fiduciary law has acquired greater influence in the financial economy in tandem with the extraordinary recent growth of institutional funds such as pension plans and insurance company portfolios. While the fiduciary prejudice against responsible investing has somewhat waned in recent years, owing mainly to reinterpretations of fiduciary and trust law, significant barriers remain.

This book advances the notion of 'nature's trust' to metaphorically signal how fiduciary responsibility should accommodate society's dependence on long-term environmental well-being. Financial institutions, managing vast investment portfolios on behalf of millions of beneficiaries, should manage those investments with regard to the broader social interest in sustaining ecological health. Even for their own financial self-interest, investors over the long-term should benefit from maintaining nature's capital. We should expect everyone to act in nature's trust, from individual funds to market regulators. The ancient public trust doctrine could be refashioned for stimulating this change, and sovereign wealth funds should take the lead in pioneering best practices for environmentally responsible investing.

Benjamin J. Richardson holds the Senior Canada Research Chair in Environmental Law & Sustainability at the University of British Columbia, Canada, and is an Adjunct Professor at the Macquarie University Law School, Australia.

Routledge Research in Finance and Banking Law

Available:

European Prudential Banking Regulation and Supervision
The Legal Dimension
Larisa Dragomir

International Secured Transactions Law
Facilitation of Credit and International Conventions and Instruments
Orkun Akseli

The Legal and Regulatory Aspects of Islamic Banking
A comparative look at the United Kingdom and Malaysia
Abdul Karim Aldohni

Banking Secrecy and Offshore Financial Centres
Money Laundering and Offshore Banking
Mary Alice Young

Fiduciary Law and Responsible Investing
In Nature's Trust
Benjamin J. Richardson

Forthcoming:

Competition Law and Financial Services
David Harrison

Redefining the Market-State Relationship
Responses to the financial crisis and the future of regulation
Ioannis Glinavos

Fiduciary Law and Responsible Investing
In Nature's Trust

Benjamin J. Richardson

LONDON AND NEW YORK

First published 2013
by Routledge
2 Park Square, Milton Park, Abingdon, Oxfordshire OX14 4RN

Simultaneously published in the USA and Canada
by Routledge
711 Third Avenue, New York, NY 10017

First issued in paperback 2015

Routledge is an imprint of the Taylor & Francis Group, an informa business

© 2013 Benjamin J. Richardson

The right of Benjamin J. Richardson to be identified as author of this work has been asserted by him in accordance with sections 77 and 78 of the Copyright, Designs and Patents Act 1988.

All rights reserved. No part of this book may be reprinted or reproduced or utilised in any form or by any electronic, mechanical, or other means, now known or hereafter invented, including photocopying and recording, or in any information storage or retrieval system, without permission in writing from the publishers.

Trademark notice: Product or corporate names may be trademarks or registered trademarks, and are used only for identification and explanation without intent to infringe.

British Library Cataloguing in Publication Data
A catalogue record for this book is available from the British Library

Library of Congress Cataloguing in Publication Data
Library of Congress Cataloging-in-Publication Data
Richardson, Benjamin J.
 Fiduciary law and responsible investing : in nature's trust / Benjamin J. Richardson.
  p. cm.
 ISBN 978-0-415-69136-9 (hardback) — ISBN 978-0-203-37033-9 (e-book) 1. Investments—Law and legislation—Moral and ethical aspects. 2. Investments—Environmental aspects. 3. Trusts and trustees—Investments—Environmental aspects. 4. Trusts and trustees—Philosophy. 5. Financial institutions—Investments—Environmental aspects. 6. Sustainability—Economic aspects. I. Title.
 K1112.R528 2013
 346'.092—dc23
 2012040379

ISBN13: 978-1-138-93010-0 (pbk)
ISBN13: 978-0-415-69136-9 (hbk)

Typeset in Garamond
by Keystroke, Station Road, Codsall, Wolverhampton

Contents

Acknowledgements vii
Abbreviations ix

1　Responsible investing in an unsustainable world　　1

2　The influence of responsible investment　　43

3　Fiduciary finance law　　101

4　Fiduciary law in retail and institutional finance　　153

5　Sovereign wealth funds　　227

6　The public fiduciary: in nature's trust　　267

Index　　319

Acknowledgements

Completion of this book would not have been possible without the support of many people. I first and foremost offer thanks to my recent student research assistants at the law schools of the University of British Columbia (UBC) and York University, especially Nicole Bakker, Amanda Branch, Zelius Kleefstra, Maziar Peihani, Zoe Si, Georgia Tanner and Meghan Trepanier. With much perseverance, they helped deepen the research and insight. They also helped me with a number of earlier publications from which portions of this book draw on, including articles in the *Nordic Journal of Commercial Law*, *European Company Law* and the *Journal of Sustainable Finance and Investment*. I am also indebted to a number of academic colleagues and experts in the finance industry whom I consulted during my research, including Peter Chapman (SHARE), Jackie Cook (Fund Votes), Ron Davis (UBC), Tessa Hebb (Carleton University), Ola Mestad (Norway's Council on Ethics) and Christie Stephenson (Ethical Funds). They enriched my outlook on the issues covered herein. Special thanks also to Lisa Gourd and Francine Geraci for their editing of the text with great care and efficiency. I also appreciate the generous financial support of the Canadian Social Sciences and Humanities Research Council, whose grant supported my fieldwork, conference participation and recruitment of student assistants. Finally, I wish to thank the editorial team at Routledge for their expertise and diligence in publishing this book expeditiously.

Abbreviations

ABA	American Bar Association
ACF	Australian Conservation Foundation
ACSI	Australian Council of Superannuation Investors
ALI	American Law Institute
ANZ	Australian and New Zealand Banking Group
ASIC	Australian Securities and Investments Commission
CalPERS	California Public Employees Retirement System
CDP	Carbon Disclosure Project
CERCLA	Comprehensive Environmental Response, Compensation and Liability Act
Ceres	Coalition for Environmentally Responsible Economies
CO_2	Carbon dioxide
CPP	Canada Pension Plan
CPPIB	Canada Pension Plan Investment Board
CRA	Community Reinvestment Act
CSA	Canadian Securities Administrators
CSR	Corporate social responsibility
DB	Defined benefit
DC	Defined contribution
EAI	Enhanced Analytics Initiative
EBSA	Employee Benefits Security Administration
EC	European Commission
EIRIS	Ethical Investment Research Services
EMAS	Eco-Management and Audit Scheme
EMS	Environmental management systems
EPs	Equator Principles
EPA	Environmental Protection Agency
ERISA	Employee Retirement Income Security Act
ESG	Environmental, social and governance
ESV	Enlightened shareholder value
EU	European Union
Eurosif	European Social Investment Forum
FRR	French Pension Reserve Funds

FSA	Financial Services Authority
GAAP	Generally Accepted Accounting Principles
GATS	General Agreement on Trade in Services
GCSD	German Council for Sustainable Development
GDP	Gross domestic product
GFC	Global financial crisis
GHG	Greenhouse gases
GNZS	Guardians of New Zealand Superannuation
GRI	Global Reporting Initiative
IASB	International Accounting Standards Board
ICCR	Interfaith Center on Corporate Responsibility
ICMIF	International Cooperative and Mutual Insurance Federation
IFC	International Finance Corporation
IIROC	Investment Industry Regulatory Organization of Canada
ILO	International Labor Organization
IMF	International Monetary Fund
ISO	International Organization for Standardization
IUCN	International Union for Conservation of Nature
JSE	Johannesburg Stock Exchange
MEA	Millenium Ecosystem Assessment
MPT	Modern portfolio theory
NBIM	Norges Bank Investment Management
NEMA	National Environmental Management Act (South Africa)
NEST	National Employment Savings Trust
NGO	Nongovernmental organization
NGPF-G	Norwegian Global Pension Fund-Global
NRTEE	National Round Table on the Environment and the Economy
NZSF	New Zealand Superannuation Fund
OECD	Organization for Economic Cooperation and Development
OPCVM	Organisme de placement collectif en valeurs mobilières
PDS	Product disclosure statement
PWMC	Pax World Management Corporation
RI	Responsible investment/investing
S&P	Standard and Poor's
SEC	Securities and Exchange Commission
SEIA	Social and environmental impact assessment
SHARE	Shareholder Association for Research and Education
SI	Sophisticated investor
SIO	Social Investment Organization (Canada)
SRI	Socially responsible investment/investing
SWF	Sovereign wealth fund
TIAA-CREF	Teachers Insurance and Annuity Association, College Retirement Equities Fund
UK	United Kingdom
UKSIF	United Kingdom Social Investment Forum

UN	United Nations
UNDP	United Nations Development Programme
UNEP-FI	United Nations Environment Programme-Finance Initiative
UNPRI	United Nations Principles for Responsible Investment
US	United States
US-SIF	US Forum for Sustainable and Responsible Investment
USS	Universities Superannuation Scheme
WBCSD	World Business Council for Sustainable Development
WEF	World Economic Forum
WTO	World Trade Organization
WWF	Worldwide Fund for Nature

1 Responsible investing in an unsustainable world

Fiduciary finance for the wealth of the planet

This book is about the influence of fiduciary law on the financial economy and its environmental performance. It focuses on how fiduciary law affects responsible investing (RI) and investigates possible reforms that might shift financial markets closer to sustainability – or 'environmentally sustainable development'. Alongside the recent growth of institutional investment, fiduciary law has assumed an ever-increasing role in the financial economy. Pension plans, insurance companies and other institutional investors that manage portfolios on behalf of millions of beneficiaries have fiduciary or fiduciary-like obligations.

In a world beset by the intertwined crises afflicting financial markets and the planetary environment, reforming fiduciary finance law in order to promote RI has never been more urgent. The global financial crisis (GFC) that erupted in 2008 revealed both profound weaknesses in the conventional paradigm of market finance and a need to rethink its fundamental tenets and purpose. Another emerging crisis stems from the rapid degradation of life-sustaining natural resources, which threatens the livelihoods and prosperity of not just future generations but also those living today. Climate change looms as the most ominous such threat. While finance capitalism has been extensively excoriated for being a vector of economic crisis,[1] its contribution to environmental *unsustainability* is less acknowledged.[2] Both the GFC and environmental crises stem from similar fundamental dysfunctions of the market economy – it lacks an innate mechanism to manage systemic risks, and it fails to take into account very long-term considerations such as global warming.

Responsible investment is a beguilingly simple yet conceptually elusive term, definable in a myriad of ways. I use it in two senses: descriptively, to

---

1 See R.J. Shiller, *Irrational Exuberance*, Princeton University Press, 2000; J. Bogle, *The Battle for the Soul of Capitalism*, Yale University Press, 2005; F. Jameson, 'Culture and finance capitalism', *Critical Inquiry* 24(1), 1997, 246–65.
2 But see W. Sun, C. Louche and R. Pérez (eds), *Finance and Sustainability: Towards a New Paradigm? A Post-Crisis Agenda*, Emerald Books, 2011.

refer to various forms of investing and financing that purport to take into account social, environmental and other non-financial criteria; and normatively, about what RI *ought* to be. The lack of any authoritative, universal agreement on RI partly reflects diverse ethical positions investors have in a socially heterogeneous world, as well as the diverse reasons that motivate people even when they share the same investment goal. For example, two investors might take the same action (e.g., to divest from a company that exploits sweatshop labour), but one might act because she believes that sweatshops are unethical, and the other because he believes that sweatshops pose a reputational risk to the company's financial prospects. Thus, although this book often refers to the RI 'movement' or 'sector', we should appreciate that its practitioners are heterogeneous, and many might not even regard themselves as RI adherents but rather as savvy investors who scrutinize social and environmental issues purely for financial prudence.

Methodologically, it is even more difficult to forge a normative position about what RI should be. However, at least in regard to very serious environmental activities or impacts, such as climate change, some parameters on which investments qualify as RI can be defined. Responsible investing should be attentive to long-term environmental issues that underpin a sustainable investing portfolio. Furthermore, in the absence of agreement on other seemingly less fundamental RI issues, investment procedures can provide a focal point around which more transparent, informed and democratic ethical deliberation about our investment decisions can occur.

Fiduciary law is a crucial element of this task. This book takes an expansive view of 'fiduciary finance law', whereby it encompasses not only conventional legal doctrine about fiduciary responsibility as pioneered by the English courts of equity but also a range of quasi-fiduciary relationships and standards found in statutory regulation, codes of conduct and other sources. While the fiduciary prejudice against RI has waned in recent years, owing mainly to reinterpretations of the law, significant barriers remain. This book advances the notion of 'nature's trust' metaphorically to signal how fiduciary responsibility should accommodate society's dependence on long-term environmental well-being. Financial institutions, as managers of vast assets for millions of people, and with the capacity for significant environmental repercussions from the businesses and projects they invest in, should have public-like responsibilities to manage those investments with regard to the social interest in sustaining ecological integrity. Even for their own financial self-interest, investors over the long term should benefit by not depleting natural capital. Acting in nature's trust should apply not only to individual funds but also to those who regulate the market. As the ultimate managers of nature's trust, government regulators must help increase or at least preserve the value of that trust. The ancient public trust doctrine could be refashioned for this task, coupled with changes to the governance of financial institutions to promote more environmentally reflective and compassionate decision-making.

Behind these proposals is the goal of 'sustainability'. This concept essentially means passing on to future generations undiminished environmental/natural capital such as clean water, predictable climate, an intact ozone layer, productive soils and ample biodiversity. Prevailing modes of capital investment tend to assume that natural and non-natural capital are interchangeable substitutes. Depletion of non-renewable natural resources such as oil and gas is assumed to be worthwhile, as their economic development converts natural resources into new forms of human capital to improve living standards for the benefit of present and future generations. The plausibility of this model is not readily extendable to multi-functional ecological services such as the nutrient cycle and the hydrologic cycle – irreplaceable complex services of enormous economic benefit.

All investing should safeguard non-substitutable natural capital by boosting funding for resource efficiency, clean and low-carbon technologies, climate adaptation, ecosystem improvement and other ways to build sustainability.[3] By prioritizing such goals, RI can help internalize the social and environmental costs of the economy so that it develops only within biosphere limits. RI implies that investors value more than mere financial returns, as they are not only investors but also customers, workers and citizens, and 'in those other roles they might be hurt by social and environmental harm caused by their investments'.[4] In these other guises, RI can serve as a crucial mechanism in the sustainability chain to link shareholders, lenders and other financiers with the global corporate sector, providing a way to reduce the agency problems of financial markets that have divorced investors from the operators of business, and thus control over their environmental and social sequelae.

Presently, RI has a long way to go before it might fulfill this vision. It has captured only a small niche in the financial economy and is rebuffed by many detractors, who fear it politicizes investment decisions or sacrifices financial returns.[5] Many social investors were also complicit in the GFC through their failure to pay attention to issues of financial stability and systemic risk.[6] The minority of mainstream financiers who have embraced RI have tended to recast it into a new paradigm of financial analysis of 'environmental, social and governance (ESG)' criteria.[7] But even this more sanitized version of RI,

---

3 T. Jackson, *Prosperity Without Growth: Economics for a Finite Planet*, Earthscan, 2009, 138–9.
4 W. Ransome and C. Sampford, *Ethics and Socially Responsible Investment: A Philosophical Approach*, Ashgate, 2010, 36.
5 E.g., A. Munnel and A. Sunden, 'Social investing: pension plans should just say "no"', *Cost and Benefits: Socially Responsible Investing and Pension Funds*, American Enterprise Institute (AEI), 7 June 2004; J. Entine, *Pension Fund Politics: The Dangers of Socially Responsible Investing*, AEI Press, 2006.
6 One group taking a more critical perspective is the online Network for Sustainable Financial Markets, comprising academics and investment practitioners: http://www.sustainablefinancialmarkets.net.
7 H. Jemel-Fornetty, C. Louche and D. Bourghelle, 'Changing the dominant convention: the role of emerging initiatives in mainstreaming ESG', in Sun, Louche and Pérez, op. cit., 85–117.

ostensibly devoid of ethical connotations, has struggled to woo converts, partly because of impediments in organizational cultures and difficulties in financially quantifying the business value of improved environmental performance.

A further reason for concern is that much investment masquerading as 'socially responsible' has not been conducted with moral rigour. While many investors and business leaders today distance themselves from the hyperbole of Milton Friedman, who once admonished corporate social responsibility (CSR) as one of the '[f]ew trends [that] could so thoroughly undermine the very foundations of our free society',[8] most are unwilling to sacrifice profits for environmental gains. Rather than ask how investment might contribute to sustainability, today's social investors are more likely to ask self-servingly how sustainability contributes to their investment returns. There is nothing objectionable about people financially benefitting from ethical investment choices; the problem arises when the financial rationale becomes their only rationale for acting.

The RI movement has tended to assume that over the long term, the financial and extra-financial values of investors will coincide.[9] While environmental protection in the long run may coincide with the financial self-interest of investors, there are too many uncertainties to reliably predict financial returns over a protracted period. Such uncertainty means that long-term considerations tend to get 'discounted'. Concomitantly, financiers face many countervailing pressures to act for the short term, in which the immediate economic benefits of depleting natural capital outweigh any long-term costs for which investors are not typically accountable under fiduciary law or other standards. Catalysts for such behaviour include 'misaligned incentives, unsustainable leverage, mis-pricing of risk, complexity, and the "quickening" of access to information and reporting requirements/regulations'.[10]

The fixation on a myopic, single-value view of commerce and investment may thus marginalize RI strategies that do not dovetail with market conventions. The older traditions of 'ethical investment' pioneered by faith-based investors have largely ceded to a business case approach. Its proponents obsess over the financial credentials of RI, sponsoring an endless stream of research about its supposed financial advantage.[11] The core belief is that companies' ability to manage ESG-related risks and opportunities is increasingly relevant to business competitiveness, profitability and organizational competence.[12]

---

8 M. Friedman, *Capitalism and Freedom*, University of Chicago Press, 1962, 133–4.
9 E.g., Assurance Asset Management, *Socially Responsible Investment (SRI) – Let's Think Long Term*, PriceWaterhouseCoopers, 2009.
10 J. Nesbitt, 'The role of short-termism in financial market crises', *Australian Accounting Review* 19(4), 2009, 314–18, 314.
11 UNEP-FI and Mercer, *Demystifying Responsible Investment: A Review of Key Academic and Broker Research on ESG Factors*, Asset Management Working Group, UNEP-FI, 2007.
12 M.J. Kiernan, 'Universal owners and ESG: leaving money on the table?', *Corporate Governance: An International Review* 15(3), 2007, 478–85.

Thus, socially-aware investors who use an ESG 'overlay' may reap added returns. Missing from this perspective is acceptance of an ethical responsibility to act regardless of immediate financial returns. Dominant industry standards, such as the United Nations Principles for Responsible Investment (UNPRI), lack explicit sustainability performance standards, instead nimbly implying that ethical and financial goals will merge through a long-term perspective on investing. If fund managers and trustees rely only on instrumental grounds to act ethically, by their own reasoning they would be justified in making an exception if ignoring those 'extraneous' values would be more profitable. Any commitment to RI thus remains fragile.

Unsustainable investment practices are also attributable to failures of the legal system. Fiduciary finance law has a problematic tendency to view financial institutions as just ordinary private trusts, despite their often public-like characteristics and social impacts. Under prevailing legal understandings, fund managers normally can accommodate sustainability considerations only if they provide investment benefits, if investors consent or if the legal instrument establishing the fund provides a mandate. Trustees' duties to invest 'prudently' and act in beneficiaries' 'best interests' are typically interpreted by courts (as documented later) to exclude consideration of social and environmental 'returns' unless they can offer at least comparable financial benefits, or unless the trust fund is established with non-financial purposes, as for a charitable foundation. Furthermore, because the duty of prudence tends to be interpreted by reference to other investors' conduct, it has become a 'lemming standard' whereby trustees slavishly follow the herd for fear of liability if they deviate from prevailing conventions. In this context, trustees may find it difficult to legally defend costly decisions that defer benefits to beneficiaries for many decades. Fiduciary law expects beneficiaries to benefit in a direct, quantifiable way, rather than amorphously, for instance as members of the greater public may benefit from cleaner air or purer water.

Yet there are elements within the corpus of fiduciary law that point to its structural capacity to be reoriented through judicial reinterpretation or legislative reform to facilitate RI. A notion of public responsibility simmers within fiduciary relationships. In the Canadian case of *Hodgkinson v. Simms*,[13] the Supreme Court noted that fiduciaries serve public interests as well as private ones, providing skilled services such as financial advising and lawyering that benefit not only their clients (or beneficiaries) but society in general.[14] This relationship, the Court noted, cannot be 'characterized by a dynamic of mutual autonomy', and consequently 'the marketplace cannot always set the rules'.[15] Instead, the law of fiduciary obligations protects the social character and public responsibilities that inhere in these relationships between market participants.

13 [1994] CanLII 70 SCC 1.
14 Ibid., 53.
15 Ibid., 54.

The law's concern with safeguarding public confidence in cooperative relationships in our fiduciary society may enable fiduciary law to evolve responsively to new social needs or concerns. Although in current interpretations of fiduciary finance law investment institutions have tended to be 'stubbornly responsive but not proactive',[16] the history of fiduciary law as later discussed in Chapter 3 reveals a record of adaptation to varying circumstances over time. When explaining the change in fiduciary finance relationships (which once treated investment in corporate shares as imprudent), the influential US *Restatement of the Law (Trusts)* observed: 'Trust law should reflect and accommodate current knowledge and concepts. It should avoid repeating the mistake of freezing its rules against future learning and developments.'[17]

In charting a new direction for social engagement with sustainability imperatives, fiduciary relationships contain some intrinsic features that make them a potentially valuable medium for nurturing environmental responsibility. The trust, the institution used for many fiduciary finance arrangements, including pension plans and some mutual funds, was born out of a conscientious necessity to ensure justice. The trust was developed in England to prevent unscrupulous guardians from failing to safeguard the property of children or other dependants. The ingenious feature of the trust was to split legal and beneficial ownership of the underlying assets – to be held in trust, by the trustees, on behalf of the designated beneficiaries.[18] Thus, from its beginnings, the trust had the makings of a customized institution of intergenerational justice to protect those who could not represent themselves adequately.

The current limitations of fiduciary law practice must be put in the wider context of financial and environmental governance that has failed to control unsustainability. Modern environmental law has had limited success, in spite of the sincere efforts of many regulators, judges, citizens and other actors dedicated to the long-term well-being of the planet. Mounting ecological problems such as climate change and loss of wildlife provoked the UN's Millennium Ecosystem Assessment in 2005 to warn that 'human activity is putting such strain on the natural functions of the Earth that the ability of the planet's ecosystems to sustain future generations can no longer be taken for granted'.[19] Many other international studies echo this view.[20] In 2012,

---

16 R.J. Gilson and J.N. Gordon, 'Capital markets, efficient risk bearing and corporate governance: the agency costs of agency capitalism' (preliminary draft, 11 May 2012), 22.
17 American Law Institute (ALI), *Restatement of the Law Third, Trusts*, volume 3, ALI, 1992, s. 227.
18 J.H. Langbein, 'The secret life of the trust: the trust as an instrument of commerce', *Yale Law Journal* 107, 1997, 165–89; M. Conaglen, 'The nature and function of fiduciary loyalty', *Law Quarterly Review* 121, 2005, 452–80; R. Flannigan, 'The core nature of fiduciary accountability', *New Zealand Law Review* 3, 2009, 375–429.
19 Millennium Ecosystem Assessment (MEA), *Living Beyond our Means: Natural Assets and Human Well-Being, Statement from the Board*, United Nations, 2005, 5.
20 UN Environment Programme (UNEP), *Global Environment Outlook GEO-5*, UNEP, 2012; Worldwatch Institute, *State of the World 2012: Moving Toward Sustainable Prosperity*, Island Press, 2012.

scientists spoke of the risk of 'threshold-induced state shifts' in the Earth's biosphere that could trigger myriad unforeseen, devastating consequences for all life.[21] Also, the crisis in global financial markets that began in the American banking system in 2008 and engendered the worst economic stress since the Great Depression is rooted in regulatory shortcomings at both national and international levels. Some of these regulatory flaws and gaps relating to the financial system have consequences for RI, including inadequate risk management, poor long-term planning and weak incorporation of environmental externalities into the cost of capital.[22]

While the RI sector has thus far been unable to overcome such problems and is not a credible alternative or supplement to official regulation, social investors are at least beginning to appreciate the importance of robust regulation for achieving their goals. For instance, 268 global investors issued a public statement prior to the 2010 UN climate change conference in Cancun, calling attention to the fact that current regulation of greenhouse gas (GHG) emission reductions fails abysmally to limit climate change to reasonably safe levels.[23] Social investors also lobby increasingly for reforms to corporate and securities law, such as introducing mandates for corporate environmental reporting and greater shareholder rights. The RI sector is thus gradually recognizing that promoting sustainability is not just a matter of voluntary action and education; it also requires partnership with government through legal reform.[24]

This book proceeds from the position that RI should not be a discretionary preference, to follow only if investors perceive a compelling business case. All investors should be socially responsible and should contribute to sustainability. The book concludes by assessing several possible legal measures that target the financial sector directly. While continued and better 'external' environmental regulation of companies and financial actors may help promote sustainability, we also need to direct legal measures at economic institutions. External regulation, ranging from pollution licensing and environmental impact assessments to carbon taxation, is reaching the limits of its effectiveness.[25] There are many reasons for this situation, as detailed in the next section of this chapter.

We need to embed environmental standards within the inner governance of economic institutions in order to minimize the tensions their managers face between reconciling expectations that they act in the public interest and

---

21 A.D. Barnosky, et al., 'Approaching a state shift in earth's biosphere', *Nature* 486, 2012, 52–7, 52.
22 E. Helleiner, S. Pagliari and H. Zimmermann (eds), *Global Finance in Crisis: The Politics of International Regulatory Change*, Routledge, 2010.
23 UNEP-FI, 'Global investor statement on climate change', November 2010, http://www.unepfi.org/fileadmin/documents/InvestorStatementClimateChange.pdf.
24 See, e.g., R. Thamotheram and H. Wildsmith, 'Increasing long-term market returns: realising the potential of collective pension fund action', *Corporate Governance: An International Review* 15(3), 2007, 438–54.
25 E.g., S. Wood, G. Tanner and B.J. Richardson, 'What ever happened to Canadian environmental law?', *Ecology Law Quarterly* 37(4), 2010, 981–1040.

serving their private interests. On the one hand, fund managers, business managers and other economic decision-makers are expected to prioritize profits or maximize shareholder wealth – goals that create powerful incentives to avoid paying for environmental externalities. On the other hand, environmental regulation seeks to assign responsibility for such externalities and to constrain profit-making. To reconcile these different goals, environmental norms should also be embedded within economic institutions so that corporate directors, fund managers and pension fund trustees see their investments and other activities as intimately tied to sustainability from the outset. Such an approach can help internalize environmental protection as a fundamental norm for investment and business. It should also thereby help improve compliance with external environmental regulation.

However, legally incorporating environmental sustainability into the purpose and decision-making of companies and other economic entities is not without some serious challenges. Legally mandating sustainability as the overall purpose of RI, for both public and private financiers, raises some major obstacles. Sustainability is neither a blueprint nor a manual to apply mechanically – rather, it is a malleable notion, the parameters and application of which require further reflection in each specific context. Asking whether a particular activity is environmentally sustainable will yield different answers depending on the time and place. One might condemn as utterly unsustainable a massive polluting factory located within New York's Central Park, while the same facility isolated in the sparsely populated and vast tracts of Siberia might pose no enduring environmental or public health concerns. We thus often need a flexible, case-by-case approach to measure the sustainability of corporate or investor behaviour. Additionally, requiring fund managers to be more responsive to their environmental performance may pose cognitively challenging problems of reconciling seeming incommensurables. The incommensurability issue refers to the difficulty of comparing and synthesizing different values into business decision-making. If a fiduciary is obliged both to seek profitability for its investors while taking into account environmental costs, how can those dissimilar values be understood in a common metric to enable coherent, integrated decision-making? Yet, many notions in law, such as the concept of negligence in the law of tort, are equally vague and context-specific but have been substantiated through repeated judicial case law over time. In meeting these challenges, fiduciary law needs to promote decision-making approaches that are sufficiently flexible and adaptable yet not so unbounded as to leave financial institutions unaccountable. Because fiduciary law looks to conventions for its substantive content, it can be trapped in prevailing mores. It needs to be grounded in governance structures and policies that can foster critical enquiry and debate to generate the necessary innovative approaches needed to modernize fiduciary standards to address the challenges outlined in this book. We need decision processes that neither privilege morally absolutist judgements about environmental protection nor leave decision-makers with open-ended discretion. Rigid, absolutist stances on appropriate environmental conduct are rarely useful except in relation to prohibiting intrinsically dangerous environmental practices, such as manufacturing highly toxic chemicals. Simplistic moral slogans such as 'respect the intrinsic value of nature'[26] tend to hinder 'genuine and enlightening debate about complex and nuanced real-world ethical issues'.[27] But while we cannot ignore the moral diversity of humankind and the often indeterminacy of language, we should rally against the 'temptation to take up a sceptical, relativist or even nihilistic view of morality, and to re-brand SRI purely as a financial market alternative, absent any overt normative dimension'.[28] Leaving the environmental conduct of companies and their financiers to their discretionary judgement and value preferences would likely not make them measurably accountable for their conduct.

While a variety of values may inform RI decision-making, they ought to be considered in a manner that is ethically reasoned and critiqued in order to choose the best justified values. The current multiplicity and shallowness of values is particularly prevalent in the retail market, where RI practice sometimes degenerates into just another customer preference, analogous to excluding emerging markets or technology stocks, whereby investors shop around for funds that focus on salesmanship rather than commitment to any overall moral purpose. Defensible positions on sustainability emanate from decision-making processes and forums that foster well-informed and nuanced evaluation of the specific circumstances and rival values. The governance of financial institutions should open a space for such dialogue; otherwise any RI might be construed as simply imposed, extraneous prescriptions. But it would be naïve to expect that more transparent, democratic and consultative decision-making within pension funds or banks will alone be transformative. Beneficiaries might be apathetic or lapse into unproductive squabbling. Alternatively, if we leave 'deliberation' solely to trustees and fund managers, such discretionary decision-making could become too removed from fiduciary standards that require beneficiaries' consent. Thus, such decision-making must be bounded within certain fundamental environmental performance standards and include oversight by state and multistakeholder regimes.

Responsible investment should heed a different model of fiduciary finance that respects ecological constraints and opportunities. This sustainability policy envelope may take the form of a number of legal mechanisms, including an overarching duty to promote long-term returns, of which one constituent element is to avoid environmental harm. Another reform is to insinuate into investment governance more transparent and democratic procedures with

---

26 J. Pietarinen, 'The principal attitudes of humanity towards nature', in H.O. Okura (ed.), *Philosophy, Humanity and Ecology*, African Centre for Technology Studies Press, 1994, 290–4, 293.
27 Ransome and Sampford, op. cit., 54.
28 Ibid., 4.

regard to consideration of a fund's environmental activities and impacts. This book considers several legal reforms for these purposes. They focus on national rather than international-level measures, because fiduciary finance law is determined by individual states (although there is some inter-jurisdictional sharing of precedents and proposals). Although not examined in detail in this book, the growing size, complexity and transnational dimension of financial markets also increasingly require internationally coordinated regulation and supervision.

This book evaluates some specific legal measures to promote environmentally responsible investing. One is to redefine investors' duty of prudent investment by extending its ambit to include a long-term perspective that incorporates sustainability considerations. This duty, at a minimum, requires making investment portfolios that cover a much longer time-frame (several decades) and taking into account environmental risks and costs that might arise during this period. Another measure is to make procedural changes to facilitate ethical dialogue and reflection within the finance sector about its impacts and how to reduce them. The governance structure of fiduciary decision-making must be altered in such ways if new investment conventions are to be generated to inform fiduciary rules which tend to be informed by prevailing conventions. Research on investor activism has tended to focus on the governance of invested companies rather than governance within investment funds.[29] Reform of decision-making within such funds is also crucial if beneficiaries are to be consulted and if they are to debate the ethical dimensions of their investments. Although beneficiaries' apathy or lack of expertise might sap such democratic procedures of meaningful participation to inform RI decisions, at the very least such procedures should improve the accountability of fiduciaries' decision-making. Both measures could help in directing investors towards sustainability while providing sufficient flexibility to enable them to make ethically informed choices on a case-by-case basis where a determination of environmental performance may depend heavily on local circumstances.

Though this book focuses on financial institutions rather than regular business corporations, complementary reforms in the latter sector are also necessary. Furthering sustainability requires multi-faceted legal responses across many sectors. Any measures that require financial institutions to respect the environment would be undermined if the companies those institutions fund were not similarly obliged. However, the fiduciary and other legal standards for business corporations are somewhat different than those for financial institutions, especially those governed by trusts law. This subject is not examined further in this book except in relation to financial

---

29 J. Franks, C. Mayer and L. Renneboog, 'Who disciplines managers in poorly performing companies?', *Journal of Financial Intermediation* 10(3/4), 2001, 209–48; S.L. Gillan and L.T. Starks, 'Corporate governance proposals and shareholder activism: the role of institutional investors', *Journal of Financial Economics* 57(3), 2000, 275–305; A. Shleifer and R. Vishny, 'Large shareholders and corporate control', *Journal of Political Economy* 94(3), 1986, 441–68.

institutions structured as corporations, such as banks and insurance companies.

Reform of fiduciary finance law must encompass the responsibilities of the state itself, which this book also addresses in its concluding chapter. As is increasingly acknowledged in the wake of the GFC, states need to better address 'the functioning and stability of the financial system as a whole'.[30] Fiduciary investors cannot achieve the goals outlined in this book unless markets are stable, well-governed, transparent and fair. Fiduciary responsibilities should be elevated beyond financiers to the state because of severe collective action problems within financial markets that hinder cooperation to address mutual concerns. Achieving sustainability requires a shift in the balance between public and private investment, and between the roles of the state and market, which fiduciary law can help institutionalize. Though fiduciary responsibilities can be publicly held,[31] fiduciary duties are commonly seen as a matter of private law. The global environmental and financial crises underscore the necessity of having more robust regulation of the financial economy as a whole, not just at the level of private financial organizations or corporations. It is unrealistic to expect individual economic actors to coordinate themselves to ensure that the economy as a whole acts appropriately to support sustainable development. To provide such coordination, we need to look to the ultimate 'universal investor' – to borrow a well-known phrase to describe large institutional funds – namely, the state.

This book draws upon the public trust doctrine as the most compelling beacon for this fundamental paradigm shift. An ancient yet enduring Western legal doctrine inherited from Roman law, the public trust is an innovative legal mechanism that contemporary scholars such as Joseph Sax and Mary Wood have argued can be used to ensure that government safeguards the environment necessary for public well-being.[32] The heart of the doctrine is the principle that every sovereign government holds important natural resources in 'trust' for the public – the present and future generations of its citizen beneficiaries. American courts have used the doctrine to oblige government to protect navigable rivers, shorelines and other public resources. The doctrine could be harnessed for new purposes in the financial economy, such as guiding the activities of sovereign wealth funds and public investment in environmental services.

The state should affirm its own fiduciary responsibilities in this manner to safeguard the integrity and fecundity of ecological systems on which

---

30 R. Lake, 'This time it has got to be different – why responsible investment needs to get seriously long-term', *Responsible-investor.com*, 13 July 2012.
31 E.g., courts have defined the Canadian government's relationship to its aboriginal citizens as of a fiduciary character: M.C. Hurley, *The Crown's Fiduciary Relationship with Aboriginal Peoples*, Parliament of Canada, 2002.
32 M.C. Wood, '"You can't negotiate with a beetle": environmental law for a new ecological age', *Natural Resources Law Journal* 50(1), 2010, 167–210; J. Sax, 'The public trust doctrine in natural resource law: Effective judicial intervention', *Michigan Law Review* 68, 1970, 471–566.

economic development and human prosperity depend. The public trust doctrine provides the appropriate legal framework to channel that fiduciary responsibility in a manner that provides sufficient flexibility and discretion to allow decision-making that is tailored to specific circumstances. The state could also provide a framework for meta-ethical debates about RI. An existing example is the Ethics Council of the Norwegian Government Pension Fund-Global, whose experience is discussed later in this book. Such ethical debate could also be nurtured within multi-stakeholder networks that represent investor, civil society and public sector interests. The best candidates for this role are the UNPRI and the UNEP-FI, although presently they are overly dominated by investor groups. If enabling institutional settings are created, the results of their ethical deliberation could help set best practice standards for the financial sector to inform a new fiduciary responsibility.

The following section examines more closely the world's financial and ecological crises that require these reforms to be considered with urgency.

The global financial and ecological crises: nature doesn't do bailouts

Reading any newspaper, listening to the radio or watching the television, one will soon notice remarks by politicians or corporate executives that our well-being depends on maintaining economic growth.[33] Despite its unsustainable burden on the biosphere, economic growth remains the foremost goal of nations worldwide. The economic trends are truly staggering. Worldwide consumer expenditure during the last century rose from US$1.5 trillion in 1900 to $24 trillion in 1998.[34] Likewise, international trade in goods soared from US$50 billion in 1870 to just over $8 trillion in 2005.[35] Adjusted for inflation, one study estimates gross world product grew from US$7 trillion in 1950 to about $77 trillion in 2011.[36] These trends vastly outstripped even the extraordinary growth in human population from some 1.6 billion in 1900 to 7 billion in 2011. In recent decades, a further impetus for economic growth has come from the financial sector. The assets of the world's 1,000 largest

---

33 E.g., 'Flaherty raises economic growth forecast', *CBC News* 2 February 2010, http://www.cbc.ca/money/story/2010/02/02/flaherty-budget.html; 'Corporate growth slow to lift markets, create jobs', *Canoe* 11 February 2010, http://money.canoe.ca/money/business/international/archives/2010/02/20100211-130228.html.
34 United Nations Development Programme (UNDP), *Human Development Report 1998*, UNDP, 1998, 1.
35 World Trade Organization (WTO), *World Trade Report 2007*, WTO, 2007, 244 (expressed in constant 1990 dollar values); see also W. Bernstein, *A Splendid Exchange: How Trade Shaped the World*, Atlantic Monthly Press, 2008.
36 Earth Policy Institute, 'Data: gross world product, 1950–2011', http://www.earthpolicy.org/datacenter/xls/indicator220121.xls. Other studies suggest slightly different numbers but, more relevantly, similar magnitudes of change: J.B. DeLong, *Estimating World GDP, One Million B.C. Present*, University of California, 1998; A. Maddison, *The World Economy: Volume 2: Historical Statistics*, OECD, 2006.

banks surged from US$23 trillion in 1990 to approximately $101 trillion by mid-2010, despite the headwinds from the GFC.[37] In 2005, approximately 40 of the world's 100 largest companies were financial firms.[38] Such majestic statistics suggest we live in an age of great prosperity.

But one dangerous consequence of such stupendous growth is that the economy has become very large compared to the ecosystems that sustain it. Natural systems provide innumerable economic and life-support benefits,[39] yet humanity often acts brazenly as though the Earth's natural bounty is infinitely abundant and free.[40] In *The Cancer Stage of Capitalism*, John McMurtry metaphorically depicts this economic plundering as a malignant tumour.[41] As ecological economists have more academically put it, infinite economic and population growth in a physically finite world is impossible.[42] The debate about such 'limits' is not recent; Thomas Malthus raised it in his influential *Essay on Population*, published in 1778, and since the early 1970s numerous scientists have warned against rampant growth at the expense of nature.[43] Natural resource scarcities are only part of the problem. There are also limits to the capacity of environmental 'sinks', which serve to assimilate the pollution and other by-products of economic activity. Climate change is the most serious of these growing sink problems. With emerging economies such as China and India rapidly industrializing and thereby intensifying the global environmental burden, grave ecological tipping points may soon be irreparably passed.

These trends are not simply an expression of some carnal human urge for greater material prosperity – though they have deep cultural and biological roots;[44] they substantially reflect prevailing economic and political systems. The market economy is particularly influential. Some economists laud the market as crucial to human welfare, a tool to solve our environmental

---

37 International Financial Services London, 'Worldwide assets of the banking industry', http://www.ifsl.org.uk/research; CityUK, 'Banking: May 2012, financial markets series', 30 April 2012, http://www.thecityuk.com/research/our-work/reports-list/banking-2012/.
38 M. Stichele, *Critical Issues in the Financial Industry: Somo Financial Sector Report*, Stichting Onderzoek Multinationale Ondernemingen, 2005, 58.
39 See G.C. Daily, *Nature's Services: Societal Dependence on Natural Ecosystems*, Island Press, 1997; Y. Baskin and P.R. Ehrlich, *The Work of Nature: How the Diversity of Life Sustains Us*, Island Press, 1998; T. Prugh, et al., *Natural Capital and Human Economic Survival*, 2nd edn, CRC Press, 1999.
40 Its economic value is undoubtedly staggering, quantified by one notorious study in 1997 at somewhere between US$16–54 trillion annually, dwarfing a then annual global gross economic product of about US$18 trillion: R. Costanza, et al., 'The value of the world's ecosystem services and natural capital', *Nature* 389, 1997, 253–60.
41 J. McMurtry, *The Cancer Stage of Capitalism*, Pluto Press, 1999.
42 H. Daly and J.B. Cobb, Jr., *For the Common Good*, Beacon Press, 1989; H. Daly, *Ecological Economics and the Ecology of Economics*, Edward Elgar, 1999; P. Victor, *Managing Without Growth*, Edward Elgar, 2008.
43 D.H. Meadows, et al., *The Limits to Growth*, Universe Books, 1972.
44 Leading works include: S. Boyden, *Western Civilization in Biological Perspective: Patterns in Biohistory*, Oxford University Press, 1987; J. Diamond, *Collapse: How Societies Choose to Fail or Succeed*, Penguin Books, 2004.

problems – by unleashing competitive pressures to pioneer innovative green technologies, efficiently use scarce resources, allocate capital for environmental protection and price pollution risks.[45] On the other hand, the market suffers from several environmental blind-spots, including its fugitive 'externalities' such as industrial pollution,[46] degradation of 'public goods' such as the atmosphere and oceans,[47] undervaluation of ecological services and amenities such as biodiversity[48] and myopic decision-making that ignores posterity's interests.[49] Geoffrey Heal optimistically contends that 'this poor [environmental] record is not intrinsic to markets. They can be reoriented in a positive direction, in which case their potential for good is immense.'[50] Similarly, through dematerialization, new technologies, better management systems and investment in a knowledge-based economy, Paul Hawken and his colleagues champion a benevolent 'natural capitalism' that respects the critical interdependency between the economy and nature.[51] Ecological economists recommend more fundamental changes that go beyond improving 'efficiency' of resource use to actually limiting economic growth.[52]

Particularly troubling is that the cornucopia of material wealth gained from the recent growth binge does not necessarily equate with heightened prosperity. Much research suggests that once basic human needs are satiated, further economic growth yields a diminishing marginal return to human happiness.[53] Data from the periodic World Values Survey also reveal that more happiness correlates with economic development, but the correlation fades above a certain level of gross domestic product (GDP) per capita – approximately US$15,000 – implying that unlimited economic growth does not correspondingly enhance human well-being.[54] Economic indicators such

---

45 See generally K. Midgley and R. Burns, *The Capital Market: Its Nature and Significance*, Macmillan, 1977.
46 A.A. John and R.A. Pecchenino, 'International and intergenerational environmental externalities', *Scandinavian Journal of Economics* 99(3), 1997, 371–87.
47 T. Cowen, *Public Goods and Market Failures: A Critical Examination*, Transaction Publishers, 1991.
48 M. Common, *Environmental and Resource Economics: An Introduction*, 2nd edn, Longman, 1996, 330–5.
49 Ibid.
50 G. Heal, 'Markets and sustainability', in R.L. Revesz, P. Sands and R.B. Stewart (eds), *Environmental Law, the Economy and Sustainable Development*, Cambridge University Press, 2000, 410–27, 427.
51 P. Hawken, L.H. Lovins and A. Lovins, *Natural Capitalism: Creating the Next Industrial Revolution*, Earthscan, 2000.
52 See, e.g., M. Common and C. Perrings, 'Towards an ecological economics of sustainability', *Ecological Economics* 6, 1991, 7–34; A.M. Jansson, et al. (eds), *Investing in Natural Capital: The Ecological Economics Approach to Sustainability*, Island Press, 1994; T. Jackson, *Prosperity Without Growth: Economics for a Finite Planet*, Earthscan, 2009, 5.
53 William Rees documents that increases in per capita expenditures on US healthcare have not improved the overall health of the American population: W.E. Rees, 'The end (of growth) is nigh', *Ecological Integrity and Sustainable Society Conference*, Dalhousie University, 23–27 June 2007.
54 See http://www.worldvaluessurvey.org/indexhtml.

as GDP undervalue the contribution of nature to overall wealth.[55] Moreover, much of this growth has delivered uneven benefits, with just a fifth of humanity earning about 2 per cent of global wealth.[56] Some economists have pioneered alternative measures of economic vitality and well-being, suggesting that the seemingly most prosperous nations do not necessarily enjoy the highest contentment.[57]

Another crisis, in global financial markets, has attracted greater attention from policy-makers and business leaders, yet its causes are entangled in some of the same processes fuelling the planetary ecological crisis – namely, excessive risk-taking, failure to incorporate social costs into the valuation of financial assets and the short-term orientation of the market.[58] Although some believe that '[t]here is nothing inherent in the structure of the financial system which necessarily leads to environmental destruction'[59] and that '[i]nvestment is the process of foregoing immediate expenditures in order to build a more prosperous future . . . to offer access to a better life',[60] such assumptions are plausible largely only at an abstract theoretical level.

The separation of ownership and management of business, the hallmark of corporate capitalism, has also leveraged the separation between investment and social responsibility. Ease of access to capital markets removes corporate financing constraints that might otherwise curb economic growth and thus its environmental consequences. Passive investors also tend to be physically distant from the activities that directly impact the environment, thus weakening their sense of responsibility for taking corrective action. Further fraying the ties between those who manage companies and those who contribute capital, investors tend to own tiny fractional stakes in a multitude of companies in their portfolio, and the ease of selling corporate securities helps diminish the perceived importance of being an owner or creditor to the company. So many intermediaries diminish the sense of moral agency of investors for the activities and companies they fund.

Whatever ethical motivations investors have, they function within a financial system whose purpose is to mobilize capital through loans and investments with the aim of delivering profit. Such returns are unlikely to accrue from investing in firms that do not expand or innovate. Financiers' desire for returns creates pressure on those firms to be profitable in order to

---

55 R. Eisler, *The Real Wealth of Nations: Creating a Caring Economics*, Berrett-Koehler Publishers, 2007.
56 Jackson, op. cit., 5.
57 H. Henderson, *Ethical Markets; Growing The Green Economy*, Chelsea Green Publishing, 2007. Consider alternative measures of prosperity, such as the 'Index of Sustainable Economic Welfare', http://www.neweconomics.org, or the 'Happy Planet Index', http://www.happyplanetindex.org.
58 K. Tienhaara, 'A tale of two crises: what the global financial crisis means for the global environmental crisis', *Environmental Policy and Governance* 20, 2009, 197–208.
59 M.A. White, 'Environmental finance: value and risk in an age of ecology', *Business Strategy and the Environment* 5, 1996, 198–206, 200.
60 R. Monks, *The New Global Investors*, Capstone, 2001, 1.

repay creditors or generate dividends for shareholders. The financial economy can play a constructive role in mobilizing investors and traders to support the fledgling carbon markets, which in 2010 totalled approximately US$141 billion in trades.[61] Financiers may also help mobilize resources for poor communities and households, such as through the microfinance movement, which in 2007 lent about US$25 billion worldwide.[62] But these are miniscule sums compared to the global financial economy managing assets of some US$212 trillion at the beginning of 2011.[63] Therefore, only a small portion of the financial economy actively contributes to the maintenance of natural capital.

In addition to squandering natural capital, financial markets' contribution to material prosperity is reproachable. Although in generic terms, the act of investing sacrifices current value and use of existing capital in order to garner greater future benefit, the financial system is prone to ephemeral and short-term tactics that can undermine long-term social and economic well-being.[64] The booms and busts driven by short-term trading and speculation become divorced from real economic value.[65] There is often a disconnection between stock markets and real investment in the productive economy, whereby the focus is on exchanging value rather than building value in underlying assets.[66]

The dominant paradigm of the finance system that arose after the 1950s is grounded on several models, particularly the efficient market hypothesis, the capital asset pricing model for the trade-off between risk and return, the modern portfolio theory (MPT) of diversified investment, and arbitrage pricing theory.[67] Over-reliance on these models, which suffer from some unrealistically simple assumptions about financial risk and investor behaviour, coupled with regulatory lacunae and lax market supervision, created vulnerabilities in the financial economy that in 2008 metamorphosed into the GFC. While financial crises are not new, growing financial market liberalization since the 1970s has contributed to the recent history of market mayhem: a World Bank study identified 112 systemic financial crises in 93 countries between the late 1970s and 2000, including the notorious Asian currency collapses in 1997 and the

---

61 CityUK, 'Carbon markets: July 2011', 11 July 2011, http://www.thecityuk.com/research/our-work/reports-list/carbon-markets-2011.
62 Deutsche Bank Research, 'Microfinance: an emerging investment opportunity', December 2007, 1.
63 C. Boxburgh, S. Lund and J. Piotrowski, *Mapping Global Capital Markets 2011*, McKinsey Global Institute, 2011, 2.
64 F. Jameson, 'Culture and finance capitalism', *Critical Inquiry* 24(1), 1997, 246–65, 247; A. Harmes, *Unseen Power: How Mutual Funds Threaten the Political and Economic Wealth of Nations*, Stoddard, 2001, 76.
65 Shiller, op. cit.
66 A.A. Berle, 'For whom corporate managers are trustees', *Harvard Law Review* 45, 1932, 1365–72; M. Kelly, *The Divine Right of Capital: Dethroning the Corporate Aristocracy*, Berrett-Koehler, 2001; S. Melman, *Profits Without Production*, University of Pennsylvania Press, 1987.
67 C.F. Lee and A.C. Lee (eds), *Encyclopedia of Finance*, Springer, 2006.

US savings and loan bust of the late 1980s.[68] The 2008 crisis was, however, of historic breadth and depth, partly because financial markets have become much more integrated than in earlier decades. It led to financial bailouts of US$4.89 trillion between 2007 and 2009 in the US and European Union (EU), equivalent to 6 per cent of GDP in each country/region.[69] One of the largest individual bailouts was the £45.5 billion of equity capital pumped into the Royal Bank of Scotland, then the world's fifth largest bank, which in 2008 suffered staggering losses from exposure to defaulting US subprime loans and over-reliance on risky short-term wholesale funding.[70]

All of these crises share the problem of systemic risks that transcend individual financial institutions to contaminate much of the entire financial and productive economy.[71] Financial markets are 'endogenous risk-generating systems' that do not just reflect the prevailing 'market mood'.[72] The fall-out from the GFC is the best recent evidence of how excessive risk-taking by financiers can precipitate wide-ranging economic and social devastation. The failure of a bank or insurance company can have a domino effect, triggering significant collateral damage to other companies and even entire economic sectors. The 2008 banking crisis began with subprime lending in the US housing market, whereby financial institutions devised new mortgage-backed securities that allowed billions in 'toxic debt' to be sold to investors seemingly far removed from the source of the problem.[73] The GFC itself was also a somewhat 'irrational' market correction, an over-reaction relative to the health of the economy; the panic that flowed from the initial collapse of these financial derivatives was so deep that their market prices likely fell below the fundamental values of the mortgage assets. Individual market actors are motivated to protect themselves, even at the expense of the system as a whole, thereby fostering collective action problems that require greater regulatory supervision.

Some commentators are hopeful that markets will sort themselves out. Gordon Clark and Dariusz Wójcik salute global finance for reshaping the economic landscape of twenty-first-century capitalism by facilitating corporate restructurings, technological innovation and economic development.[74] In

---

68 World Bank, *Finance for Growth: Policy Choices in a Volatile World*, World Bank, 2001.
69 J. Black, 'Restructuring global and EU financial regulation: capacities, coordination and learning', Working Paper 18/2010, London School of Economics, 2010, 8.
70 Financial Services Authority, 'The failure of the Royal Bank of Scotland: Financial Services Authority Board Report', December 2011, 6.
71 S.L. Schwarcz, 'Systemic risk and markets', in R.W. Kolb (ed.), *Lessons from the Financial Crisis: Causes, Consequences, and Our Economic Future*, John Wiley and Sons, 2010, 495–500.
72 D. Satchov, 'The new paradigm in risk management', in Jemel-Fornetty, Louche and Bourghelle, op. cit., 299–318, 316.
73 The mortgages were known as 'subprime' because they catered to less suitable borrowers who made tiny down payments and had unverified income.
74 G.L. Clark and D. Wójcik, *The Geography of Finance: Corporate Governance in the Global Marketplace*, Oxford University Press, 2007.

particular, they and others see the growing presence of institutional investors as a generally positive phenomenon that can help align corporate behaviour with social norms. Clark and Tessa Hebb, whose writings focus on pension funds, contend that these actors have helped re-group dispersed shareholders with unprecedented concentrations of ownership, enabling them to pressure firms to raise their business practices and standards on a range of issues, including accountability, transparency, and social and environmental performance.[75] Similarly, other commentators such as Robert Monks have observed a willingness on the part of institutional investors to collaborate in order to amplify their influence over the governance of their investee firms.[76] The voice of institutional funds, whose beneficiaries are millions of ordinary workers and 'mum and dad' investors, are promoting corporate social responsibility not only in response to broad societal demands but also because improved social and environmental standards should lower financial risk over the long term.[77]

The debate about the capacity and willingness of enlightened investors to address such challenges is examined later in this book. Suffice to say at this point that institutional funds and the RI movement largely failed to predict the 2008 financial crisis, let alone do anything to prevent it. Many social funds were preoccupied with *ad hoc* or specific issues of corporate conduct, while giving insufficient attention to the structural and systemic dimensions of the financial economy that are also determinative of progress towards sustainability. While some banks and other financial behemoths were saved through massive financial bailouts, nature wasn't: long-term ecological damage such as climate change can be irreparable or simply too expensive to recover from. The purpose of this book isn't, however, to investigate the wide array of reforms proposed to ensure greater stability of global financial markets other than incidentally in relation to issues directly relevant to the RI industry, such as calls for greater disclosure and transparency of financial and ESG risks.[78]

Before examining further the barriers and opportunities within existing RI practices to address these economic and environmental challenges, we should pause to consider the limitations of conventional environmental regulation. Why can we not rely on such regulation to discipline environmentally irresponsible companies and their investors?

A damp squib: environmental law and the conflicted state

By and large, environmental law is a damp squib. Nature is sicker than ever, despite the vast swathe of regulations enacted in many countries in recent decades. We continue to edge closer to the precipice of an anthropogenic

---

75 G.L. Clark and T. Hebb, 'Pension fund corporate engagement. The fifth stage of capitalism', *Industrial Relations* 39(1), 2004, 142–71.
76 Monks, op. cit., 2001.
77 Clark and Hebb, op. cit., 158.
78 R. Alembakis, 'Superannuation to heed call for greater disclosure', *The Sustainability Report* 13 January 2012.

collapse in planetary ecological systems. Species are disappearing at unprecedented rates as the planet's sixth mass extinction is forecast,[79] while atmospheric carbon dioxide reportedly jumped to the highest in the last 15 million years[80] and continues to rise.[81] We should not be misled by law's occasional triumphs, such as the phasing out of atmospheric ozone-depleting chemicals[82] or the rescue of iconic species from the brink of extinction.[83] At most, we could concede that environmental law is mitigating what would be a direr situation.

Until now, environmental law has tended to function as a set of external controls on economic activity rather than as norms embedded within the very institutional structure of companies, financiers and other economic agents. Companies and other business entities have had to obtain licences or approvals to harvest resources, pollute or cause other environmental impacts, and these processes are overseen by a labyrinth of administrative agencies and procedures. The function of environmental law, therefore, remains limited to alleviating the worst effects of the dominant model of economic development rather than to fundamentally challenging or transforming it. It is rare for a major project, especially one that promises many jobs and other economic benefits, to be vetoed on the basis of environmental protection.

Several negative factors have converged to undermine the effectiveness of environmental law, including its political–economic context and its methods of governance,[84] in addition to more fundamental characteristics of humankind's evolutionary disposition.[85] The modern environmental administrative state is structured largely to legalize environmental damage, for under most legislation, the governing agency has the authority – or discretion – to permit the very pollution or resource destruction that the regulations were drafted to prevent or reduce. Further, within this context, government agencies often confront and succumb to political pressure and lobbying by vested interest groups, especially the corporations they are supposed to police, in order to issue permits and sanction other harmful actions.

---

79 A.D. Barnosky, et al., 'Has the Earth's sixth mass extinction already arrived?' *Nature* 471, 2011, 51–7.
80 A.K. Tripati, C.D. Roberts and R.A. Eagle, 'Coupling of CO_2 stability over major climate transitions of the last 20 million years', *Science* 326(5958), 2009, 1394–7.
81 J. Amos, 'Deep ice tells long climate story', *BBC News* 4 September 2006, http://news.bbc.co.uk/2/hi/science/nature/5314592.stm.
82 Montreal Protocol on Substances That Deplete the Ozone Layer, ILM 28, 1989, 649.
83 A notable example is the American Bald Eagle (*Haliaeetus leucocephalus*), the national symbol of the US, which was saved by the Endangered Species Preservation Act, Pub. L. 89-669, 1966.
84 See e.g., D. Boyd, *Unnatural Law: Rethinking Canadian Environmental Law and Policy*, UBC Press, 2003; B.A. Ackerman and R.B. Stewart, 'Reforming environmental law: the democratic case for market incentives', *Stanford Law Review* 37, 1985, 1333–65; A. Gillespie, *The Illusion of Progress: Unsustainable Development in International Law*, Earthscan, 2001.
85 B.J. Richardson, 'A damp squib: environmental law from a human evolutionary perspective', *Law and Prosociality eJournal* 3, 2011.

A further fundamental weakness of environmental law is its focus on frontline companies (e.g., manufacturing firms or mining companies) that most visibly pollute or exploit natural resources, rather than on their financial sponsors. The latter have systemically been viewed as remote to these environmental and social consequences,[86] despite the capital they provide and their ability as shareholders or creditors to voice concerns to the firms they fund. Causal relationships between finance and environmental impacts are separated widely across time and space, frequently obscuring holistic responsibility for environmental degradation.[87]

States can hesitate to stringently protect the environment because their political fortunes hinge on their success as economic managers. Driven by the imperatives of national housekeeping, the state acts as the '*parens patriae*' with responsibility to sustain economic growth.[88] Yet because economic activity can also produce politically contentious environmental impacts, the state must reconcile the antagonistic imperatives of curbing the worst pollution while allowing market actors enough freedom to grow the economy.[89] Unresolved contradictions between these imperatives have prompted major disputes over forestry, nuclear power, mining and other resource issues.[90] Governments have sought to manage their conflicting roles and the attendant challenges to their legitimacy by devolving more authority to market actors.[91] Particularly since the 1980s, states have increasingly privatized public services and assets and liberalized market controls in the hope of reducing the regulatory burden on industry and of creating more opportunities to harness market efficiencies.[92] This strategy, however, carries its own risks. The GFC led governments worldwide to intervene to restore market stability in a way not seen since the Great Depression.[93] By contrast, the looming crisis of climate change prompted in 2009 only a luke warm political accord in

---

86 J. Rada and A. Trisoglio, 'Capital markets and sustainable development', *Columbia Journal of World Business* 27(3–4), 1992, 42–50; W. Thomas, 'The green nexus: financiers and sustainable development', *Georgetown International Environmental Law Review* 13, 2001, 899–947.
87 The connections between financial institutions and social problems are being made in other contexts. One example is litigation by Holocaust survivors against Swiss and German banks for their collusion with the Nazi expropriation of Jewish property: P. van der Auweraert, 'Holocaust reparation claims fifty years after: the Swiss banks litigation', *Nordic Journal of International Law* 71(4), 2002, 557–83.
88 H. Arendt, *The Human Condition*, University of Chicago Press, 1957.
89 See K. Walker, 'The state in environmental management: the ecological dimension', *Political Studies* 37(1), 1989, 25–38.
90 E.g., R. Falkner, *Business Power and Conflict in International Environmental Politics*, Palgrave Macmillan, 2007; I. Watson, *Fighting Over the Forests*, Allen and Unwin, 1990.
91 D. Boaz and E. Crane (eds), *Market Liberalism: A Paradigm for the 21st Century*, Cato Institute, 1993.
92 B. Bortolotti and D. Siniscalco, *The Challenges of Privatization: An International Analysis*, Oxford University Press, 2004.
93 'Adding up the government's total bailout tab', *New York Times* 4 February 2009, http://www.nytimes.com/interactive/2009/02/04/business/20090205-bailout-totals-graphic.html.

Copenhagen.⁹⁴ And the economic hardship created by the GFC prompted some governments to curb environmental protectionist measures,⁹⁵ such as the Obama administration's scrapping of stricter limits on urban smog pollution,⁹⁶ as well as the Canadian government's repeal of fisheries habitat protection controls and cutbacks on environmental impact assessments of development proposals.⁹⁷ The financial sector itself also responded to the GFC with reduced environmental investment; in 2008, investment in clean energy firms via the world's stock markets tumbled 51 per cent to US$11.4 billion.⁹⁸

The effectiveness of environmental law is blunted not only by its political and economic context but also by its *methods* of regulation. The rise of modern environmental law in Western countries was closely associated with the norms and institutions of the welfare state, including reliance on instruments of public ownership and prescriptive standards.⁹⁹ While these techniques helped mitigate such acute pollution problems as lead in gasoline, their suitability for resolving complex environmental issues is increasingly doubted.¹⁰⁰ The main elements of the critique are now quite familiar:¹⁰¹ the conventional techniques of 'command and control' regulation were too rigid, complex, burdensome, costly, inefficient, adversarial and ineffective; they stifled entrepreneurial innovation, eliminated jobs and hindered competitiveness in return for diminishing environmental benefits; and they were prone to industry capture. Their proliferation resulted in a dense maze of legal controls, the effectiveness of which was increasingly outweighed by their administrative costs and economic burden, threatening finally to collapse under their own weight or to seize up in a process of 'juridification'.¹⁰² According to one influential account, '[t]he present regulatory system wastes tens of billions of dollars every year, misdirects resources, stifles innovation, and spawns massive and often counterproductive litigation'.¹⁰³ While this isn't an

---

94 'Copenhagen accord climate pledges too weak: UN', *Reuters*, 31 March 2010, http://www.reuters.com/article/idUSTRE62U13M20100331.
95 V. Anbumozhi and A. Bauer, 'Impact of global recession on sustainable development and poverty linkages,' Working Paper 227, Asian Development Bank Institute, 2010.
96 D. Cappiella, 'Obama's smog decision draws lawsuit from environmental groups', *The Huffington Post*, 11 October 2011, http://www.huffingtonpost.com/2011/10/11/groups-sue-obama-for-epa-rulesn1005129.html.
97 D. Crocker, L. Finney and J. Todres, 'Federal government seeks to overhaul the environmental assessment process', *Davis LLP*, 8 May 2012.
98 S. Fritz-Morgentha, et al., 'The global financial crisis and its impact on renewable energy finance', UNEP, 2009.
99 C. Sunstein, 'Paradoxes of the regulatory state', *University of Chicago Law Review* 57, 1990, 407–41; M. Moran, 'Understanding the regulatory state', *British Journal of Political Science* 32, 2002, 391–413.
100 See e.g., P. Yeager, *The Limits of Law: The Public Regulation of Private Pollution*, Cambridge University Press, 1991.
101 See e.g., C. Abbott, 'Environmental command regulation', in B.J. Richardson and S. Wood (eds), *Environmental Law for Sustainability*, Hart Publishing, 2006, 61–95.
102 G. Teubner, 'Juridification: concepts, aspects, limits, solutions', in R. Baldwin, C. Scott and C. Hood (eds), *A Reader on Regulation*, Oxford University Press, 1998, 389–440, 398.
103 Ackerman and Stewart, op. cit., 1333.

accurate depiction of all environmental regulation, which sometimes has been characterized by a consultative style in which environmental rules are negotiated and enforced in a largely non-coercive way via closed-door, bilateral deals between government and industry,[104] it does reflect much of the history of modern environmental law.

Criticism of the efficacy of the regulatory state and its reliance on coercive 'command-and-control' regulation has fostered in recent decades experimentation with alternate approaches that cede some responsibility for environmental governance to the market or civil society. These realignments have been described by commentators in various terms, such as 'mutual regulation',[105] 'self-organization',[106] 'responsive regulation',[107] 'smart regulation'[108] and 'post-regulatory governance'.[109] Among the common elements of these so-called 'decentered' forms of regulation are the preference for legal systems that are 'less heavy-handed, and more responsive to the demands and possibilities of their context',[110] as well as the enlistment of non-state actors in regulatory governance.

Gunther Teubner describes reflexive law as one of these approaches – a system of regulation that does not seek coercive policy direction but confines itself to the 'regulation of organization, procedures and the redistribution of competences'.[111] With the vision that governance should no longer arise out of external regulation but rather occur through the internal reconfiguration of decision-making within corporations, detailed regulatory prescription is somewhat replaced by mechanisms encouraging internal reflection, learning and behavioural change. Thus, the function of law is recast from direct control

---

104 M. Howlett, 'Policy instruments and implementation styles: the evolution of instrument choice', in D. VanNijnatten and R. Boardman (eds), *Canadian Environmental Policy: Context and Cases*, Oxford University Press, 2002, 25–45.
105 See P. Simmons and B. Wynne, *State, Market and Mutual Regulation? SocioEconomic Dimensions of the Environmental Regulation of Business*, Lancaster University, 1994.
106 G. Teubner, L. Farner, and D. Murphy (eds), *Environmental Law and Ecological Responsibility: The Concept and Practice of Ecological Self-Organisation*, John Wiley and Sons, 1994.
107 I. Ayres and J. Braithwaite, *Responsive Regulation: Transcending the Deregulation Debate*, Oxford University Press, 1992.
108 N. Gunningham and P. Grabosky, *Smart Regulation: Designing Environmental Policy*, Oxford University Press, 1998.
109 D. Levi-Faur, 'Regulation and regulatory governance', in D. Levi-Faur (ed.), *The Handbook on the Politics of Regulation*, Edward Elgar, 2012, 2–23.
110 J. Steele and T. Jewell, 'Law in environmental decision-making', in T. Jewell and J. Steele (eds), *Law in Environmental Decision-Making. National, European and International Perspectives*, Clarendon Press, 1998, 1–28, 14; see further D. Osborne and T. Gaebler, *Reinventing Government: How the Entrepreneurial Spirit is Transforming the Public Sector*, Addison-Wesley Publishing, 1992; J. Black, 'Decentring regulation: understanding the role of regulation and self-regulation in a "post-regulatory world"', *Current Legal Problems* 54, 2011, 103–46.
111 G. Teubner, 'Social order from legislative noise? Autopoietic closure as a problem for legal regulation', in G. Teubner (ed.), *State, Law, Economy as Autopoietic Systems: Regulation and Autonomy in a New Perspective*, Giuffrè, 1992; G. Teubner, 'After legal instrumentalism?' in G. Teubner (ed.), *Dilemmas of Law in the Welfare State*, Walter De Gruyter, 1986, 229–325.

to 'procedural' control.¹¹² For environmental policy, Eric Orts describes reflexive law as seeking 'to encourage internal self-critical reflection within institutions about their environmental performance [and] . . . to set up processes that encourage institutional self-reflective thinking and learning about environmental effects'.¹¹³ Thus, many jurisdictions increasingly rely on informational policy instruments, norms of self-governance, economic incentives and contractual agreements to govern markets' environmental impacts.¹¹⁴

However, the effectiveness of such new strategies in promoting sustainability has not yet been demonstrated. Instead, they have served to reduce pressure on the regulatory system by offering a seemingly more efficient and cost-effective environmental governance. These mechanisms leave unaltered basic assumptions about the purpose and value of economic development; they fail to provide tools to steer the economy towards long-term horizons and to provide a mechanism to scale the economy within biosphere limits.

Other regulatory failures and gaps that contribute to unsustainability inhere in business law, including companies' legislation, securities regulation and financial markets controls. In these domains the primary problem from a sustainability perspective is the general lack of environmental standards per se. Indirectly, they are a problem as well. Corporate governance rules can hinder shareholder activism and engagement by social investors to change companies from 'within'.¹¹⁵ The deregulation of financial markets since the 1980s until the GFC has generally aimed to loosen legislative restrictions – such as asset ratios and investment rules – and replace them with disclosure standards and self-regulation under government supervision.¹¹⁶ This book focuses on one of these areas of law – fiduciary responsibility – that is of particular significance for RI.

A fiduciary is essentially someone who has undertaken to act on behalf of another, vulnerable party. The distinguishing obligation of a fiduciary relationship therefore is one of loyalty. Furthermore, there are several recurring features of fiduciary relationships. The fiduciary likely has custody of some of the assets of the person to whom the fiduciary duty is owed, or the relationship between the parties is such that the fiduciary has considerable

---

112 J. Black, 'Proceduralising regulation: part I', *Oxford Journal of Legal Studies* 20, 2000, 597–614.
113 E.W. Orts, 'Reflexive environmental law', *Northwestern University Law Review* 89(4), 1995, 1227–340, 1254.
114 See D.A. Farber, 'Taking slippage seriously: noncompliance and creative compliance in environmental law', *Harvard Environmental Law Review* 23, 1999, 297–326; A. Iles, 'Adaptive management: making environmental law and policy more dynamic, experimentalist and learning', *Environmental and Planning Law Journal* 13, 1996, 288–308; E.W. Orts and K. Deketelaere (eds), *Environmental Contracts: Comparative Approaches to Regulatory Innovation in the United States and Europe*, Kluwer Law, 2000.
115 R. Aguilera, et al., 'Corporate governance and social responsibility: a comparative analysis of the UK and the US', *Corporate Governance and Social Responsibility* 14(3), 2006, 147–58.
116 On Canadian reforms, see A.M. Abdalyan, 'The Porter Commission Report revisited', *Banking and Finance Law Review* 11, 1995, 57–75, 64.

discretionary authority or influence over the person's affairs to whom the duty is owed. Typical fiduciary relationships include trustee–beneficiary, director–corporation, guardian–ward, principal–agent and so forth. Fiduciary responsibility has also migrated from these established categories to various *ad hoc* circumstances, as determined by the courts. Fiduciary responsibility is also closely intertwined with other related legal doctrines that govern the investing activities of some financial institutions; for instance, trusts law applies to pension and mutual funds that are organized as trusts.

The legal framework governing fiduciary finance affects RI in myriad ways, as will be examined in detail in Chapter 3. In common law systems, institutional investors owe fiduciary and trusts law duties to their beneficiaries, which require that they invest prudently in beneficiaries' best interests.[117] Some British and American court rulings[118] suggest trustees and fund managers are liable to their beneficiaries if they negligently sacrifice financial returns for ethical causes.[119] Fiduciary law also relegates beneficiaries to a passive role, without rights to be consulted or to issue instructions, thus limiting the potential for RI policies to evolve through democratic processes within funds.[120] While banks generally do not owe fiduciary duties to their depositors or clients, they may if they provide financial advisory services: and the directors of banks typically owe a separate duty of care to the bank and parties it deals with.[121]

At an international level, an even larger regulatory lacuna exists. Global environmental rules are typically quarantined within designated 'environmental treaties', such as those governing biodiversity conservation or transboundary pollution, while treaties governing investment and other economic activities are largely devoid of sustainability considerations. Market liberalization and technological advances have greatly accelerated the mobility and liquidity of financial capital across borders, and consequently, the capacity for more unsustainable development has only risen.[122] Largely missing from these policy prescriptions are mechanisms to ensure that transnational firms and their investors who benefit from the liberal economic framework adhere to high standards of corporate governance and environmental responsibility.

---

117 Somewhat similar legal concepts exist in civil law systems: F.J. Preu and B.J. Richardson, 'German socially responsible investment: barriers and opportunities', *German Law Journal* 12(3), 2011, 865–900.
118 *Cowan v. Scargill*, [1985] 1 Ch. 270; *Martin v. City of Edinburgh District Council*, [1988] SLT 329; *Bishop of Oxford v. Church Commissioners for England*, [1992] 1 WLR 1241; *Board of Trustees of Employee Retirement System of the City of Baltimore v. City of Baltimore*, (1989) 317 Md. 72; 562 A.2d 720.
119 See R. Thornton, 'Ethical investments: a case of disjointed thinking', *Cambridge Law Journal* 67, 2008, 396–422.
120 B.J. Richardson, 'Fiduciary relationships for socially responsible investing: a multinational perspective', *American Business Law Journal* 48(3), 2011, 597–640.
121 J. Glover, 'Banks and fiduciary relationships', *Bond Law Review* 7(1), 1995, 50–66.
122 C. Williams, 'Corporate social responsibility in an era of economic globalization', *University of California Davis Law Review* 35, 2002, 705–77, 731.

While globalization has helped disseminate and universalize voluntary standards for RI and business ethics, regulation of financial markets at an international level remains sparse and deeply fragmented. The 1997 General Agreement on Trade in Services (GATS) subsidiary Agreement on Financial Services[123] aims to eliminate discriminatory and market access-impairing measures so that insurers, banks and other institutions have access to the financial markets of all member states,[124] but the Agreement lacks organizational machinery to supervise financial markets and also lacks any RI-related standards. An assortment of institutions, such as the Bank for International Settlements and the International Organization of Securities Commissions, provides a very loose regulatory framework at a global level.[125] Such associations serve primarily to facilitate cooperation among national regulators and to promote cross-border movement of capital.[126]

The GFC has provoked much debate among policy-makers, academics and other observers about the future governance of the financial economy, but so far politicians have struggled to forge long-term solutions. The financial implosion revealed serious drawbacks in capital adequacy regulations, which proved to be set too low and were pro-cyclical, excessively reliant on internal risk modelling and credit ratings, and insufficiently protective against liquidity and market risk.[127] The crisis also exposed the frailties of the prudential investment law standard, which fuelled inaction to the crisis as trustees blindly followed investing conventions that were collectively and egregiously irrational. When the financial turmoil erupted in early 2008, most trustees were just 'deer in the headlights', paralyzed by indecision on what course of action to take to fulfill their fiduciary responsibilities. Mainly *ad hoc*, expedient or temporary measures have since been adopted in response to the GFC, such as controls on short-selling, tighter regulation of financial derivatives, more robust capital adequacy standards, closer scrutiny of lending conditions, and bailouts and partial nationalizations of insolvent financial institutions.[128] The measures have tended to serve restoration of business-as-usual rather

---

123 V. Presti, 'Barings bar none: the financial service agreement of the GATS and its potential impact on derivatives trading', *Maryland Journal of International Law and Trade* 21, 1997, 145–202. The legal text of the GATS, including the *Annex on Financial Services* and the *Understanding on Commitments in Financial Services*, are part of the *Final Act Embodying the Results of the Uruguay Round of Multilateral Trade Negotiations*: see http://www.wto.org/english/docse/legale/finale.htm.
124 The Agreement entered into force on 1 March 1999. See further A. Mattoo, *Financial Services and the WTO: Liberalization in the Developing and Transition Economies*, WTO, 1998.
125 See M. Giovanoli, 'A new architecture for the global financial market: an outline of legal issues', in M. Giovanoli (ed.), *International Monetary Law: Issues for the New Millennium*, Oxford University Press, 2000, 3–59.
126 See generally K. Alexander, R. Dhumale and J. Eatwell, *Global Governance of Financial Systems*, Oxford University Press, 2006.
127 M. Peihani, 'The Global Financial Crisis of 2008: an analysis of contributing trends, policies and failures', *Banking and Finance Law Review* 27(3), 2011, 465–94, 487–9.
128 K. Davis, *Regulatory Reform Post the Global Financial Crisis: An Overview*, Australian Centre for Financial Studies, 2011.

than engineer fundamental, structural reforms. The environmental sustainability agenda has not been part of these policy-making discussions.

In conclusion, around the world environmental law of frontline companies of the productive economy has generally been of limited success, and environmental standards have hardly extended to the financial economy. Serious deficiencies exist in the capacity or willingness of states to regulate markets for sustainability, provoking a search for alternative or supplementary means of environmental governance that draw on the expertise and influence of the market itself and civil society. Responsible investment is one of these means.

What is responsible investment?

Historical evolution

In recent decades a global movement for RI has emerged, raising the spectre of more enlightened investing that is predicated not solely on maximizing financial returns.[129] It can be interpreted as a reaction to the impacts of a flawed economic system and the failure of states to regulate it. As the economy falls short of fulfilling people's preferences and values, and governments fail to intervene, some consumers and investors reach for alternatives. The fair trade movement, green consumerism and social investment are all examples of citizens seeking other means for expressing their values in the economic system to influence corporate behaviour. Some activists without financial resources to participate in this new 'market governance' prefer to voice their concerns in more confrontational or unorthodox ways, as exemplified by the recent Occupy Movement.[130]

RI, which has a long history of challenging the status quo, draws upon a variety of methods that traditionally involve two choices: screening investments in certain industries or companies because of the characteristics of their products or operations; or engaging with businesses to make them change their behaviour. These methods are respectively known as portfolio screening (typically either by excluding 'bad' companies or including 'good' ones in an investment portfolio) and corporate engagement and activism (such as through shareholder rights or lenders' influence). A more detailed treatise on this subject would elaborate on the various other practices within these principal categories, such as positive community investing, drafting codes of conduct, integrating ESG analysis and so on.

---

129 Examples of the pioneering literature include A. Domini and P. Kinder, *Ethical Investing*, Addison Wesley, 1984; P. Kinder, S. Lydenberg and A. Domini, *The Social Investment Almanac: A Comprehensive Guide to Socially Responsible Investing*, Henry Holt, 1992; R. Sparkes, *The Ethical Investor*, HarperCollins, 1995; M. Jeucken, *Sustainable Finance and Banking: The Financial Sector and the Future of the Planet*, Earthscan, 2001.
130 K. Adam, 'United in anger, Occupy Wall Street protests go global', *Washington Post*, 16 October 2011, A20.

The history of RI is one of serial attachment to disparate causes, which probably began in the eighteenth century when the Quakers proscribed financial ties to the global slave trade. During the early twentieth century, many churches likewise screened their portfolios to avoid alcohol, tobacco, gambling and other 'sin stocks'.[131] In the 1970s, a global divestment campaign began against firms profiting from South Africa's apartheid regime – a campaign led by faith-based investors and some pension funds and foundations.[132] These early forms of RI that serenaded as moral crusades relied mainly on negative portfolio screens and occasionally confrontational shareholder activism. Today, RI includes a larger pot-pourri of causes and issues, including climate change, animal welfare, tobacco and much more. Issues connected with sustainability have become increasingly salient in the sector. Geographically, the RI industry has also spread and diversified, taking root in a number of emerging economies, including India and South Africa, while gaining strength in its major markets in North America and Western Europe.[133]

In this context, RI parades as a style of market governance, supplementing official regulation. It allows ethical investors to challenge corporate irresponsibility when states do not. Since many companies rely on debt or equity funding to sustain their activities, in theory investors can influence corporate behaviour by making finance subject to environmental and social considerations.[134] RI suggests that economic agents need not only a legal licence to operate but also a 'market licence' or 'social licence'. Companies and financial institutions should not only operate within juridical boundaries but also respect extra-legal social standards of reasonableness, fairness and environmental responsibility.

Recent proponents of RI have distanced themselves somewhat from this idealistic stance, partly because it has long been perceived to be financially imprudent,[135] and most financiers today would reject any pretensions to 'policing' the market. As mainstream investors have embraced RI – for a variety of reasons, including to placate NGO pressure, to stave off state regulation and to pursue their financial self-interest – they have refashioned it, purging RI's more radical ethical agenda and reframing it as a technical paradigm of financial risk management. This business case style of RI is increasingly known as 'ESG analysis' and has been described by some as 'a

---

131 J. Brill and A. Reder, *Investing from the Heart*, Crown Publishers, 1992.
132 'World Council ends relations with three banks over apartheid', *Ecumenical Review* 34(1), 1982, 82–3; R.K. Massie Jr., 'Corporate democracy and the legacy of divestment', *Christian Century* 108(22), 1991, 716–21.
133 R. Bakshi, 'Transforming markets in the 21st century: socially responsible investing as a tool', *Futures* 39, 2007, 523–33, 528.
134 P. Rivoli, 'Making a difference or making a statement? Finance research and socially responsible investment', *Business Ethics Quarterly* 13(3), 2003, 271–87.
135 J.M. Leger, 'Socially responsible funds pique interest, but results often have been unimpressive', *Wall Street Journal* 200, 18 November 1982, 33; D. Shapiro, 'Social responsibility mutual funds: down the down staircase', *Business and Society Review*, winter, 1974–75, 90–3.

fundamentally different approach than RI'.[136] Numerous ESG research providers have emerged since 2000, and the Enhanced Analytics Initiative (EAI), launched in 2004, is perhaps the most influential collaborative mechanism for sharing ESG information among financiers.[137] Rather than view RI as an agent of social change, ESG issues are packaged as a cluster of 'extra-financial' values that sometimes have financial consequences for investors. This RI 'industry' – a now more accurate expression than 'movement' – has become preoccupied with the financial returns of RI rather than the evaluation of its social and environmental returns and ability to improve corporate behaviour.[138]

Under this new guise, RI has emerged from its haphazard and episodic foundations to become a global phenomenon.[139] It is increasingly unified around standards, mostly drafted by the financial industry.[140] These include the Equator Principles,[141] UNPRI[142] and UNEP-FI.[143] These are voluntary codes or regimes to which institutions may subscribe on a take-it-or-leave-it basis, furnishing both normative standards for improved performance and procedures for more transparent and accountable financial decisions.[144] As well, the RI industry has coalesced around new RI methods of financial due diligence, corporate engagement and 'best-in-class' portfolio screening.

Although it continues to grow in importance, RI has not yet become particularly extensive or influential, as Chapter 2 explains. Ostensibly, it has acquired some respectability in Western Europe and North America, with some industry-sponsored research trumpeting that between 10 to 20 per cent of investment portfolios are now managed for RI purposes.[145] This seeming

---

136 Jemel-Fornetty, Louche and Bourghelle, op. cit., 87.
137 See http://www.uss.co.uk/Documents/enhancedanalyticsinitiative.pdf.
138 Although the 'business case' has become the dominant theme of the RI narrative only since the early 2000s, it was present as early as the mid-1980s: A.L. Domini and P.D. Kinder, 'Your money or your ethics: a choice investors no longer have to make', *Environmental Action* 17, 1985, 16–20.
139 S. Fahrer, '*Socially responsible* investing comes of age', *Dollars and Sense* 218 (July/August), 1998, 32–6; K. Burgess, 'Investors jump on environmental wagon', *Financial Times*, 3 June 2008, 7.
140 B.J. Richardson, 'Socially responsible investing through voluntary codes', in P.M. Dupuy and J.E. Viñuales (eds), *Harnessing Foreign Investment to Promote Environmental Protection: Incentives and Safeguards*, Cambridge University Press, 2013, *in press*.
141 Http://www.equator-principles.com.
142 Http://www.unpri.org.
143 Http://www.unepfi.org.
144 See K. Miles, 'Targeting financiers: can voluntary codes of conduct for the investment and financing sectors achieve environmental and sustainability objectives?', in K. Deketelaere, et al. (eds), *Critical Issues in Environmental Taxation*, volume 5, Oxford University Press, 2008, 947–62; O. Perez, 'The new universe of green finance: from self-regulation to multi-polar governance', in O. Dilling, M. Herberg and G. Winter (eds), *Responsible Business. Self-Governance and Law in Transnational Economic Transactions*, Hart Publishing, 2008, 151–80.
145 E.g., Social Investment Organization (SIO), *Canadian Socially Responsible Investment Review 2010*, SIO, 2010; Social Investment Forum (US-SIF), *2010 Report Socially Responsible*

trend is uneven, with some jurisdictions such as Germany lacking much RI growth.[146] Flawed survey methodologies have likely exaggerated the extent of RI.

Philosophical approaches to RI

RI's ability to govern the market has been undermined by its fungible standards and unprincipled foundations.[147] Diverse labels for RI abound, including 'ethical investment', 'mission investment', 'social investment' and 'sustainable finance'. The terminological differences are not in themselves necessarily significant, as they partly reflect cultural, historical and political differences in international markets. More important are the underlying conceptual differences and lack of 'definitional clarity'.[148] All investors, whether or not they identify themselves as 'social' ones, share a desire for financial returns, in contrast to philanthropists who donate money to charitable causes without expecting financial benefit. Some proponents believe RI involves merely 'taking into account' social and environmental issues that might have bearing on financial performance,[149] while others prioritize ethical considerations.[150] Although these issues parallel in some ways similar debates in the corporate social responsibility literature about the economic and social values and purposes that should inform business conduct, few researchers have sought to develop a coherent theory of ethics specifically for RI.[151]

Ethics, which is about how we ought to act and how we should live our lives, informs a range of philosophical approaches to RI.[152] Deontological ethics places the moral status of our actions in specific features of the acts themselves, regardless of their consequences. One version of deontological ethics closely associated with faith-based investing is the divine command doctrine, which tends to cast itself in morally absolutist terms. Another deontological approach is Immanuel Kant's theory that morality rests not on divine authority but on inherent moral duties discoverable by rational people through reasoning.[153] Kant believed that through reasoning, rational

---

Investing Trends in the United States, US-SIF, 2010; European Social Investment Forum (Eurosif), *European SRI Study 2010*, Eurosif, 2010.
146 Preu and Richardson, op. cit.
147 J. Sandberg, et al., 'The heterogeneity of socially responsible investment', *Journal of Business Ethics* 87(4), 2009, 519–33.
148 Ransome and Sampford, op. cit., 9.
149 UNEP-FI, *The Materiality of Social, Environmental and Corporate Governance Issues in Equity Pricing*, UNEP-FI, 2004.
150 B.J. Richardson and W. Cragg, 'Being virtuous and prosperous: SRI's conflicting goals', *Journal of Business Ethics* 92(1), 2010, 21–39.
151 See, e.g., J.D. Cronin, *From Ethical Investment to Investment Ethics*, PhD, Queensland University of Technology, 2004.
152 This discussion draws partially on Ransome and Sampford, op. cit., 57–85; and A. Lewis, *Morals, Markets and Money: The Case of Ethical Investing*, Financial Times and Prentice Hall, 2002.
153 See B. Aune, *Kant's Theory of Morals*, Princeton University Press, 1979.

individuals would reach the same conclusions, providing an objective and universal morality. Natural law theory is yet another variant of the deontological tradition.[154] These deontological approaches can inform social investing that calls for respect for universal, 'fundamental' human rights, as well as investing that aims to avoid complicity in activities deemed morally objectionable by religious scriptures, such as 'sinful' gambling or alcohol businesses.[155]

These ethical theories are problematic for RI in a culturally and morally diverse world. The moral absolutism of divine command provides no guidance for situations in which moral imperatives clash, such as a blanket prohibition against violence and the right to self-defence. Moral judgements in Kantian theory are also problematic to defend, since as the theory focuses on the reasons underlying actions rather than on actions themselves, it can be difficult in the absence of intimate knowledge to morally evaluate some behaviour. In other words, it is hard to universalize moral axioms without knowing the motivating reason behind someone else's action.

Rather than base morality on any intrinsic goodness or wrongness, by deference to human reasoning or divine will, teleological theories judge morality by the *consequences* of our actions. The classic utilitarianism of Jeremy Bentham and John Stuart Mill is one type of teleological ethics, rationalizing decisions by weighing the relative pleasure or pain, or other metrics.[156] The use of cost-benefit analysis in contemporary environmental regulation is one widespread application of the instrumental, calculative approach of utilitarianism. It has also influenced ethical investors wishing to improve the environmental or social behaviour of companies – as opposed to just avoiding association with morally offensive firms.[157] Some social investors try to leverage positive change through targeted community investment. Even religious investors have increasingly embraced teleological ethics, working in coalition to exert social change, such as the US-based Interfaith Center for Corporate Responsibility's campaigns on climate change and environmental justice.[158]

The notion of 'complicity' has become an increasingly critical ethical concept for understanding RI because investing in companies can lead to one being regarded as an accessory or accomplice to the companies' delicts.[159] The

---

154 B. Bix, 'Natural law: the modern tradition', in J.L. Coleman and S. Shapiro (eds), *Oxford Handbook of Jurisprudence and Philosophy of Law*, Oxford University Press, 2002, 61–103.
155 P. Triolo, M. Palmer and S. Waygood, *A Capital Solution: Faith, Finance and Concern for a Living Planet*, Pilkington Press, 2000.
156 See G. Scarre, *Utilitarianism*, Routledge, 1996.
157 J.C. Baker, et al., 'Institutional Investors attitudes toward corporate social responsibility', *Arkansas Business and Economic Review* 7, 1974, 14–20; N. Carter and M. Huby, 'Ecological citizenship and ethical investment', *Environmental Politics* 14(2), 2005, 255–72; P. Dembinski, et al., 'The ethical foundations of responsible investment', *Journal of Business Ethics* 48(2), 2003, 203–13.
158 See http://www.iccr.org/issues/globalwarm/goalsobjectives.php.
159 See especially G. Nystuen, A. Follesdal and O. Mestad (eds), *Human Rights Corporate Complicity and Disinvestment*, Cambridge University Press, 2011.

notion of ethical complicity is potentially wider than its legal understanding in criminal law, but both notions are mired in uncertainty regarding the requisite degree of causality or association to render one culpable. Some commentators believe the teleological approach can offer a robust framework for RI, enabling 'a clear, simple and direct link . . . between harmful corporate behaviour and the moral reasons for opposing it'.[160] But Christopher Kutz points out that '[g]iven the complex intertwining of capital in a globalized world, it is inevitable that any investment decision would link one to wrongdoing in some form'.[161] While investing significantly expands one's potential agency in human rights abuses or environmentally harmful development in the companies one owns stock in or buys bonds from, individual investors have limited ability to influence corporate managers.

From a legal perspective, such a 'link' can sometimes be only tenuously established because the chain of causation between the investing and the resulting harm may be faint. The notion of 'complicity', as a legal principle, can be defined in various ways in order to attribute liability to actors, such as direct complicity (where an actor knowingly assists another to commit a legal violation) and beneficial complicity (where an actor benefits directly from the violation committed by someone else).[162] On these tests, demarcating clearly the necessary degree of proximity or complicity between investors and the resulting harm to trigger moral or legal responsibility is fraught with challenges.

Utilitarianism's reductionism can sometimes be a drawback when a more nuanced analysis of competing moral considerations is required. For example, some social investors categorically oppose investing in companies that 'exploit' child labour, yet in some deprived communities employment opportunities for older minors can be justified as economically beneficial.[163] Alternatively, some might condone environmental pollution that results from economically worthwhile activity despite the accompanying despoliation. Furthermore, by putting all morality at the service of happiness, the utilitarian approach can overwhelm other values we might cherish, such as justice and equality (unless they make us 'happy'). Peter Singer, a utilitarian, thus recommends we should speak of human 'preferences' rather than happiness as the metric of comparison.[164]

Among other major philosophical approaches available to RI, virtue ethics is important. Derived from Aristotelian theory, it focuses on one's character, such as having a sense of justice and practical wisdom. Cultivation of a

---

160 Ransome and Sampford, op. cit., 72.
161 C. Kutz, 'Responsibility beyond the law?', in G. Nystuen, A. Follesdal and O. Mestad (eds), *Human Rights, Corporate Complicity and Disinvestment*, Cambridge University Press, 2011, 64–78, 74.
162 S.H. Kadish, 'Complicity, cause and blame: a study in the interpretation of doctrine', *California Law Review* 73, 1985, 323–410.
163 See P. Rivoli, 'Labor standards in the global standards: issues for investors', *Journal of Business Ethics* 43(3), 2003, 223–32.
164 P. Singer, *A Practical Ethics*, Cambridge University Press, 2009.

virtuous character is both an end in itself as well as a means to human flourishing. Aristotle believed that an underlying virtue – which he called *'phronesis'*, or practical wisdom – informed all other ethical virtues, and the polity's overriding purpose was to create a space to cultivate the virtuous good life.[165] While virtue ethics avoids the prescriptive moral absolutism of some other ethical theories, it is too open-ended and lacks sufficient guidance for routine ethical judgements about actions.

All these ethical approaches to RI, especially in a global context, face a further legitimization problem because of the pervasive sense of 'ethical relativism' across different societies. As RI has grown into an international phenomenon, its proponents have increasingly shied away from taking moral positions, on the basis that moral belief and practice differ across societies, cultures and historical eras.[166] The annual World Values Survey, which provides unique insights into values and attitudes in the majority of the world's population, shows that opinions vary widely on many issues.[167] Yet the survey also shows increasingly pro-environment attitudes and behaviours worldwide, and that a substantial majority prefer positive action on the environment; although surveys also show some 'critical gaps between what people say and do'.[168]

Thus, in this global setting where no universal objective moral truths are assumed beyond a degree of self-interest in economic development and the absence of major environmental damage, a kind of moral relativism is paraded. Taken to one extreme, this position can lead to a 'moral subjectivism' whereby ethical judgement is reduced to personal moral conviction on the assumption that different cultural worldviews are just the aggregate of many different individual views. This outlook has opened RI to criticism for frequently being an expression of 'personal ideological convictions'.[169] Often, one is left with the impression that the RI industry simply treats ethics as an investment strategy that caters to personal value preferences rather than as a matter of how one ought to behave.

Often intertwined with moral relativist beliefs is *cognitive* relativism. Doubting that there is any 'truth' that is objectively knowable to people, this perspective views 'facts' as merely social constructs. Post-structuralist and postmodernist philosophies are a seminal source of this tradition, suggesting that the conventions of language filter how people interpret the world, and language does not provide any stable window to represent the world. Such cognitive relativism has fuelled many of the heated 'science wars', such as that

---

165 P. Simpson, 'Contemporary virtue ethics and Aristotle', *Review of Metaphysics* 45(3), 1992, 503–24.
166 Ransome and Sampford, op. cit., 77, and 102–3 (discussing the Australian RI market).
167 Http://www.worldvaluessurvey.org/indexhtml.
168 A.A. Leiserowitz, R.W. Kates and T.M. Parris, 'Do global attitudes and surveys support sustainable development?', *Environment* 47(9), 2005, 22–38, 33.
169 J. Entine, 'The politicization of public investments', in J. Entine (ed.), *Pension Fund Politics: The Dangers of Socially Responsible Investing*, AEI Press, 1–12, 8.

presently raging on the science of climate change where the integrity and methodology of researchers is increasingly disputed.[170]

However, moral relativism poses a much greater threat to RI than cognitive relativism, as the financial industry already is well accustomed to scientific epistemologies in its dogma about maximizing financial returns and monetizing risk. Investors are much more likely to doubt or misunderstand the *ethical* significance of climate change, for instance, than to dispute the factual existence of climate change. The RI narrative has increasingly jettisoned pretensions to having any fundamental ethical basis in favour of what the industry sees as morally neutral, financial assessment of the 'materiality' of ESG issues. Such attitudes permeate the industry-sponsored research and practice guides.[171] The 2005 Freshfields report on the legality of RI similarly believes that financial materiality is legally the safest basis for such investing.[172]

There is an alternative to the foregoing philosophical approaches to RI that rejects moral absoluteness and rigidity while avoiding the slide towards irresolvable relativism or morally vacuous business-case RI. While there is undeniably much diversity in our moral outlook, and there should be representation of some of this plurality in RI, representation of any moral variety would render RI incoherent and indefensible. Instead, a pluralist values approach can accept ethical variety – which is necessary given the often complex and ethically contested circumstances that investors face – but 'not at the cost of abandoning reflective rigour or accountability, let alone the capacity to distinguish between good from bad and right from wrong'.[173] Ransome and Sampford contend that at the 'core of the pluralist view is the belief that while no single theory succeeds in exclusively accounting for morality overall, each of the range of different ethical theories and their many varieties ... captures some essential element or facet of what we mean by normative morality'.[174]

The notion of sustainability or sustainable development is one candidate for the philosophical and practical framework that offers this flexible yet not wholly unbounded ethical approach to RI. Indeed, sustainability is already an influential concept in the RI industry, as well as in the related CSR sector. The following section explores its meaning as a potential guiding framework for RI's environmental agenda.

---

170 P. Kitcher, 'The climate change debates', *Science* 328(5983), 2010, 1230–4; S. Funtowicz and J. Ravetz, 'Science for the post-normal age', *Futures*, September 1993, 739–55.
171 UNEP-FI, *Show Me the Money: Linking Environmental, Social and Governance Issues to Company Value*, UNEP-FI, 2006, 4.
172 Freshfields Bruckhaus Deringer, *A Legal Framework for the Integration of Environmental, Social and Governance Issues into Institutional Investment*, UNEP-FI, 2005, 6 (referring to RI's 'financial materiality').
173 Ransome and Sampford, op. cit., 82.
174 Ibid.

Sustainability

The concept of 'sustainability' emerged in the late twentieth century as the dominant concept in environmental policy and law. In its most prevalent formulation, 'sustainable development', it has been widely endorsed as a goal of states, international bodies, businesses and NGOs. For example, sustainability has been enshrined in the European Community's Treaty as a core objective[175] and is featured in many international environmental conventions, multilateral development policies, national environmental strategies and legislation.[176] In the context of business enterprise, sustainability has been incarnated in the motifs 'sustainable companies', 'sustainable finance' and similar phrases that imply economic activity within acceptable environmental parameters.[177]

In contrast to the older environmentalist terminologies that prioritized 'nature conservation', the sustainability discourse seeks to integrate the environmental and economic agendas. It purports to seek a responsible balance between the otherwise incongruous imperatives of unfettered economic exploitation of natural resources and the dependence of all life on healthy ecosystems. Most fundamentally, sustainability implies consumption of renewable resources at their regeneration rate, as well as limiting waste and pollution to the assimilative capacity of the biosphere, thereby maintaining critical ecological processes and the biodiversity of the planet.[178] Sustainability also implies rejecting capitalism's assumption that natural and non-natural resources are interchangeable substitutes. Depletion of non-renewable resources such as oil and gas is assumed as worthwhile if their economic development generates new forms of human capital to improve living standards for the benefit of present and future generations. This model is not readily extendable to multi-functional ecological services of incalculable economic benefit.

Sustainability is supported by several specific policy principles that give it some operational traction. The 'polluter pays' principle expects polluters to bear the expenses of waste or contamination prevention and remediation.[179] The precautionary principle provides a guide for acting in situations of uncertainty regarding the environmental risks of development choices.[180] Sustainability also adheres to principles of social justice by requiring fair

---

175 Article 2, Consolidated version of the Treaty establishing the European Community, OJ C 340, 10 November 1997.
176 M.C. Cordonier Segger and A. Khalfan, *Sustainable Development Law: Principles, Practices, and Prospects*, Oxford University Press, 2005; S.A. Atapattu, *Emerging Principles of International Environmental Law*, Transnational Publishers, 2006; Revesz, Sands, and Stewart, op. cit.
177 Jeucken, op. cit.
178 H.E. Daly, 'Toward some operational principles of sustainable development', *Ecological Economics* 2, 1990, 1–6.
179 OECD, *The Polluter Pays Principle: OECD Analyses and Recommendations*, OECD, 1992.
180 N. de Sadeleer (ed.), *Implementing the Precautionary Principles: Approaches from the Nordic Countries, the EU and USA*, Earthscan, 2007.

distribution of the benefits and burdens of environmental policy, as reflected in the cognate principles of inter- and intra-generational equity.[181] These principles have ostensibly informed vast swathes of modern environmental governance and policy,[182] including strategic plans, framework laws and reconfigured regulatory agencies, as well as procedural reforms that widen participation in environmental decision-making.[183] Considerable effort has also been expended to set 'sustainability indicators' to measure progress.[184]

Part of sustainability's appeal is its ambiguity and open-endedness, enabling numerous actors with divergent objectives to commonly embrace it.[185] The success of the sustainability ideal also derives from how business and political elites have tamed its broad possible implications to avoid radical economic changes. The prevailing rhetoric seeks to reassure us that environmental protection and economic growth can mutually reinforce each other.[186] Sustainability is presented as a supporting means to gain competitive advantages, build new markets and improve production efficiency, rather than to impose rigid ecological limits on business activity.[187] It also implies soft business advantages, such as improved relations with employees and local communities, and therefore fewer costly disputes.[188]

This incremental and reformist approach to sustainable development has not gone uncontested. The anti-globalization movement represents the most visible form of resistance.[189] Diverse campaigns from civil society advocacy networks have exposed the environmental and social impacts of firms and investors, keeping their influence on the sustainable development discourse somewhat in check.[190] The recent global 'Occupy Movement' has extended this discontentment to the sustainability and equity of the

---

181 I. Voinovic, 'Intergenerational and intragenerational equity requirements for sustainability', *Environmental Conservation* 22(3), 1995, 223–8; J.E. Roemer, *Intergenerational Equity and Sustainability*, Palgrave Macmillan, 2007.
182 See K. Bosselammn, *The Principle of Sustainability: Transforming Law and Governance*, Ashgate, 2008.
183 J.C. Dernbach, 'Sustainable development as a framework for national governance', *Case Western Reserve Law Review* 4(1), 1998, 1–103; K. Ginther, et al. (eds), *Sustainable Development and Good Governance*, Graham and Trotman; Martinus Nijhoff, 1995; G.C. Bryner, 'Policy devolution and environmental law: exploring the transition to sustainable development', *Environs: Environmental Law and Policy Journal* 26, 2002, 1–32.
184 S. Bell and S. Morse, *Sustainability Indicators: Measuring the Immeasurable*, Earthscan, 1999.
185 A.D. Basiago, 'Methods of defining sustainability', *Sustainable Development* 3, 1995, 109–19; K. Pezzoli, 'Sustainable development: a transdisciplinary overview of the literature', *Journal of Environmental Planning and Management* 40(5), 1997, 549–74.
186 On the potential symbiosis, see M.E. Porter and V. der Linde, 'Green and competitive: ending the stalemate', *Harvard Business Review* 73(5), 1995, 120–34.
187 E.g., WBCSD and UNEP, *Cleaner Production and Eco-Efficiency, Complementary Approaches to Sustainable Development*, WBCSD, 1998.
188 M. Grieg-Gran, *Financial Incentives for Improved Sustainability Performance: The Business Case and the Sustainability Dividend*, Institute for the Environment and Development, WBCSD, 2002, 5–6.
189 N. Klein, *No Logo: Taking Aim at the Brand Bullies*, Vintage Canada, 2000.
190 D. Szablowski, *Transnational Law and Local Struggles: Mining, Communities and the World Bank*, Hart Publishing, 2007, 64.

financial economy.¹⁹¹ The movement, which declares it 'aims to fight back against the system that has allowed the richest 1% to write the rules governing an unbalanced and inequitable global economy, and thus foreclosing on our future',¹⁹² has however not yet advanced a concrete agenda for reform.

Likewise, this book's advocacy of sustainability as a guiding framework for RI is informed by a critical stance that views the planetary environmental crisis as requiring substantial changes in the governance and purpose of investment. The hallmarks of such RI are that it is procedurally managed in a more transparent and democratic manner, and substantively it is accountable to robust environmental performance standards. The financial sector – not just its RI niche – must accept a greater ethical responsibility, especially for its environmental burden. Investing cannot be viewed as merely a financial strategy to stimulate local economic activity but rather must be seen as a global trend of environmental and economic significance. The treatment of ethics as an idiosyncratic personal or cultural choice is hardly acceptable as financial markets become a global phenomenon, impacting upon a variety of ecosystems and human communities worldwide.

Of course, sustainability is not simply a matter of environmental protection and improvement. It has important social justice dimensions, such as respect for basic human rights, because environmental management is about not just humankind's relationship with nature but also the relations among ourselves over access to scarce resources and the distribution of environmental benefits and burdens. For example, the livelihood of indigenous peoples and their land rights and other legal claims are often closely intertwined with environmental protection.¹⁹³ The principle of intra-generational equity most directly engages with sustainability's social dimensions.

The analysis and reforms proposed by this book focus on sustainability's environmental side for several reasons. Notably, social concerns such as abuse of human rights often have stakeholders who are willing to speak out, protest or initiate legal action, because those stakeholders' personal well-being is directly affected. By contrast, the environment, especially its long-term integrity, tends to be a mute stakeholder, unable to represent itself except indirectly through environmental NGOs who advocate on its behalf. While some environmental problems directly menace individuals, such as pollution of one's property or person, in many cases the impacts are so widely dispersed across space or time that they lack sufficient proximity to motivate people to take costly action. In particular, the long-term interests of future generations

---

191 Writers for the 99%, *Occupying Wall Street: The Inside Story of an Action That Changed America*, OR Books, 2011.
192 Occupy Movement, http://occupytogether.org.
193 B.J. Richardson, 'The ties that bind: indigenous peoples and environmental governance', in B.J. Richardson, S. Imai and K. McNeil (eds), *Indigenous Peoples and the Law: Comparative and Critical Perspectives*, Hart Publishing, 2009, 337–70.

in environmental well-being are less likely to be represented in public policy debates or business decision-making than the immediate interests of people alive today. Because many environmental impacts are irreversible, such as climate change or species extinction, it will not be possible for future generations to obtain justice later. Thus, there is a much greater imperative to address sustainability's environmental dimensions at their inception, in business and economic decision-making. By contrast, while RI can be an important means to champion sustainability's social side, it is sometimes better addressed through external regulation, such as labour standards, human rights codes and access to justice procedures.

Legal structures for RI values

The function of fiduciary finance law should therefore not merely be to keep investments within acceptable ecological parameters; rather, because of the ambiguity and complexity in defining and applying sustainability in specific circumstances, fiduciary finance law must also facilitate ethical dialogue within financial institutions. Law should empower beneficiaries, trustees and other participants to adopt a critical and morally reflective approach, which includes well-informed examination of particular circumstances, and also help participants to understand the reasons for and consequences of their moral judgements on environmental issues. Such ethical reflection and debate should further extend to industry, multi-stakeholder and regulatory approaches that oversee the RI sector and financial markets. The prospect of apathy by beneficiaries and the difficulties of coordinating response by numerous individual funds suggest that sector-wide forums are a crucial part of this agenda.

Even in the absence of shared ethical norms, Jurgen Habermas' model of communicative practice suggests we might at least find greater legitimacy in decisions that follow democratic procedures that foster a practical form of *rational* decision-making designed to ensure that the decisions reached serve generalizable, and not particular, interests.[194] Concomitantly, the notion of 'reflexive law' advanced by Gunther Teubner projects an approach to governance that accommodates such discursive practices, because rather than dictating the details of regulated behaviour, it aims to provoke self-reflection and self-correction by regulated actors in line with governments' goals.[195] Self-reflection may be fostered by requiring investors and companies to disclose their environmental performance, justify decisions and assess impacts. Such a philosophical and legal approach may lead to more knowledgeable, legitimate and defensive RI policies, as well as policies that are more congruent

---

194 J. Habermas, *The Theory of Communicative Action 1: Reason and the Rationalization of Society*, T. McCarthy trans., Beacon Press, 1984.
195 G. Teubner, 'Substantive and reflexive elements in modern law', *Law and Society Review* 17, 1983, 239–85.

with fiduciary law's requirements of acting in beneficiaries' best interests. Although, as earlier noted, reflexive law approaches alone may be insufficient to motivate change in the absence of other legal mechanisms of accountability.

A further way through which this approach to RI can flourish is more corporate engagement and activism. Sometimes this can offer better strategies for ethical reflection and dialogue because, unlike inflexible and morally absolutist portfolio screens, engagement can allow for more nuanced negotiation of complex and disputed moral issues. Moreover, 'the use of a priori criteria is potentially misleading' about the 'actual impacts of the company's products and services'.[196] And in some relatively undiversified economies that are dominated by one sector, such as mining, morally rigid screens may be impractical.[197] Corporate engagement strategies are more compatible than portfolio screening with fiduciary law because they do not per se narrow the investment universe or diversity of a portfolio. Moreover, active investing such as filing or supporting shareholder resolutions is increasingly viewed as an integral part of fiduciary responsibility. Investor rights are valuable fiduciary assets that should be utilized and protected.

Corporate engagement strategies are presently not practised extensively to make RI influential, as Chapter 2 reveals. One reason is they can be costly and time-consuming, and there are impediments to collaboration among investors. Another reason is legal obstacles from securities regulation and corporate governance. For example, securities regulation can constrain institutional investors' engagement with companies through protective provisions that seek to limit individual funds from acquiring a controlling stake or having access to insider information.[198] Engagement and active styles of investment therefore may require some institutional and legal changes in order to flourish.

Law thus has a role in helping to overcome the poorly articulated or vague ethical dimensions of RI. The sustainability paradigm provides the best available framework for providing greater moral clarity in RI. Paradoxically, therefore, whereas RI once stood for change when governments failed to act, the RI industry's ability to flourish and be a force for sustainability now requires a helping hand from the state itself. Curiously, if perfect environmental regulation existed, such as robust controls on carbon polluters that reduced the threat of climate change, social investing would lose much of its justification. We wouldn't need social investors to correct market failures,

---

196 S. de Colle and J.G. York, 'Why wine is not glue? The unresolved problem of negative screening in socially responsible investing', *Journal of Business Ethics* 85, 2009: 83–95, 83.
197 Canadian investors face such a dilemma where resource and energy stocks comprise a major part of the market; according to Michael Jantzi, a leading figure in the Canadian RI community, '[e]liminating all resource stocks is unrealistic, because it wipes out about 40 per cent of the Toronto market and causes an investor to lose diversity': S. Won, 'Ethical summa above average', *Globe and Mail*, 29 November 1995, B17.
198 R. Davis, *Democratizing Pension Funds: Corporate Governance and Accountability*, UBC Press, 2009, 136–7.

because governments would have already done the job. RI would likely retreat to its original domain as a means for individuals and eleemosynary institutions to advance their own ethical preferences, such as shunning companies that produce intoxicants or operate casinos. But the track record of public regulation suggests this is a sisyphean task. RI needs law, but a more diverse kind than only blunt external regulation.

The concept of 'nature's trust' offers a beacon to guide the legal reform of fiduciary finance law to facilitate investing that is environmentally responsible. Fiduciaries should no longer define their responsibilities as simply maximizing financial returns for investors; rather, those financial returns must be earned without depleting natural capital. Investing in nature's trust is about a new fiduciary standard that comes from the assumption that beneficiaries' best interests fundamentally include, over the long term, ensuring social and environmental returns as well.

Method, plan and terminology of the book

This book builds on my scholarship over the past decade on RI and its governance.[199] This effort focuses on what I regard as the single most important legal issue shaping RI – fiduciary law. The aim is to deepen our understanding of how fiduciary finance law affects the prospects of RI and to suggest better legal arrangements. Reorienting markets towards sustainability, of course, is not just a task for social investors; the social economy also has an enabling role through its non-profit and charitable sectors as well as public–private partnerships and other vehicles for promoting community-oriented development.[200] But there are limits to the scope of any book, and those issues aren't considered here.

Throughout this work, I examine RI and fiduciary law in a comparative context, discussing legal precedents and issues from a number of countries. Significant emphasis is given to common law jurisdictions, especially the UK and US, which are the cradle of fiduciary law and also where disproportionately many global-equity institutional funds are domiciled. In 2010, the US accounted for about 45 per cent of global investment assets under management, and the UK (the world's second ranked) accounted for 8 per cent.[201] Somewhat functionally equivalent legal rules exist in civil law systems such as Germany, which are sometimes discussed as a point of comparison. The Norwegian, New Zealand and French sovereign wealth funds are also assessed for their RI practices and innovative legal mandates. Through this multi-jurisdictional

---

199 Such as B.J. Richardson, *Socially Responsible Investment Law: Regulating the Unseen Polluters*, Oxford University Press, 2008; B.J. Richardson, *Environmental Regulation Through Financial Organisations: Comparative Perspectives on the Industrialised Nations*, Kluwer Law, 2002.
200 See, e.g., work of the Canadian-based Social Economy Network: http://socialeconomy centre.ca.
201 CityUK, 'Fund management', October 2011, 2.

focus, this book aims to fill the gap in the literature that has focused on RI's governance in individual countries.[202]

A multinational focus is worthwhile for several reasons. First, financial institutions function in an increasingly global market, having beneficiaries from and making investments in a diverse number of jurisdictions. The transnational character of modern investment requires attentiveness to the jurisdictional variations of fiduciary law and other relevant laws. Second, over the past decade a major debate about the legality of RI and its legal reform has erupted, involving scholars, lawyers and policy-makers worldwide. The seminal Freshfields Report,[203] commissioned by UNEP-FI, emphasized the importance of examining RI's legal framework in an international context in order to compare the effects of different legal regimes and to identify the best innovations to guide reform. Third, among common law jurisdictions particularly, courts and regulators sometimes draw upon each other's legal precedents for guidance, including dealing with novel fiduciary law disputes.[204] The recent crisis in global financial markets has also stimulated the search for more robust, common methods of regulating investments worldwide.

In addition to this multi-jurisdictional sweep, this book canvasses a variety of financial institutions. A limitation of the extant scholarship is its obsessive focus on pension funds.[205] Most discussions about the interaction between fiduciary law and RI treat occupational pension funds not only as the paradigmatic example but as seemingly the *only* example. Yet fiduciary relationships govern many types of financial intermediaries, including within financial corporations – banks and insurance companies – as well as in mutual funds and sometimes even between individual clients and their financial advisers. Moreover, RI itself can reach across the entire financial economy, including bank lending and the bond market, in addition to equity investing by pension funds. A comprehensive assessment of RI's legal context requires that all forms of corporate financing be analysed. This book focuses primarily on investments in equities (shares) and corporate debt, as these asset classes provide the clearest link between investment and corporate activities.

This book is replete with specialized terminology. As already introduced, the term 'responsible investment' (RI) is problematic for some. Traditionally, it was more commonly known as 'ethical investment' (especially in the UK)

---

202 See, e.g., M. O'Brien Hylton, '"Socially responsible" investing: doing good versus doing well in an inefficient market', *American University Law Review* 42 1992, 1–52; Thornton, op. cit.; J. Scharlau, *Socially Responsible Investment: Die Deutschen und Europarechtlichen Rahmenbedingungen*, Walter de Gruyter, 2009.
203 Freshfields, op. cit.
204 E.g., English courts have examined US precedents when hearing cases about RI, as in *Cowan*, op. cit., 291.
205 Among numerous examples, see A.G.F. Hoepner, M. Rezec and S. Siegl, 'Does pension funds' fiduciary duty prohibit the integration of environmental responsibility criteria in investment processes? A realistic prudent investment test', Working Paper, SSRN, 2011; G. Yaron, 'The responsible pension trustee: reinterpreting the principles of prudence and loyalty in the context of socially responsible institutional investing', SHARE, 2001.

or 'socially responsible investment (SRI)' (in the US). In recent years both terms have tended to wane in usage in favour of the seemingly more neutral phrase 'responsible investment'. While some observers favour maintaining these distinctions and see RI as watered down and less stringent than ethical investment or SRI,[206] such terms risk ghettoizing efforts to foster responsible investing throughout the financial economy. *All* investment should be ethical and socially responsible.

Another terminological issue to clarify is 'fiduciary law'. Some lawyers emphasize that there is only one fiduciary rule, namely to control opportunism and self-interested behaviour when 'an actor has access to the assets of another for a defined or limited purpose'.[207] It is commonly enunciated as the duty of loyalty, requiring the fiduciary to avoid conflicts of interest or profiting at the expense of the beneficiary. Many further fiduciary-like responsibilities belong in other categories of law, such as trust law's duty of prudent investment. Commentators often gloss over such distinctions,[208] conflating trust and fiduciary law. This book refers to 'fiduciary law' in a broad sense to cover a range of situations that involve fiduciary-like relationships in financial decision-making, in which not only the foregoing narrow sense of fiduciary law applies but also some other areas of related law (but where appropriate, distinctions between specific legal norms are made, such as in relation to the triggers of liability and available remedies for breach of legal obligations). This expansive approach is justified because investment management, at a general level, has a fiduciary character, and traditional fiduciary law interacts closely with a range of quasi-fiduciary standards in statutory regulation, codes of conduct and other legal mechanisms.

The research for this book took place over several years, with funding gratefully received from Canada's Social Sciences and Humanities Research Council. The research included many interviews with investment practitioners and other participants in the financial sector. The interviews were conducted informally through face-to-face or telephone discussions, with questions formulated to elicit a range of experiences and perceptions relevant to RI and its governance. To maintain the confidentiality of interviewees where requested, not all such discussions are formally cited in this book. Additional sources of empirical information were examined, including surveys and case studies conducted by RI industry associations, consultancy reports, graduate theses and other materials. Much research also was gleaned from traditional library sources. Numerous academic articles, books, policy papers and corporate documentation on RI and its regulation have been published in

---

206 Cronin, op. cit., 112–13.
207 R. Flannigan, 'Fiduciary duties of shareholders and directors', *Journal of Business Law* 2004, 277–302, 281.
208 P. Birks, 'The content of fiduciary obligation', *Israel Law Review* 34, 2000, 3–38; A. Hudson, 'The regulation of trustees', in M. Dixon and G. Griffiths (eds), *Contemporary Perspectives on Property, Equity, and Trusts Law*, Oxford University Press, 2007, 163–80.

recent years, although the fiduciary law dimension remains under-researched. Many students from the law faculties at York University and the University of British Columbia assisted with much of this laborious research, as named in this book's acknowledgements page.

Over five further chapters, this book attempts to substantiate its central claim that fiduciary law remains a significant hindrance to investing for sustainability, which requires not only legal and governance changes at the level of individual funds but also new responsibilities on the part of the state. Chapter 2 explains why RI has had little success in disciplining the financial economy and thereby has largely failed to improve corporate environmental behaviour. The impact of fiduciary and trusts law on RI is discussed in Chapter 3, highlighting both constraints and opportunities for social investors. Chapter 4 extends the fiduciary law analysis by comparing its application to different kinds of financial entities in the retail and institutional sectors, particularly banks, pension plans, mutual funds and insurance companies. Sovereign wealth funds in France, New Zealand and Norway are considered in Chapter 5 to illustrate the capacity for RI through public sector funds and their putative fiduciary responsibilities. The final chapter outlines potential legal reforms to facilitate RI that reflects 'nature's trust', including the public trust doctrine to frame the state's overarching responsibilities for environmental stewardship.

2 The influence of responsible investment

Introduction

It has been said that finance is 'grease to the economy',[1] a metaphor that suggests financial markets are pivotal to facilitating economic activity. Likewise, some social investors suppose they can 'encourage corporations to improve their practices on environmental, social, and governance issues'.[2] Large institutional investors, in particular, are believed to 'occupy an influential position and are capable of achieving many objectives with such financial power'.[3] So far, however, RI's societal impact has received relatively little careful attention from scholars or practitioners, who obsess with RI's financial performance.[4] While investors increasingly encourage companies to report on their sustainability performance, they have paid scant attention to the robustness of the targets that companies have set themselves or their long-term impact.[5]

One example of the hope some might have that RI can improve corporate environmental behaviour is the Gunns pulp mill controversy in Australia. In May 2008, the Australian and New Zealand (ANZ) Bank declined to fund a pulp mill proposed by Gunns, a major forestry operator.[6] Although the ANZ

---

1 B. Scholtens, 'Finance as a driver of corporate social responsibility', *Journal of Business Ethics* 68(1), 2006, 19–33, 19.
2 US-SIF, 'Sustainable and responsible investment facts', http://ussif.org/resources/sriguide/ srifacts.cfm. See also D. Ross and D. Wood, 'Do environmental and social controls matter in Australian capital investment decision-making', *Business Strategy and the Environment* 17(5), 2008, 294–303; Worldwide Fund for Nature (WWF) and BankTrack, *Shaping the Future of Sustainable Finance: Moving from Paper Promises to Sustainable Performance*, WWF, 2008.
3 R. Koo, 'Ethical finance: can ethical objectives be achieved through financial investments?', *Company and Securities Law Journal* 26, 2008, 127–39, 133.
4 M. Barnett and R. Salomon, 'Beyond dichotomy: the curvilinear relationship between social responsibility and financial performance', *Strategic Management Journal* 27, 2006, 1101–22; N. Kreander, et al., 'Evaluating the performance of ethical and non-ethical funds: a matched pair analysis', *Journal of Business Finance and Accounting* 32(7–8), 2005, 1465–93; R. Bauer, J. Derwall and R. Otten, 'The ethical mutual fund performance debate: new evidence from Canada', *Journal of Business Ethics* 70, 2007, 111–24. J. Derwall, et al., 'The eco-efficiency premium puzzle', *Financial Analysts Journal* 61(2), 2005, 51–63; M. Kiernan, *Investing in a Sustainable World: Why Green is the New Color of Money on Wall Street*, AMACOM, 2008.
5 R. Sullivan, *Valuing Corporate Responsibility*, Greenleaf Publishing, 2011, xi.
6 M. Wilkinson and B. Cubby, 'ANZ exit from pulp mill project confirmed', *Melbourne Age*, 28 May 2008, 3.

publicly declined to elaborate its reasons for shunning the project,[7] which was worth about AUD$2 billion, the bank was concerned about the pulp mill's potential environmental legacy.[8] ANZ incurred much bad press and hostility from some of its shareholders,[9] despite commissioning a technical review of Gunns' proposal that included some scrutiny of its environmental dimensions. As a signatory to the Equator Principles,[10] a global voluntary code for responsible project financing, the ANZ was surely conscious of the environmental due diligence standards it had pledged to follow. The lender's stance is particularly enlightening given that the pulp mill had largely met government regulatory requirements.[11] Gunns subsequently struggled to raise the cash to launch its pulp mill, which remains mothballed. As of October 2012, it still hadn't managed to find new financial backers, and the company's share value also reportedly dropped from over AUD$4 in 2004 to $0.95 in early 2012.[12]

This episode raises the spectre of investors and financiers acting in effect as surrogate environmental 'regulators' of the market. As sources of corporate finance, the financial sector can in theory sway both firms' development choices and, cumulatively, wider economic trends.[13] Also, as shareholders, investors acquire a voice within companies to hypothetically leverage change. Thereby, RI might complement official regulation by improving the social responsibility of the market. The extent of (and need for) RI in any given country may thus correlate with how social and environmental issues are addressed through ordinary regulation, with RI perhaps being more extensive where such issues are under-regulated or, conversely, less extensive where they are well-governed. In Germany, where RI has historically been rather weak, one explanation is that some issues that might be targeted by social investors, such as labour standards, are already closely regulated under German legislation.[14] Its system of labour 'co-determination' has possibly led companies to

---

7 'ANZ quiet on Gunns funding', *Sydney Morning Herald*, 22 May 2008, http://www.smh.com.au/business/anz-quiet-on-gunns-funding-20080522-2h52.html.
8 'Lobby group ups pressure on ANZ', *ABC News*, 7 April 2008, http://www.abc.net.au/news/2008-04-07/lobby-group-ups-pressure-on-anz/2395140.
9 M. Bowman, 'The role of the banking industry in facilitating climate change mitigation and the transition to a low-carbon global economy', *Environmental and Planning Law Journal* 27, 2010, 448–68, 456.
10 Http://www.equator-principles.com.
11 A. Darby and D. Welsh, 'Contentious pulp mill wins federal approval', *Sydney Morning Herald*, 11 March 2011, 7.
12 A. Crook, 'Race to find financier as Gunns pulp mill faces facts', *Crikey*, 5 April 2012, http://www.crikey.com.au/?p=283898; 'Gunns share price hits all time low', ABC News *The Examiner*, 10 January 2012, http://www.abc.net.au/news/2012-01-10/gunns-shares-hit-new-low/3766328.
13 J. Froud, A. Leaver and K. Williams, 'New actors in a financialised economy and the remaking of capitalism', *New Political Economy* 12(3), 2007, 339–47.
14 *Law on Codetermination (Mitbestimmungsgesetz (MitbestG))*, 4 May 1976, (1976) BGBl. I 1153; *Law on Works Councils (Betriebsverfassungsgesetz (BetrVG))*, 25 September 2001, (2001) BGBl. I 2518.

be more mindful of stakeholder interests,[15] and thus social investors might view it as less important to voice concerns in German firms than comparable investors in Anglo-American companies. Peter Waring and Tony Edwards agree that 'in the countries without a strong tradition of social regulation, such as the US, SRI is becoming the functional equivalent of such regulation in that it imposes constraints on the employment practices implemented by management'.[16] Yet in other jurisdictions with similarly small RI markets, other factors seem to be operative. For example, Spain, whose RI market was in 2009 described by researchers as 'incipient and virtually nonexistent', suffers from a lack of relevant knowledge, inhospitable organizational cultures in funds and a weak societal interest in CSR.[17]

Most social investors no doubt would disavow any pretence of being surrogate regulators, as they don't view themselves as qualified, capable or authorized to police the market. Only a minority of deeply ethical investors, such as those associated with religious and activist groups, would regard their mission as including to change market behaviour. Some other investors may be willing to play this role but likely doubt that they have the means to exert influence. On the whole, the financial industry has viewed itself as mostly just passively tied to its clients and borrowers, and not meant to meddle in their policies and operational practices unless those policies and practices jeopardize the industry's financial interests. For example, they might be jeopardized if a borrower sinks into insolvency or its share price dives because of burdensome pollution fines.[18] Otherwise, it appears naïve to hope that financiers will manipulate their market position to promote sustainability, since they might price themselves out of the market as clients look for funding from less scrupulous sources. Or financiers might suffer if they shoulder the costs of promoting sustainability without being able to monopolize the benefits and prevent other investors from free-riding on their efforts. Although dedicated social investors might be willing to incur these financial costs and disadvantages, today they tend to either be too few in number or lack clout.

However, RI's underlying rationale is tied to its capacity to yield social benefits by enlightening the market. As the previous chapter explained, historically, ethical investors were often teleologically driven, seeking to reform the behaviour of companies and governments. While social investors have strong financial objectives, which the RI industry increasingly prioritizes,

---

15 K.J. Hopt and P.C. Leyens, 'Board models in Europe – recent developments of internal corporate governance structures in Germany, the United Kingdom, France, and Italy', *European Company and Financial Law Review* 7, 2004, 135–68.
16 P. Waring and T. Edwards, 'Socially responsible investment: explaining its uneven development and human resource management consequences', *Corporate Governance* 16(3), 2008, 135–45, 137.
17 L.A. Vivo and M. Franch, 'The challenges of socially responsible investment among institutional investors', *Business and Society Review* 114(1), 2009, 31–57, 46.
18 See J. Lipton, 'Project financing and the environment: lender liability for environmental damage in Australia', *Journal of International Banking Law* 11, 1996, 7–17.

the legitimacy of RI still hinges on its reputation to offer 'social returns' in addition to financial gains. In other words, the rhetoric says one can 'do well while doing good'.[19] Providing 'social returns' implies that RI has influence, it being not just about avoiding complicity in 'sin stocks' but also about reducing the amount of ongoing sin.

The purpose of this chapter is to demonstrate that RI's capacity to generate social returns is presently rather limited. It critiques five ways RI has sought to exert influence:

1. by promoting RI as a profitable alternative to conventional investment;
2. by altering the cost of capital of targeted companies, such as by divestment, and thereby creating pressure for improved corporate behaviour, or through positive investment such as community impact investing;
3. by advocating change within companies, as shareholders or lenders, such as by filing shareholder resolutions and through informal engagement with corporate management;
4. by drafting codes of conduct for more systemic changes across the market; and
5. by reforming public policy and official regulation pertaining to the financial economy.

The notion of having 'influence' as used in this chapter is about possessing some power to affect a thing or course of events. It denotes some degree of leverage that financial institutions may exert over borrowers, clients or portfolio companies regarding their social and environmental performance. Such influence might range from dissuading a company from initiating a project that is environmentally harmful, to making modest adjustments to its operations or even to encouraging a business to take positive measures to improve its sustainability performance. Importantly, investors' influence might transcend individual targeted companies to acquire broader strategic significance in shaping the public policy and regulatory agenda, such as lobbying for changes to securities regulation or environmental standards. Investors might fail to change the behaviour of a specific firm yet nonetheless exert subtle influence over the long term by raising awareness about aspects of corporate behaviour among investors, the general public and policymakers. This impact can help improve the legitimacy of taking action on such issues and ultimately lead to regulatory reform.

We can thus gauge RI's impact on corporate behaviour along a spectrum of ambition. Initially, social investors might aim to avoid sponsoring companies that perpetrate environmental and social wrongs. With this minimalist approach, investors deny finance to those planning to commit such harm. The

---

19 H.G. Fung, S.A. Law and J. Ya, *Socially Responsible Investment in a Global Environment*, Edward Elgar, 2010, 46.

rationale for this approach might be that eschewing *complicity* with irresponsible companies and denying them tacit support will prevent reputational damage to investors. Alternatively, some social investors seek more positive change, such as through community impact investing and the financing of 'green and clean tech' start-ups. And in the wake of global financial crises, some social investors believe they should try to influence the entire financial *system*, shifting the market as a whole towards long-term, sustainable investment.

Therefore, in reflecting on RI's influence, we need to keep in mind distinctions about the relative ambition of social investors. It is the latter two types of RI that are potentially the most transformative with regard to sustainability. When we consider the influence of RI codes of conduct or shareholder engagement, for instance, their success has to be seen in light of their ambitiousness – from aiming to avoid complicity with harmful behaviour to actively promoting positive change. It is much easier for a social investor to achieve the former, which doesn't require any action by the companies targeted.

Measuring or quantifying such influence is difficult because changes in the behaviour of targeted firms should be correlated to the actions of investors. For instance, evaluations of the effectiveness of shareholder resolutions usually try to compare specific filings with particular managerial decisions of targeted corporations within a given period. But there may be a prolonged delay before desired changes are made – beyond the period surveyed by researchers – and various other causal factors may be at work, making it hard to verify the impact of a specific shareholder resolution. Furthermore, shareholder resolutions that don't pass or are withdrawn may provide leverage at the corporate bargaining table to achieve changes in business practice. Jeanne Logsdon and Harry van Buren recorded nearly 400 separate discussions between companies and members of the Interfaith Center on Corporate Responsibility in their survey covering 1999 to 2005.[20] Thus, an assessment of the influence of RI is invariably somewhat conjectural and qualitative.

Because of these methodological challenges, especially when considering RI's influence on a large scale, this chapter takes a tentative approach. The argument proceeds in a mainly conceptual and conjectural manner, as a basis for facilitating more systematic and precise enquiries into RI's influence. There is sufficient evidence now to doubt the influence of social investors on corporate behaviour and the market more generally, as many social investors already agree.[21] One of the most powerful pieces of evidence is the size of the RI market, as examined in the next section. The main inference of this chapter is that, despite serving investors who wish to seek change through the market

---

20 J.M. Logsdon and H.J. van Buren III, 'Beyond the proxy vote: dialogues between shareholder activists and corporations', *Journal of Business Ethics* 87, 2009, 353–659.
21 Research on the Australian market, for example, reveals considerable scepticism on the part of fund managers of the level of RI influence or potential influence on the corporate sector: W. Ransome and C. Sampford, *Ethics and Socially Responsible Investment: A Philosophical Approach*, Ashgate, 2011, 99–101.

when governments don't act, paradoxically, RI's influence is constrained without an enabling policy and legal framework. This book concentrates on one key part of that legal framework – fiduciary law.[22]

Size of the RI market

The media and popular literature can paint a misleading picture of the extent of RI,[23] and formal surveys tend to overstate the size of its market. While recent research by leading RI industry associations in North America and Western Europe heralds the sector as having captured between 10 to 20 per cent of these investment markets,[24] the survey methodologies as discussed below are flawed and exaggerate the amount of RI. We lack similar data for responsible lending in the banking sector, although some qualitative research raises concerns about its extent.[25] Nonetheless, some academic research suggests in recent years there has been a clear improvement in banks' social responsibility, and the leading lenders in this regard are in the Netherlands, Germany and the UK, while the least responsible are allegedly Japanese and Swedish banks.[26]

The fundamental problem is that the surveys take an overly inclusive or broad understanding of RI. In part, this methodological bias reflects a trend in the RI industry to distinguish or broaden itself beyond traditional ethical investing to a more morally neutral approach that focuses on long-term investing and integration of ESG issues into financial analyses.[27] But such a stance potentially allows a wide range of practices to be deemed 'responsible investing' because there is often much discretionary judgement about the necessary depth and quality of ESG analysis or long-term horizon. Thus some surveys count an entire fund's portfolio as 'RI' even though it ethically screens only on a single or limited number of issues, or engages with just a few of its investee firms. In the US market, the Forum for Sustainable and Responsible Investment (US-SIF) estimates that about 12 per cent of assets under

---

22 B.J. Richardson, *Socially Responsible Investment Law: Regulating the Unseen Polluters*, Oxford University Press, 2008.
23 E.g., P. Aburdene, *Megatrends 2010: The Rise of Conscious Capitalism*, Hampton Roads Publishing, 2005, 140; T. Grant, 'Social investment assets soar', *Globe and Mail*, 22 March 2007, B17.
24 Eurosif, *European SRI Study 2010*, 2010; US-SIF, 'Socially responsible investing assets in US top $3 trillion; nearly 1 out of every 8 dollars under professional management', Press release, 9 November 2010, http://www.socialinvest.org/news/releases/pressrelease.cfm?id=168.
25 One 2006 study concluded that 'with few exceptions bank policies are lagging significantly behind relevant international standards and best practices': WWF and BankTrack, op. cit., 4; see also International Finance Corporation (IFC), *Banking on Sustainability: Financing Environmental and Social Opportunities in Emerging Markets*, World Bank, 2007.
26 B. Scholtens, 'Corporate social responsibility in the international banking industry', *Journal of Business Ethics* 86, 2009, 159–75.
27 See notably R. Urwin, *Sustainable Investing Practice: Simplified Complexity*, Towers Watson, 2009.

professional management are linked to RI.[28] Yet, US-SIF includes in this figure funds that screen merely against tobacco, alcohol or gambling – indeed, 25 per cent of notional RI funds screen on the basis of only *one* of these activities.[29]

Another illustration of this defective surveying comes from the Canadian RI market. The 2010 study made by the Social Investment Organization trumpets that Canadian RI is worth CAD$530 billion and holds about one fifth (19.1 per cent) of all assets under management in the country.[30] Nearly 90 per cent of this figure is based on the estimated value of investment portfolios that do not ethically screen but rather engage with a small number of firms in these portfolios.[31] The Canadian survey egregiously counts the *entire* value of these investment portfolios rather than the tiny portion targeted for corporate engagement. A likely more realistic figure for Canadian RI is about 2 to 3 per cent of the market, as recognized by the same Canadian study in its separate measurement of the proportion of funding tied to 'core' ethical screens.[32]

The extent of the RI market in any individual country may also be shaped by a number of local factors. In Japan, the RI retail market in 2007 was estimated at just 1.2 per cent of total retail fund assets,[33] reputedly due to various factors, including the lack of corporate sustainability reporting, the lack of environment-oriented business groups and insulated corporate governance structures.[34] Local factors are also significant determinants of Germany's historically tiny RI sector. Until the 1990s, a large segment of the German economy was closed to equity investors. The *Mittelstand* (small- and medium-sized, often family-run companies), often considered a backbone of the German economy,[35] were not always incorporated, and if they were, they would be largely run as *GmbHs* (limited liability companies) that are not publicly traded.[36] (The number of public stock corporations in Germany remains fairly small.[37]) A further factor is that until the mid-1990s Germany

---

28 US-SIF, op. cit.
29 US-SIF, *2005 Report on Socially Responsible Investing Trends in the United States: A 10-Year Review*, US-SIF, 2005, 9.
30 Social Investment Organization (SIO), *Canadian Socially Responsible Investment Review 2010*, SIO, 2011, 7.
31 Ibid., 9.
32 Ibid.
33 E. Adachi, *SRI in Asia: Its Trends and Challenges*, Asian Development Bank Institute, 2007.
34 J. Park, 'Sustainable consumption and the financial sector: analysing the markets for responsible investment in Hong Kong and Japan', *International Journal of Consumer Studies* 33, 2009, 206–14, 211–13.
35 J.W. Cioffi, 'Corporate governance reform, regulatory politics, and the foundations of finance capitalism in the United States and Germany', *German Law Journal* 7, 2006, 533–62, 551.
36 H. Schaefer, 'Ethical investment of German non-profit organizations – conceptual outline and empirical results', *Business Ethics: A European Review* 13(4), 2004, 269–87, 271.
37 There were approximately 15,000 stock corporations in 2005: U. Noack and D. Zetzsche, 'Corporate governance reform in Germany: the second decade', *European Business Law Review* 16(5), 2005, 1033–64, 1034.

lacked sufficient institutional mechanisms to facilitate the growth of capital markets, a precondition for RI through equity investment and shareholder engagement.[38]

RI's financial rationale

If you scan recent literature on social investing, you'll quickly observe a preoccupation with its financial justification. Rather than assess how RI contributes to sustainability as an ethical goal valuable in its own right, both practitioner and academic writings dwell obsessively on RI's financial advantages.[39] In the case of institutional funds such as pension plans, this stance is due partly to how such funds interpret their fiduciary responsibilities to beneficiaries. Chapter 3 examines closely fiduciary law, showing that part of the legal prejudice against RI stems from problematic, narrow interpretations of the law. Moreover, similar investment practices and philosophies are found in the retail funds supposedly liberated from many of the fiduciary constraints on institutional investors. RI's philosophy is thus changing dramatically away from ethical investment, paralleling the same trend in the CSR discourse.

Historically, religious investors pioneered RI with the aim to avoid financial ties to intoxicants, gambling or other 'sin stocks'.[40] During the early 1970s, the aspirations of the RI movement shifted in its divestment campaign against South Africa's apartheid regime. No longer were social investors satisfied merely to avoid profiting from immorality; instead, they also sought to improve the moral behaviour of others.[41] While the ethical rationale has continued to enlighten the protest wing of the RI sector through their campaigns on a miscellany of causes spanning land mines to animal welfare, the dominant oeuvre of RI has gravitated elsewhere.

In trying to woo more adherents, many RI proponents have rebranded it as a savvy business strategy.[42] Investors are asked to scrutinize the ESG performance of their firms, not primarily for ethical reasons but because financial returns are at stake. In contrast to the belligerent divestment campaigns and shareholder activism of earlier styles of RI, 'business-case RI'

---

38 B.J. Richardson, 'Greening the financial sector: legal reforms in the European Union', *Yearbook of European Environmental Law* 7, 2007, 159–203, 168.
39 The literature is vast, but see e.g., Kiernan, op. cit.; P. Camejo, *The SRI Advantage: Why Socially Responsible Investing Has Outperformed Financially*, New Society Publishers, 2002; M. Barnett and R. Salmon, 'Beyond dichotomy: the curvilinear relationship between social responsibility and financial performance', *Strategic Management Journal* 27(11), 2006, 1101–22.
40 N. Kreander, K. McPhail and D. Molyneaux, 'God's fund managers: a critical study of stock market investment practices of the Church of England and UK Methodists', *Accounting, Auditing and Accountability Journal* 17(3), 2004, 408–41.
41 J. Davis, J. Cason and G. Hovey, 'Economic disengagement and South Africa: the effectiveness and feasibility of implementing sanctions and divestment', *Law and Policy in International Business* 15, 1983, 529–63.
42 I. Cherneva (ed.), *The Business Case for Sustainable Finance*, Routledge, 2012.

is typically implemented through light-touch screens, filtering only the most pernicious companies from investment portfolios, polite engagement with corporate management, and nuanced ESG evaluations for financial due diligence. RI is emptied of its ethical connotations and redefined as a new model of financial analysis in which ESG factors are assessed for materiality and effect on risk and returns. The UNEP-FI has advised: 'The first – and arguably for investors the most important – reason to integrate environmental, social and governance issues is, simply, to make more money.'[43] Another UNEP-FI report cautions investment analysts to '[c]ommunicate on issue-specific, proven, quantifiable, material links to business value; . . . [and to] avoid moral arguments'.[44] Some studies suggest social investors are willing to accept lower returns for ethical gains, although their willingness to accept a steep trade-off is limited.[45]

Much research asserts that RI offers comparable, and occasionally superior, risk-adjusted financial returns relative to conventional portfolios.[46] This might occur because socially irresponsible businesses presumably excluded from such portfolios tend to lose value due to litigation costs, reputational damage, labour disputes, inefficient resource consumption or many other possible variables.[47] However, the reliability of the data is reproachable because investigators use diverse methodologies and criteria, including small samples and short performance periods, as well as inadequate controls for industry, country and other factor biases. Without authoritative agreement on the parameters of an RI portfolio, comparisons can at most be made between funds that apply specific screening criteria against market performance, with conclusions inferred only from that specific screening style or other methods. In other words, it isn't possible to extrapolate from such research conclusions

---

43 UNEP-FI, *Show Me the Money: Linking Environmental, Social and Governance Issues to Company Value*, UNEP-FI, 2006, 4.
44 UNEP-FI, *Generation Lost: Young Financial Analysts and Environmental, Social and Governance Issues. Executive Summary*, UNEP-FI, 2004, 5.
45 L. Renneboog, T. Horst and C. Zhang, 'Socially responsible investments: institutional aspects, performance, and investor behavior', *Journal of Banking and Finance* 32, 2008, 1723–42; J. McLachlan and J. Gardner, 'A comparison of socially responsible and conventional investors', *Journal of Business Ethics* 52, 2004, 11–52.
46 UNEP-FI and Mercer Consulting, *Demystifying Responsible Investment Performance: A Review of Key Academic and Broker Research on ESG Factors*, UNEP-FI, 2007; M. Orlitzky, F. Schmidt and S. Rynes, 'Corporate social and financial performance: a meta-analysis', *Organization Studies* 24(3), 2003, 403–41; M. Schroeder, 'The performance of socially responsible investments: investment funds and indices', *Financial Markets and Portfolio Management* 18(2), 2004, 122–42; G.A. Mill, 'The financial performance of a socially responsible investment over time and a possible link with corporate social responsibility', *Journal of Business Ethics* 63(2), 2006, 131–48; N. Kreander, et al., 'Evaluating the performance of ethical and non-ethical funds: a matched pair analysis', *Journal of Business Finance and Accounting* 32(7–8), 2005, 1465–93; M. Statman, 'Socially responsible indexes: composition, performance, and tracking errors', *Journal of Portfolio Management* 32 (spring), 2006, 100–9.
47 L. Renneboog, J.T. Horst and C. Zhang, 'Socially responsible investments: institutional aspects, performance, and investor behavior', *Journal of Banking and Finance* 32(9), 2008, 1723–42, 1734.

about the relative financial performance of RI generally. Even if we could, there is another fundamental methodology weakness associated with the similarity between RI portfolios and the underlying market. That many studies suggest RI portfolios' returns track the market very closely likely reflects the laxity of the inclusion criteria of such funds. The claim that these portfolios substantially out-perform the market is thus counterintuitive. A major study of the Australian RI market concluded that '[t]he criteria that funds employ appear ineffective, with practically all listed companies being acceptable to at least one social or ethical fund. Due to such indiscriminate screening practice, much of what is called ethical investment . . . has little to do with ethics at all.'[48] In other words, RI is too inclusive.[49] Such inclusivity can be justified only if social investors engage actively with their portfolio companies, which they generally don't, as explained later in this chapter.

Modern corporate finance theory suggests that if RI were to exclude significant portions of the market on ethical grounds, it could not financially outperform the market.[50] One of its principal concepts, MPT, holds that a diversified investment universe is more likely to produce optimal, risk-adjusted returns than a narrowly constructed portfolio.[51] Exclusionary ethical screens that reduce the investment pool therefore should augment risks without compensatory higher returns.[52] Even if markets in the 'real world' do not behave strictly as theory predicts, as some commentators plausibly contend,[53] RI does not necessarily enjoy an advantage because an 'inefficient' market may under- or over-rate both ethical and unethical businesses equally.[54] RI that relies on corporate engagement rather than exclusionary screens should retain a reasonably diversified portfolio, although both methods may carry higher expenses and administrative overheads than incurred by regular funds due to the additional ESG research and activism.[55]

Even the more principled members of the RI industry, often associated with NGOs and public sector funds, show signs of being lured by financial

---

48 J.D. Cronin, *From Ethical Investment to Investment Ethics*, PhD, Queensland University of Technology, 2004, 136.
49 For research that suggests otherwise, see K.L. Benson, T.J. Brailsford and J.E. Humphrey, 'Do socially responsible fund managers really invest differently?', *Journal of Business Ethics* 65(4), 2006, 337–57.
50 J. Langbein and R. Posner, 'Social investing and the law of trusts', *Michigan Law Review* 79, 1980, 72–112; M. Knoll, 'Ethical screening in modern financial markets: the conflicting claims underlying socially responsible investment', *Business Lawyer* 57, 2002, 681–726.
51 H. Markowitz, 'Portfolio selection', *Journal of Finance* 7(1), 1952, 77–91. Returns, for instance, include dividends paid by firms as well as appreciation of the firms' stock prices.
52 A. Rudd, 'Social responsibility and portfolio performance', *California Management Review* 23(4), 1981, 55–61.
53 See, e.g., R. Ball, 'The theory of stock market efficiency: accomplishments and limitations', *Journal of Applied Corporate Finance* 30(2–3), 1995, 4–18.
54 Knoll, op. cit., 706.
55 S. Croome-Carther, 'Funds with values', *forbes.com*, 14 November 2007.

considerations. The Darfur divestment campaign is one example.[56] The Vermont State Treasurer, who oversees the state's pension funds, explained that 'it would be prudent, from a fiduciary position, to refrain from owning securities in companies listed on the Sudan Divestment Task Force Highest Offenders list, because the value of our portfolio could suffer if we continue holding those securities while other investors take affirmative action to sell securities on the list'.[57] The director of the Sudan Divestment Task Force says the market reaction has changed the argument from 'purely a moral argument ... [to] much more of a financial argument'.[58] Even the most socially responsible public sector pension plans, such as CalPERS, stress their primary goal is profit-making for their beneficiaries.[59]

By appealing to the market's logic, business-case RI seductively promises to solve the movement's historic marginalization. In contrast, for moral arguments to prevail among investors, there likely needs to be some substantial preponderance of public opinion, for example, on the immorality of profiting from apartheid or genocidal dictatorships. In the divestment campaign against South Africa's apartheid regime, the ethical case carried fervent support only among faith-based investors and a few public pension plans, while for their private counterparts the financial rationale for divestment was determinative.[60] Financial self-interest of course can be a very persuasive reason to act: vividly depicting climate change as a financial threat or opportunity can galvanize many investors more than ambiguous pious talk.[61]

For several reasons, the business case is not yet a viable basis for a comprehensive approach to RI. ESG due diligence is still far from integrated into conventional financial practices.[62] Certainly, a flourishing ESG research industry has emerged,[63] helping to inform new sustainability performance standards. A pioneering example is the Climate Bonds Standard and Certification Scheme, which assures investors of the low-carbon quality of screened assets such as corporate bonds.[64] But such initiatives are not widespread, and a

56 S. Grene, 'Ambiguity cloaks ethical investment message', *Financial Times*, 4 February 2008, 13.
57 J. Spaulding, 'Vermont pension funds axe investments in Sudan', News release, Office of the State Treasurer, 20 February 2007.
58 'Activists hail data as reason to avoid Sudan-linked firms', *Investment News* 12, 2008, 2.
59 T. Hebb, *No Small Change: Pension Funds and Corporate Engagement*, Cornell University Press, 2008, 39.
60 Ibid., 32.
61 Mercer, *Climate Change Scenarios: Implications for Strategic Asset Management*, Mercer, 2011.
62 D. Campbell and R. Slack, 'Environmental disclosure and environmental risk: skeptical attitudes in the UK sell-side bank analysis', *British Accounting Review* 43(1), 2011, 54–64; McKinsey, 'Valuing corporate social responsibility', *McKinsey Global Survey Results*, McKinsey Quarterly, February 2009, at http://www.mckinseyquarterly.com; European Centre for Corporate Engagement, 'Use of extra financial information by research analysts and investment managers', 2007, http://www.gmiratings.com/noteworthy/ECCESurveyMarch 2007.pdf.
63 E.g., Trucost (UK) and Jantzi Sustainalytics (Canada).
64 The credibility of the scheme is enhanced by the representation of environmental NGOs in its supervisory body. Climate Bond Certified: http://standards.climatebonds.net.

variety of impediments to robust ESG analysis have been identified, including: scepticism about the link between ESG factors and investment performance; behavioural impediments rooted in the organizational culture of institutional funds and their agents, wherein short-term outlooks prevail; difficulty in monetizing intangible ESG information; and dissatisfaction about the quality and reliability of ESG information.[65] Relatedly, corporate ESG reporting 'remains unsatisfactory in the eyes of many investors' because reports are 'inconsistent in scope and content', and they cherry-pick good news while glossing over the bad. Furthermore, 'how companies are performing against their own corporate responsibility policies and commitments' is difficult to measure.[66] By contrast, investment professionals are accustomed to 'hard' financial data such as return on equity, sales growth, price/earnings ratios and other technical indicia of financial performance.[67]

Thus, sustainability issues must be *perceived* to have financial implications, otherwise investors might ignore them. Research into UK pension funds suggests that climate integrity is often seen by fund managers and trustees as too nebulous for workable financial quantification and thus not warranting serious consideration.[68] Environmental issues cannot be accurately reflected in conventional accounting systems unless they manifest as specific expenses or income attributable to an entity.[69] The RI industry is trying to develop new valuation methods,[70] and the value of environmental performance to a company's brand name is one area where firms might be responsive. Robert Eccles states that 'studies have found that only twenty-five percent of a company's market value can be attributed to accounting book value, with the remaining seventy-five percent based on an assessment of value created by intangibles, such as strategy, product innovation, people and customer loyalty'.[71] Yet, reputational risk to companies or their financiers is not an echo for all underlying societal concerns, as sometimes the most disadvantaged groups or victims of environmental hardship can't publicize their plight adequately.

---

65 H. Jemel-Fornetty, C. Louche and D. Bourghelle, 'Changing the dominant convention: the role of emerging initiatives in mainstreaming ESG', in W. Sun, C. Louche and R. Pérez (eds), *Finance and Sustainability: Towards a New Paradigm? A Post-Crisis Agenda*, Emerald Group, 2011, 85–117, 89–91; C. Juravle and A. Lewis, 'Identifying impediments to SRI in Europe: a review of the practitioner and academic literature', *Business Ethics: A European Review* 17(3), 2008, 285–310.
66 Sullivan, op. cit., 3.
67 Jemel-Fornetty, Louche and Bourghelle, op. cit., 90.
68 J. Solomon, *Pension Fund Trustees and Climate Change*, Association of Certified Chartered Accountants, 2009, 21–3.
69 S. Goodman and T. Little, *The Gap in GAAP: An Examination of Environmental Accounting Loopholes*, Rose Foundation for Communities and the Environment, 2003.
70 S. McGeachie, M. Kiernan and E. Kirzner, *Finance and the Environment in North America: The State of Play of the Integration of Environmental Issues into Financial Research*, Innovest, 2005, 57.
71 R. Eccles, 'Enhanced business reporting consortium releases framework to promote greater transparency in corporate reporting', *The Free Library*, 18 October 2005.

A second objection is that a countervailing business case for financing environmentally damaging companies can prevail. Ubiquitous market and regulatory failures to control environmental externalities provide temptations for financiers. The recent international commodities market boom is one such example of intensified exploitation of natural resources.[72] Growing investment in the fossil fuel economy, such as Canada's oil sands, persists despite talk about the menace of climate change.[73] In other words, if RI is contingent on profitability, that logic will also sometimes give reasons to act unethically. Dan Ahrens, a US mutual fund industry executive, advocates investments in sin stocks such as casinos and adult entertainment industries – the very stocks that RI eschews – to maximize returns.[74] While social investors increasingly argue that the business case for investing responsibly strengthens over the long term,[75] many factors impede acting as though the future mattered: fund managers hired on two-year performance contracts tend to act for the short term; corporations themselves are structured around short-term financial measurements, such as quarterly financial reporting; and uncertainty about the financial cost of distant environmental harms, which depends partly on the extent of government regulation to penalize polluters, persists.[76]

Beyond these disincentives, there are also obstacles to acting collectively that inhibit investing responsibly. The financial market contains no intrinsic ordering mechanism to keep the economy as a whole within ecosystem-based limits, such as restraining pollution within the overall assimilative capacity of the environment.[77] While many investors are surely aware that climate change is both a serious environmental problem and an economic one, in a competitive market they struggle to coordinate their activities to limit investment in fossil fuel industries or other sources of global environmental pressure. Such coordination typically requires governmental intervention, such as through a carbon cap-and-trade scheme.

The prevalence of business drivers for RI varies somewhat depending on the type of financial organization, although both the retail and institutional sectors are highly attentive to financial returns. Some retail banks have branded themselves as social or ethical banks, professing to give precedence to ethical principles; examples include Banca Etica (Italy), Ekobanken

---

72 'The commodities boom on 2011: coal will be the new gold', *MoneyMorning.Com* 23 February 2011.
73 E. Crooks, 'Oil sands: ice thaws on Canadian projects', *Financial Times*, 11 March 2011, http://www.ft.com/cms/s/0/2bf6bb96-50f9-11e0-8931-00144feab49a.html#axzz1a LC3tPKE.
74 D. Ahrens, *Investing in Vice: The Recession-Proof Portfolio of Booze, Bets, Bombs, and Butts*, St. Martin's Press, 2004.
75 S. Lyndenberg, 'Universal investors and socially responsible investors: a tale of emerging affinities', *Corporate Governance: An International Review* 15(3), 2007, 467–77, 471 (stating that pension funds have 'inherently long investment horizons').
76 Richardson, *Socially Responsible Investment Law*, op. cit., 120–58.
77 H. Daly, 'Allocation, distribution and scale: towards an economics that is efficient, just and sustainable', *Ecological Economics* 6, 1992, 185–93.

(Sweden) and Mibanco (Peru).[78] In the institutional fund sector, which includes pension plans, several factors can constrain investing ethically. Such funds commonly act on behalf of thousands of unrelated beneficiaries holding diverse and often conflicting values about social and environmental issues. In contrast to the seemingly subjective or arbitrary nature of ethics, financial returns tend to be perceived as a measurable, objective standard to hold fiduciaries to account.[79] Furthermore, as subsequent chapters in this book elaborate, the fiduciary responsibilities of institutional investors have tended to be interpreted conservatively as requiring pursuit of optimal financial returns for beneficiaries without collateral ethical considerations. While the institutional sector sometimes acknowledges human rights, climate change and other issues as potential investment concerns, they garner attention primarily when perceived as financially material.

Altering the cost of finance

Another way RI may nudge companies towards sustainability is by altering firms' cost of finance. Social investors might believe they can financially reward ethical companies by channelling additional investment to them while punishing or disciplining unethical ones by divesting, thereby imposing higher costs of raising capital.[80] If sufficient social investors dominate the market, they might be able to alter the cost of capital for polluters and thereby, in effect, create something analogous to a Pigouvian tax.[81] If responsible financiers could differentiate the cost of capital on the basis of environmental or social impacts, they could motivate companies to improve their behaviours in order to entice cashed-up social investors. In this manner, the RI industry may fulfill its rhetoric to create 'a better, more just and sustainable economy'.[82]

Corporate finance theory, however, suggests otherwise. The literature suggests that in an efficient stock market, there are limitations to investors' ability to affect the price of a firm's shares or bonds.[83] The standard textbook theory is that the current price of a firm reflects a combined assessment of the current value of the firm relative to reported earnings and expectations of any changes in value in the near to medium terms. The notion of 'elasticity' is

---

78 O. Weber and S. Remer, 'Social banking: introduction', in O. Weber and S. Remer (eds), *Social Banks and the Future of Sustainable Finance*, Routledge, 2011, 1–14.
79 See L. Renneboog, J.T. Horst and C. Zhang, 'Socially responsible investments: institutional aspects, performance, and investor behavior', *Journal of Banking and Finance* 32(9), 2008, 1723–42.
80 Hebb, *No Small Change*, op. cit., 22; R. Sparkes and C. Cowton, 'The maturing of socially responsible investment: a review of the developing link with corporate social responsibility', *Journal of Business Ethics* 52, 2004, 45–57, 45.
81 A. Pigou, *The Economics of Welfare*, Macmillan, 1932.
82 US-SIF, *2003 Report on Socially Responsible Investing Trends in the United States*, US-SIF, 2003, 3.
83 C. Loderer, et al., 'The price elasticity of demand for common stock', *Journal of Finance* 46, 1991, 621–51.

used by economists to describe the fractional change in the quantity demanded for each fractional change in price, and there tend to be important differences in the demand curve (elasticity) for corporate securities compared to many goods and services in the productive economy. Whereas in a stock market investors may buy and sell blocks of shares without any significant consequence for the share price, in the case of many commodities, such changes in demand can dramatically alter price. Thus, an Israeli boycott against cottage cheese in 2011, aimed at protesting against recent food price rises in Israel, led to a reduced demand, and the decrease in cottage cheese sold led major supermarkets to slash the retail price of this food staple.[84] Conversely, because corporate stock is often highly fungible with many similar substitutes for investors (e.g., a variety of companies operating in a particular economic sector, such as IT or energy), the demand for its securities is more elastic. Consequently, a small change in share price will trigger a large change in the quantity demanded, or conversely, a large increase in the quantity demanded will result in only a small price change.

The essential implication of this model for RI is that social investors are price takers rather than price makers. It assumes that any changes in the price for stock will only reflect underlying changes in the perceived financial prospects of the company (i.e., stock price based on the present discounted value of anticipated future cash flows to the company). As any divesting by a social investor on ethical criteria does not per se alter that formula, its stock prices should not change.[85] Thus, divestment on ethical grounds should simply lead to change of ownership, not a change of price for the corporate securities, as other (conventional) investors stand by ready to buy the stock. Furthermore, punitive divestment as a strategy cannot reach unlisted, private companies. On the other hand, business-case RI that educates the market to the financial consequences of firms' ESG performance might wield some influence. But, as already explained, it presently offers an imperfect view of corporate behaviour.

A further crucial variable is the extent to which a firm needs to raise funds, as some commentators believe 'SRI is more likely to be relevant whenever companies are heavily dependent on the stock market as a financing instrument'.[86] Yet corporate financing data suggests that most companies, especially well-established firms, can mostly self-finance operations through retained earnings rather than by borrowing or issuing securities.[87] Indeed,

---

84 R. Rozenberg and A.D. Meseritz, 'Cottage cheese sales plummet as Israeli consumers revolt over price', *Haaretz*, 19 June 2011, http://www.haaretz.com/themarker/cottage-cheese-sales-plummet-as-israeli-consumers-revolt-over-price-1.368458.
85 W. Davidson, D. Worell and A. El-Jelly, 'Influencing managers to change unpopular corporate behavior through boycotts and divestitures', *Business and Society* 34(2), 1995, 171–96.
86 A. Beltratti, *Socially Responsible Investment in General Equilibrium*, Fondazione Eni Enrico Mattei, 2003, 21.
87 J. Corbett and T. Jenkinson, 'The financing of industry, 1970–1989: an international comparison', *Journal of the Japanese and International Economies* 10, 1996, 71–96; but compare to A. Hackethal and R. Schmidt, *Financing Patterns: Measurement Concepts*

through increasing stock repurchases and buy-backs, in some economies equity's contribution in net terms has been negative.[88] The 2012 Kay Review into British stock markets found that they 'are no longer a significant source of funding for new investment by UK companies. Most publicly traded UK companies generate sufficient cash from their day-to-day operations to fund their own corporate projects.'[89] Thus, a study of efforts by environmental NGOs and social investors to challenge the mining activities of Freeport McMoRan Copper and Gold found that the multinational was largely insulated from investor pressure because it could self-finance.[90] However, even mature companies are not entirely insulated from investors' demands;[91] a declining stock price can affect a firm's market capitalization and thus stock market listing, and corporate management's remuneration is often tied to stock options, thus motivating them to adopt measures that keep stock prices high.

Some other research highlights variables that might enable social investors to exert market influence in specific circumstances. Pietra Rivoli, who extrapolates from the reality that markets don't always reflect textbook theory, predicts that social investors may alter the cost of capital when the stock is particularly unique (i.e., has few substitutes) or trades in small, restrictive markets.[92] Such conditions might exist for a firm that operates a niche, boutique business or is a market leader and innovator. Some research also examines change in stock prices flowing from the addition or removal of stocks from widely tracked stock indexes, such as the S&P 500. Index tracking funds typically adjust their own portfolios to reflect changes in the underlying index, and some indexes cater to social investors such as the Dow Jones Sustainability Indexes. Standard finance theory would predict that changes in demand for a stock added or removed from an index should not affect the stock price, because they do not per se reflect changes in the company's financial prospects. But several studies of the S&P 500 found such an effect, mainly owing to the accompanying benefits of increased liquidity and inclusion in a larger investor base.[93]

Presumably if all or the overwhelming majority of investors were socially-oriented, then by their sheer numeracy they might sway companies. We lack

---

    and Empirical Results, Working Paper, Department of Finance, University of Frankfurt, 2003.
88 S. Deakin, 'The rise of finance: what is it, what is driving it, what might stop it?', *Comparative Labor Law and Policy Journal* 30, 2008, 67–75, 68.
89 J. Kay, *Kay Review of UK Equity Markets and Long-Term Decision-Making*, Department of Business, Innovation and Skills, 2012, 10.
90 J. Emel, 'An inquiry into the green disciplining of capital', *Environment and Planning A* 34, 2002, 827–43.
91 M. Jensen and K. Murphy, 'CEO incentives – it's not how much you pay, but how', *Harvard Business Review* 68(3), 1990, 138–53.
92 P. Rivoli, 'Making a difference or making a statement? Finance research and socially responsible investment', *Business Ethics Quarterly* 13(3), 2003, 271–87.
93 A. Lynch and R. Mendenhall, 'New evidence on stock price effects associated with changes in the S&P 500 Index', *Journal of Business* 70(3), 1997, 351–83.

research that predicts informatively the tipping point for such an effect,[94] but as already noted, RI markets are small and probably nowhere near this threshold. Heinkel and others developed a model of corporate environmental responsibility that predicted social investors would need to hold at least 20 per cent of the market in order to induce targeted businesses to make environmental improvements.[95] Other researchers suggest RI needs a much higher market share, although even 20 per cent exceeds quite substantially the current RI market.[96] Under current market conditions, no individual financier or coalition of investors could ever come close to monopolizing all sources of development and corporate finance to make RI obligatory. We should thus concur with George Gay and Johann Klassen that 'screening alone is not likely to have a significant impact on corporate behaviour – or on an individual company's share price – until the vast majority of investors are all screening the same group of stocks out of their portfolios'.[97]

But if social investors could convince major stock exchanges to require listed companies to meet sustainability and corporate governance performance standards, then RI could substantially amplify its influence. These stock exchanges would become gatekeepers to the market and could make it more difficult for companies to access the capital markets, especially raising finance from the issuance of shares. A number of major global stock exchanges in New York, Toronto, Sydney and Johannesburg already have adopted corporate governance and reporting standards for listed companies, though currently none appear to include any environmental listing standards except indirectly.[98] For instance, the Johannesburg Stock Exchange (JSE) Listings Requirements Relating to Corporate Governance[99] include compliance with the King Code III, and thus listed companies are expected to report annually on their environmental performance and sustainability issues affecting their business.[100] Bursa Malaysia requires listed companies to disclose their corporate social responsibility activities,[101] and the Shanghai Stock Exchange requires listed companies to disclose certain environmental information.[102]

---

94 Yet see the limited stab at modeling an answer: R. Heinkel, A. Kraus and J. Zechner, 'The effect of green investment on corporate behavior', *Journal of Financial and Quantitative Analysis* 36(4), 2001, 431–49.
95 R. Heinkel, A. Kraus and J. Zechner, 'The effect of green investment on corporate behavior', *Journal of Financial and Quantitative Analysis* 36(4), 2001, 431–49.
96 J. Angel and P. Rivoli, 'Does ethical investing impose a cost upon the firm? A theoretical perspective', *Journal of Investing* 6(4), 1997, 57–61.
97 G. Gay and J. Klassen, 'Retirement investment, fiduciary obligations and socially responsible investing', *Journal of Deferred Compensation* 10(4), 2005, 34–40, 36.
98 EIRIS, 'Taking stock: how leading stock exchanges are addressing ESG issues and the role they can play in enhancing ESG disclosure', 2009.
99 JSE, 'Service Issue 14 of the JSE Listings Requirements', 29 May 2012, http://www.jse.co.za/How-To-List/Listing-requirements/JSE-listing-requirements.aspx.
100 Institute of Directors in Southern Africa and the King Committee on Governance, *King Code of Governance Principles*, 2009, http://www.ecgi.org/codes/documents/king3.pdf.
101 Http://www.klse.com.my.
102 Http://www.sse.com.cn/en_us/cs/about/news/en_news_20080514a.html.

Companies may be delisted in the exchanges for failure to comply. Adoption of stronger sustainability standards by leading exchanges would spur corporations to raise their performance and also help safeguard the competitiveness of those markets in light of rapid regulatory developments in foreign markets to promote CSR.

A further piece to this discussion is empirical evidence of the impact of specific RI campaigns. The South African boycott is the most comprehensively studied example, and many researchers conclude it had at best only a modest impact on the economic fate of targeted companies.[103] A common research finding is reflected by one study's conclusion that '[o]verall, we cannot find any strong statistical evidence that firms operating in South Africa have suffered declines in their share prices as a result of divestment'.[104] The more recent crusade against the tobacco industry also appears to have only dabbed targeted firms' stock prices.[105] Talisman Energy's foray into Sudan's oil industry is another studied example, as its share prices were apparently discounted because of the reputational risks suffered due to its association with this regime.[106] Other research examining changes in the cost of capital in light of information released to the market about firms' environmental behaviour, such as news of a pollution scandal or, conversely, commendations for exemplary achievements, suggests such factors can affect stock prices or the cost of borrowing,[107] but the effect tends to be short-lived.[108]

The discussion so far has related to equity investors, but we must also account for debt financing, an alternate source of funding that is primarily made through bank loans and issuance of corporate bonds. Banks also have influence through provision of financial advice. They may exert reasonable influence over borrowers, especially small, private enterprises with few

---

103 S. Teoh, I. Welch and C.P. Wazzan, 'The effect of socially activist investment policies on the financial markets: evidence from the South African boycott', *Journal of Business* 72, 1999, 35–89; but compare to R. Kumar, W. Lamb and R. Wokutch, 'The end of South African sanctions, institutional ownership, and the stock price of boycotted firms', *Business and Society* 41(2), 2002, 133–65.
104 W.H. Kaempfer, J.A. Lehman and D. Lowenberg, 'Divestment, investment sanctions, and disinvestment: an evaluation of anti-apartheid policy instruments', *International Organization* 41(3), 1987, 457–73, 466.
105 T. Burroughes, 'Ethical investors losing out as tobacco stocks burn up Britain's equity markets', *The Business*, 24 February 2007.
106 C. Cattaneo, 'Lingering "Sudan effect" likely to tarnish Talisman', *Financial Post*, 24 February 2000, D1; S.J. Kobrin, 'Oil and politics: Talisman Energy and Sudan', *New York University Journal of International Law and Policy* 36, 2003–04, 425–56.
107 N. Lorraine, D. Collison and D. Power, 'An analysis of the stock market impact of environmental performance information', *Accounting Forum* 28, 2004, 7–26; S. Dasgupta, B. Laplante and N. Mamingi, *Capital Market Responses to Environmental Performance in Developing Countries*, World Bank, 1998; J. Hamilton, 'Pollution as news: media and stock market reactions to the toxics release inventory data', *Journal of Environmental Economics and Management* 28(1), 1995, 98–113.
108 D. Cormier, M. Magnan and B. Morard, 'The impact of corporate pollution on market valuation: some empirical evidence', *Ecological Economics* 8, 1993, 135–55.

financing options, as well as larger, public firms seeking massive loans.[109] A thriving social banking sector, comprising lenders focusing on poverty alleviation (mainly in developing countries) and ethical banking (mainly in Western countries), is providing targeted financial support for businesses, communities and households that contribute to sustainable development.[110] Banks may also influence the environmental and social behaviour of their suppliers, thus giving them 'the potential for *exponential* change through client and supplier networks'.[111] Westpac, an Australian bank reputed to be an RI leader, believes that '[t]he role of the leader is not just to look at themselves but to also look outwardly at who they can influence. As a bank we are in a good position to do that because nearly all businesses have a banking relationship.'[112] Westpac gained publicity in 2011 when it pulled out of financing a new brothel in Sydney, touted as the world's largest.[113] Gunns (discussed earlier in this chapter) was likewise denied loans by the ANZ bank for a proposed AUD$2 billion Tasmanian pulp mill. Lenders usually scrutinize borrowers' environmental practices when they might engender costly liabilities and may consequently adjust the cost of a loan to reflect unresolved environmental risks, require the borrower to adopt specific safeguards or demand more valuable security against the loan. There is a debate among RI commentators over whether banks should shun problematic companies or projects altogether, or try to engage with borrowers in order to mitigate the risk or extent of harm.[114]

In a competitive credit market, lenders also have incentives not to be too demanding for risk of losing clients to less scrupulous financiers. While banks' influence has increased as market deregulation has enabled them to extend their range of services to include insurance and retail investing, direct lenders' influence has correspondingly waned as alternative sources of cash have become available to firms through institutional investors. In the US, banks' and other depository institutions' share of financial assets declined from 54.9 per cent in 1967 to 23.7 per cent in 2007, while pension funds' and mutual funds' share surged from 15.4 to 37.8 per cent.[115] The trend has

---

109 M. Jeucken, *Sustainable Finance and Banking: The Financial Sector and the Future of the Planet*, Earthscan, 2001; P. Thompson, 'Bank lending and the environment: policies and opportunities', *International Journal of Bank Marketing* 16(6), 1998, 243–52.
110 Weber and Remer, op. cit., 2.
111 Bowman, op. cit., 464.
112 G. Paterson, Westpac, quoted in A. De Lore 'How the companies compare: a network of high achievers is showing the way', *Sydney Morning Herald*, 20 May 2008, 2.
113 M. West, 'Westpac pulls out of brothel project', *Sydney Morning Herald*, 15 August 2011, 3.
114 P. Watchman, *Banking on Responsibility. Part 1 of Freshfields Bruckhaus Deringer Equator Principles Survey 2005: The Banks*, Freshfields Bruckhaus Deringer, 2005, 36; compare to A.B. Coulson, 'How should banks govern the environment? Challenging the construction of action versus veto', *Business Strategy and the Environment* 18, 2009, 149–61.
115 J. D'Arista and S. Griffith-Jones, 'Agenda and criteria for financial regulatory reform', in S. Griffith-Jones, et al. (eds), *Time for a Visible Hand: Lessons from the 2008 World Financial Crisis*, Oxford University Press, 2010, 126–49, 133–4.

benefitted both public and private companies, as the growth of private equity funds since the 1970s has boosted capital for private companies.[116]

Even if lenders lack influence over the sustainability performance of the market, they have self-interested reasons to heed it. 'Climate risk' has become a specialized area of environmental risk assessment that banks increasingly incorporate into their due diligence protocols.[117] Climate risks might arise from tightening regulation on GHG emissions, reputational risks to borrowers perceived as 'climate sceptics', and physical risks to investment assets from rising sea levels and harsher storms.[118]

Other parts of the financial sector that seek to alter the cost of finance for social or environmental concerns are community impact investing and microfinance. They can channel funds to low-income households, small businesses and organizations that provide facilities such as affordable housing. But this 'positive' investing sector in most countries is fragmented and lacks established market infrastructure to have widespread effects. The microfinance sector in 2007 had an estimated total loan volume of about US$25 billion.[119] The majority of impact investors surveyed in a report produced by J.P. Morgan with data collected by the Global Impact Investing Network agreed that the impact investing industry is 'in its infancy'.[120] In contrast to the vast majority RI funds that invest in large publicly-traded companies, impact investors aim to support small and local businesses and communities by helping to finance and subsidize neighbourhood infrastructure, job-creation schemes, poverty alleviation ventures and local environmental improvements. Inherent in this model is the notion that part of the 'return' of investment is the social and environmental benefit it represents. In recent years this approach to financing has also been labelled 'slow money', in reference to these patient investors' aspiration for long-term, gradual returns.[121]

There are numerous examples of impact financing, though isolated successes do not equate to a market trend. The financiers include public sector pension plans, such as CalPERS, and community development banks and credit unions that lend money in underserved communities. Examples include Triodos (Netherlands), Shorebank (US) and Gemeinschaftsbank (Germany).[122] Among

---

116 E. Talmor and F. Vasvar, *International Private Equity*, John Wiley and Sons, 2011.
117 Among reports that have evaluated banks' climate-related policies and practices, see: D.G. Cogan, *Corporate Governance and Climate Change: The Banking Sector*, Ceres, 2008; B. Furrer, M. Swoboda and V. Hoffman, *Banking and Climate Change: Stumbling into Momentum? An Analysis of Climate Strategies in More Than 100 Banks Worldwide*, WWF and SAM, 2009.
118 Bowman, op. cit., 454.
119 Deutsche Bank Research, 'Microfinance: an emerging investment opportunity', December 2007, 1.
120 Y. Saltruk, A. Bouri and G. Leung, 'Insight into the impact investment market: an in-depth analysis of investor perspectives and over 2,200 transactions', Global Impact Investing Network, 2011, http://www.thegiin.org/cgi-bin/iowa/resources/research/334.html.
121 See http://www.slowmoney.org/invest.
122 Weber and Remer, op. cit., 3–8.

Canadian examples, VanCity Credit Union offers deposit accounts that channel funds into environmental and social enterprises,[123] while Fondaction invests in the Quebec social economy by supporting businesses developing technologies or products that promote efficient use of natural resources or reduce waste.[124] In the US, a targeted investing programme of the New York City and State public pension funds achieved competitive returns for its plan participants and beneficiaries while investing in urban revitalization.[125] Since 1973, ShoreBank has invested over US$1.7 billion in priority communities and companies, and rehabilitated 38,000 housing units.[126] CalPERS's Double Bottom Line initiative has targeted investments in urban neighbourhoods to produce returns for the fund and stimulate local economic development, and its Environmental Technology Investment Program backs firms that meet stringent environmental technology standards.[127] These and other initiatives will hopefully reach a critical mass of market influence through networks such as the Global Alliance on Banking for Values,[128] Mission Investors Exchange[129] and the MicroFinance Network.[130]

Corporate engagement

Shareholder activism and dialogue

Social investors may seek to influence companies through dialogue and pressure from within, rather than by divestment or exclusionary screening. Designed primarily to address corporate under-performance, engagement procedures may include monitoring investee companies, meeting with senior management and directors, and policies on shareholder voting and voting disclosure. The justification for engagement is grounded in the agency problems that arise from the gap between owners and managers and the potential for misalignment of interests between them; shareholder engagement is intended to narrow this gap. Yet it is not necessarily desirable for shareholders to micromanage or second-guess the management of a company, as they may not be in a position to identify and assess specific business or operational issues. Thus, engagement focuses on areas where shareholder influence could increase the long-term value of firms or target specific controversies. This commonly includes the quality of corporate senior management, ensuring

---

123 C. Strandberg and B. Plant, *Scan of the Community Investment Sector in Canada*, National Round Table on the Environment and the Economy, 2004, 12.
124 Ibid., 16.
125 L. Hagerman, G. Clark and T. Hebb, 'New York case study: competitive returns and a revitalized New York', Oxford University Centre for the Environment and Harvard Law School, 2005, 2.
126 Strandberg and Plant, op. cit., 19–20.
127 Ibid., 22.
128 Http://www.gabv.org.
129 Http://www.missioninvestors.org.
130 Http://www.mfnetwork.org.

that the board and its committees are composed appropriately and function effectively; evaluating the company's strategies and the company's performance in delivering them; and assessing the company's remuneration policy.[131]

Corporate engagement may involve a range of actors and diverse goals. It is occasionally used, explains Jackie Cook, 'by well-organized shareholder coalitions to achieve public policy changes, thereby extending their reach beyond targeted firms'.[132] Faith-based investors and public sector pension funds have tended to be in this vanguard, such as Canada's Taskforce on the Churches and Corporate Social Responsibility,[133] which was most active in the 1980s and 1990s, and the ongoing US-based Interfaith Center on Corporate Responsibility.[134] Church groups are credited with having 'revitalized the shareholder resolution system' in the South African divestment campaign.[135] There are also important inter-jurisdictional differences in terms of the subject matter and extent of corporate engagement. Engagement, especially of the activist style, is more common in North America than Europe, partly due to different legal milieus.

Occasionally, non-profit NGOs and individuals (notably Ralph Nader) have bought corporate stock in order to acquire an additional platform to voice their concerns,[136] and some have even targeted fund managers directly. A UK-based group, Forest Monitor, wrote to fund managers to 'apprise them, from the perspective of financial prudence, of a logging company's egregious and unsustainable practices.... [It] successfully convinced many money managers to divest from the logging company'.[137] The effectiveness of such campaigns is often enhanced when they are conducted in concert with social investors, as discussed later in this chapter.

---

131 R. Barker, 'Ownership structure and shareholder engagement: reflections on the role of institutional shareholders in the financial crisis', in W. Sunn, et al. (eds), *Corporate Governance and the Global Financial Crisis: International Perspectives*, Cambridge University Press, 2011, 144–64, 151–2.
132 J. Cook, 'Political action through environmental shareholder resolution filing: applicability to Canadian oil sands?', *Journal of Sustainable Finance and Investment* 2(1), 2012, 26–43.
133 See the Taskforce's annual reports, at http://www.share.ca/about/responsible-investment/taskforce-on-the-churches-and-corporate-responsibility/taskforce-on-the-churches-and-corporate-responsibility-annual-reports.
134 See http://www.iccr.org.
135 'World Council ends relations with three banks over apartheid', *Ecumenical Review* 34(1), 1982, 82–3; R.K. Massie Jr., 'Corporate democracy and the legacy of divestment', *Christian Century* 108(22), 1991, 716–21, 719.
136 For instance, in light of atrocities in Sudan and other areas, in 2008 Amnesty filed a proposal at Citigroup's annual general meeting of shareholders requesting against the wishes of the bank's management that the company 'prepare a report to shareowners which discusses how policies address or could address human rights' in relation to its investments, operations, supply chains and other business ties. Citigroup, *Definitive Proxy Statement, Pursuant to Section 14(a) of the Securities Exchange Act of 1934*, 13 March 2008, proposal 10, 88–9.
137 J. Emel, 'An inquiry into the green disciplining of capital', *Environment and Planning A* 34, 2002, 827–43, 833.

The rise of institutional investors in global markets over recent decades has raised hopes for greater shareholder oversight of corporate management. Adolf Berle and Gardiner Means's pioneering work in the 1930s on corporate governance suggested that the twentieth-century ascendancy of public corporations entailed a growing dispersal of shareholding across much of the general public, with a consequential loss of shareholder control over corporate managers.[138] Today, some commentators see burgeoning institutional funds as challenging those assumptions, re-concentrating share ownership and providing greater economies of scale and incentives to monitor and discipline managers.[139] Legislation commonly restricts the number of voting shares an institutional fund can hold in any one corporation; such policies are designed to prevent the risky concentration of ownership of commercial businesses.[140] But importantly, the re-concentration is not simply at the level of individual funds but also occurs through funds' ability to collaborate. While each institutional fund typically holds only a small fraction of the stock of any single firm, together they can hold a sufficient stake to potentially exert influence.

Until recently, the shift in shareholding from retail to institutional investors has not been paralleled by increased activism by major institutional investors. The latter have traditionally not actively exercised their shareholder rights to supervise management, instead relying on reactive correctives such as hostile takeovers to address poor performance. A European Commission policy paper in 2010 explained that the GFC 'has shown that confidence in the model of the shareholder-owner who contributes to the company's long-term viability has been severely shaken'.[141] Institutional shareholders can be unwilling or unable to exert influence through engagement owing to lack of knowledge and incentives to monitor companies because of the costs involved; difficulties of coordinating action and conflicts of interest; and aversion to potential increased political visibility.[142] The increased opportunities for free riders, who benefit from any share price increases resulting from corporate engagement without shouldering any of its costs, can undermine the incentive to engage with managers to address ESG issues. The traditional lack of

---

138 A. Berle and G. Means, *The Modern Corporation and Private Property*, Transaction Publishers, 1932.
139 Hebb, *No Small Change*, op. cit., 28.
140 For instance, Canadian pension fund legislation usually restricts a fund to holding a maximum of 30 per cent of the shares of any one corporation: R. Bauslaugh, 'Let the chickens run the henhouse?', *Alberta Law Review* 47(1), 2009, 285–90, 287.
141 European Commission (EC), *Green Paper: Corporate Governance in Financial Institutions and Remuneration Policies*, COM (2010) 285 final, 8.
142 J. Parkinson, *Corporate Power and Responsibility: Issues in the Theory of Company Law*, Clarendon Press, 1995, 168–9; P. Myners, *Institutional Investment in the United Kingdom: A Review*, HM Treasury, 2001; B.S. Black, 'Shareholder activism and corporate governance in the United States', in P. Newman (ed.), *The New Palgrave Dictionary of Economics and the Law*, Palgrave, 1998; A. Shleifer and R.W. Vishny, 'Value maximization and the acquisition process', *Journal of Economic Perspectives* 2(1), 1988, 7–20.

investor-related activism is also partly attributable to legal barriers to shareholder voice and networking, though increasingly these have been removed or mitigated by legislative reform.

Institutional investors' adherence to the principles of MPT can also hinder their willingness to engage with companies. MPT holds that the optimal investment strategy is to diversify across a broad portfolio, and because markets are assumed to be efficient, active investing is not a cost-effective long-term investment strategy. The result is investments spread over many companies, making it hard to justify paying much attention to individual firms.[143] In such a situation, it seems natural to abandon engagement in favour of trading when companies under-perform.[144] Overall, MPT provides a rationale for passively holding a pool of stocks and assets representative of the market as a whole, and treating individual shares as fungible components in a wider strategy of investment management.

In addition, outsourcing of investment management on the pretext of the complexity and scale of investment portfolios can hinder active investing and effective oversight by fiduciaries. Gordon Clark and Eric Knight explain that 'the accumulated size, complexity, and time-sensitivity of global financial markets have effectively disenfranchised pension fund trustees from direct operational responsibility for investment management. . . . Only rarely, and mostly in public pension funds, do trustees seek to influence the trajectory of particular stocks.'[145]

Where institutional funds engage with companies on ESG concerns, as the following section discusses, their impact can be episodic and fleeting, unless it results in more enduring policy and regulatory changes governing the market more widely. Investors' motivation to engage is primarily being driven by awareness of the financial materiality of ESG issues and the increasingly influential notion of their 'universal owners' status (i.e., as funds holding large, diversified portfolios, they are vulnerable to the performance of the economy as a whole). Investors commonly invoke long-term profit maximization arguments rather than ethical considerations. A further possible driver is the widespread practice of holding assets in passive indexes that limits funds' option to sell off stock from individual companies that suffer from poor governance practices or subpar financial performance. On the other hand, the very appeal of indexed holdings managed by computer programs is the cheaper portfolio management costs than active engagement, so the impact of indexing tracking on engagement can work both ways.

---

143 J.G. MacIntosh, 'Institutional shareholders and corporate governance in Canada', *Canadian Business Law Journal* 26, 1996, 145–88, 158 71.
144 Barker, op. cit., 151–2.
145 G.L. Clark and E. Knight, 'Implications of the UK Companies Act 2006 for institutional investors and the market for corporate social responsibility', *University of Pennsylvania Journal of Business Law* 11(2), 2009, 256–96, 268.

Current patterns of engagement

The quality and extent of institutional investors' engagement have been mixed in recent years. CalPERS in the US and Hermes in the UK have good records of active ownership, but many investors don't. Research on the ascendance of institutional investors has highlighted both their cumulative victories as active shareholders that challenge corporate management on RI issues and some corresponding, wider political influence over policy-makers.[146] The effectiveness of shareholder campaigns appears to be more pronounced in the largest firms and businesses operating close to their ultimate consumers, as presumably these corporations' brand images and reputational value are more significant and sensitive to challenge.[147] But measuring the extent and impact of corporate engagement is methodologically challenging given that much of it is informal and 'behind the scenes', and there are difficulties in showing the cause and effect of engagement and changes in corporate behaviour.

A prominent recent example of activism is the proposed Enbridge Northern Gateway Project, which involves twin pipelines through Western Canada and has attracted considerable shareholder action, ranging from informal dialogue to formal resolutions calling on Enbridge to adopt mitigating measures or abandon the environmentally controversial project altogether. A group of RI funds led by Ethical Funds (formerly known as NEI Investments) filed a shareholder proposal on risks associated with First Nations opposition to the Northern Gateway pipeline at Enbridge's AGM in May 2012, with 28.5 per cent voting for and 10.7 per cent abstaining.[148] This was a relatively strong result and is an indication of growing investor unease with this massive project.

An array of engagement strategies is utilized by investors. Most commonly, corporate engagement takes the form of polite, informal dialogue between investors and company executives, active proxy voting and occasionally filing or supporting dissent shareholder proposals. The Universities Superannuation Scheme (USS), one of the UK's most active funds, has singled out climate change as a specific issue for engagement.[149] It is difficult, however, to gauge

---

146 M.P. Lee and M. Lounsbury, 'Domesticating radical rant and rage: an exploration of the consequences of environmental shareholder resolutions on corporate environmental performance', *Business Society* 50(1), 2011, 155–88; W.T. Proffitt and A. Spicer, 'Shaping the shareholder activism agenda: institutional investors and global social issues', *Strategic Organization* 4(2), 2006, 165–90.
147 G.L. Clark, J. Salo and T. Hebb, 'Social and environmental shareholder activism in the public spotlight: US corporate annual meetings, campaign strategies, and environmental performance, 2001–04', *Environment and Planning A* 40(6), 2008, 1370–90; Lee and Lounsbury, op. cit.
148 A. Hasham, 'Pipeline protest rolls into T.O. First Nations group taking fight to Enbridge', *Toronto Star*, 9 May 2012, A6. Details of the shareholder proposal at: http://www.neiinvestments.com/NEIFiles/PDFs/5.2.2%20Shareholder%20Resolutions/2012%20Resolutions/Shareholder%20Resolution%20Enbridge.pdf.
149 Universities Superannuation Scheme (USS), *Climate Change: A Risk Management Challenge for Institutional Investors*, USS, 2001.

the extent and quality of USS's corporate engagement because it relies on a discrete, behind-the-scenes approach to raising its concerns.[150] By contrast, the Californian financial behemoth CalPERS takes a dramatically more public and confrontational style of engagement, often using the media to 'name and shame' recalcitrant companies.[151] Also, CalPERS sometimes puts pressure not on individual companies but on entire countries, because the problems are more systemic. Its exclusion of some emerging markets from its huge portfolio reportedly had an adverse reputational affect on markets and precipitated a capital flight by foreign investors.[152] Fund managers acting on behalf of financial institutions often may undertake such engagement. Given its informal and sometimes covert nature, some research suggests fund managers can exercise 'private corporate governance influence' over investee companies on an ongoing basis.[153]

There is, however, research suggesting that institutional investors engage little with investee companies.[154] A study conducted by the Riskmetrics and some other business organizations on behalf of the European Commission found that 'the institutional investor community consists of two distinct parts: a small active minority and a majority of more passive investors'.[155] Recent research suggests UK institutional investors do not routinely monitor investee firms.[156] Stephen Choi and Jill Fisch found that many US public pension funds typically keep a low and non-confrontational profile.[157] Furthermore, many institutions rely on proxy advisers either to advise on voting or to exercise their voting rights.[158] A wide-ranging survey by the International Corporate Governance Network in 2009 found that 'insufficient trust' between companies and investors hindered constructive engagement.[159]

---

150 Hebb, *No Small Change*, op. cit., 63.
151 Ibid., 65.
152 Ibid., 82.
153 J. Holland, 'Financial institutions, intangibles and corporate governance', *Accounting, Auditing and Accountability Journal* 14(4), 2001, 497–529, 497.
154 Barker, op. cit., 149.
155 Riskmetrics Group, et al., *Study on Monitoring and Enforcement Practices in Corporate Governance in the Member States*, September 2009, 15, http://ec.europa.eu/internal_market/company/docs/ecgforum/studies/comply-or-explain-090923_en.pdf.
156 M. Goergen, et al., 'Do UK institutional shareholders monitor their investee firms?' Working Paper, European Corporate Governance Institute, 2007, 12.
157 S. Choi and J.E. Fisch, 'On beyond CalPERS: survey evidence on the developing role of public pension funds in corporate governance', *Vanderbilt Law Review* 61, 2008, 315–54, 329. The survey found: '53.9% of our funds [which participated in the survey] never submitted a letter to management, and 64.1% never met with management. More openly confrontational activity is even less frequent; fewer than 20% of funds had submitted a shareholder proposal or actively engaged in the solicitation of proxies. . . . None of our funds reported nominating a director candidate, and fewer than 15% had even submitted the name of a potential director candidate to a board member, CEO, or nominating committee'.
158 Ibid., 318.
159 S.C.Y. Wong, 'Shareholder-company engagement: a comparative overview', *International Corporate Governance Network Yearbook* 61, 2009, http://papers.ssrn.com/sol3/papers.cfm?abstract_id=1490724.

There was also the concern that not all shareholders had the resources and expertise to make informed decisions on corporate governance issues. In addition, the lack of coordination between corporate governance specialists and fund managers can be frustrating for companies, as it causes conveyance of inconsistent messages and adoption of contrary decisions.[160]

The Walker Report, commissioned by the UK government in the wake of the GFC, identified various barriers to corporate engagement, and considered them to be some of the factors leading to the financial crisis. The barriers included: the scale of the resources that fund managers must commit to effective dialogue; concern that such dialogue cannot be relied upon to remain confidential and might cause embarrassment to shareholders or fund managers; specific legal and governance barriers, including communications and collaboration among shareholders, share blocking and short notice periods; and concern that a vote against a firm may cause the stock prices to fall, which could be damaging to ultimate beneficiary investors.[161] Furthermore, the financial returns that accrue to clients from good governance are hard to quantify, and thus they are hard to attribute to diligent fund managers, in addition to the problem that such 'returns' may accrue over a time-frame longer than the quarterly performance scrutiny that fund managers are subject to.[162]

Shareholder advocacy has been predominantly a US tradition and is not as widely practised in other markets.[163] In Canadian companies, between 1982 and 1995 only 18 shareholder proposals were circulated, whereas 701 were filed in US companies in 1994 alone.[164] Investor-related activism reportedly 'neither has tradition nor meaning in the system of German corporate governance',[165] though ostensibly there is negligible difference between the current German Stock Corporations Act of 1965[166] and laws in Anglo-American jurisdictions regarding shareholders' rights such as calling meetings, filing proposals and voting. Curiously, the more concentrated patterns of shareholding found in Germany and other EU continental jurisdictions, such as the presence of creditors holding a dominant equity stake, in theory 'provides shareholders with a stronger position in management control than those of Anglo-American countries'.[167]

The number of shareholder resolutions on RI issues that went to vote in the US has fluctuated little between 180 and 205 per year between 2004 and

---

160 Ibid.
161 D. Walker, *A Review of Corporate Governance in UK Banks and Other Financial Industry Entities: Final Recommendations*, UK Treasury, 2009, 73–4.
162 Ibid.
163 Corporate Monitor, *Responsible Investment: A Benchmark Report on Australia and New Zealand by the Responsible Investment Association Australasia*, Corporate Monitor, 2008, 23.
164 J. Yang, E. Wang and Y. An, 'An empirical analysis of Canadian shareholder proposals', Administrative Sciences Association of Canada conference, Ottawa, 2007, 2.
165 Schaefer, op. cit.,271.
166 (BGBl. I S. 1089) FNA 4121-1; extensively amended since.
167 S. Wen, 'Institutional investor activism on socially responsible investment: effects and expectations', *Business Ethics: A European Review* 18(3), 2009, 308–33, 311.

2011, although over this period the average supporting vote jumped from 10.02 per cent to 15.83 per cent.[168] Climate change has been the dominant environmental issue raised by shareholders; from 2004 to 2011, resolutions on climate change and energy issues that went to a vote annually rose from 11 to 50.[169] Many resolutions are filed but never voted on, sometimes because shareholders withdraw their resolutions if management agrees to come to the table. Shareholder activists often target large corporations; 79 per cent of shareholder resolutions voted on in the US in the 2011 proxy season targeted firms listed in the S&P 500 Index, which comprises the 500 largest public companies in the country by market capitalization.[170]

Shareholder proposals or resolutions rarely garner a majority of votes and are often only precatory and may thus be ignored by corporate management.[171] In addition, the effective exercise of voting rights is often hindered by problems such as cross-border voting restrictions,[172] short notice periods,[173] share blocking[174] and shareholder-unfriendly practices of fund managers.[175] Occasionally, defeated shareholder resolutions may induce management to cooperate, as they might interpret even modest dissent as reflective of broader unease about company policies and decisions. When management signals its willingness to listen, the resolution is commonly withdrawn. Research on shareholder activism by TIAA-CREF[176] revealed that although only one of its resolutions ever achieved a majority vote during the survey period, more than 95 per cent of the time when TIAA-CREF contacted management to suggest changes, the company adopted them.[177]

---

168 FundVotes, 'Shareholder resolutions: average shareholder support by category', http://www.fundvotes.com/resolutionsbycategory_countavg.php. Shareholder resolutions filed on corporate governance issues during this period fluctuated between 300 and 500 annually, with average voting support of about 33 to 43 per cent.
169 FundVotes, 'Shareholder resolutions: average shareholder support by sub-category', http://www.fundvotes.com/resolutionsbysubcategory_countavg.php.
170 Cook, op. cit., 29.
171 S. Davis, J. Lukomnik and D. Pitt-Watson, *The New Capitalists. How Citizen Investors are Reshaping the Corporate Agenda*, Harvard Business School Press, 2006, 16–18.
172 Cross-border voting refers to voting by non-resident shareholders at shareholder meetings of investee companies. Manifest, *Cross-Border Voting in Europe – A Manifest Investigation into the Practical Problems of Informed Voting Across EU Borders*, May 2007, 15.
173 In many countries, regulation provides a minimum notice of five to ten days before the shareholders' meeting. Many believe this minimum period should be increased so that shareholders can make informed decisions and communicate those decisions through intermediaries to the company: OECD, *Methodology for Assessing the Implementation of the OECD Principles of Corporate Governance*, OECD, 2007, 45–6.
174 This practice requires investors to deposit shares at a designated institution for a specific period before the general meeting, during which shares are blocked from trading: Manifest, op. cit., 17.
175 The fund manager may have legal responsibility for a customer's securities. The main functions of this custodian include: processing the trades, keeping the assets safe and servicing the associated portfolios. Ibid., 15.
176 Teachers Insurance and Annuity Association – College Retirement Equities Fund.
177 W.T. Carleton, J.M. Nelson and M.S. Weisbach, 'The influence of institutions on corporate governance through private negotiations: evidence from TIAA-CREF', *Journal of Finance* 53(4), 1998, 1355–62.

Outsourcing corporate governance to proxy advisers, as is ubiquitous among institutional investors, is not without drawbacks. The quality of voting recommendations made by proxy advisers can vary dramatically by company and market. The market for proxy voting in North America and Western Europe has become highly concentrated, and conflicts of interest may arise from advisers who serve both companies and their institutional investors.[178] Dominant proxy advisory providers such as ISS and Glass Lewis reportedly have business ties to companies whose shares are being voted on their advice, such as providing consultancy services on corporate governance and selling data about companies' comparative ESG performance and rating.[179] Not all proxy advisory services face such ostensible conflicts of interest; the Vancouver-based Shareholder Association for Research and Education (SHARE) provides proxy voting advice to Canadian shareholders based on its own research and without collateral business ties to the corporate sector.[180] A competitive and effectively regulated market for proxy advice with more actors like SHARE has the potential to assist institutional investors with their engagement responsibilities.[181] Alternatively, funds could devote more resources to drafting their own proxy voting guidelines.

In the retail fund sector including RI funds, fierce competition leads fund managers to:

> focus on straightforward [trading] strategies and quarterly performance metrics in an effort to attract and retain investors. With some exceptions, mutual funds tend not to invest significant monies in their analysis of corporate governance issues. The result is that some mutual funds defer to proxy advisors to determine how to vote their shares and focus their resources on determining when to buy, hold and exit.[182]

Dominated by the triumvirate of Fidelity, Vanguard and American Funds, the huge US mutual fund industry tends not to vote against corporate management. These mutual fund groups compete on returns and low fees and appear to have little incentive to invest in ESG analysis and active shareholding. By contrast, however, the proxy voting record of dedicated RI mutual funds in North America suggests they are 'far less supportive of management' and commonly offer 'strong support for shareholder initiatives'.[183]

---

178 OECD, *Corporate Governance and the Financial Crisis: Key Findings and Main Messages*, OECD, 2009, 54.
179 J. McFarland, 'Rules urged for proxy advisory firms', *Globe and Mail*, 21 August 2012, B5.
180 Http://www.sharevancouver.org.
181 Barker, op. cit., 156.
182 American Bar Association (ABA), *Report of the Task Force of the ABA Section of Business Law Corporate Governance Committee on Delineation of Governance Roles & Responsibilities*, ABA, 2009, 19.
183 L. O'Neill and J. Cook, *Proxy Voting by Canadian Mutual Funds 2006–2009*, SHARE and FundVotes, 2010, 3.

An additional disincentive that US mutual funds have to challenging corporate management is that they obtain lucrative business from them in managing section 401(k) personal plans allowed under taxation law for workers.[184] Skewed proxy voting on shareholder resolutions concerning executive compensation is related to mutual fund business ties with companies. In 2011, Fund Votes co-sponsored a study of how the 26 largest US fund families voted on proxies relating to executive compensation, finding that funds *supported* management compensation proposals 80 per cent of the time and, by contrast, voted in favour of shareholder proposals that would *limit* executive pay 48 per cent of the time.[185] Furthermore, when a mutual fund becomes a section 401(k) plan trustee, it tends to over-weight that company's stocks in its portfolio and holds those stocks when others are selling, sometimes resulting in large costs to the 401(k) plan beneficiaries.[186]

Advocacy and engagement may flourish also when retail and institutional investors collaborate. Although single investors may hold small stakes in individual companies, they could increase their control over companies through collaboration. Hebb traces a trend since the late 1990s in collaboration among institutional funds, especially among public sector pension plans in North America and the UK; the collaboration has been directed towards improving corporate governance, including greater accountability to shareholders, more transparency and managerial oversight. The desire to establish best practices for corporate governance within institutional funds encompasses a search for well-qualified and independent directors.[187] Corporate pension funds, however, remain largely disinterested in such strategies.

Much of this institutional collaboration is clustering around specific RI codes of conduct, such as the Carbon Disclosure Project (CDP) and the UNPRI. The effect of these, as well as of collaborative forums such as the Council of Institutional Investors, the UK's National Association of Pension Funds and the International Corporate Governance Network is noted later in this chapter. Especially in emerging markets, some funds now hold companies accountable to global corporate governance and other business standards. Such funds include the Extractive Industries Transparency Initiative and the Global Reporting Initiative.[188]

---

184 Pub. L. No. 93-406. Section 401(k) allows employers to create tax-qualified personal pension plans to which employees can elect to contribute a portion of their cash wages, as an alternative to a traditional group pension scheme. The management of these 401(k) plans is typically assigned to external mutual funds, and the pension plan options for employees may include RI funds.
185 Discussed in L. Braham, 'When your 401(K) provider doesn't vote your interests', *Bloomberg*, 4 May 2012, http://www.bloomberg.com/news/2012-05-04/when-your-401-k-provider-doesn-t-vote-your-interests.html.
186 L. Cohen and B. Schmidt, 'Attracting flows by attracting big clients: conflicts of interest and mutual fund portfolio choice', Working Paper, Harvard Business School, 2008, http://www.hbs.edu/research/pdf/08-054.pdf
187 Hebb, *No Small Change*, op. cit., 1–2.
188 See http://eiti.org; and https://www.globalreporting.org.

Some sovereign wealth funds such as the New Zealand Superannuation Fund (NZSF) and the Norwegian Government Pension Fund-Global (NGPF-G) are becoming active shareholders and supporting shareholder resolutions on sustainability issues.[189] Their work suggests that divestment and engagement are not necessarily mutually exclusive. The NGPF-G uses both techniques to fulfill its legal mandate to invest ethically, and its policy is to engage with targeted companies before potentially excluding them. The Fund's ethical investment regulations require that companies proposed for exclusion be given a chance to respond to the stated reasons for the proposed exclusion.[190] This process may trigger some dialogue and persuade the firms to make amends (e.g., by cancelling controversial projects).[191] Corporate engagement may also occur after exclusion; for example, excluded Rio Tinto sought re-admission and communicated with the NGPF-G about how it might redeem itself.

Because corporate engagement can be tedious and labour intensive, it is usually done very selectively. Even the ability to monitor companies – a precondition to engagement – can be beyond the resources of many pension funds and other financial institutions.[192] Active, one-to-one interaction with firms is typically done in a handful of cases at any one time. With over 3,000 firms in its portfolio, the Canada Pension Plan engages closely with only about 15 firms annually, although it communicates on RI issues with many more investee companies through questionnaires and proxy voting.[193] Likewise, as of early 2010, the NGPF-G held shares in approximately 8,300 companies, with an average ownership stake in each of about 1 per cent,[194] and therefore engaged with only a miniscule number. Like the Canada Pension Plan, the NGPF-G also votes on thousands of shareholder proposals.[195] Most institutional investors have far fewer resources than the Norwegian Fund and therefore face even greater disincentives to active ownership.

The most concerted corporate engagement is often found in funds that practise 'relationship investing', which is a strategy to acquire large equity stakes in public companies, typically greater than 10 per cent and as high as 30 per cent, as a way to build shareholder value. The Ontario Teachers Pension

---

189 B.J. Richardson, 'Sovereign wealth funds and the quest for sustainability: cases from Norway and New Zealand', *Nordic Journal of Commercial Law*, Fall (2), 2011, 1–27.
190 *Guidelines for Observation and Exclusion from the Government Pension Fund Global's Investment Universe*, 2010, s. 5(3).
191 This option tends to not be available for companies liable to be excluded because of the very *nature* of their business (e.g., producing tobacco).
192 Hebb, *No Small Change*, op. cit., 76.
193 Canada Pension Plan Investment Board, *2011 Report on Responsible Investing*, Government of Canada, 2011, 8–20.
194 Norwegian Ministry of Finance, *The Management of the Government Pension Fund in 2009*, Report No. 10 (2009–2010) to the Storting, 2010, 65.
195 A. Halvorssen, *Addressing Climate Change through the Norwegian Sovereign Wealth Fund (SWF) – Using Responsible Investments to Encourage Corporations to take ESG issues into account in their decision-making*, Legal Studies Research Paper Series, No. 2010-06, Faculty of Law, University of Oslo, 2010, 29.

Plan, for instance, selects companies for relationship investing that it 'perceive[s] as undervalued but poised for long-term capital appreciation'.[196] Most funds, however, are unwilling to make such a commitment to a single company because of the additional due diligence required.

Legal context to engagement

Law influences the scope and methods of corporate engagement. Securities and corporate governance law may affect the filing of shareholder resolutions or proposals by restricting the eligibility to file, the content of proposals, voting mechanisms and the legal effect of prospective proposals. Overall, the power of shareholders to control a corporation in which they have invested is rather limited. Their principal right is to elect or remove the board of directors. Shareholders generally lack the power to make or pass proposals that would dictate the corporation's operations, and such proposals may be barred if they have little support from fellow shareholders.[197] Nonbinding proposals, while commonly provided for in most jurisdictions,[198] serve only to signal shareholders' wishes.[199] While shareholder approval is often required for certain major corporate actions, such as to amend the firm's articles of incorporation or amalgamations, it tends to be limited to approving a proposal originating from the directors; and even where shareholders can initiate fundamental changes to the articles or bylaws, these generally cannot be used to override the discretion of the directors. Moreover, while corporate law may allow for all shareholders of a corporation to enter into a 'unanimous shareholder agreement' with significant powers to control the firm, it requires an unrealistically high threshold.[200]

There are further legal hindrances to shareholder activism relating to mandatory disclosures and restrictions in communicating and colluding. Australian institutional investors have expressed concern that their collaboration on corporate governance outside shareholder meetings would violate provisions of the Corporations Act.[201] In Britain, the provisions of Rule 9 of the Takeover Code and the FSA's rules on controlling shareholders may deter

---

196 Ontario Teachers Pension Plan, 'How we invest', http://www.otpp.com/wps/wcm/connect/otpp_en/home/investments/public+equities/relationship+investing/how+we+invest.
197 In Canada, an Albertan company may refuse to circulate a shareholder proposal if the filer holds less than 5 per cent of the company's shares: Business Corporations Act, 2000, RSA s. 136(1); Business Corporations Regulation, Alta. Reg. 118/2000, s. 18.1(c). In contrast, other Canadian jurisdictions typically set shareholding thresholds for filing at a more reasonable 1 per cent or CAN$2,000 in value.
198 L.A. Bebchuk, 'The case for increasing shareholder power', *Harvard Law Review* 118, 2005, 833–917, 877.
199 J. Sarra, 'The corporation as symphony: are shareholders first violin or second fiddle?', *UBC Law Review* 36, 2003, 403–41, 413.
200 E.g., Canada Business Corporations Act, RSC 1985, s. 146.
201 R. McKay, *Collective Action by Institutional Investors is More Than a Passing Fad*, Australian Council of Superannuation Investors, 2007, 2.

collective engagement.[202] In the US, levels of engagement have remained low partly due to concerns over potential infringement of the Regulation Fair Disclosure (Regulation FD),[203] which provides that when a company discloses material non-public information to certain individuals or entities, it must also publicly disclose that information.

In recent years, legal reform – to facilitate communication between shareholders and to lower their transactions costs in both monitoring and coordinating responses – has helped increase the scope for investor activism. Allaying concerns about the extent to which engagement is inconsistent with regulation, the UK's FSA issued guidance affirming that the existing regulatory regime 'do[es] not prevent collective engagement by institutional shareholders designed to raise legitimate concerns on particular corporate issues, events or matters of governance with the management of investee companies'.[204] The UK Takeover Panel has issued similar guidance on the relevant provisions of the Takeover Code.[205] In Germany, the Risk Limitation Act of 2008 has reaffirmed that coordinated conduct in single cases (i.e., regarding issues raised in general meetings or arrangements to affect the composition of a supervisory board) will not be deemed as 'acting in concert' and is thus spared the onerous regulatory consequences.[206] Significantly, the US Department of Labor advised in 1998 that shareholder rights are valuable fiduciary assets that should be utilized by pension fund managers in beneficiaries' interest.[207] US and Canadian securities regulators made bold regulatory decisions in 2003 and 2005 respectively to encourage more active shareholding.[208] Their requirements for mutual fund companies to disclose their shareholder voting policies and practices encourage funds to exercise these responsibilities more vigilantly.

Another area of legal reform improves shareholder rights to file proposals and challenge corporate management. In Germany, revisions to the 2009 Law

---

202 Rule 9.1 (a) of the City Code on Takeovers and Mergers provides that a mandatory offer should be made to all shareholders when any person acquires, whether by a series of transactions over a period of time or not, an interest in shares which (taken together with shares in which persons acting in concert with him are interested) carry 30% or more of the voting rights of a company: Panel on Takeovers and Mergers, 'City Code on Takeovers and Mergers', 129, http://www.thetakeoverpanel.org.uk/wp-content/uploads/2008/11/code.pdf.
203 SEC, *Fair Disclosure, Regulation FD*, http://www.sec.gov/answers/regfd.htm.
204 S. Dewar, 'Shareholder engagement and the current regulatory regime', FSA, 19 August 2009.
205 Takeover Panel, 'Practice Statement No.26 – Shareholder Activism', 2009, http://www.thetakeoverpanel.org.uk/wp-content/uploads/2008/11/ps26.pdf.
206 *Risikobegrenzungsgesetz*, Bundesgesetzblatt, 2008, 1666.
207 See letter from US Department of Labor to William M. Tartikoff, Senior Vice President and General Counsel of Calvert Group, 28 May 1998, http://www.calvert.com/nrc/literature/documents/sri_dol_letter.pdf?litID=DOLSRI (discussing the ERISA legislation governing private pension funds).
208 SEC, 'Disclosure of proxy voting policies and proxy voting records by registered management investment companies', 31 January 2003; Canadian Securities Administrators, *National Instrument 81-106 Investment Fund Continuous Disclosure and Companion Policy 81-106CP*, 2005.

on the Implementation of the Directive of Shareholder Rights (ARUG)[209] have this purpose.[210] Amendments to the Canadian Business Corporations Act in 2001 curbed company management's discretion to disallow a shareowner proposal that promotes political, social or similar objectives, with the revised rule requiring a shareowner to 'demonstrate that the proposal relates in a significant way to the business or affairs of the corporation'.[211] Shareholder proposals have since flourished, from fewer than three in each year during the 1980s and first half of the 1990s, to 40 in 2001 and 134 by 2005.[212]

In some countries, corporate governance codes rather than strict regulation are used to encourage shareholder engagement. While the 2009 Walker Report's principal recommendation is for institutional investors to become more active owners and also be vigilant and engage with their investee companies before problems arise, Walker's desire to see collaborative and peaceful relations between investors and their portfolio companies led him to recommend against tough legal reforms to foster change. Instead, as a result of his recommendations, the Stewardship Code for institutional investors was adopted in 2011.[213] A voluntary code of best practices, the Code lacks a robust enforcement mechanism and expects investors to 'comply or explain'.[214] Consequently, fund managers should publicly disclose how they fulfill their stewardship obligation or explain their alternative approach if they are unwilling to assume such a commitment. It remains to be seen if this approach will succeed in improving engagement between companies and shareholders. Notably, it does not respond to one of the underlying causes of poor engagement – the diversified portfolio strategies of most fund managers. Many are deterred from devoting sufficient resources to engagement due to the costs involved and the free-rider benefits that accrue to competitors.[215]

Creditors' engagement

Corporate engagement can also be undertaken by creditors. Through lending, banks may have close, ongoing relationships with borrowers, and the contractual terms of a loan can give a bank leverage to scrutinize a company's activities and even impose covenants regarding its handling of environmental activities and risks. On current evidence, however, most banks are unwilling or disinterested to engage closely with clients' environmental performance.

---

209 *Gesetz zur Umsetzung der Aktionaersrichtlinie*, 30 July 2009, BGBl. I 2479.
210 Waring and Edwards, op. cit., 141.
211 Section 137(5)(b)(i).
212 Yang, Wang and An, op. cit., 5.
213 Financial Reporting Council, *The UK Stewardship Code*, July 2010, http://www.frc.org.uk/FRC-Documents/FRC/The-UK-Stewardship-Code.aspx.
214 R.A.G. Monks, 'A review of corporate governance in UK banks and other financial industry entities: the role of institutional shareholders', in Sunn, et al., op. cit., 134–43, 139.
215 Ibid.

Andrea Coulson, who has researched this issue quite extensively, explains that 'the power of a bank to exercise control over a borrower is limited, and participation in management would be deemed inappropriate bank behaviour and outside the normal course of business'.[216] This leverage, if deployed, may be strongest in the traditionally bank-based economies of continental Europe and East Asia, where lenders have been more important than the capital markets for corporate financing. In Germany, such intimate relationships between banks and companies gave rise to the *Hausbank* phenomenon, involving loans to corporate clients being secured by the bank holding substantial shares in the firm.[217] From 1993 to 2000, bank financing represented on average about 37 per cent of German companies' financial liabilities, compared to only about 24 per cent from equity finance.[218] In the US and UK, by contrast, such relationships have traditionally been more at arm's length, with banks generally distancing themselves from clients' corporate and operational affairs, in addition to lenders being relatively less important for corporate financing.

These jurisdictional differences regarding creditors' engagement practices are, however, diminishing. Legal and market reform in Germany is shifting the country's corporate financing and governance model closer to the UK approach, though German banks still have a strong presence on corporate supervisory boards.[219] Frederick Tung finds that Anglo-American banks increasingly influence corporate managerial decision-making, including routine operational matters rather than simply when borrowers are in distress.[220] Banks may also exert influence through research and advisory work: Megan Bowman discusses how some banks have partnered with NGOs and companies 'to commission and disseminate research that influences policy-makers as well as corporate actors', citing the work of Westpac partnering with other parties through the Australian Business Roundtable on Climate Change to commission research on the business case to address global warming.[221]

For significant ESG concerns, banks may occasionally either deny financing or extract greater loan security. One seminal precedent from Australia is the ANZ Bank's rejection of a loan worth AUD$2 billion sought by Gunns, which wanted to build a giant pulp mill in Tasmania. Although the ANZ publicly declined to elaborate its reasons,[222] it was almost certainly concerned

---

216 Coulson, op. cit., 155.
217 A. Onetti and A. Pisoni, 'Ownership and control in Germany: do cross-shareholdings reflect bank control on large companies?', *Corporate Ownership and Control* 6(4), 2009, 54–77, 55.
218 Ibid., 57.
219 Ibid., 59–60, 73.
220 F. Tung, 'Leverage in the board room: the unsung influence of private lenders in corporate governance', *UCLA Law Review* 57, 2009, 115–81, 118–19.
221 Bowman, op. cit., 463.
222 'ANZ quiet on Gunns funding', *Sydney Morning Herald*, 22 May 2008, http://www.smh.com.au/business/anz-quiet-on-gunns-funding-20080522-2h52.html.

about the environmental impacts of the project, or at least negative publicity from environmental protesters, even though the project had obtained most necessary government approvals.[223] Yet the practical effect of such measures can be undermined by the availability of money from unscrupulous sources such as in China and Russia.[224]

Bondholders are other corporate creditors that potentially wield enormous influence given that the global bond market is worth about US$28.6 trillion as of March 2012[225] and that in most OECD countries, bonds are the dominant asset class, accounting on average for 50 per cent of the total assets of pension funds.[226] Surprisingly, however, the level of engagement between bondholders and corporate borrowers is much lower than that between stockholders and investee companies.[227] One might attribute the passivity of bondholders to their lack of voting rights in corporations. But this is not conclusive, as creditors can exert influence through the inclusion of ESG covenants in bond agreements, analogous to bank lenders using contractual covenants to constrain borrowers.[228] Some institutional investors have declared that their RI policies cover all asset classes, including bonds. But as CalPERS conceded in its 2011 announcement, 'The opportunities for investors to engage with debt issuers can be more limited than in other asset classes'.[229] CalPERS is working with the Credit Roundtable, a group of institutional investors, to protect the bondholders rights, but its white paper on this subject omits reference to ESG covenants in bond agreements.[230] An institutional investor that engages more actively with bondholders is BT Pension Scheme. Its sustainability policy purports to cover all asset classes,[231] and it reports being engaged with approximately 150 corporate borrowers each year on ESG issues.[232]

---

223 M. Wilkinson and B. Cubby, 'ANZ exit from pulp mill project confirmed', *Melbourne Age*, 28 May 2008, 3.
224 In Gunns' case, it is trying to relaunch its project by courting a wealthy joint venture partner: F. Ogilvie, 'Financial backing Gunns' next pulp mill hurdle', *ABC News*, 11 March 2011, http://www.abc.net.au/news/2011-03-11/financial-backing-gunns-next-pulp-mill-hurdle/2660914.
225 Bank of International Settlements, 'International bonds and notes – all issuers', 2012, http://www.bis.org/publ/qtrpdf/r_qa1206_anx14b.pdf.
226 OECD, 'Pension fund assets climb back to pre-crisis levels but full recovery still uncertain', *Pension Markets in Focus* 8, 2011, 1–22, 2.
227 M. Gull, 'Engagement for corporate bond holders', *Financial Times*, 11 July 2010, 6.
228 Tung, op. cit., 135–7.
229 CalPERS, 'Responsible investment's second decade: summary report of the state of ESG integration, policy and reporting', August 2011, 37–8.
230 Credit Roundtable, 'Improving covenant protections in the investment grade bond market', 2007, http://www.iimemberships.com/dl/creditroundtable/Covenant%20White%20Paper%20revised%207-2-08.pdf.
231 BT Pension Scheme, *BTPS Sustainability Policy*, 2012.
232 BT Pension Scheme, 'Bond engagement report Q1/2012', http://www.btpensions.net/download/194/BTPS+Bonds+Engagement+Summary+Q1+2012.pdf.

RI codes of conduct and investor collaboration

Collective action barriers to RI

A major limitation of the scope and ambition of RI has been its traditional emphasis on targeting discrete issues such as tobacco, weapons or apartheid, rather than addressing systemic, economy-wide concerns. Though an increasing number of investors are attentive to more pervasive problems such as climate change, even here the potentially broader perspective may dissipate because of their focus on specific issues such as GHG emissions of individual companies rather than the overall sustainability of the fossil fuel economy.

Significant collective action problems in financial markets hinder social investors from cooperating to address these systemic, big-picture concerns. The problems stem from the 'public good' nature of many social and environmental amenities. Investors – and companies themselves – tend to avoid taking costly actions that improve social and environmental well-being (i.e., providing positive externalities) unless they can exclusively capture that value financially. RI actions often take time and resources, while the benefits generated from those activities (such as reducing GHG emissions) may accrue to all investors and society as a whole, not just those taking the initiative. Presumably, the individual financier bears all the costs and only, at best, a small portion of the benefits. Consequently, there tends to be reduced investment than otherwise in the collective, long-term interests of financiers and their beneficiaries.

The 'universal owner' thesis, proposed by Robert Monks and elaborated by James Hawley and Andrew Williams, implies that large institutional owners are sufficiently diversified in the economy to be motivated to curb environmental externalities.[233] Large banks also commonly hold substantial and diverse lending portfolios and thus may also be considered to have such 'universal' characteristics. Hawley and Williams contend that universal owners, investing broadly across the economy, should be self-interested in the health and long-term sustainability of the entire economy because they 'have no interest in abetting behavior by any one company that yields a short-term boost while threatening harm to the economic system as a whole'.[234] Acting as a universal investor implies that any 'externality' of an individual company can result in a costly 'internality' for an investor's total portfolio that should be addressed. Moreover, as they commonly hold assets on behalf of millions of investors, such as pension plan members, whose investment portfolios are closely tied to the overall health of the economy, universal investors should be concerned about any social or ecological impacts that might erode financial returns for their beneficiaries.

---

233 J. Hawley and A. Williams, *The Rise of Fiduciary Capitalism*, University of Pennsylvania Press, 2000; R.A.G. Monks and N. Minnow, *Corporate Governance*, Basil Blackwell, 1995, 132.
234 Davis, Lukomnik and Pitt-Watson, op. cit., 18.

Franck Amalric develops a related view in his characterization of pension funds as 'civic investors'.[235] He reasons that such investors should care about broader sustainability issues and the prevention of costly externalities for the following reasons: investors' 'ability to meet their future liabilities is linked to the trajectory of societal change'; 'pension funds influence that trajectory via their investment decisions'; and such funds 'should aim to influence the economy and to promote those trajectories of social change that will maximize their expected ability to meet their liabilities'.[236] In addressing these issues, Amalric suggests that pension funds should not only modify their investment strategies but also lobby public authorities to encourage greater oversight of the market and corporate miscreants.

Expressed differently, the universal owner or civic investor thesis suggests a way to resolve, in the context of financial markets, the generic collective action problems mapped by Garrett Hardin[237] and Mancur Olson,[238] where seemingly rational choices for individuals are irrational for society collectively. In contrast to individual investors with incentives to exploit market failures for personal gain – which ultimately leaves all worse off as the externalities accumulate – universal owners should be motivated to act in the interests of all for the long term.

Nonetheless, the universal owner thesis has theoretical weaknesses, and it certainly does not accurately reflect prevailing investment practices. One fundamental weakness of the thesis is that it can't explain how environmental externalities in aggregate may become internalized in the economy. Many externalities, such as the disappearance of species or toxics in the food chain, can occur without manifesting any discernible economic cost, at least not in the near term. Some noble attempts have been made to measure such losses; for example, a study by the UNEP-FI and the UNPRI secretariat sought to quantify the cost of the major types of ecological negative externalities caused by the world's largest 3,000 companies, estimating their cost in 2008 at US$2.15 trillion.[239] However, it is misleading to extrapolate, as James Hawley does, that 'a large proportion of these externalities were internalized by firms owned by universal investors, actively reducing the value of other firms in the portfolio'.[240]

While an economy-wide investor might be willing to scrutinize the externalities of individual companies, the economy as a whole doesn't necessarily

---

235 F. Amalric, 'Pension funds, corporate responsibility and sustainability', *Ecological Economics* 59(4), 2006, 440–50.
236 Ibid., 441.
237 G. Hardin, 'The tragedy of the commons', *Science* 162, 1968, 1243–8.
238 M. Olson, *The Logic of Collective Action: Public Goods and the Theory of Groups*, Harvard University Press, 1965.
239 UNEP-FI and the UNPRI Secretariat, *Universal Ownership: Why Environmental Externalities Matter to Institutional Investors*, UNEP-FI, 2011.
240 J.P. Hawley, 'Towards a fiduciary capitalism perspective on business ethics', in Sun, Louche and Pérez, op. cit., 19–37, 21.

internalize all those costs. Markets innately lack a mechanism to constrain the economy's total resource use or pollution load within biosphere limits.[241] Many environmental values are also too temporally or spatially remote for markets to recognize.[242] In any event, any concern for externalities that an investment fund harbours will presumably be not in relation to their impact on social welfare but rather in relation to their adverse effect on the prosperity of the economic assets that the fund holds. Thus, we cannot assume that the current health of the economy as a whole is an adequate proxy for the long-term health of the biosphere.

Relatedly, it is unclear whether universal owners could or should take into account beneficiaries' interests beyond the economic value of the fund portfolio, to consider their indirect interests as consumers, employees and citizens. Differences in demographics, geography and job status might engender conflicts of interest among a universal owner's beneficiaries. Moreover, even if they are united in their interest in the overall sustainability of the economy, the universal owner may lack the resources or means to exert influence, or the cost of doing so might exceed any improved values that can be captured by the universal investor. It is thus not good enough to simply proclaim that because an investor with an economy-wide portfolio is potentially exposed to an array of externalities, that investor will thereby 'internalize' those costs in its financial decisions.

Further criticisms of the universal owner thesis or its assumptions can be made. One is that financiers commonly focus on the credit risks of individual borrowers or the financial risks of a specific security. While investors design diversified portfolios to minimize overall financial risks, they tend to evaluate assets on a case-by-case basis. Thus, constraints arise when institutions have characteristics of universal owners but rely on one-off or narrowly framed analytical techniques in evaluating financial transactions. Another criticism derives from the management of investment portfolios. The portfolio of any large institutional investor is commonly dispersed over several asset management companies, possibly resulting in each portfolio being narrower than the original 'universal' portfolio.[243] Moreover, as portfolio management is commonly delegated to specialist fund managers hired on limited-term performance contracts, pressures for short-term or opportunistic investing arise.[244] Finally, the argument that universal owners invest responsibly because they are accountable to a broad investment base is questionable. While institutional intermediaries have given mass society a stake in the

---

241 H. Daly, 'Allocation, distribution and scale: towards an economics that is efficient, just and sustainable', *Ecological Economics* 6, 1992, 185–93.
242 An IUCN report concluded that the financial sector generally has a poor understanding of the diffuse risks posed by biodiversity loss: I. Mulder, *Biodiversity, the Next Challenge for Financial Institutions?*, IUCN, 2007.
243 C. Mackenzie, 'The scope for investor action on corporate social and environmental impacts', *Responsible Investment*, op. cit., 22.
244 Ibid., 32–3, 37.

financial markets, these funds do not represent all stakeholders in society, especially the poor or unemployed, and they do not represent future generations.[245]

The retail fund sector and asset management business contain a further dynamic that can inhibit cooperation for RI. They are fiercely competitive, as funds vie for investors on the basis of financial or 'ethical' returns. Individual funds have incentives to avoid sponsoring measures, such as engagement actions, which might increase corporate value for the benefit of all shareholders and thus their rival funds.[246] Similarly, insurance companies compete both with each other and increasingly with banks offering savings products and other financial services. Ostensibly, pension funds are not competitive, as they usually are monopolistic providers of retirement benefits to employees within a given organization. Nonetheless, competitive pressures may arise surreptitiously at the asset manager level, as funds outsource investment management. Furthermore, the development of portable, personal pension plans, as in Australia, allow superannuitants to shift their savings into funds of their choice, thereby feeding competitive pressures into the pension sector. Among banks, lenders who raise environmental standards too high may lose business to less scrupulous competitors. A lender who charges a higher interest rate for loans to environmentally risky projects or refuses finance altogether may lose clients to less stringent lenders.[247] However, it would be misleading to imply an inevitable race-to-the-bottom in financing – only a tendency exists – as sometimes borrowers and financiers want the RI imprimatur on a project because it brings additional credibility and reputational value.[248]

Some examples of collaboration in the RI sector, with funds pooling their expertise or leverage, indicate the potential for change. This collaboration may occur at two levels: at a company level, involving shareholder activism within individual firms; and at a sector- or economy-wide level, such as targeting whole industry groups or environmental issues involving many firms. Codes of conduct (such as the UNPRI and Equator Principles) and cooperative forums (such as UNEP-FI) are among the most developed examples of economy-wide collaboration. The following section examines the potential of codes to succeed. Among some of the more useful sectoral initiatives, the work of the UK's USS on the pharmaceutical industry is

---

245 M. Patry and M. Poitevin, 'Why institutional investors are not better shareholders', in R.J. Daniels and R. Morck (eds), *Corporate Decision-Making in Canada*, University of Calgary Press, 1995, 341–77.
246 E. Becker and P. McVeigh, 'Social funds in the United States: their history, financial performance, and social impacts', in A. Fung, T. Hebb and J. Rogers (eds), *Working Capital: The Power of Labor's Pensions*, Cornell University Press, 2001, 44–66, 64 (referring to pitiful levels of shareholder resolutions sponsored by US ethical mutual funds).
247 ISIS Asset Management, op. cit., 24.
248 B. Kingsbury, 'Operational policies of international institutions as part of the law making process: the World Bank and indigenous peoples', in G. Goodwin-Gill and S. Talmon (eds), *The Reality of International Law: Essays in Honor of Ian Brownlie*, Oxford University Press, 1999, 323–42.

exemplary. Through the Pharmaceutical Shareowners Group[249] and the Pharma Futures project,[250] USS led a campaign of engagement concerning drug companies' business models to address the risks associated with the public health crisis in developing countries.[251] Among religious investors, the ICCR and the 3iG help coordinate religious investment and campaigns for policy reforms on environmental justice, mitigating global warming and maintaining food quality.[252]

The principal shortcoming of these collaborative forums is that they cater mainly to investors with similar values. They lack commensurate influence over the behaviour of funds with different priorities or goals. Thus, for instance, while the ICCR has extensive support from mainstream and socially liberal religious denominations, it has virtually no members from the evangelical and conservative Christian sects. Codes of conduct offer one potential solution to this need to stimulate wider cooperation and level the playing field.

RI codes

Another seminal measure of RI's influence is the plethora of codes of conduct that, at their best, help to coordinate, standardize and facilitate action. Mostly drafted by financial institutions, though sometimes also by or with governments, NGOs or individuals, such codes have proliferated greatly in recent years. The first was the Sullivan Principles, crafted by the Reverend Leon Sullivan in 1977 for corporations doing business in South Africa; adherence to the code was taken into account by divestment campaigners. Such codes are only voluntary and may attract considerable interest from mainstream financial players.[253] Some commentators hail the trend as highly beneficial. Bowman asserts that 'voluntary action by the banking industry has potential to facilitate climate change mitigation and the transition to a low-carbon economy',[254] while Kate Miles believes 'voluntary codes for the financing sector are making a positive impact', including 'through the rejection or modification of environmentally damaging projects, the raising of environmental awareness amongst the financing sector ... and the harmonization of lending standards'.[255] On the other hand, the drawbacks of

---

249 Http://www.pharmashareownersgroup.org.
250 Http://www.pharmafutures.org.
251 P. Casson and D. Russell, 'Universities Superannuation Scheme: implementing responsible investment', in *Responsible Investment*, op. cit., 164–5.
252 ICCR, http://www.iccr.org.
253 B.J. Richardson, 'Financing sustainability: the new transnational governance of socially responsible investment', *Yearbook of International Environmental Law* 17, 2007, 73–110.
254 Bowman, op. cit., 448.
255 K. Miles, 'Targeting financiers: can voluntary codes of conduct for the investment and financing sectors achieve environmental and sustainability objectives?', in K. Deketelaere, et al. (eds), *Critical Issues in Environmental Taxation*, vol. 5, Oxford University Press, 2008, 947–62, 948.

such codes include lax compliance controls and a lack of standards concerning financial markets' broader structure. While individual codes may target specific environmental concerns (e.g., climate change), specific actors (e.g., institutional investors) or methods of accountability (e.g., greater transparency and disclosure), the systemic constraints that the financial economy poses to sustainability are hardly acknowledged.

RI codes span a range of methods, structures and objectives that can be broadly categorized into two types, though a single instrument may combine both. Some are normative frameworks that enunciate substantive principles and guidance on desirable performance; they include the Collevecchio Declaration on Financial Institutions[256] and the UNPRI.[257] Process standards, enabling the assessment, verification and communication of performance, constitute a second approach to governing the market. A good example is the Equator Principles.[258] Process standards don't dictate social and environmental outcomes but rather establish procedures such as environmental reporting that may spur improvements in signatories' performance. Table 2.1 lists existing RI codes. Most entries were selected because they explicitly address the financial sector or RI; but two examples – the Ceres Principles and the Sullivan Principles – have wider application to the business community beyond financial organizations.

Also, the RI industry has established several collaborative mechanisms that, although not setting performance standards, address collective action impediments, for instance by facilitating exchange of information. One is the EAI, founded in 2004 by a group of institutional investors to encourage financial analysts to produce more and better ESG research. Accordingly, EAI members agreed to allocate, on an individual basis, at least 5 per cent of their brokerage commission budgets to research houses that effectively deliver robust extra-financial research to investors.[259]

These initiatives are complemented by numerous voluntary standards for CSR and corporate governance that indirectly or implicitly touch the financial sector. Conversely, some RI-related codes such as the Ceres Principles may influence non-financial companies.[260] While financial entities are not commonly signatories to CSR codes, they may assist social investors by providing information about best practice standards in a particular industry sector, as well as insights into the behaviour of individual companies. Some codes deal generally with CSR in any business context, while others focus exclusively on specific sectors: the former type includes the ISO's Social Responsibility 26000 standard, UN Global Compact, OECD Principles of

---

256 See http://www.foe.org/camps/intl/declaration.html.
257 See http://www.unpri.org.
258 See http://www.equator-principles.com/index.shtml.
259 J. O'Loughlin and R. Thamotheram, *Enhanced Analytics for a New Generation of Investor*, USS, 2006, 5.
260 W. Cragg (ed.), *Ethics Codes, Corporations and the Challenge of Globalization*, Edward Elgar, 2005.

Table 2.1 RI-related codes and standards

Code	Principal Sponsor	Year Established
Global Sullivan Principles	Reverend Leon Sullivan	1977 (redrafted 1985)
Ceres Principles	Coalition for Environmentally Responsible Economies (Ceres)	1989
UNEP Statement by Financial Institutions on the Environment and Sustainable Development	United Nations Environment Programme – Finance Initiative (UNEP-FI)	1997
Carbon Disclosure Project (CDP)	Rockefeller Philanthropy Advisors	2002
London Principles of Sustainable Finance	UK Department of Environment and Corporation of London	2002
Collevecchio Declaration on Financial Institutions	Coalition of NGOs	2003
Equator Principles	Multinational banks and the World Bank's International Finance Corporation	2003
Investor Network on Climate Risk Action Plan	Ceres	2003
Eurosif Transparency Guidelines	European Social Investment Forum (Eurosif)	2004
UN Principles for Responsible Investment (UNPRI)	United Nations	2005
ClimateWise Principles	Global insurance companies	2007
Carbon Principles	Consortium of US banks	2008
Climate Principles	Climate Group	2008
UK Stewardship Code	UK Financial Reporting Council	2010
Natural Capital Declaration	UNEP-FI, Global Canopy Programme, & Getulio Vargas Foundation	2011
Principles for Sustainable Insurance	UNEP-FI and insurance industry	2012

Corporate Governance and OECD Guidelines for Multinational Enterprises, while the latter includes Responsible Care (designed for the chemical industry) and the Extractive Industries Transparency Initiative.[261] Some CSR codes also manifest as environmental management systems (EMSs) to provide frameworks for organizations to routinely manage their environmental and social impacts. Of the two main international EMSs – the European Community's Eco-Management and Audit Scheme (EMAS)[262] and the International Organization for Standardization (ISO) 14001 standard[263] – neither is

---

261 For citations and discussion of most of these codes, see K. McKague and W. Cragg, *A Compendium of Ethics Codes and Instruments of Corporate Responsibility*, York University, 2007.
262 European Commission, 'EMAS': http://ec.europa.eu/environment/emas/indexen.htm.
263 ISO, 'ISO 1400 essentials': http://www.iso.org/iso/iso14000essentials.

particularly well suited to capturing the environmental or social footprint of financiers.[264]

The main potential advantages of RI codes are to coordinate action on shared concerns, facilitate exchange of information and best practices, and build a network for peer pressure to minimize unscrupulous and unethical financing. Some codes have been heavily subscribed to; most notably, as of October 2012, the UNPRI boasted approximately 1,100 signatories, including many mainstream actors.[265] As for influencing corporate behaviour – the ultimate indicator of success – evidence is less verifiable. The most successful demonstrated effect has been greater disclosure of corporate ESG performance, such as pursuant to the CDP, which crucially enables social investors to better discriminate between corporate leaders and laggards on GHG emissions and to apply pressure accordingly. Transparency standards may also foster reflection and learning among participants about their practices and impacts, in turn stimulating positive behavioural changes.[266]

As *voluntary* mechanisms, RI codes raise doubts about their potential for credible governance of financial markets.[267] Voluntary instruments tend to lack independent monitoring and enforcement mechanisms, do not contain robust performance metrics to evaluate compliance and are not certifiable. Considerable literature has scrutinized these dimensions of corporate self-regulation through voluntary codes and other mechanisms.[268] Consider British Petroleum (BP), to illustrate: despite a reputation as being 'green' – it was listed on the Dow Jones' Sustainability Index and was a signatory to the UN Global Compact – BP was responsible for the Deepwater Horizon explosion in 2010 that spawned massive environmental and economic costs, including to the company itself.[269] Apart from the quality of codes' standards, seminal factors that shape implementation are the presence of independent monitoring of signatories' commitments and sanctions against poor performance.

The substance of RI codes varies considerably, with some rather open-ended and others fairly prescriptive. Some impose generic performance targets (e.g., to prevent pollution or minimize adverse environmental impacts) while

---

264 B.J. Richardson, 'Implications of recent changes to the EMAS and Eco-label regulations for the financial services sector', *Environmental Law and Management* 14(2), 2002, 131–5.
265 Listed at http://www.unpri.org/signatories.
266 A. Kolk, D. Levy and J. Pinkse, 'Corporate responses in an emerging climate: The institutionalization and commensuration of carbon disclosure', *European Accounting Review* 17(4), 2008, 719–45.
267 See I. Maitland, 'The limits of business self-regulation', *California Management Review* 27(3), 1995, 132–47.
268 E.g., J. Moon, 'The firm as citizen? Social responsibility of business in Australia', *Australian Journal of Political Science* 30(1), 1995, 1–17; R. Gibson (ed.), *Voluntary Initiatives: The New Politics of Corporate Greening*, Broadview Press, 1999; S. Wood, 'Voluntary environmental codes and sustainability', in B.J. Richardson and S. Wood (eds), *Environmental Law for Sustainability*, Hart Publishing, 2006, 229–76.
269 J. Balmer, 'The BP Deepwater Horizon débâcle and corporate brand exuberance', *Journal of Brand Management* 18, 2010, 97–104.

others are specific (e.g., to reduce GHG emissions by a specific quantity and within a specific time-frame). A good example of the more prescriptive approach is the Collevecchio Declaration, while the UNPRI reflects the more discretionary, general style. More stringent standards have drawbacks; investors have shunned the Collevecchio Declaration, drafted by NGOs. Investors usually favour more discretionary and procedural-based standards, such as self-reporting. While transparency measures can have beneficial effects, they probably won't induce major changes in investors' underlying goals, especially if there is no independent auditing and verification. Information on pollution or human rights violations must compete for attention in a crowded field with often seemingly more pressing and tangible concerns. Voluntary mechanisms also typically depend on peer pressure, market discipline or NGO scrutiny to motivate compliance.

Apart from their voluntariness, the most distinctive characteristic of RI codes is their global reach. Most are pitched as universal standards for an international market. Their broad scope contrasts with the presently rudimentary intergovernmental regulation of financial markets. Globalization, spurred by technological advances and market deregulation, has greatly accelerated the mobility of financial capital across national borders.[270] Globalization can distance financiers from the social and environmental sequelae of the companies they fund, hinder nuanced consideration of such impacts on a case-by-case basis and widen the sources of capital for companies, thereby enabling polluters to find alternatives to any ethical investors who shun them.[271] These trends have concomitantly diminished the capacity and willingness of states to govern financial markets, though the GFC has politically strengthened the case for re-regulation.[272]

RI codes can be differentiated along several other dimensions as well. The extent to which their terms are legally binding is one such facet. Simply because participation in a code is voluntary doesn't mean that the code, once accepted, lacks legal consequences. It may be legally binding by virtue of contracts among participating institutions; a bank may include in its contract with a borrower a term that the parties adhere to the Equator Principles' provisions regarding environmental assessment. A code may also have consequences for regulatory compliance; for example, Denmark's Financial Statements Act provides that an investment institution's requirement to report annually on its social and environmental performance may be met if it has submitted a progress report in connection with its accession to the

---

270 C. Williams, 'Corporate social responsibility in an era of economic globalization', *University of California Davis Law Review* 35, 2002, 705–76, 731.
271 Chinese banks, for instance, have been accused of predatory lending: 'EIB warns Africa may suffer as Chinese banks move in', *Environmental Finance*, March 2007, www.environmental-finance.com/2007/0703mar/news.htm#on2.
272 K. Alexander, R. Dhumale and J. Eatwell, *Global Governance of Financial Systems*, Oxford University Press, 2005.

UNPRI.[273] Also, codes differ in their degree of specificity; some contain brief aspirational declarations, as in the London Principles of Sustainable Finance, while others posit near-byzantine rules and performance indicators, such as EMAS. The significance of such differences is that the less specific codes may not be self-executing without additional effort to define their working requirements. Another variable is the regulatory function performed by codes, including agenda-setting, rule-making, target-setting, administration (such as facilitating exchange of information and verification of compliance) and dispute settlement.[274] Typically, most codes straddle several of these regulatory functions rather than merely performing one.

The most successful codes – although it is empirically hard to quantify their effect – appear to possess two attributes: they were drafted through multi-stakeholder processes, and they are embedded in wider institutional regimes for ongoing dialogue, education and monitoring. These forms of 'civic regulation', as some commentators describe them, are providing frameworks for business and non-profit NGOs to work collaboratively.[275] The UNEP-FI perhaps best exemplifies these traits, and it has garnered considerable support from many investors.[276] Research by John Conley and Cynthia Williams on the Equator Principles, which apply to bank-based project financing, suggests the Principles have generally improved the culture among lenders; and they identify the presence of NGO watchdogs as instrumental in operationalizing the Principles.[277]

The following sections examine in more detail three RI codes – the Equator Principles, UNPRI and UNEP-FI – that provide contrasting examples. The Equator Principles apply to bank lending, whereas the UNPRI govern institutional investors, and the UNEP-FI has a stronger multi-stakeholder approach and application. These examples are highlighted because of their widespread support in the financial community, and thus one might presume that they are relatively more influential than other RI codes.

Equator Principles

The Equator Principles (EPs) provide lenders with a framework to manage the social and environmental impacts associated with projects such as dams, factories and mines.[278] Formulated mainly by the banking industry under the

---

273 Act amending the Danish Financial Statements Act ('Årsregnskabsloven'), 8 October 2008. s. 99a(7).
274 See M. Priest, 'Five models of self-regulation', *Ottawa Law Review* 29, 1997–98, 233–316, 239.
275 D.J. Vogel, 'Private global business regulation', *Annual Review of Political Science* 11, 2008. 261–82.
276 Http://www.unepfi.org.
277 J. Conley and C. Williams, 'Global banks as global sustainability regulators? The Equator Principles', *Law and Policy* 33(4), 2011, 542–75.
278 T. O'Riordan, 'Converting the Equator Principles to Equator stewardship', *Environment* 47(4), 2005, 1.

auspices of the International Finance Corporation (IFC), the EPs target private, commercial lending, especially in developing countries and emerging economies, where competent environmental regulation may be lacking. Motivated to evade both public criticisms of controversial projects and the loss of business to less scrupulous lenders, a cohort of banks sought to level the playing field for responsible project financing by drafting the Principles.[279] Involvement of the IFC, the World Bank's private-sector lending arm, boosted the credibility of the EPs.

The EPs are not entirely self-contained but incorporate references to the IFC's Safeguard Policies for social and environmental impact assessment (SEIA), forestry, dam safety, indigenous peoples and other topics. The EPs were released in 2003[280] and revised in 2006,[281] and in July 2010 a set of governance rules were adopted, introducing integrity measures to improve implementation of the EPs and establishing the Equator Principles Association, comprised of representatives of member signatories.[282] All signatories pledge to provide loans only to borrowers who conform to the Principles. The EPs apply to projects with a total capital cost of at least US$10 million (US$50 million before the 2006 revisions). They require lenders to rate proposed projects based on the magnitude of potential impacts and risks in accordance with the screening criteria of the IFC.[283] These criteria categorize projects as A, B or C (high, medium and low), depending on their potential consequences. While for category C projects no further assessment is required, A or B project borrowers must undertake a SEIA based on IFC standards to address the issues identified by the screening. Project financing banks must also prepare an Action Plan based on the conclusions of the SEIA.[284]

Lenders of category A and B projects must also ensure that borrowers have consulted with affected local communities 'in a structured and culturally appropriate manner'.[285] This requirement falls short of the 'prior informed consent' standard demanded by indigenous peoples and other vulnerable communities, as reflected in some international legal instruments.[286] Nonetheless, the EPs offer higher transparency and accountability standards than most financier codes such as the UNPRI. Proponents must make the SEIA report and Action Plan available in a local language for public comment

---

279 N. Affolder, 'Cachet not cash: another sort of World Bank group borrowing', *Michigan State Journal of International Law* 14, 2006, 141–65, 156.
280 See http://www.equator-principles.com.
281 See E. Morgera, 'Significant trends in corporate environmental accountability: the new performance standards of the international finance corporation', *Colorado Journal of International Environmental Law and Policy* 18 (Winter), 2007, 151–88.
282 Equator Principles Association, *Governance Rules*, July 2010.
283 Principle 1.
284 Principle 4.
285 Principle 5.
286 C. Charters, 'Indigenous peoples and international law and policy', *Public Law Review* 18(1), 2007, 22–58.

and for independent expert review.[287] Financiers must include a 'grievance mechanism' to hear complaints 'by individuals or groups from among project-affected communities'.[288] And prior to drawing on a loan, the borrower must covenant with the lender to implement an environmental management plan and to provide ongoing monitoring of impacts.[289]

Given that the banking sector largely designed the EPs, its embrace of the Principles is unsurprising. As of September 2012, 77 banks and related financial institutions, accounting for about 95 per cent of the global project financing market, had endorsed the EPs. Most signatories are North American or Western European lenders, especially large banks with international operations.[290] A study by the British law firm Freshfields Bruckhaus Deringer concluded that the Principles' 'impact on the financial market generally, and their success in redefining banking considerations has been far greater than anyone could have predicted'.[291] Through common standards and procedures for earlier and more granular risk assessment, the EPs have helped signatory banks to minimize the reputational risks associated with development projects and have offered public relations benefits to deflect the scrutiny of NGO.[292]

The 2006 revisions to the EPs improved their accountability, transparency and enforceability, although weaknesses remain.[293] A lender's categorization of a project or the scope of an SEIA or management plan cannot readily be challenged. The categorization of a project crucially influences the types of environmental standards and procedures that subsequently apply. Further, while affected groups may publicly comment on a SEIA or a proposed management plan, they cannot legally challenge their adequacy.

Implementation of the EPs has received mixed reviews. BankTrack, an umbrella organization of NGOs pooling their advocacy on financial issues, has found various deficiencies.[294] Conversely, a report by Freshfields suggested more optimistically that the Principles have led some Equator banks 'into more structured dialogue with stakeholders and NGOs about social and environmental aspects of their lending'.[295] Several international project financing deals have tested the credibility of the EPs. These include the Baku-Tbilisi-Ceyhan pipeline project to bring Caspian Sea oil to Western

---

287 Principle 7.
288 Principle 6.
289 Principle 8.
290 P. Kulkarni, 'Pushing lenders to over-comply with environmental regulations: a developing country perspective', *Journal of International Development* 22(4), 2010, 470–82.
291 Freshfields Bruckhaus Deringer (FBD), *Banking on Responsibility*, FBD, 2005, 1.
292 See D. Schepers, 'The impact of NGO network conflict on the corporate social responsibility strategies of multinational corporations', *Business and Society* 45(3), 2006, 282–99.
293 B. Baue, 'Revised Equator Principles fall short of international best practice for project finance', *SocialFunds.com* 2 July 2006; A. Missbach, 'The Equator Principles: drawing the line for socially responsible banks? An interim review from an NGO perspective', *Development* 47, 2004, 78–84.
294 M. Chan-Fishel, *Unproven Principles: The Equator Principles at Year Two*, BankTrack, 2005.
295 Freshfields, op. cit., 10.

Europe,[296] the Sakhalin II oil and gas project in Eastern Russia[297] and the Uruguayan pulp mills bordering Uruguay and Argentina.[298] The latter project, financed by Calyon and other lenders, has been particularly controversial, leading to litigation between these states in the International Court of Justice.[299] Furthermore, the Equator Principles only address project financing and leave untouched the majority of banking operations that can also sometimes be environmentally problematic. The total value of the global project finance market in 2011 was US$214.5 billion,[300] compared to the total assets of the world's 1,000 largest banks in 2010 of approximately US$101 trillion.[301]

UN Principles for Responsible Investment (UNPRI)

Designed primarily for institutional investors, the UNPRI were developed by the investment community under the auspices of the UN through its UNEP-FI and UN Global Compact initiatives. The UNPRI, however, cannot be defined as an intergovernmental initiative in the same manner as many UN initiatives, such as the international environmental treaties sponsored by the UN. While a multi-stakeholder working group with representatives from environmental NGOs, academia and other non-commercial stakeholders was consulted in preparing the Principles, the financial sector dominated. The present governance of the UNPRI includes the Advisory Council of 11 elected representatives from investor signatory organizations and two representatives from the UN, while daily operations are managed by the UNPRI secretariat, which is financed by fees levied on signatories.

The UNPRI combine process and performance standards in its six brief principles and supplementary guidance on 'possible actions'. The expectations are broadly defined and do not provide yardsticks to which investors can easily be held measurably accountable. Principle 1 vaguely declares: 'We will incorporate environmental, social and corporate governance (ESG) issues into investment analysis and decision-making processes'. Principle 2 calls for active ownership practices. Principles 3 and 4 essentially emphasize an advocacy role for signatories beyond active ownership. Principle 5 expects

---

296 BankTrack, *Principles, Profit or Just PR?*, 2004.
297 M. Bradshaw, 'The "greening" of global project financing: the case of the Sakhalin-II offshore oil and gas project', *Canadian Geographer* 51(3), 2009, 255–79.
298 M. Spek, *Financing Pulp Mills: An Appraisal of Risk Assessment and Safeguard Procedures*, Center for International Forestry Research, 2006, 57.
299 *Pulp Mills on the River Uruguay (Argentina v. Uruguay)*, ICJ, 13 July 2006; ILM 45 2006, 1025.
300 Thomson Reuters, 'Global project finance review –Full Year 2011' (2012) online: Thomson Reuters http://dmi.thomsonreuters.com/Content/Files/4Q11_Project_Finance_Review.pdf.
301 International Financial Services London, 'Worldwide assets of the banking industry', http://www.ifsl.org.uk/research; CityUK, 'Banking: May 2012, financial markets series', 30 April 2012, http://www.thecityuk.com/research/our-work/reports-list/banking-2012/.

cooperation or partnership among investors. In Principle 6, signatories commit to report on their own activities in regard to the UNPRI.

More helpful as an educative tool is the supplementary guidance; for example, for the second principle on active shareholding, the suggested actions include to 'exercise voting rights', 'develop an engagement capability' and 'file shareholder resolutions consistent with long-term ESG considerations'. Through such actions, the UNPRI secretariat sees several benefits: 'Implementing the Principles will lead to a more complete understanding of a range of material issues, and this should ultimately result in increased returns and lower risk. There is increasing evidence that ESG issues can be material to performance of portfolios, particularly over the long term.'

Apart from this somewhat narrow business-case rationale, the UNPRI have various limitations. Among the list of possible actions for the first principle, there is no stated expectation that investors will actually incorporate ESG factors into their ultimate portfolio choices; the principle focuses on 'investment analysis' and 'decision-making processes' but not on ensuring that final decisions achieve specific targets, such as avoiding carbon-intensive developments. Human rights and sustainability are not explicitly mentioned in the Principles or in the list of accompanying actions, and thus signatories do not need to demonstrate any particular performance standards with regard to these outcomes. The UNPRI do not refer to divestment; rather, active engagement, shareholder resolutions, ESG analysis and reporting are proposed as methods of RI. However, nothing is said about the eventual outcome of these actions and what should be done if they are ineffectual. Another lacuna is that the second principle on active ownership focuses on participation in investee companies but ignores the possible need to democratize decision-making within financial institutions.

More positively, the UNPRI secretariat has started to bolster the disclosure and verification of the quality of signatories' implementation. Since 2006 it has required asset-owner and money-manager signatories to annually complete a questionnaire that details their progress in integrating the six principles in their investment frameworks. The secretariat then interviews about a third of those surveyed for verification purposes, and in 2009 it expelled five signatories who failed to complete the survey.[302] In a further tightening of the disclosure standards, in 2012 the UNPRI Secretariat began to trial a public reporting process for all signatories.[303]

Overall, the UNPRI secretariat reassures investors that '[t]here are no legal or regulatory sanctions associated with the Principles. They are designed to be voluntary and aspirational . . . a direction to head in rather than a prescriptive checklist with which to comply.'[304] Finally, in addition to being

---

302 T. Hua, 'U.N. Boots 5 from responsible investing group', *Pensions and Investments*, 20 August 2009.
303 UNPRI, *Reporting Framework – Pilot 2012 Introduction*, June 2012.
304 UNPRI secretariat, 'Frequently asked questions', http://www.unpri.org/faqs.

voluntary principles, the UNPRI caution that 'investors publicly commit to adopt and implement them, *where consistent with our fiduciary responsibilities*'.[305] Thus, any regard to ESG factors is potentially constrained by the fiduciary position of institutional investors, an issue that we will return to in the following two chapters.

UNEP-FI *and other multi-stakeholder regimes*

Some of the obstacles to robust and legitimate codes may be overcome by multi-stakeholder, integrated norm-making regimes, in contrast to the more lopsided codes that are somewhat characteristic of the Equator Principles and UNPRI. The UNEP-FI has some of these preferable regime traits. Collaboration through multi-stakeholder forums for ongoing governance – involving business, public authorities and non-profit actors – has similarities to the 'corporatist' modes of interest group intermediation found in some Western states in the 1970s and 1980s as a supplement to the traditional polyarchal mechanisms of political decision-making.[306] The process of negotiation between diverse parties on a code of conduct can lead to a more legitimate and influential agreement. But sometimes it is difficult to distinguish multi-party codes from purely financier codes because the investors who implement them can have over-weaning influence. On the other hand, tripartite negotiated codes are helpfully displacing the closed-door industry–government bargaining that characterized many of the early negotiated environmental codes and agreements.

Established in 1991, UNEP-FI is a global partnership of investor, civil society and government representatives to promote governance standards, education and research on RI,[307] although in practice financial institutions are its dominant stakeholder. In 1992, it released its first code, the Statement by Banks on Environment and Sustainable Development, to help lenders manage their environmental risks.[308] UNEP-FI sponsored in 1995 a similar statement for the insurance industry.[309] In 1997, UNEP-FI issued a more comprehensive code for all financiers, known as the Statement by Financial Institutions on the Environment and Sustainable Development, which as of September 2012 had just over 200 signatories.[310] In 2007, UNEP-FI issued a Declaration on Climate Change by the Financial Services Sector, cajoling greater action,

---

305 UNPRI, http://www.unpri.org/principles (emphasis added).
306 L. Panitch, 'The development of corporatism in liberal democracies', *Comparative Political Studies* 10(1), 1977, 61–90.
307 See e.g., UNEP-FI, 'Managing environmental risks in project finance', Fact Sheet No. 1, 1999.
308 UNEP, Advisory Committee on Banking and the Environment, *Statement by Banks on Environment and Sustainable Development*, UNEP, 1992.
309 See http://www.unepfi.org/signatories/statements/ii/index.html.
310 Ibid. These UNEP-FI signatories in 2007 represent about 15 per cent of global capital assets under management: N. Purcell, Group General Manager, Westpac, UNEP-FI Global Roundtable, Melbourne, 24–25 October 2007.

including integration of climate change considerations into financial decision-making and reduction of financiers' direct carbon footprint.[311] Paralleling the growth of RI over the past decade, UNEP-FI has greatly expanded its collateral activities to include convening workshops, taskforce meetings and global and regional roundtables, and conducting education and training.[312]

UNEP-FI's 1997 Statement, its main doctrinal achievement, speaks to financiers' environmental performance with regard to internal operations (e.g., energy and resource use); environmental risk assessment; and promotion of financial products and services to enhance environmental protection. Appropriately, the Statement also targets financiers' relationships with borrowers and clients, and ambitiously expects signatories to 'regard sustainable development as a fundamental aspect of sound business management', 'support the precautionary approach to environmental management' and 'foster openness and dialogue relating to environmental matters with relevant audiences'.[313] However, UNEP-FI does not systematically monitor signatories' compliance, let alone exert sanctions for nonfulfillment. A 2007 survey by BankTrack of 45 international banks, including 30 UNEP-FI signatories, found discouraging results, concluding that 'voluntary standards and initiatives are no substitute for stringent policies developed by banks themselves'.[314]

Anxiety about global warming has also fomented new coalitions dedicated to standardizing climate finance. The Climate Principles: A Framework for the Financial Sector were adopted in 2008 to provide a 'common global standard of best practice not only to assist the finance sector in managing its own climate impact but also to assist the sector in supporting its clients and stakeholders in managing their own impacts'.[315] The Principles were devised by the Climate Group, a confederation of NGOs, business and public sector members, in dialogue with some 20 financial institutions. Unlike most RI codes, the Climate Principles contain provisions tailored to specific parts of the finance industry. The insurance sector is expected to advise clients on climate risks and GHG mitigation technologies, while investment banks should facilitate financing of low-carbon technologies and GHG reduction projects, as well as assess the climate consequences of their investments. For financiers of projects that involve emission of at least 100,000 tonnes of CO_2 equivalent annually, the Climate Principles expect them to request that their clients 'quantify and disclose' GHG emissions associated with the project, to 'monitor and report GHG emissions annually in accordance with internationally-recognised methodologies' and to 'evaluate technically and financially feasible options to reduce or offset project-related GHG

---

311 Available at http://www.unepfi.org/fileadmin/documents/ccstatementjun2007.pdf.
312 E.g., UNEP-FI, *2009 Overview*, UNEP-FI, 2010.
313 See http://www.unepfi.org/signatories/statements/fi/index.html.
314 BankTrack, *Mind the Gap: Benchmarking Credit Policies of International Banks*, 2007, xi.
315 Climate Group, http://www.theclimategroup.org/programs/the-climate-principles.

emissions'.³¹⁶ The Climate Principles thereby provide more concrete performance standards than most RI codes, and the Climate Group monitors compliance and publishes performance reviews.³¹⁷ Yet like many other examples, individual signatories aren't obliged to report their progress, and any detected failure to make meaningful progress does not formally incur sanctions.

Public policy and legal reforms

In addition to targeting the market, some social investors try to impress market regulators. Investors can advocate for legal and policy reforms to overcome the limitations of voluntary approaches to RI. Once self-regarded as an alternative to official regulation, the RI sector increasingly concedes the need for state intervention, such as reforms to corporate governance to facilitate shareholder activism, improved financial incentives and environmental reporting standards to enable investors to scrutinize firms' sustainability performance.³¹⁸ The financial sector's dependence on the state is most acute in pricing climate change-related behaviour and impacts, which may necessitate carbon taxes or cap-and-trade schemes to help value GHG emissions.³¹⁹ Investors' attitude to law and official policy is an important metric for assessing the integrity of their RI practices. David Vogel, a leading US commentator, stresses that the definition of CSR must include not only what companies do voluntarily but also the position they take with respect to public policy.³²⁰ If a business opposes public authority initiatives that would strengthen industry-based responsibility, can it really be considered socially responsible?

A few telling examples illustrate the emerging trend of investors and financiers engaging with regulators. In Australia, several banks made submissions to the federal government's Garnaut Review about the proposed introduction of a carbon emission trading scheme, and some such as Westpac explicitly advocated it to ensure an efficient carbon pricing mechanism.³²¹ In Canada, the Social Investment Organization (SIO), which represents most of the country's RI industry, and the Shareholder Association of Research and Education (SHARE) lobbied provincial and federal government for reform,

---

316 Article 2.7.
317 Climate Group, *Climate Principles: Progress Review*, January 2011.
318 Richardson, *Socially Responsible Investment Law*, op. cit., 303–75; T. Hebb and D. Wójcik, 'Global standards and emerging markets: the institutional investment value chain and CalPERS' investment strategy', *Environment and Planning* A 37(11), 2005, 1955–74. 1971.
319 See S. Labatt and R. White, *Carbon Finance: The Financial Implications of Climate Change*, John Wiley and Sons, 2007; B.J. Richardson, 'Climate finance and its governance: moving to a low carbon economy through socially responsible financing?', *International and Comparative Law Quarterly* 58(3), 2009, 597–626.
320 D. Vogel, *The Market for Virtue: The Potential and Limits of Corporate Social Responsibility*, Brookings Institution Press, 2005.
321 Bowman, op. cit., 463.

particularly for greater disclosure of RI policies by pension funds.[322] In 2011, they influenced the Ontario government to declare its intention to adopt a British precedent to oblige occupational pension funds to disclose their RI policies.[323] Earlier in 2001, the SIO and other Canadian RI groups, including Michael Jantzi Research Associates (now known as Sustainalytics) and Ethical Funds, successfully campaigned for revisions to the Canadian Business Corporations Act to reduce barriers to filing shareholder proposals on RI issues.[324] SHARE was also a seminal voice in several other Canadian reforms, including the establishment of the former National Roundtable on Environment and the Economy's Task Force on Capital Markets and Sustainability. In the US, major public sector pension funds such as CalPERS in early 2010 effectively petitioned the Securities and Exchange Commission (SEC) to issue guidance to improve companies' disclosure of climate change investment risks.[325] Not all such efforts, however, are successful; the UKSIF proposed an amendment to the Financial Services and Markets Act 2000 to include the provision of environmental financing within the Financial Services Authority's mandate, a proposal resolutely rejected by UK authorities.[326]

Social investors not only target national regulators; they also occasionally lobby international standard-setters. Ethical Funds in March 2012 wrote the Office of the High Commissioner for Human Rights in response to the call for input for the UN Secretary-General's report on implementation of the Ruggie Guiding Principles on business and human rights throughout the UN system.[327] It asked that the concept of fiduciary duty be added to the list of influential areas of policy and business law that require review with a human rights lens. Another example is the work of UNEP-FI, which has sought to alter the narrative of how fiduciary duties affect institutional investors, such as through commissioning the 2005 Freshfields report, which helped encourage a more liberal interpretation of fiduciary duties.[328]

---

322 See L. O'Neil, *Pension Fund Investment and Disclosure: Acknowledging Environmental, Social and Governance Considerations*. Submission to the Federal Department of Finance, Financial Sector Division, SHARE, 2009.
323 E. Ellmen, 'Ontario budget announces mandatory disclosure of pension ESG policies', *SRI Monitor*, 30 March 2011, http://srimonitor.blogspot.com/2011/03/ontario-budget-announces-mandatory.html.
324 M.R. MacLeod, *Forging Private Governance of Climate Change: The Power and Politics of Socially Responsible Investment*, PhD, Columbian College of Arts and Sciences, George Washington University, 2008, 148.
325 SEC, 'SEC issues interpretive guidance on disclosure related to business or legal developments regarding climate change', 27 January 2010, http://sec.gov/news/press/2010/2010-15.htm.
326 UKSIF, 'UK Social Investment Forum tells MPs of need to include environment in framework for financial services regulator', Press release, 19 April 1999.
327 Submission from NEI, 26 March 2012, http://www.neiinvestments.com/neifiles/PDFs/5.5%20Public%20Policy%20and%20Standards/Business%20and%20Human%20Rights%20Framework%20Implementation%20UN%20System.pdf.
328 Freshfields Bruckhaus Deringer, op. cit.

Shareholder campaigns are one means by which social investors sometimes undertake strategies to achieve these changes at the policy or regulatory level. Michael Macleod and Jacob Park describe collaboration among institutional shareholders on issues such as climate change as 'investor-driven governance networks'.[329] Two quite successful examples from the US, both focusing on environmental issues, were organized by Ceres, addressing climate change, and another, coordinated by Investors Environmental Health Network, targeting hydraulic fracturing.

In seeking changes to the behaviour of companies, investors and policy-makers, Ceres' climate campaign highlighted the significant risks to shareholders from global warming in four areas: litigation, regulation, physical damage and reputation impacts. Among its strategies, Ceres coordinates the filing of shareholder resolutions, and networks and engages with targeted companies, institutional investors and government policy-makers. The number of climate-related shareholder resolutions filed in the US has grown from 25 in 2004 to 109 in 2011, of which about half went to vote, and many were led by major public pension funds and labour groups.[330] Voter support for these climate resolutions has fluctuated between 7.68 per cent and 19.5 per cent on average each year between 2004 and 2011.[331]

The Ceres' campaign is conducted at several levels: sector-based, targeting fossil fuel industry sectors; issue-based, addressing activities posing reputational risks under-estimated by the market, such as palm oil cultivation; and solutions-based, such as energy efficiency improvements for building designs and improved disaster risk management such as from offshore oil drilling.[332] In her analysis of the Ceres' climate campaign and other examples, Cook reveals that 'resolution filing with broad investor appeal and linked to a policy agenda can achieve change beyond targeted companies'.[333] The impact on the policy agenda arose because 'management is forced to publicly defend its position when activists use the SEC-mediated proxy process'.[334] Shareholder resolutions published in proxy materials become part of the public record, and the issues contained therein are brought to the attention of securities regulators. Concomitantly, their impact on the policy agenda can be amplified when shareholder activists utilize other channels of influence, including 'participation on policy committees, meetings with politicians and regulators and the production of research with policy implications'.[335]

---

329 M. MacLeod and J. Park, 'Financial activism and global climate change: the rise of investor-driven governance network', *Global Environmental Politics* 11(2), 2011, 54–74.
330 Cook, op. cit., 32.
331 FundVotes, 'Shareholder resolutions: average shareholder support by sub-category', http://www.fundvotes.com/resolutionsbysubcategory_countavg.php.
332 Cook, op. cit.
333 Ibid., 32.
334 Ibid., 29.
335 Ibid., 30.

The Ceres' campaign concentrated on reform of SEC's disclosure regulations. With support from major public sector pension funds such as CalPERS and CalSTERS, from 2007 to 2009 the campaign petitioned the SEC to oblige public companies to disclose the way climate change might affect their shareholders' investments.[336] In January 2010, the SEC responded favourably by releasing new interpretative guidance on existing SEC disclosure regulations relating to climate change.[337] Some researchers portray this guidance as a major step towards regulators' recognizing the materiality of climate disclosures,[338] while Graham Erion views the SEC's response as strengthening the prospects for litigation to request climate risk information from public companies that do not adequately disclose.[339]

Ceres has also been active in a Canadian investor campaign that has sought to highlight the business and financial risks from oil sands projects and has called for improved monitoring and disclosure. Canadian oil sands developments are among the most carbon-intensive and environmentally polluting industries worldwide. The investor activism has been led by the Vancouver-based SHARE and Ethical Funds, as well as the Pembina Institute, a Canadian research and policy advocacy body focusing on sustainable energy solutions. They have undertaken research that identifies the litigation and regulatory risks that oil sands ventures face in relation to both environmental law and aboriginal rights. These risks are presently poorly understood or quantified. A report by SHARE concluded that 'investors currently do not have enough information to assess whether significant reclamation liabilities are being deferred by companies into the future'.[340]

Ethical Funds has been leading corporate engagement and investor awareness-raising, as well as making submissions to governmental policy consultations. In 2009, it published an important report explaining the investment risks of oil sands projects.[341] In recent years, Ethical Funds and other shareholder activists such as the Dogwood Initiative have also filed several shareholder resolutions in the Canadian oil and gas industry to raise such concerns. For example, resolutions filed at Enbridge over 2010 to 2012

---

336 L. Riddell, 'Pension funds throw green weight around', *Carbon Insider*, 16 July 2008, http://carboninsider.com/?p=25.
337 SEC, 'SEC issues interpretive guidance on disclosure related to business or legal developments regarding climate change', 27 January 2010, http://sec.gov/news/press/2010/2010-15.htm.
338 M.P. Allen, E.M. Jamison and M.J. Bennett, 'SEC opens the door for climate change-related shareholder proposals and disclosure requirements, with potential new liabilities for public companies', *Securities Regulation and Law Report* 42, 1 March 2010.
339 G. Erion, 'The stock market to the rescue? Carbon disclosure and the future of securities-related climate change litigation', *Review of European Community and International Environmental Law* 18(2), 2009, 164–71.
340 P. Barrios and D. Putt, *Investor Briefing Note: What Investors Need to Know About Reclamation Risks in the Oil Sands*, SHARE, March 2010, 10.
341 Northwest and Ethical Investments (NEI), *Lines in the Sands: Oil Sands Sector Benchmarking*, NEI, 2009.

requested more disclosure on the financial risks relating to the Northern Gateway Pipeline proposal.[342] However, Cook says that 'as yet, shareholder actions remain largely uncoordinated', and there have been no discernible policy or regulatory changes due to the campaign targeting oil sands operations.[343] The Canadian Securities Administrators (CSA) has since issued environmental reporting guidance[344] to clarify obligations under existing securities legislation to disclose material risks relating to environmental matters.[345] But unlike the SEC's example, climate change is not identified by the CSA as a specific issue for disclosure. The CSA's reporting guidance flowed from an Ontario Securities Commission review of corporate environmental disclosures practices and incorporates advice from a submission by the Climate Change Lawyers Network supported by others, including Ceres and the British Columbia Investment Management Corporation.[346]

While the RI industry is sometimes willing to advocate such reform, the financial industry more generally is not, mainly because of concerns of increased regulatory compliance costs. In 1996, the American banking industry successfully lobbied Congress to amend the Superfund legislation to immunize itself from lender liability suits for the costs of remediating contaminated lands.[347] The mutual fund industry in North America fiercely resisted new securities regulations in the mid-2000s to make fund managers disclose how they vote shareholding rights belonging to beneficiaries.[348] Extraordinarily, in the wake of the GFC, which exposed deep structural failings in the banking world and capital markets, many financial institutions that were happy to accept government bailouts baulked at many of the proposals to tighten regulatory oversight.[349] For example, Barclays opposed on cost and efficiency grounds some of the recommendations of the Vickers' report to reform the vulnerable UK banking sector, including an increase in banks' ability to absorb financial losses and to minimize risks by requiring 'ring-fencing' between retail banking and investment banking.[350] Another example is the highly unreceptive attitude of JP Morgan Chase to the 2009

---

342 J. Berkow, 'Enbridge braces for more pipeline backlash as annual meeting nears', *Financial Post*, 8 May 2012, http://business.financialpost.com/2012/05/07/enbridge-braces-for-more-pipeline-backlash-as-annual-meeting-nears/?__lsa=4932100c.
343 Cook, op. cit., 38.
344 CSA, Staff Notice 51-333: Environmental Reporting Guidance, 2010.
345 National Instrument 51-102 Continuous Disclosure Obligations.
346 Submission by the Climate Change Lawyers Network, 14 October 2009, http://www.ceres.org/files/Submission_to_Ontario_Securities_Commission_October_2009.pdf.
347 Asset Conservation, Lender Liability and Deposit Insurance Protection Act 1996, Pub. L. No. 104-208, ss. 2501–04.
348 Davis, Lukomnik and Pitt-Watson, op. cit., 73.
349 See W. Grant and G.K. Wilson (eds), *The Consequences of the Global Financial Crisis: The Rhetoric of Reform and Regulation*, Oxford University Press, 2012.
350 Independent Commission on Banking (ICB), *Interim Report: Consultation on Reform Options* (ICB, April 2011), 6–7; Barclays, 'Response to Independent Commission on Banking Interim Report: Consultation on Reform' (4 July 2011), 3.

proposals of the Basel Committee on Banking Supervision aimed at strengthening the resilience of the banking sector.[351]

These stances help explain why legal reforms to promote RI that have emerged in some countries since 2000 have generally just tinkered with the underlying problems of the financial economy that impede sustainability. The reforms have concentrated on market-based and informational tools that alter the procedures of RI decision-making, without seriously facilitating or obliging RI. The more ambitious reforms have been reserved for public financial institutions; sovereign wealth funds, for example, have been mandated to avoid unethical investments.

Conclusions

So far, RI has been a measured mutation rather than a maelstrom. The upbeat rhetoric in some popular literature and media is misleading about the extent and influence of RI in the market. While it has certainly moved beyond its traditional status as a quirky, fringe sector, it is still far from mainstream financial practice. And even if RI eventually attracts a larger crowd, it might be only because the movement has had to jettison its more radical, transformative agenda in favour of a self-serving business case that prioritizes financial returns. This chapter has canvassed the major means of influence that social investors might use in improving corporate sustainability performance, and in each case it has found them presently to be wanting. The anecdotal evidence and reasoning laid out in this analysis, while not comprehensive, shows that social investors are not yet particularly influential.

The RI industry should focus on addressing two issues. Firstly, do more research to measure both the influence of RI on corporate sustainability behaviour and the ways that means of influence such as divestment, positive investment or engagement can be more effective. Rather than continuing to produce often dubious research about RI's financial returns or financial advantage, the RI industry and academic researchers should examine more closely how RI might generate greater social and environmental returns. Secondly, because public regulation is probably indispensable to effective RI, at least in some contexts, the industry should devote more attention to working with governments and other stakeholders to develop governance frameworks that can facilitate change. The choice and mix of regulatory and other legal tools for this task remains a matter of some debate. The following chapters examine the current fiduciary law framework for retail and institutional investing, to help understand the nature of this task.

---

351 Basel Committee on Banking Supervision (BCBS), *Strengthening the Resilience of the Banking sector – Consultative Document*, BCBS, 2009; JP Morgan Chase, Letter to BCBS, 16 April 2010, http://www.bis.org/publ/bcbs165/jpmorganchase.pdf.

3 Fiduciary finance law

Social responsibility or fiduciary folly?

This chapter assesses whether investing with regard to social and environmental considerations is compatible with fiduciary responsibility. We previously identified barriers to RI, of which one is potentially fiduciary finance law. Other researchers also recognize that 'the most pertinent barrier which surrounds ethical investment is the ambiguous legal territory which it occupies'.[1] Investment management often occurs where the parties are in a fiduciary relationship, in contrast to when individuals manage their own investments, without relying on an agent, trustee or other type of intermediary. When someone manages investments on behalf of others, these intermediaries will likely have fiduciary responsibility and associated obligations to invest prudently in the interests of the fund's members.

The notion of 'fiduciary finance law' is used expansively in this chapter, encompassing not only the traditional doctrinal elements that centre on the duty of loyalty, as developed in the English courts of equity, but also various quasi-fiduciary responsibilities and procedures associated with government regulations, trusts law and other sources of law of relevance to financial activities. This expansive approach is appropriate both because investment management is, through its reliance on financial intermediaries, imbued with a fiduciary-like character at a general level and because, secondly, investment governance is enmeshed within a labyrinth of rules including securities regulation and company law, which apply concurrently with traditional fiduciary norms in various ways. Thus, to discuss fiduciary law only in a narrow sense, isolated from the broader legal framework of the financial economy, would convey an incomplete and misleading picture. This chapter focuses, however, mainly on the traditional core of fiduciary law and the cognate rules in trusts law.

In common law systems, these constituent elements of fiduciary finance law are primarily duties to: (i) act loyally in the interests of beneficiaries/principals;

---

1 R. Koo, 'Ethical finance: can ethical objectives be achieved through financial investments?', *Company and Securities Law Journal* 26, 2008, 127–39, 136.

(ii) treat them even-handedly or impartially; (iii) treat them with the care, skill and prudence expected of similarly placed professionals; and (iv) act in accordance with the prevailing law and any governing instruments (such as the trust deed). Among subsidiary duties, financial fiduciaries must administer their responsibilities so that incurred costs are appropriate and reasonable. In most jurisdictions, these duties have been enshrined and modified by regulation, such as pension fund legislation.[2] Somewhat comparable legal duties for financial intermediaries have been codified in civil law systems such as in Japan and Germany. This chapter takes a multi-jurisdictional approach in its analysis of trusts and fiduciary law, focusing on the Anglo-American jurisdictions of North America, the UK and Australia. The subsequent chapter elaborates on some of the nuanced permutations of fiduciary finance law in specific contexts, in particular highlighting differences between the retail and institutional sectors, and between specific institutional types such as insurance companies and pension plans.

Fiduciary law exerts a significant influence over the extent to which institutional investors can practise RI. The UNPRI, the RI code most widely endorsed by institutional funds, are prefaced by the proviso that 'where consistent with our fiduciary responsibilities, we commit . . .'.[3] Hence, signatories' implementation of this code may hinge on compliance with fiduciary obligations. Yet much uncertainty and controversy persists regarding the legality of RI from a fiduciary perspective. This quagmire partly reflects the underlying state of fiduciary law, which the UK Law Commission in 1992 described as 'highly complex, poorly delimited and in a state of flux'.[4] FairPensions surmises that 'the legal position remains unclear, and statutory clarification may be needed to restore common sense to the law and resolve a debate that has generated more heat than light'.[5]

Fiduciary law's seemingly exclusive focus on the interests of investors, especially their financial interests, clashes with a vision of RI advancing social responsibility.[6] The South African divestment campaign in the 1970s and 1980s led to a plethora of academic commentary and some litigation about the fiduciary law consequences.[7] Today, many academic commentators view funds' 'fiduciary duty [as] to act solely in the long-term "financial" interest of

---

2 ERISA, s. 404.
3 UNPRI, http://www.unpri.org/principles.
4 Law Commission of England and Wales, *Fiduciary Duties and Regulatory Rules*, Consultation Paper No. 124, HMSO, 1992, para. 2.4.
5 C. Berry, *Protecting Our Best Interests: Rediscovering Fiduciary Obligation*, FairPensions, 2011, 5.
6 See A. Emid, 'The ethical choice: it takes a steady hand to balance fiduciary responsibility with ethical goals', *Benefits Canada* 21(4), 1997, 89–92; D. Hayton, 'English fiduciary standards and trust law', *Vanderbilt Journal of Transnational Law* 32, 1999, 555–609; D. Tennent, 'Ethical investment in superannuation funds: can it occur without breaching traditional trust principles?', *Waikato Law Review* 17, 2008, 98–114.
7 E.g., D. Pederson, 'Divestment of securities in companies doing business in South Africa: conflicting moral and legal imperatives?', *Inquiry and Analysis* 1, 1986, 1; J.C. Dobris, 'Arguments in favour of fiduciary divestment of "South African" securities', *Nebraska Law Review* 65, 1986, 209–41.

their beneficiaries ... [and thus] to be long-term profit maximizers'.[8] One Canadian report concluded, 'current interpretations of the fiduciary duties of pension fund managers may unnecessarily constrain their ability to address the full range of relevant corporate responsibility considerations related to prospective investments'.[9] In South Africa, institutional investors have been warned that they may 'not be fulfilling their fiduciary responsibilities if they make socially responsible investments'.[10] Some others view fiduciary law less problematically. The 2005 Freshfields report commissioned by UNEP-FI suggested that RI might be compatible with fiduciary responsibilities when ESG issues are financially material to investment performance:

> The question is not a zero-sum equation of either maximizing returns or favouring ESG issues, but of taking all relevant factors into consideration in a prudent and properly motivated investment analysis. It is not a breach of fiduciary duties per se to have regard to ESG considerations while pursuing the purposes of the trust. Rather, in our opinion, it may be a breach of fiduciary duties to fail to take account of ESG considerations that are relevant and to give them appropriate weight.[11]

Likewise, a 2006 Australian parliamentary report declared that 'consideration of social and environmental responsibility is in fact so far bound up in long-term financial success that a superannuation trustee would be closer to breaching the sole purpose test by ignoring corporate responsibility'.[12] The American Law Institute's authoritative guidance stresses that fiduciary responsibility to promote the financial success of a business does not extend to violating established laws just because illegal behaviour might be more profitable than the applicable penalties.[13]

Determining fiduciary law's latitude for RI depends heavily on how we define 'social responsibility', as well as the specific legal obligations included in any given fiduciary relationship. As Lord Browne-Wilkinson cautioned, 'the phrase "fiduciary duties" is a dangerous one, giving rise to a mistaken assumption that all fiduciaries owe the same duties in all circumstances. This is not the case.'[14] We'll come back to this observation shortly. As already noted in this book, 'responsible investing' is a contentious and ambiguous term, rivalling the related debate on 'sustainable development' in complexity

---

8 T. Hebb, *No Small Change: Pension Funds and Corporate Engagement*, Cornell University Press, 2008, 26.
9 Stratos, *Corporate Disclosure and Capital Markets*, National Roundtable on the Environment and the Economy, 2004, 12.
10 A. Gillingham, 'Money follows morality', *Sunday Times (South Africa)*, 24 June 2007, 22.
11 Freshfields Bruckhaus Deringer, *A Legal Framework for the Integration of Environmental, Social and Governance Issues into Institutional Investment*, UNEP-FI, 2005, 100.
12 Parliamentary Joint Committee on Corporations and Financial Services, *Corporate Responsibility: Managing Risk and Creating Value*, Commonwealth of Australia, 2006, 74.
13 American Law Institute (ALI), *Principles of Corporate Governance: Analysis and Recommendations*, ALI, 1994, s. 2.01(B)(1) and s. 4.01.
14 *Henderson v. Merrett Syndicates Ltd*, [1995] 2 AC 145 HL, 206.

and passion.[15] While some people hope sustainability is achievable without major structural change to capitalism,[16] others, such as Tim Flannery[17] and George Monbiot,[18] advocate more fundamental transformation. Thus, if RI implies that investment fiduciaries should merely 'take into account' environmental and social issues they perceive to be financially material to investment performance, such practice is probably lawful. Indeed, if trustees ignore such issues and consequently incur avoidable financial losses, legal liabilities might arise. Alternatively, if RI infers radical changes, such as ridding investment portfolios of all fossil fuel producers or extractive industries, legal problems might ensue because of possible short-term financial losses.

Fiduciary law of course is not the only legal influence on RI. Extensive public regulation governs finance, including statutory duties on funds to disclose their investment policies and quantitative restrictions on investing in certain markets or assets. Corporate law affects the prospects for RI, as it determines the opportunities for shareholders to exert influence within public corporations by voting proxies, filing or supporting shareholder resolutions and seeking dialogue with management, as well as directly shaping the governance of financial institutions that have a corporate form, (notably banks). Securities regulation is also relevant, especially in governing financial reporting and disclosure of financially material environmental performance. Without such disclosure, investors might struggle to differentiate companies' sustainability records. Private law, particularly tort and contract law, also has a role, including protecting retail investors from being misled or cheated by sellers of financial products and services. Contractual arrangements are themselves sometimes relevant to the presence, ambit and content of a fiduciary relationship.[19] Parties may contractually modify or displace fiduciary obligations. More broadly, human rights and environmental regulation also influence financial markets, such as by creating environmental risks for investors in companies exposed to pollution liabilities. Ultimately, if environmental problems such as climate change were legally controlled, there would undoubtedly be far fewer social investors; RI is largely a symptom of the weaknesses of conventional regulation in controlling market externalities.

Overall, this chapter will show that fiduciary finance law may accommodate RI in principally four situations:

1. When ESG issues are judged to be financially material to investment performance. This approach fulfills the duty to invest prudently.

---

15 K. Pezzoli, 'Sustainable development: a transdisciplinary overview of the literature', *Journal of Environmental Planning and Management* 40(5), 1997, 549–74.
16 World Business Council for Sustainable Development (WBCSD), *Catalyzing Change: A Short History of the WBCSD*, WBCSD, 2007.
17 T. Flannery, *The Weather Makers*, HarperCollins, 2006.
18 G. Monbiot, *Heat: How to Stop the Planet from Burning*, South End Press, 2007.
19 J.K. Maxton, 'Contract and fiduciary obligation', *Journal of Contract Law* 11, 1997, 222–40, 229.

2. When alternative investments or investment portfolios are equally financially prudent, then ethical considerations may be the 'tie breaker'.
3. When a trust deed, investment prospectus or other governing instrument provides a mandate for RI, as for an endowment fund that is established to fulfill philanthropic goals.
4. When beneficiaries consent. In a pension plan, while beneficiaries might agree to an RI policy, these funds tend to be subject to legislative duties that restrict trustees' latitude to follow non-financial criteria.

Evolution of fiduciary law and trusts

In broad terms, a 'fiduciary' is a person in a position of trust or confidence with respect to another person, who is often referred to as the 'beneficiary' or 'principal'. The term derives from the Latin words 'fides' and 'fiducia', meaning faith and trust.[20] Central to this relationship is 'the scope for exercise of discretion or power by the fiduciary, the ability of a fiduciary to affect the legal or practical interests of the beneficiary and the vulnerability of the beneficiary'.[21] This bond of responsibility and dependency thus has two distinctive features.[22] First, considerable discretion vests in the fiduciary to exercise within broad parameters of care and loyalty to protect the beneficiary's 'structural vulnerability to exploitative misuse of power by the fiduciary'.[23] Second, the beneficiary is typically precluded from exercising any control over that area. As will be shortly observed, both attributes have important implications for RI in terms of both prioritizing the interests of beneficiaries and also limiting their voice. Fiduciary law's concern with the maintenance of fidelity, as reflected in its expectations of impeccable conduct by fiduciaries, 'reflects public policy considerations, not least of which is the need to maintain public confidence in the integrity and utility of a range of relationships perceived to be socially important'.[24]

Fiduciary status in an investment management context is most often associated with trust relationships, in which a distinct set of trusts law obligations arises, including the obligations to obey the trust deed and to exercise care and prudence.[25] A pension fund trust is a common example. Robert Flannigan contends that the function of fiduciary law has traditionally

---

20 J. Morwood (ed.), *Pocket Oxford Latin Dictionary*, Oxford University Press, 2001, 56.
21 J. Edelman, 'When do fiduciary duties arise?' Legal Research Paper Series, No. 65, Oxford University, 2010, 15.
22 See generally R. Flannigan, 'The boundaries of fiduciary accountability', *Canadian Bar Review* 83, 2004, 35–90; J.C. Shepherd, 'Towards a unified concept of fiduciary relationships', *Law Quarterly Review* 97, 1981, 51–79.
23 P. Miller, 'A theory of fiduciary liability', *McGill Law Journal* 36, 2011, 235–88, 269.
24 A. Tuch, 'Investment banks as fiduciaries: implications for conflicts of interest', *Melbourne University Law Review* 29(2), 2005, 478–517, 481.
25 See P. Birks, 'The content of fiduciary obligation', *Israel Law Review* 34, 2000, 3–38; A. Hudson, 'The regulation of trustees', in M. Dixon and G. Griffiths (eds), *Contemporary Perspectives on Property, Equity, and Trusts Law*, Oxford University Press, 2007, 163–80.

been only to control opportunism and self-interested behaviour when 'an actor has access to the assets of another for a defined or limited purpose'.[26] Thus, the fiduciary accountability of trustees is established through their privileged access to the assets of the trust fund. Such fiduciary accountability, by this analysis, should be regarded as functionally distinct from other legal duties in trusts law, which include investing prudently in the case of a trust fund. To commingle fiduciary law with trusts law (or other legal duties) might thus be problematic, explains Flannigan, given that 'there are different triggers for liability . . . and different remedial consequences'.[27] While this distinction is valid in some contexts, many discussions about fiduciary law and investing elide it;[28] John Langbein, a leading US scholar on this subject, declares, 'The law of fiduciary administration, the centerpiece of the modern law of trusts, resolves into two great principles, the duties of loyalty and prudence.'[29] And Peter Birks, a UK expert, described the duty of care as the 'backbone' of fiduciary responsibility.[30]

Another way to make sense of the legal situation is summarized by one Australian court in *Permanent Building Society (in liq.) v. Wheeler*, where Justice Ipp advised, 'It is essential to bear in mind that the existence of a fiduciary relationship does not mean that every duty owed by a fiduciary to the beneficiary is a breach of fiduciary duty. In particular, a trustee's duty to exercise reasonable care, though equitable, is not specifically a fiduciary duty.'[31] In other words, not all investment trustees' duties should be regarded as strictly fiduciary, notwithstanding the fact that the trust relationship, at a general level, is undoubtedly fiduciary.

In understanding these taxonomic issues, we should also be mindful of some important inter-jurisdictional differences. One significant difference is between jurisdictions that recognize fiduciary obligations as prescriptive in nature, Canada and the US, for instance, and those that more narrowly define them as only proscriptive, such as Australia.[32] Canadian courts have been a

---

26 R. Flannigan, 'Fiduciary duties of shareholders and directors', *Journal of Business Law* 2004, 277–302, 281; and R. Flannigan, 'The core nature of fiduciary accountability', *New Zealand Law Review* 3, 2009, 375–429.
27 Flannigan, ibid., 425.
28 Notably, Freshfields, op. cit.; M.B. Leslie, 'Trusting trustees: fiduciary duties and the limits of default rules', *Georgetown Law Journal* 94, 2005, 67–119, 95. Interestingly, while Ron Atkinson, like Flannigan, agrees on the need to scale down the essence of fiduciary responsibility, he describes that essence as a 'duty of obedience' – the fiduciary's duty to obey the will of the principal: R. Atkinson, 'Rediscovering the duty of obedience: toward a trinitarian theory of fiduciary duty', in K.J. Hopt and T. Von Hippel (eds), *Comparative Corporate Governance of Non-Profit Organizations*, Cambridge University Press, 2010, 564–618.
29 J.H. Langbein, 'The contractarian basis for the law of trusts', *Yale Law Journal* 105, 1995, 625–75, 655.
30 Birks, op. cit., 36.
31 (1994) 11 WAR 187; 14 ACSR 109, 157.
32 While the boundaries of fiduciary law may differ between some jurisdictions, there is near consensus on its essence, namely the cardinal duty of loyalty: E.J. Weinrib, 'The fiduciary obligation', *University of Toronto Law Journal* 25, 1975, 1–22, 16 (the duty of loyalty is 'the

pioneer, 'showing unusual ambition in a protracted and deliberate effort to develop a broad conceptual framework for fiduciary duties'.[33] In *Breen v. Williams*, Justices Gaudron and McHugh explained:

> The Canadian cases also reveal a tendency to view fiduciary obligations as both proscriptive and prescriptive. However, Australian courts only recognise proscriptive fiduciary duties ... In [Australia] fiduciary obligations arise because a person has come under an obligation to act in another's interests. As a result, equity imposes on the fiduciary proscriptive obligations – not to obtain any unauthorised benefit from the relationship and not to be in a position of conflict. If these obligations are breached, the fiduciary must account for any profits and make good any loss arising from the breach. But the law in [Australia] does not otherwise impose positive legal duties on the fiduciary to act in the interests of the person to whom the duty is owed.[34]

In Australia, as well as to some extent in the UK, the proscriptive paradigm is embedded in case law, and therefore any positive obligations to actively produce a beneficial outcome for a beneficiary tend to belong to other areas of law. The extent to which fiduciary law embodies proscriptive versus prescriptive duties has triggered much academic debate, though for this book resolution of this debate is less important, given that related positive duties of relevance to investment management are readily found in statutory regulation and trusts law.[35]

Fiduciary and trusts law has ancient roots. Trusts are found in Roman, Salic and Islamic law.[36] The legal norms of *fideicommisum* and *salmannus* evolved in Roman and Salic law, respectively, to facilitate the transfer of property between generations. The Islamic *waqf* arose to serve charitable purposes, by allowing for endowments to be created in perpetuity.[37] The modern trust developed most strongly in English law from civil law antecedents as a device to overcome feudal restrictions on the transfer of land.[38] In the Middle Ages the first trusts reminiscent of their current form were created by knights

---

irreducible core of the fiduciary obligation'); also D.A. DeMott, 'Beyond metaphor: an analysis of fiduciary obligation', *Duke Law Journal* 37, 1988, 879–924, 882.
33 D. Sarro and E. Waizter, 'The public fiduciary', draft paper (20 July 2012), 6.
34 (1996) 186 CLR 71, 113; see also Australian case *Pilmer v. Duke Group Ltd*, (2001) 207 CLR 165, and UK case *R. v. Mid Glamorgan FHSA, ex p. Martin*, [1995] 1 All ER 356.
35 See D. Jensen, 'Prescription and proscription in fiduciary obligations', *Kings Law Journal* 21, 2010, 333–54; R. Lee, 'Rethinking the content of the fiduciary obligation', *Conveyancing and Property Lawyer* 73, 2009, 236–53.
36 A. Avini, 'The origins of the modern English trust revisited', *Tulane Law Review* 70, 1996, 1139–63.
37 M.M. Gaudiosi, 'Influence of the Islamic law of Waqf on the development of the trust in England: the case of Merton College', *University of Pennsylvania Law Review* 136, 1987–88, 1231–61.
38 M. Lupoi, 'The civil law trust', *Vanderbilt Journal of Transnational Law* 32, 1999, 967–88.

to safeguard their wealth while they were away on military service.[39] Legal title of a knight's estate would be assigned to a trusted friend, on the understanding that ownership would revert to the knight if he returned. The trust institution gradually extended to ameliorate situations in which existing legal obligations had failed to protect the assets of minors or dependants from unscrupulous guardians. The ingenious feature of the trust was to separate legal and beneficial ownership of the underlying assets – to be held in trust, by the trustees, on behalf of the designated beneficiaries.[40] Trusts law also serves to align the behaviour of trustees with the interest of beneficiaries by obliging trustees to act for beneficiaries.[41]

While the trust continues to be a popular mechanism in property conveyancing,[42] it has evolved dramatically over time and been extended to other purposes. Trusts are now widely used as the underlying legal structure for pension plans, charitable endowment funds and some mutual funds.[43] Concomitantly, many relationships in the finance world, such as between financial advisers and their clients, have been legally characterized as sometimes fiduciary in nature. Today, the US has the most detailed legal framework for fiduciary finance; and fiduciary and trusts duties are defined through legislation and court cases in both state and federal law. The American Law Institute's *Third Restatement* of the law of trusts and the associated Uniform Trust Code provide the principal benchmark for both jurisdictional consistency and investment guidance for financial fiduciaries and trustees.[44]

Although sometimes compared to company directors' legal duties, the standards of both care and loyalty have traditionally been stricter in the law of investment trusts than in the equivalent law governing for-profit corporations.[45] Though expected to seek optimal returns, trustees are not obliged to raise capital.[46] Unlike corporations, there are fewer market controls on trustees, and a trust's beneficiaries lack the freedom to sell their interest on the market and cannot remove trustees (unless they have breached their trust contrary to the duty of loyalty, as most courts have inherent or statutory

---

39 J. Youngdahl and C. Haynes, 'Comparative visions of fiduciary duty', in D. Campbell (ed.), *Comparative Law Yearbook of International Business 2010*, Kluwer Law, 2010, 273–306, 275.
40 J.H. Langbein, 'The secret life of the trust: the trust as an instrument of commerce', *Yale Law Journal* 107, 1997, 165–89.
41 M. Conaglen, 'The nature and function of fiduciary loyalty', *Law Quarterly Review* 121, 2005, 452–80.
42 Langbein, op. cit.
43 P. O'Hagan, 'The use of trusts in finance structures', *Journal of International Tax, Trust and Corporate Planning* 8(2), 2000, 85–92.
44 American Law Institute (ALI), *Restatement of Law Third, Trusts*, volume 3, ALI, 1992; National Conference of Commissioners on Uniform State Laws, *Uniform Trust Code*, 2004; also R.J. Aalberts and P.S. Poon, 'The new prudent investor rule and the modern portfolio theory: a new direction for fiduciaries', *American Business Law Journal* 34, 1996, 39–72.
45 J. Hawley, K. Johnson and E. Waitzer, 'Reclaiming fiduciary law fundamentals', PRI Academic Conference, Stockholm, May 2011, 13.
46 Langbein, op. cit.

jurisdiction to replace trustees where their continuance threatens the beneficiaries' interests in the trust). Furthermore, trustees are not entrepreneurs and thus subject to legal norms that discourage the kind of active risk-taking associated with company directors.[47] If a trustee is alleged to have breached his/her fiduciary duty, this claim will be scrutinized more discerningly than if the standard were the business judgement rule, which protects corporate directors from reasonable business decisions made in good faith.[48] Fiduciary law governing investment management has traditionally focused on preservation of trust assets through avoidance of conflicts of interest by fund custodians. Finally, a key distinction between these areas of fiduciary law is that a director under corporate law owes her obligation to the company itself, whereas the duty of loyalty in a trust is for the beneficiaries (rather than to the trust).

While some commentators believe that the definitional content of fiduciary law is sufficiently malleable to accommodate changing social needs,[49] the culture of investment markets inhibits change. One particular issue to address, which can be traced to the infusion of prudence standards, is the increasing tendency for 'herding' behaviour and short-term investment horizons. Concerning fund managers' tendency to follow the crowd, Raghuram Rajan notes that there is an 'incentive to herd with other investment managers on investment choices because herding provides insurance the manager will not under perform his peers', even though herding can collectively shift asset values away from fundamentals.[50] Furthermore, as the relevant legal standard hinges on what typical prudent investors do, this 'duty to herd' induces fiduciaries to eschew actions that are at odds with common practice in order to mitigate any legal liability. Clinging to the herd, however, can stifle innovative investment practices and 'distracts fiduciaries from focusing on the interests of [beneficiaries]',[51] as verified by studies of the cautious and dogmatic practices of investment managers who increasingly invest passively by tracking indexes.[52] James Hawley and others despair that 'there remains a strong cognitive resistance' to understanding the dynamic context to fiduciary law that must address the systemic risks associated with financial markets.[53] These risks relate to the instability or collapse of the entire or a substantial part of the financial system, as opposed to risks associated with

---

47 See O' Hagan, op. cit.
48 *Oberly v. Kirby*, (1991) 592 A. 2d 445, 467 (Del.).
49 E.C. Halbach, Jr., 'Trust investment law in the Third Restatement', *Iowa Law Review* 77, 1992, 1151–85, 1154–5.
50 R. Rajan, 'Risky business', *Finance and Development* 42(3), 2005, 54–6, 55.
51 J. Hawley, K. Johnson and E. Waizter, 'Reclaiming fiduciary duty balance', *Rotman International Journal of Pension Management* 4(2), 2011, 4–17, 7.
52 D.G. Del Guercio, 'The distorting effect of the prudent man laws on institutional equity investments', *Journal of Financial Economics* 40(1), 1996, 31–62; A. Thomas and I. Tonks, 'Equity performance of segregated pension funds in the United Kingdom', *Journal of Asset Management* 1(4), 2001, 321–43.
53 Hawley, Johnson and Waizter, op. cit., 7.

any individual entity. The classic example is a panic run of a bank, but it also includes the global fallout from the collapse of the subprime mortgage market in the US banking sector in 2008.

Financial actors' fiduciary responsibilities

Ascertaining fiduciary relationships

Fiduciary relationships may arise under a number of circumstances.[54] They may exist not only between parties that have a proprietary connection, as typically occurs in management of a trust asset, but also in established categories, such as doctors and patients or company directors and companies, because of their inherent purpose or the status of the parties. Other relationships are not considered innately fiduciary but may attract such responsibilities because of the specific factual situation and undertakings the parties make. A basic ingredient of all fiduciary relationships is some discretionary control; E.J. Weinrib explains that 'the hallmark of a fiduciary relation is that the relative legal positions are such that one party is at the mercy of the other's discretion'.[55] But it is important to recognize, as Justice La Forest did in *McInerney v. MacDonald*, that not all fiduciary relationships and not all fiduciary obligations are alike: '[T]hese are shaped by the demands of the situation.'[56] It is necessary to ascertain the content of the fiduciary duty in each circumstance. In an investing context, therefore, a fiduciary relationship typically arises when someone exercises control or discretionary authority over investment assets or acts in a professional capacity of confidence to render investment advice.

The trust is the quintessential example of a fiduciary relationship. The relationship is actually trilateral, not bilateral, in which the principal, the trust's settlor or grantor, provides property to his or her 'agent' (i.e., the trustee) for the purposes of undertaking the terms of the trust and in the interests of a third party, the beneficiaries. The fiduciary's fundamental duty is thus to obey the principal's directive to serve the beneficiary. The fiduciary is the trustee of the trust assets, and the beneficiary the equitable owner of that property.[57] This entitlement gives the beneficiary rights not only against the trustee but also against third parties not to interfere with the trustee–beneficiary relationship. The fiduciary obligations may extend to a variety of actors in the case of an institutional fund. For example, for an occupational pension fund, under Canadian law both the employer who sponsors the

---

54 *Hodgkinson v. Simms*, (1994) 3 SCR 377, 1994 Carswell BC 438, para. 32.
55 Weinrib, op. cit., 7.
56 [1992] 2 SCR 138, 149.
57 A.W. Scott, 'The nature of the rights of the cestui que trust', *Columbia Law Review* 17, 1917, 269–90; D.W.M. Waters, 'The nature of the trust beneficiary's interest', *Canadian Bar Review* 45(2), 1997, 219–83, 274.

pension fund and the board of trustees owe fiduciary loyalty to the plan members.[58] Although a charitable trust such as an endowment fund normally has no specific beneficiaries, the fiduciary's obligations may be enforceable by the state Attorney-General.[59]

Some fiduciary relationships, while not innate to a given relationship, may also arise because of specific factual circumstances. This second category can be referred to as *ad hoc* relationships.[60] They are open-ended and may continue to be found in novel situations.[61] 'Thus, outside the established categories', explained one court, 'what is required is evidence of a mutual understanding that one party has relinquished its own self-interest and agreed to act solely on behalf of the other party'.[62] One judicial decision observed, 'The fiduciary's undertaking may be the result of the exercise of statutory powers, the express or implied terms of an agreement or, perhaps, simply an undertaking to act in this way.'[63] A widely accepted circumstance is an undertaking by one party in a position to exercise some discretionary power over another, and the reposing of trust and reliance on the other.[64] But courts have been watchful to avoid imposing fiduciary duties in ordinary business relationships even where one party could exploit a disparity of bargaining power.[65]

Ad hoc fiduciary obligations may be found in the relationship between a financial professional and her client, depending upon their circumstances; financial brokers acting only as such generally are not fiduciaries, but they can be if they provide investment advice.[66] Fiduciary duties may also apply to fund managers or asset managers, depending on the nature of the specific principal–agent relationship.[67] Legislation typically also makes fund managers effectively subject to the same prudential obligations as their

---

58 See *Re Indalex Ltd*, [2011] ONCA 265.
59 D.B. Parker, A.R. Mellows and A.J. Oakley, *Parker and Mellows: The Modern Law of Trusts*, Sweet and Maxwell, 1998, 440.
60 P.D. Maddaugh, 'The centrality of undertaking in identifying fiduciary relationships: Galambos v. Perez', *Banking and Finance Law Review* 26(2), 2011, 315–26.
61 See the Canadian case of *Guerin v. R*, (1984) 13 DLR (4th) 321, para 99, where Justice Dickson observed: 'It is sometimes said that the nature of fiduciary relationships is both established and exhausted by the standard categories of agent, trustee, partner, director, and the like. I do not agree. It is the nature of the relationship, not the specific category of actor involved that gives rise to the fiduciary duty. The categories of fiduciary, like those of negligence, should not be considered closed.'
62 *Hodgkinson v. Simms*, [1994] 3 SCR 377, para. 33.
63 *Galambos v. Perez*, [2009] 3 SCR 247, para. 77.
64 J.C. Shepard, *The Law of Fiduciaries*, Carswell, 1981.
65 E.g., *Committee on Children's Television*, 35 Cal. 2d 197, 221 (1983) (California Supreme Court rejected plaintiffs' argument that the seller of breakfast cereals owed fiduciary obligations to children, who were said by plaintiff to be uniquely susceptible to misleading advertising claims that eating such cereals would confer health benefits on them).
66 G.A. Clarke, *Liability and Damages in Unsuitable Investment Advice Cases*, Fasken Martineau DuMoulin LLP, 2005.
67 See S. Willey, 'Investment management and fiduciary duties', in D. Frase (ed.), *Law and Regulation of Investment Management*, Sweet and Maxwell, 2004, 237–63.

principals.[68] Investment consultants may also be recognized as having fiduciary status.[69] But often legislation will designate certain relationships as fiduciary in nature. In pension plans, ERISA defines three types of fiduciaries: (i) those who exercise authority over the management or disposition of plan assets; (ii) providers of investment advice for a fee with respect to pension plan assets; and (iii) administrators of a plan.[70] ERISA thus 'defines "fiduciary" not in terms of formal trusteeship, but in *functional* terms of control and authority over the plan, . . . thus expanding the universe of persons subject to fiduciary duties'.[71]

Fiduciary responsibilities in institutional contexts

Fiduciary and cognate responsibilities materialize in somewhat different ways across the financial sector. The distinguishing quality of any fiduciary relationship, however, is the obligation of loyalty. Its nature is encapsulated in the following remarks of Millett L.J. in *Bristol and West Building Society v. Mothew*:

> The principal is entitled to the single-minded loyalty of his fiduciary. This core liability has several facets. A fiduciary must act in good faith; he must not make a profit out of his trust; he must not place himself in a position where his duty and his interest may conflict; he may not act for his own benefit or the benefit of a third person without the informed consent of his principal. This is not intended to be an exhaustive list, but it is sufficient to indicate the nature of fiduciary obligations.[72]

Beyond this expectation of fidelity, a range of cognate legal responsibilities, which may come from trusts law, statutory regulation and other realms, may be impressed upon fiduciary finance relationships. Trusts law is particularly applicable to pension plans, which have distinct beneficiaries. Likewise, investment foundations are typically governed by trust principles. Commercial banks do not owe their depositors a fiduciary duty in regard to management of deposited funds, but they are covered by detailed banking regulations, and

---

68 E.g., UK Pensions Act, 1995, s. 36 (duties to assess the suitability of each investment and have regard to the need for diversification); see further J. Franks and C.P. Mayer, *Risk, Regulation and Investor Protection: The Case of Investment Management*, Oxford University Press, 1989.
69 C. Berry, *Protecting Our Best Interests: Rediscovering Fiduciary Obligation*, FairPensions, 2011, 4.
70 Pub. L. No. 93-406; and R.K. Matta, 'ERISA for securities professionals', *Journal of Investment Compliance* 5(1), 2004, 69–83.
71 *In re Enron Corp. Securities, Derivative and ERISA Litigation*, (2003) 284 F. Supp. 2d 511, 587.
72 [1998] Ch. 1, 18.

fiduciary responsibility may arise when investment banks provide financial advisory services.[73] In most jurisdictions, insurance companies, which are major institutional investors, do not owe a fiduciary duty to insured policy-holders regarding their investment activities. Fiduciary responsibilities may arise when insurance companies provide pension-type investment services through agreements with individual savers, although contract and consumer protection law largely governs such relationships. Furthermore, insurers' investment decisions tend to be regulated to protect insurers' loss reserves and to maintain liquidity.[74] Although fiduciary principles also arise in mutual fund governance, contract law and securities regulation primarily serve to align investment decisions with the interests of fund members. Trustees of mutual funds, pension plans and other types of investment funds often delegate many of their decision-making powers to professional asset managers. Contrary to the common law prohibition on such delegations, legislation typically authorizes deputation of fund management so long as the fiduciary retains ultimate control and carefully supervises fund managers.[75] Financial advisers, acting independently or employed by financial institutions such as banks and insurance companies, may and often do have fiduciary obligations. They may arise between a financial adviser and her client where the adviser professes to be an expert on financial issues and performs a financial advisory role for the client.[76]

Within a single financial sector such as pension funds, there can be further significant cross-jurisdictional differences in the legal and institutional characteristics of consequence for fiduciary relationships. Compare Canadian and British pension fund governance, for example. In the UK, the trustees of pension funds have played a pre-eminent role in supervising the administration of pension investments since the 1991 Maxwell scandal.[77] In Canada, by contrast, trustees of employer-sponsored pension funds tend to play a more notional role of keeping custody of the trust funds, while employer corporations appoint or act as plan administrators, who make key decisions. An employer thus owes a fiduciary duty to plan members.[78] Canadian pension funds jointly sponsored by both employers and employees (through their trade union) have a fiduciary structure that is closer to the UK model, with strong, independent boards of trustees.[79]

---

73 Tuch, op. cit., 497–9.
74 S. Randall, 'Insurance regulation in the United States', *Florida State University Law Review* 26, 1999, 625–99.
75 Willey, op. cit.
76 Tuch, op. cit.
77 The scandal, in which media entrepreneur Robert Maxwell stole more than £400 million from 32,000 members of company pension plans, led to tighter legal controls: 'Could it happen again?', *BBC News*, 30 March 2001, http://news.bbc.co.uk/2/hi/business/1251019.stm.
78 See *Re Indalex Ltd* (2011) ONCA 265.
79 See further R. Davis, *Democratizing Pension Funds: Corporate Governance and Accountability*, UBC Press, 2009.

Obey governing documents

An investment fund must be managed in accordance with its governing instrument, such as a trust deed, in the case of a pension plan or investment foundation, or an investment prospectus, in the case of a mutual fund. The following comments focus on the trust deed, while Chapter 4 looks at the investment prospectus in the context of its analysis of retail funds. A trust deed is the legal document that creates the framework within which a trustee must operate. To illustrate, the New South Wales (NSW) Trustee Act 1925 states: 'A trustee must exercise a power of investment in accordance with any provision of the instrument (if any) creating the trust that is binding on the trustee.'[80] The 'settlor' is the person who creates the trust deed by assigning legal control of assets to the trustees, to be dealt with in accordance with the deed. Apart from describing the purposes of the trust, the deed typically enumerates the powers and responsibilities of the trustees, their appointment and removal, the preferred approach to investment and ancillary matters such as record-keeping. If a deed drafted by a settlor expressly requires trustees to follow ethical investment criteria, they must respect those criteria.[81]

The trust deed is important for a foundation or eleemosynary institution – so-called 'mission-based investors'. Although some foundations lack an explicit RI mandate, it may be implied that they should not invest contrary to their mission.[82] A foundation that promotes research into lung cancer treatment presumably should allow its trustees to eschew investing in tobacco companies. Britain's Charity Commission, which supervises UK charities under the Charities Act of 1993, advises that charities may choose investments that do not necessarily seek the best financial returns if they advance their philanthropic mission.[83]

While the trust deed is particularly determinative of fiduciary obligations in the context of a charitable foundation or a private trust established to manage family assets, it is less decisive for financial institutions that manage or sell investments to the general public. For employee pension funds, the trust deed is embedded within a legislative framework that elaborates rules on investment decision-making. Where legislation provides for the conferment of investment management powers on trustees, they must exercise their

---

80 Section 14A(3).
81 Law Reform Commission (LRC), *Trust Law: General Proposals*, LRC, 2008, 134.
82 Parker, Mellows and Oakley, op. cit., 543.
83 Charity Commission, *Guidance on Programme-Related Investment*, Charity Commission, 2001.

powers for that purpose. Some commentators regard this requirement as having 'overarching application, subordinating other "duties" owed by the trustee'.[84]

It would surely be very rare or strange to find a trust fund established with an explicit purpose to engage in environmentally harmful investing or to harm the non-economic interests of beneficiaries. As Ron Davis explains, 'It is much more likely that the trust agreement or declaration and the applicable legislation will be silent. . . . Thus, the real issues are whether or not trustees are required to exercise the trust funds . . . to further the non-economic interests of the . . . beneficiaries.'[85] In the absence of an express clause in a trust deed on a specific point, the rules of trust law and any legislation supplement the terms of the trust. Sometimes legislation may vitiate any trust provisions contrary to public policy. Typically, trusts law accords trustees very wide powers of investment; the NSW Trustee Act 1925 declares that 'a trustee may, unless expressly forbidden by the instrument (if any) creating the trust: (a) invest trust funds in any form of investment, and (b) at any time vary any investment'.[86] Where a trust has several stated purposes, such as to invest assets for financial return while fulfilling an ethical agenda, conflicts may arise. Litigation is illustrated by the English case of *Bishop of Oxford v. Church Commissioners for England*.[87] The bishop wanted the Commissioners to uphold Christian doctrine strictly, or at least his interpretation of it, even if this heightened financial risk. Although the Commissioners had an RI policy for managing the Church's assets, it applied only to the extent that it would not be financially injurious. The court explained:

> It is axiomatic that charity trustees, in common with all other trustees, are concerned to further the purposes of the trust of which they have accepted the office of trustee. That is their duty. To enable them the better to discharge that duty, trustees have powers vested in them. Those powers must be exercised for the purpose for which they have been given: to further the purposes of the trust. That is the guiding principle applicable to the issues in these proceedings.[88]

The Church Commissioners' investment policy stated that '[w]hile financial responsibilities must remain of primary importance (given our position as trustees), as responsible investors . . . we do not invest in companies whose main business is armaments, gambling, alcohol, tobacco and newspapers'.[89]

---

84 S. Donald and N. Taylor, 'Does "sustainable" investing compromise the obligations owed by superannuation trustees?', *Australian Business Law Review* 36, 2008, 47–61, 55.
85 Davis, op. cit., 53.
86 Section 14.
87 [1992] 1 WLR 1241.
88 Ibid., 1242–3.
89 Ibid., 1249.

The court took no issue with these goals, but it found the declarations sought by the plaintiff as exceeding the legal obligations of the trustees:

> In most cases the best interests of the charity require that the trustees' choice of investments should be made solely on the basis of well-established investment criteria, having taken expert advice where appropriate and having due regard to such matters as the need to diversify, the need to balance income against capital growth, and the need to balance risk against return.[90]

The court also felt that where the aims of the charity and the objects of investment would directly conflict, the trustees must balance the extent of financial loss from offended supporters of the Church against the financial risks of RI.

In the US, by contrast, legal commentators have observed a trend facilitated by the Uniform Trust Code (UTC) for prudence standards to supersede the terms of the trust deed. As Jeffery Cooper explains:

> Whereas trust law typically accorded a trust settlor nearly unfettered latitude to determine which trust terms and restrictions would benefit her chosen beneficiaries, one can read the UTC to deny her this power. . . . [T]he 'benefit' of a trust provision is determined by reference to objective notions of prudence and efficiency rather than the settlor's subjective intent.[91]

A controversial trend, for some observers, it has apparently been rationalized as a way 'to aid the beneficiaries of settlors who have made mistakes or failed to anticipate changed circumstances'.[92]

Duty of loyalty

The core duty of a fiduciary is the duty of loyalty, which obligates that the fiduciary put the interests of the beneficiaries or principals first, ahead of the fiduciary's self-interest or that of any third-party parties. In a charitable trust, as just discussed, fidelity is owed to the purposes of the trust rather than to any specific class of beneficiaries. Courts and legislatures have developed several constituent elements of this duty over the years, which typically include the obligation on fiduciaries to avoid conflicts of interest, to act honestly and in good faith, the duty not to delegate responsibility and the

---

90 Ibid., 1246.
91 J. Cooper, 'Empty promises: settlor's intent, the uniform trust code, and the future of trust investment law', *Boston University Law Review* 88, 2008, 1165–216, 1168–9.
92 Ibid., 1216.

duty to act impartially towards different beneficiaries.[93] As previously mentioned in this chapter, in North America the duty of loyalty has tended to be interpreted as going beyond this basic proscriptive duty to encompass also a positive obligation to act in the best interests of beneficiaries. Furthermore, in financial entities governed by trusts law, the duty of loyalty is often framed around an expectation to act in beneficiaries' best interests.[94] The following discussion encompasses both this narrow and broad legal conception of loyalty, and focuses on its application in financial trusts. However, we should keep in mind the potentially different triggers of liability and available remedies, as discussed later in this chapter, between breach of a pure fiduciary duty of loyalty and its application in a trusts law context.

The duty of loyalty is sometimes framed in positive terms to act in beneficiaries' 'sole interests' or their 'best interests', with the latter possibly more accommodating of wider societal concerns, given that 'sole' interests implies a more exclusive relationship. The EU's Occupational Pensions Directive provides that 'assets shall be invested in the best interests of the members and beneficiaries. In the case of a potential conflict of interest, the institution, or the entity that manages its portfolio, shall ensure that the investment is made in the sole interest of members and beneficiaries.'[95] The UK's Occupational Pension Schemes (Investment) Regulations 2005 characterize a trustee's chief duty to beneficiaries as acting in their 'best interests', except 'in the case of a potential conflict of interest, [where they must act] in the sole interest of members and beneficiaries'.[96] The American ERISA uses a 'sole interests' standard,[97] and US courts have expressed this duty as one of 'undivided loyalty'.[98]

Fiduciary law does not per se prescribe what beneficiaries' interests are, but in the management of trust assets the terms of the governing trust deed or investment prospectus will be relevant. In financial institutions, the duty of loyalty is commonly interpreted as directed to safeguarding beneficiaries' financial interests. Lord Nicholls of Birkenhead has observed, 'A pension fund trustee is not the guardian of the moral welfare of the fund members, and modern developments in social conditions do not compel the conclusions that he should assume this role.'[99] In the English case of *Cowan v. Scargill*, which involved a dispute among trustees of a mining industry pension fund about whether its investment policy should exclude investment abroad and in

---

93 A.B. Laby, 'Resolving conflicts of duty in fiduciary relationships', *American University Law Review* 54, 2004, 75–149, 99–108.
94 J.H. Langbein, 'Questioning the trust law duty of loyalty: sole interest or best interest?', *Yale Law Journal* 114, 2005, 929–90.
95 Directive 2003/41/EC of the European Parliament and of the Council of 3 June 2003 on the activities and supervision of institutions for occupational retirement provision, OJ L. 235/10, art. 18.
96 Clause 4(2).
97 Section 404.
98 *Meinhard v. Salmon*, (1928) 164 NE 545 (NY).
99 D. Nicholls, 'Trustees and their broader community: where duty, morality and ethics converge', *Australian Law Journal* 70(3), 1995, 205–16, 211.

industries in competition with the domestic coal industry, Vice-Chancellor (VC) Robert Megarry held:

> When the purpose of the trust is to provide financial benefits for the beneficiaries, as is usually the case, the best interests of the beneficiaries are normally their best financial interests. ... In considering what investments to make, trustees must put to one side their own personal interests and views. Trustees may have strongly held social or political views. They may be firmly opposed to any investment in South Africa or other countries, or they may object to any form of investment in companies concerned with alcohol, tobacco, armaments or many other things. In the conduct of their own affairs, of course, they are free to abstain from making any such investments. Yet under a trust, if investments of this type would be more beneficial to the beneficiaries than other investments, the trustees must not refrain from making the investments by reasons of the views that they hold.[100]

But Megarry also conceded that if beneficiaries share a moral objection to a particular investment, they might benefit if their trust fund avoids it, possibly even to their financial detriment. He reasoned, '"Benefit" is a word with a very wide meaning, and there are circumstances in which arrangements which work to the financial disadvantage of a beneficiary may yet be for his benefit ... But I would emphasise that such cases are likely to be very rare.'[101] Likewise, in one US case about the use of state school lands of environmental significance held in trust by authorities, the Supreme Court of Utah stressed the importance of the trustees safeguarding 'unique scenic, paleontological, and archaeological values that would have little economic value on the open market'.[102] Even where there is no ambiguity about prioritizing financial returns, fiduciaries must focus on *risk-adjusted* returns (standard investment practice) rather than absolute returns. Incorporating a risk-sensitive approach to the pursuit of investment returns gives fiduciaries some room to take ESG issues into account, at least where they are financially material.

Related to this recognition that beneficiaries' interests may go beyond financial goals, some commentators affirm that fiduciary law may countenance RI if it fulfills the will of beneficiaries. The seminal Freshfields Report acknowledged this by stating that 'a decision-maker may integrate ESG considerations into an investment decision to give effect to the views of the beneficiaries in relation to matters beyond financial return'.[103] A practice of consulting beneficiaries would seem congruent with the purposes of fiduciary law, in that it

---

100 [1985] Ch. 270, 286.
101 Ibid., 287; see also P. Palmer, et al., *Socially Responsible Investment: A Guide for Pension Schemes and Charities*, Key Haven Publications, 2005, 97.
102 *National Parks and Conservation Association v. Board of State Lands*, (1993) 869 P.2d 909, 921. However, the Court held the trustees were not obliged to give priority to these environmental values over their concomitant duty to maximize economic returns (ibid.).
103 Freshfields, op. cit., 12.

could help fiduciaries to fulfill their duty of loyalty by improving their understanding of the interests and preferences of their beneficiaries. A fiduciary may also learn more about the best interests of its beneficiaries while minimizing any specific disadvantage to the interests of some classes of beneficiaries, thereby enabling fulfillment of the concomitant duty of impartiality. But so far the law has tended to recognize only beneficiaries' right to be informed[104] rather than a right to be consulted. Beneficiaries have traditionally assumed a passive role in fund governance as a matter of practice and legal precedent.

The principal concern with allowing consultation rights is that it might lead to beneficiaries taking an active role in fund governance, contrary to the basic structure of the fiduciary relationship. As the Ontario Law Reform Commission once explained:

> To allow beneficiaries to direct the ongoing administration of the trust confuses the role of trustee and beneficiary and is inconsistent with the trust concept. If the creator of a trust wishes the beneficiary to be actively involved in the administration of the trust, such person may always be appointed as trustee.[105]

Historically, trusts arose in England primarily to protect family wealth and to provide for wives and children, who were socially constructed as passive and dependent.[106] From such private trusts also came the corollary principle that trustees do not need to disclose their reasons for exercising a discretionary power in a particular way, on the assumption that it might cause embarrassment or family disharmony.[107]

While beneficiaries' right to information is now well established in fund government, modern investment law has transplanted the corollary attribute of private trusts – lack of consultation – into a wholly different context in which such familial considerations carry little or no relevance. Treating beneficiaries as passive parties continues to be rationalized on the assumption that investment management is a complex, specialized activity that few lay persons could competently undertake or understand.[108] Despite emerging judicial pronouncements that it is 'good discipline' for trustees to consult beneficiaries concerning investment matters that may closely affect them,[109] trustees are not yet obliged to consult except in specific legislated contexts. Ontario pension legislation, for instance, requires administrators to consult with beneficiaries before seeking to amend a pension plan in a way 'that

---

104 D. Hayton, 'The irreducible core content of trusteeship', *Journal of International Trust and Corporate Planning* 5, 1996, 47–62, 49.
105 Ontario Law Reform Commission (OLRC), *Report on the Law of Trusts*, OLRC, 1984, 74.
106 For history of trusts, see A. Hudson, *Principles of Equity and Trusts*, Cavendish, 1999.
107 See, e.g., *Wilson v. Law Debenture Trust Corporation*, [1995] 2 All ER 337; *Edge v. Pensions Ombudsman*, [1998] Ch. 512.
108 B.J. Richardson, 'Fiduciary relationships for socially responsible investing: a multinational perspective', *American Journal of Business Law* 48(3), 2011, 597–640, 602–3.
109 *X v. A*, [2000] 1 All ER 490. 496.

would . . . adversely affect the rights or obligations of a . . . person entitled to payment from the pension fund'.[110] Perhaps the quintessential example is Canada's legal requirement that the state consult with Aboriginal peoples to whom it owes a fiduciary obligation.[111] This, however, is a *sui generis* fiduciary relationship, unlike the fiduciary finance relationships discussed in this book.

When investment funds come into existence through agreements or pursuant to statutory mandate (or a combination of both) there may be some scope at the commencement of the trust to influence investment strategy. Beneficiaries' involvement in investment policy might be rationalized as a matter of contract law given that occupational pension schemes typically arise through collective bargaining processes between employees and employers, where pension benefits form part of the total compensation packages for workers.[112] As the court in the New Zealand case of *Re UEB Industries Ltd Pension Plan* remarked, 'Pension plans are different in nature from traditional trusts. There is an interrelationship of contract law and trust law in any pension scheme . . . [It] is fundamentally a contract entered into by an employer to fund the payment of defined benefits to members of the plan.'[113] Employees may also, with their employer, be construed as joint settlors of the pension trust by virtue of their financial contributions to the plan.[114] Therefore, Megarry erred in *Cowan* by equating the legal context of a pension scheme to a private family trust when the latter is 'funded exclusively by the original settlor as a gift'.[115] Framing the scheme as a private trust wrongly limits beneficiaries' contractual rights of participation and consultation. In civil law systems, pension plans also tend to be seen as primarily a matter of contract law within a regulatory envelope.

In a trust fund exclusively created and funded by the employer,[116] it would be more difficult to sustain the foregoing argument for beneficiaries. Trustees are bound to follow the express intentions of the settlor with regard to their administration of the trust property. Without legislative authority, courts cannot alter the trust's terms, apart from a few limited exceptions. Under English and Canadian law, a court could vary the terms of a trust in order to address urgent, unforeseen circumstances that threaten the trust property.[117]

---

110 Ontario's Pension Benefits Act, RSO 1990, s. 26(1).
111 D.G. Newman, *The Duty to Consult: New Relationships with Aboriginal People*, Purich Publishing, 2009.
112 Ibid.
113 [1992] 1 NZLR 294, 298.
114 Davis, op. cit., 64.
115 J.K. Maxton and J. Farrar, 'Social investment and pension scheme trusts', *Law Quarterly Review* 102, 1986, 32–5, 34.
116 However, labour economics suggests that a rational employer would include funding the pension in its total employee compensation cost and bargain accordingly with workers; thus, the pension fund should be understood as deferred compensation, the cost of which effectively reduces current cash wages: D. McCarthy, et al., *Pensions and Economics: The Way Ahead*, Staple Inn Actuarial Society, 2004, 10–12.
117 A.J. McClean, 'Variation of trusts in England and Canada', *Canadian Bar Review* 43(2), 1965, 181–261, 184.

Even here, courts rationalize their variation of the trust by invoking the assumed intent of the settlor had he or she foreseen the circumstances.[118] In England, the rule established in *Saunders v. Vauthier* putatively allows beneficiaries to modify or extinguish the trust, provided they are adults with full legal capacity and their consent is unanimous.[119] Fiduciary law also allows a fiduciary to engage in a conflicting situation or profit from his/her position so long as informed consent is obtained from the beneficiary with full disclosure.[120] But in the context of modern pension fund governance, this rule may not be applicable. The Supreme Court of Canada ruled in *Rogers Communication v. Buschau*[121] that the position in *Saunders* is inapplicable to a modern pension trust – only termination by regulator or employer is available. In the US, under general trusts law, the settlor's power is more intact, and beneficiaries may alter the trust only if they all consent and the proposed change would not defeat a material purpose of the trust's creator.[122] The current US UTC, however, signals a trend towards offering more leeway for courts to allow beneficiaries to alter a settlor's wishes due to unforeseen circumstances, for instance when the change would benefit the beneficiaries.[123] Under regulated financial trusts such as ERISA pension funds, it isn't possible to interpret the rights of members and employers only from a strict trust law perspective; financial prudence standards thus cannot be overridden, for instance.

For a defined benefit plan in which an employer assumes greater financial risks and liability for any shortfall in benefits, the 'employer could legitimately object to the use of non-financial criteria . . . on the grounds that this increased its risk of having to make additional contributions'.[124] But in a broader sense, the financial risk is also implicitly shared between the shareholders and employees (beneficiaries), both in the form of reduced future wage increases and an insolvency risk to the company. The pension trust in the *Cowan* case was a defined-benefit scheme. Legislation commonly restricts the ability of trustees to fulfill any investment preferences expressed by beneficiaries. British Columbia's Pension Benefits Standards Act provides that 'pension plan investments . . . must be made . . . in the *best financial* interests of plan members, former members and other plan beneficiaries'.[125] While an agency relationship may be imputed where the trustees hold merely legal title to act on the beneficiary's wishes, courts may not let beneficiaries interfere in cases where a trustee possesses significant discretionary powers.

---

118 Ibid., 194–200.
119 (1841) 4 Beav. 115, 49 ER 282.
120 E.g., *Chan v. Zacharia*, (1984) 154 CLR 178, 198–9.
121 (2006) 1 SCR 973.
122 See *Claflin v. Claflin*, (1889) 149 Mass. 19, 20 NE 455; *Shelton v. King*, (1913) 229 US 90.
123 NCCUSL, *Uniform Prudent Investor Act*, 7 B ULA 18, supplement 1997.
124 Davis, op. cit., 67. Though, Davis notes that this argument is undermined where 'the costs of additional contributions will be passed on to the employees through lower future wage rises' (ibid).
125 Section 44(1).

Any legal mandate allowing trustees to respond to the will of beneficiaries might also give rise to other potential problems. If beneficiaries can instruct trustees and thereby influence investment decisions, trustees might be considered their agents, and consequently beneficiaries might be liable as principals to third parties for any compensable losses. The extent to which American and Commonwealth jurisprudence recognizes an agency relationship in a trust where beneficiaries exert control has been debated by legal scholars without conclusive agreement.[126]

Another way trustees might act on the will of beneficiaries, albeit indirectly, is by responding to the broader societal values they belong to. Scott's *The Law of Trusts*, a leading US scholarly authority, explains that trustees may properly consider the social performance of a corporation in investment decisions:

> They may decline to invest in, or to retain, the securities of corporations whose activities, or some of them, are contrary to fundamental and generally accepted ethical principles. They may consider such matters as pollution, race discrimination, fair employment and consumer responsibility.[127]

The Freshfields Report also suggests that trustees could rely on well-established social customs as a proxy for the values of beneficiaries, such as to exclude 'investments that are linked to clear breaches of widely recognised norms, such as international conventions on human rights, labour conditions, tackling corruption and environmental protection'.[128] One reason such social customs may be considered a proxy, Gifford explains, is '[g]iven the ubiquity of pension fund membership, especially in the developed world, it can also be argued that the interests of members of funds are broadly consistent with those of the society in which the members live'.[129]

Many international treaties govern issues of interest to social investors, including environmental protection, human rights and labour standards. Some are widely ratified and thus putatively reflect a near-consensus of international opinion. As of July 2012, in a world of 195 recognized independent states, the International Labor Organization's Worst Forms of Child Labor Convention[130] of 1999 has 175 state ratifications, the Convention on Biological Diversity of 1992 has 193 ratifications[131] and the Convention

---

126 See, e.g., R. Flannigan, 'The political path to limited liability in business trusts', *Advocates Quarterly* 31, 2006, 257–92; M. Cullity, 'Liability of beneficiaries: a rejoinder', *Estates and Trusts Quarterly* 7, 1985–86, 35–52.
127 A.W. Scott and W.F. Fratcher, *The Law of Trusts*, 4th edn. Little Brown and Company, 1988, 227.17.
128 Freshfields, op. cit., 96.
129 J. Gifford, 'Measuring the social, environmental and ethical performance of pension funds', *Journal of Australian Political Economy* 53, 2004, 139–60, 140.
130 ILM 38, 1999, 1207.
131 ILM 31, 1982, 818.

on the Elimination of All Forms of Discrimination against Women of 1979 has 187 ratifications.[132] However, in each of these examples, the US is not a state party. Thus, reliance on international treaties (or national legislation) as evidence of social custom has shortcomings. While certain social norms embodied in such legal instruments may reflect democratically determined decisions or a preponderance of global opinion, invariably not everyone agrees with them, and it is unclear how substantially the majoritarian position should be in order to qualify as 'public opinion'. Moreover, many standards embodied in such treaties and laws are drafted too vaguely to provide concrete guidance for financial decision-makers in hard cases.

Apart from the foregoing options, the duty of loyalty may allow trustees or other fiduciaries to make investments that incidentally benefit third parties, such as a local community. While it is legally well established that fiduciaries must put the interests of beneficiaries first, disagreement rages on about whether they must consider the interests of beneficiaries solely as beneficiaries or whether they may also consider their interests as employees, consumers and members of society more generally. The narrower view is rationalized on the basis that otherwise fiduciaries might favour investments based on benefit to the community or other stakeholders rather than maximizing financial benefits for beneficiaries, or fiduciaries might act surreptitiously in their own self-interest.[133] The alternative view suggests that benefits may incidentally be provided to third parties so long as the financial impact is trivial.[134]

Some case law on pension fund governance hints that the latter view of fiduciary responsibility prevails. Among UK authorities, *Evans v. London Cooperative Society*[135] acknowledged the interests of beneficiaries as employees. Within US case law on ERISA, the District Court observed in *Donovan v. Walton* that the legislation 'simply does not prohibit a party other than a plan's participants and beneficiaries from benefiting in some measure from a prudent transaction with the plan'.[136] The pension plan trustees in *Donovan* constructed a building on property owned by the pension fund and leased part of the premises to the employee-beneficiaries' union, as well as providing mortgage loans to plan participants with the fund's assets at an interest rate below commercial rates. The court found that the financial and property arrangements were carefully researched and offered a reasonable rate of return, and the collateral benefits to third parties did not undermine the financial integrity of the pension plan. The *Donovan* ruling also clarified that the discretion of pension trustees to seek a lower rate of return in order to

---

132 UNTS 1249, 1980, 13.
133 J.D. Hutchinson and C.G. Cole, 'Legal standards governing investment of pension assets for social and political goals', *University of Pennsylvania Law Review* 128(4), 1980, 1340–88, 1367.
134 R.J. Lynn, 'Investing pension funds for social goals requires changing the law', *University of Colorado Law Review* 53(1), 1981, 101–16, 113.
135 *Evans v. London Co-operative Society Limited*, [1976] CLY 2059.
136 *Donovan v. Walton*, (1985) 609 F. Supp. 1221, 1245.

accommodate competing interests of beneficiaries required that such interests and intentions be enunciated in the pension plan's investment policy or by the plan beneficiaries directly.[137] Likewise, in 1998 the US Department of Labor interpreted ERISA as 'not preclud[ing] consideration of collateral benefits, such as those offered by a "socially-responsible" fund . . . [so long as] it is expected to provide an investment return commensurate to alternative investments having similar risks'.[138] In another US case, *City of Baltimore*[139] (discussed below), the Maryland Court of Appeal suggested trustees could consider third-party interests if the financial consequences were *trivial*, while *Blankenship v. Boyle*[140] may suggest otherwise, though each ruling turns heavily on its facts.

In *Blankenship*, trustees of the United Mine Workers of America Welfare and Retirement Fund were challenged by some beneficiaries for buying shares in power utilities in an effort to strengthen demand for coal mined by the Mine Workers Union. Presiding Judge Gesell ruled that the trustees' actions breached their duty of loyalty because they sought to benefit the Union rather than the Fund beneficiaries.[141] While the case affirms trustees' duty to act only in beneficiaries' interest, it does not necessarily imply that a trustee cannot ever consider non-financial criteria. The District Court of Columbia did not canvass what constitutes the 'best interests' of the beneficiaries when admonishing the trustees for seeking collateral benefits for the Union; in this case arguably the beneficiaries' interests could have been furthered by investing in companies that would improve demand for Union-mined coal given that the financial health of its fund depended on a market for its resource.

In the UK, the duty of loyalty's constraint on RI was considered in the seminal case of *Cowan v. Scargill*.[142] Trustees appointed jointly by the National Coal Board and the National Union of Mine Workers disagreed about the investment strategy for the workers' pension plan. The union trustees wished to ban further foreign investment of the plan's assets, including, in particular, investment in energy industries that competed with coal mining. The Coal Board trustees commenced legal proceedings against the union trustees, claiming their proposed investment restrictions would breach fiduciary duties. The court summarized the union trustees' defence as follows:

> The general thrust of the defendants' evidence in support of the restrictions that they seek to impose was along the following lines.

---

137 On appeal, the *Donovan* court appeared to go further on the scope for providing incidental benefits to third parties, by emphasizing the evidence provided of the many ways in which the trustees took steps to ensure this was a sound investment in the interests of the beneficiaries: *Brock v. Walton*, 1986, 794 F.2d 586, 588.
138 R.J. Doyle, Advisory opinion, Pension and Welfare Benefits Administration, Office of Regulations and Interpretations, 28 May 1998.
139 *Board of Trustees of Employee Retirement System of the City of Baltimore v. City of Baltimore*, (1989) 317 Md. 72; 562 A.2d 720.
140 *Blankenship v. Boyle*, (1971) 329 F. Supp. 1089.
141 Ibid., 1095.
142 [1985] Ch 270.

Pension funds in Britain have enormous assets. If all, or nearly all, of these assets were invested in Britain, and none, or few, were invested overseas, this would do much to revive this country's economy and so benefit all workers, especially if those investments were in the form not of purchasing established stocks and shares but of 'real' investment in physical assets and new ventures. For the mineworkers' scheme, the property of the coal industry would aid the prosperity of the scheme, and so lead to benefits for the beneficiaries under the scheme.[143]

The presiding judge, V.C. Megarry, thought otherwise. Drawing upon US court decisions concerning the responsibilities of pension fund trustees, Megarry held that trustees must treat beneficiaries' interests as paramount, and he reasoned that where a trust's purpose is to provide financial benefits, the best interests of the beneficiaries normally are financial in character. If the beneficiaries of a trust share strict ethical views, such as 'condemning all forms of alcohol, tobacco and popular entertainment, as well as armaments',[144] Megarry conceded that it might not be for their 'benefit' to invest in such activities. But he thought such a situation would be rare. He also concluded that the benefits to beneficiaries projected to flow from investing in British industry were 'too speculative and remote' to justify the investment restrictions.[145]

In light of *Cowan*, some financial trustees believe they must seek the highest financial returns. However, the decision is seriously deficient.[146] The pension fund was a fully funded and defined benefit plan, and therefore the investment restrictions proposed by the union trustees would not adversely affect the beneficiaries' retirement income. Second, the case turns heavily on its unique facts, in particular, the fact that the union trustees were trying to prop up an entire industry, the failing British coal industry, which was not in the interests of all the beneficiaries. Third, there was no previous authority on point for the judge to rely on, and the ruling is only that of an English lower court. Fourth, the mining union trustees' proposal sought a sweeping ban on an entire class of investments rather than a more nuanced approach, and their proposal 'bore little or no resemblance to a modern ESG investment policy'.[147] Writing extra-judicially in a later academic article, Megarry explained that his *Cowan* judgement didn't mean profit maximization alone was consistent with the legal duties of a pension fund trustee.[148] Moreover, if the trustees in *Cowan* had framed their investment policy as a preference rather than an absolute prohibition, then it would have been difficult to admonish.

---

143 Ibid., 295.
144 Ibid., 288.
145 Ibid., 296.
146 Some of the criticisms were acknowledged by Freshfields, op. cit., 89 and 101.
147 Ibid., 89.
148 R. Megarry, 'Investing pension funds: the mineworkers case', in T.G. Youdan (ed.), *Equity, Fiduciaries and Trusts*, Carswell, 1989, 149–59.

Allowing trustees to consider third-party interests does not give the latter any rights against the trust; their interests remain discretionary considerations. This limitation is illustrated by the unsuccessful 1987 lawsuit in *Associated Students of the University of Oregon v. Oregon Investment Council*.[149] The students sought a judicial declaration that the Investment Council must follow a directive of the Oregon Board of Higher Education that the Council not invest the state's university endowment funds in corporations doing business in South Africa, Zimbabwe and Namibia. The substantive legal issues were never litigated, since the Oregon Court of Appeals denied the students standing, noting that they did not 'allege any legally recognized injury, and neither agreement with plaintiffs' opposition to apartheid nor the desirability of encouraging students to become concerned with social and moral wrongs and to seek to right them can turn the alleged "injuries" into legally recognized ones'.[150]

A related situation arose in the 1988 case of *Regents of the University of Michigan v. State of Michigan*.[151] The Michigan state legislature directed public universities to divest from South Africa and the Soviet Union. The Michigan Court of Appeals held that the legislature lacked such authority based on the state constitutional clause that allows only the university to dictate investment of its endowment funds. Whether the university itself could choose to divest from companies doing business in the aforementioned countries was left unanswered by the court.

Duty of impartiality

Fiduciaries must act not only on behalf of beneficiaries; they must treat them even-handedly. A derivative of the duty of loyalty, the duty of impartiality obliges fiduciaries to identify and impartially consider the conflicting interests of different beneficiary groups. While rigid equality is not decreed, the duty of impartiality expects that 'conduct in administering a trust cannot be influenced by a trustee's personal favoritism . . . nor is it permissible for a trustee to ignore the interests of some beneficiaries merely as a result of oversight or neglect'.[152] In addition to ensuring their ultimate decisions reflect due regard for all beneficiaries' interests, trustees must follow the procedural requirement of the duty of impartiality that the 'process of administration itself' be impartial.[153] In sum, the duty expects fiduciaries to

---

149 (1987) 82 Or. App. 145, 728 P.2d 30.
150 Ibid., 150.
151 (1988) 164 Mich. App. 314, 419 NW 2d 723.
152 ALI, op. cit., s. 79, comment b.
153 In *McNeil v. Bennett*, 792 A.2d 190 (2001), the Delaware Court stated, 'The fact that the [trustees] might have properly decided to choose the same course of action had they engaged in an unbiased and adequately informed process does not excuse how they went about reaching this course of action.'

make diligent and good faith efforts to identify and balance respectfully the various beneficial interests.[154]

Though the fiduciary duty of loyalty implies that beneficiaries may authorize trustees to practise RI, the duty of impartiality may create obstacles. In the most famous RI case, *Cowan*, Megarry stressed 'the duty of trustees to exercise their powers in the best interests of the trust, holding the scales impartially between different classes of beneficiaries'.[155] What, then, if the beneficiaries aren't unanimous in their views on ethical investing? In *Bishop of Oxford v. Church Commissioners for England*, it was ruled that 'trustees should not make investment decisions on the basis of preferring one view of whether on moral grounds an investment conflicts with the objects of the charity over another. This is so even when one view is more widely supported than the other.'[156] The likelihood that beneficiaries of a modern institutional fund with numerous members would hold similar views on the desirability of RI is far-fetched. The ability of beneficiaries to 'consent' to RI is essentially a way by which they can approve or give trustees a defence to depart from their trust obligations, such as by making investments that are not financially prudent.[157] But in a large financial institution with many beneficiaries, lack of consensus is likely to inhibit such consent.

The issue of whether and how a fiduciary can act in the interests of numerous parties whose interests don't coincide is not unique to financial trusts. In corporate law, directors routinely must deal with many conflicting claims from different stakeholders. This quandary was the focus of the Supreme Court of Canada's ruling in *BCE Inc. v. 1976 Debentureholders*,[158] where it held that corporate directors' duty of loyalty to act in the best interest of a corporation includes an expectation to a 'good corporate citizen'.[159] In resolving tensions among the firm's stakeholders, the Court advised there is 'no principle that one set of interests . . . should prevail over another set of interests. Everything depends on the particular situation faced by the directors and whether . . . they exercise business judgment in a responsible way'.[160]

Because impartiality requires fair treatment rather than equal outcomes, complete unanimity among beneficiaries of a financial trust would appear to be setting the bar too high, contrary to the obiter in *Cowan* and the *Bishop of Oxford* cases. To illustrate, in the Canadian case of *Anova*,[161] the court allowed

---

154 ALI, op. cit., s. 227, comment k.
155 [1985] Ch. 270, 287.
156 [1992] 1 WLR 1241, 1247.
157 Equity has developed several defences for a defendant facing a claim for breach of fiduciary duty; one of them, the doctrine of laches and acquiescence, is particularly applicable to this context.
158 [2008] 3 SCR 560.
159 Ibid., para. 81.
160 Ibid., para. 84.
161 *Anova Inc. Employee Retirement Pension Plan (Administrator of) v. Manufacturers Life Insurance Co.*, (1994) 121 DLR (4th) 162.

an employer to provide early retirement inducements to only some of the pension plan beneficiaries because this benefitted the company funding the plan, and thus the plan's financial viability as a whole, and it didn't impair the plan administrator's ability to meet its existing obligations to other plan beneficiaries.[162] But nonetheless, because of the assumed unlikelihood of any consensus of values amongst beneficiaries in a large institutional fund, trustees tend to retreat to the belief that beneficiaries' only common interest is maximization of financial returns. One experienced Canadian lawyer suggests otherwise: 'Unanimity is not the test. One cannot assume that beneficiaries would be unanimous about the question of maximizing raw dollar return. This is a false assumption. There will always be beneficiaries who disagree with investment decisions made by trustees.'[163] Furthermore, whether or not unanimity is legally required, courts have never obliged trustees to poll beneficiaries to ascertain their interests.[164] Instead, courts tend to judge whether trustees have acted impartially and loyally by looking for evidence that they reasonably believed on the facts that they were acting in the beneficiaries' best interest.

In the sole known instance where a government sought to quantify the extent of unanimity required among beneficiaries, the Ontario South African Investment Act (which has since been repealed) authorized trustees to divest or refuse to acquire a South African investment, provided that a majority of identifiable beneficiaries with combined interests of at least 50 per cent of the fund's assets did not object or there were reasonable grounds to believe they would consent. Though one might view the Ontario legislation as motivated to negate an assumed common law stipulation of unanimity, just as plausibly it was motivated to provide greater legal certainty in the context of some ambiguous case law.

Conceivably, fiduciary law could allow RI in order to appease a majority of beneficiaries if it would not pose any material financial risks or losses. In his subsequent ruminations about the famous case, Megarry, the judge in *Cowan v. Scargill*, opined that an investment motivated by ethical considerations that does not risk a financial penalty 'will in general be for the benefit of the beneficiaries at large' because by 'gratifying the majority, [the investment] will neither harm nor benefit the minority'.[165] British pension law expert Charles Scanlan has gone further to doubt whether it is even necessary that the beneficiaries who are gratified by the decision represent a clear majority, contending that '[o]n the assumption that the scheme suffers no financial harm ... there is no trust law requirement to obtain the views of all

---

162 Ibid., para. 58.
163 P. Lane, 'Ethical investment: towards the best interest of everyone', *The Advocate*, 1986, 171–82, 176.
164 In *Cowan v. Scargill*, op. cit., the court rejected that the mining union had received unanimous support from a poll of its members, as this was not viewed as being reflective of all the membership of the plan including dependants and retired miners.
165 Megarry, op. cit., 158.

beneficiaries. If the trustees can confer a non-financial benefit on a significant number of their beneficiaries, that should be sufficient justification.'[166] But if a minority of beneficiaries would be financially harmed, they could request a court to intervene in the administration of the trust.

Moreover, in some circumstances trustees cannot avoid making a decision despite disunity among beneficiaries. Ron Davis identifies one such situation as voting the shares held by a pension fund in a particular corporation when an issue raised by a dissident shareholder, rejected by the company's management, has been put on the firm's meeting agenda. Davis explains:

> If there was conflict among the beneficiaries on these issues, between those who wished to support current management and those who did not, abstention would not be a third, neutral option. Abstention would, in effect, support management, since all proxies that are not returned are treated as votes for the management's position. Therefore, a decision by a majority of the beneficiaries about how the proxies should be voted in their best interests ought to govern the way the shares are voted.[167]

Disagreements among trustees on RI may be just as common as they are among beneficiaries. Trusts law generally requires that trustees act unanimously, although the trust deed or legislation might alter that requirement. Pension fund legislation in many countries typically allows for boards of trustees to make decisions on a majoritarian basis, although trusts law continues to hold each trustee personally responsible for her fiduciary duties. In the *Cowan* case, the litigation arose because the 10 trustees, providing equal representation of the mining union and employer interests, could not reach unanimity as required. The case was just as much about the politics of fund governance as about a disagreement over investment policy. Where trustees are deadlocked, courts have jurisdiction to intervene where necessary to carry out the terms of the trust in the interest of the beneficiaries.[168]

A policy for investing ethically might be acceptable in the absence of beneficiary consensus when there are several classes of beneficiaries spanning different generations. American case law recognizes that the duty of impartiality can include an intergenerational equity dimension, mandating trustees to consider the long-term consequences of their investment decisions. In *Withers v. Teachers' Retirement System*,[169] the court held that a New York City pension fund must be managed to meet future as well as present financial obligations:

> [T]he trustees . . . would have violated their fiduciary obligation had they exhausted the assets of an underfunded actuarially reserved pension

---

166 Palmer, op. cit., 98. See also Freshfields, op. cit., 97 (endorsing Scanlan's views).
167 Davis, op. cit., 69.
168 E.g., *Kordyban v. Kordyban*, [2003] BCJ No. 793.
169 (1978) 447 F. Supp. 1248 (SDNY), affirmed, 595 F.2d 1210.

system on a single class of beneficiaries (retirees). Their obligation, plainly, was to manage the fund . . . [for] not only . . . current retirees, but also . . . those scheduled to retire in the future.[170]

On this basis, trustees may justify long-term, sustainable investment as a way to ensure that investments better meet the needs of future beneficiaries, even if this approach reduces financial returns for current retirees of the pension plan. The potential value of this approach to reorienting prevailing understandings of fiduciary law towards a better accommodation of RI will be further explored later in this book.

Duty of care and prudence

Evolution of the prudent investment standard

The duty of care, along with the duty of loyalty, forms the core legal responsibilities of investment fiduciaries. Known more commonly as the 'duty of prudent investing' in this context, it stems from the relationship of vulnerability and trust between the beneficiary and fiduciary, protecting the beneficiary from any 'careless, inept, or inattentive' use of the fiduciary's discretionary power.[171] The trust duty of care, whose parameters include exercising diligence and skill, posits a higher standard than the conventional duty of care found in contract or tort law. The latter imposes only a negative obligation to avoid conduct that may foreseeably harm the recipient of the duty.[172] In a trust context, the duty of care also carries positive responsibility to exercise diligence and apply specialist skill. In the context of investing, the duty of care has two specific performance dimensions: producing income and preserving trust assets. The former obliges a trustee to assess potential and comparative rates of return; the latter requires the trustee to assess the risks of potential investments. The integrity of a fiduciary's conduct is judged with regard to when the investment decision was made, not the performance of the investment with 'the prescience of hindsight'.[173]

As explained earlier, some legal commentators view the duty of care as not a true fiduciary duty, instead belonging to other realms of law, such as trusts law in the case of management of trust funds.[174] Some disagreement also stems from the view that the duty of prudent investment entails a positive, *prescriptive* duty to act for beneficiaries, as against the conception

---

170 Ibid., 1257–8.
171 Miller, op. cit., 284.
172 E.g., *Cooper v. Hobart*, [2001] 3 SCR 537.
173 *Fales v. Canada Permanent Trust Company*, [1977] 2 SCR 302, 317.
174 See W.A. Gregory, 'The fiduciary duty of care: a perversion of words', *Akron Law Review* 38, 2005, 181–206; M. Conaglen, *Fiduciary Loyalty: Protecting the Due Performance of Non-Fiduciary Duties*, Hart Publishing, 2010, 35.

in some jurisdictions of a narrower, *proscriptive* standard in the case of the duty of loyalty.[175] In other words, while the duty of loyalty tends to be understood as avoiding conduct that would create a conflict of interest, the duty of prudent investment today has connotations of active, positive conduct about maximizing financial returns to trust funds in addition to preserving capital. Essentially, therefore, 'the trustee's duty of care is part of the trustee's equitable duty to defend and promote the beneficiary's best interests, with loyalty as a hedging set of duties ensuring proper performance of such positive performance duties'.[176] The fiduciary must therefore invest on behalf of beneficiaries whose values, risk tolerance and time horizons may differ from hers.

The duty of prudent investment has evolved significantly over the centuries, with important implications for RI. One seminal transformation was the shift from quantitative to prudential standards. Following the scandalous collapse of the South Sea Company in the early 1700s, English courts of equity required trustees to restrict their investments to sovereign debt and well-secured mortgages.[177] This was the genesis of the 'legal list' approach to restricting permitted fiduciary investments.[178] This injunction was primarily directed to the preservation of beneficiaries' capital. In time, economic changes facilitated the widening of the allowable list, but the suspicion that some asset classes (e.g., investment in corporate shares) might be innately imprudent lingered for years. Also importantly, fiduciaries were expected to evaluate the merits of presumptively allowable investments on an investment-by-investment basis rather than by evaluating the overall asset portfolio.[179] Consequently, it was difficult to offset any heightened risks in an equity investment with seemingly safer investments in government securities.

Some American states took a different approach, which paved the way for the now dominant prudential investment standard that underpins the duty of care. In *Harvard College v. Amory*,[180] which dealt with a suit against a trustee for losses incurred by funds invested in seemingly risky insurance and manufacturing stocks, the Massachusetts Supreme Court declared:

> [The trustee] shall conduct himself faithfully and exercise a sound discretion. He is to observe how men of prudence, discretion and intelligence manage their own affairs, not in regard to speculation but in regard to the permanent disposition of their funds, considering

175 Birks, op. cit., 28; Conaglen, ibid., 202–3.
176 J. Getzler, 'Fiduciary investment in the shadow of financial crisis: was Lord Eldon right?', *Journal of Equity* 3, 2009, 1–31, 9–10.
177 J. Carswell, *The South Sea Bubble*, Cresset Press, 1960.
178 G. Keeton, 'Modern developments in the law of trusts', *Northern Ireland Legal Quarterly* 4, 1971, 48–62.
179 P. Ali and K. Yano, *Eco-Finance*, Kluwer, 2004, 131.
180 (1830) 26 Mass. (9 Pick) 446.

the probable income, as well as the probable safety of the capital to be invested.[181]

The court thus propagated a legal standard that focused on prudent conduct, as judged by similarly placed individuals with the same goals and consequent responsibilities, rather than rigidly prescribing specific types of investment. But the flexibility of this approach was curbed 40 years later. In *King v. Talbot*,[182] a New York court held that it was imprudent for trustees to buy corporate stock and limited them to investing in government bonds and mortgage-backed instruments.[183] This restrictive judicial approach, similar to the English approach of the time, was also often reinforced in legislation.

Gradually, changing market conditions rendered the restrictive nature of quantitative rules impractical, and the 'prudent person' standard of fiduciary responsibility eventually superseded the laundry list of permissible investments.[184] The shift was also influenced by the recognition of the need for trustees to effectively hedge against inflation and acceptance of MPT. The latter theory predicts that optimal returns are best achieved through large, diversified portfolios, where risk-adjusted returns are judged by reference to entire portfolios rather than by discretely considering each specific investment asset.[185]

A concomitant change was the need to ensure trustees and other fiduciaries possessed suitable expertise for the increasingly sophisticated requirements of modern fund management. Consequently, the 'prudent person' standard ceded to a higher 'prudent investor' standard of care for a trustee representing himself to be a skilled professional (as required for other professionals, such as doctors).[186] The original objective standard of care and diligence required of a trustee in administering a trust was that of an 'ordinary prudent person in managing his own affairs'.[187] That standard has shifted from someone investing in their own affairs to someone investing in someone else's affairs, coupled, in an investment context, with a 'prudent professional' standard. As ERISA declares, 'a fiduciary shall discharge his duties . . . with the care, skill, prudence, and diligence under the circumstances, then prevailing that a prudent man acting in a like capacity and familiar with such matters would use in the conduct of an enterprise of a like character and with like

---

181 Ibid., 461.
182 (1869) 40 NY 76.
183 J.A. Taylor, 'Massachusetts' influence in shaping the prudent investor rule for trusts', *Massachusetts Law Review* 78, 1993, 51–64, 55.
184 See e.g., US Employee Retirement Income Security Act 1974, s. 404; and Australia's Superannuation Industry (Supervision) Act 1993, s. 52(2)(f)(ii).
185 P.G. Haskell, 'The prudent person rule for trustee investment and modern portfolio theory', *North Carolina Law Review* 69, 1990, 87–111; W.F. Sharpe, *Portfolio Theory and Capital Markets*, McGraw-Hill, 1970, 20–4.
186 B.J. Stanley, 'A standard for trustees stricter than the prudent man standard: the past and the future', *Oklahoma City University Law Review* 9, 1984, 485–503.
187 E.g., *Fales v. Canada Permanent Trust Co.*, [1977] 2 SCR 302, 70 DLR (3d) 257.

aims'.[188] The trend-setting US Uniform Prudent Investor Act,[189] a model statute, adopted in the great majority of US states, provides: 'A trustee who has special skills or expertise, or is named trustee in reliance upon the trustee's representation that the trustee has special skills or expertise, has a duty to use those special skills or expertise.'[190]

As recognition of the trust's utility for holding financial assets grew, the legal framework that restricted the powers of trustees shifted to a new paradigm conferring broad managerial discretion within an umbrella of fiduciary obligations. These legislatively-driven changes included: removing all category-based restrictions on types of investment, prescribing diversification as integral to prudent investing, focusing on total portfolios rather than individual investments and repealing the non-delegation rule with regard to assignment of investment management functions, subject to safeguards. These changes were reflected in ERISA, which imposes a fiduciary regime on trustees of US federal pension and employee pension plans sponsored by non-state employers that is separate from the general law of trusts,[191] as well as the American Law Institute's revision to the *Restatement (Second) of Trusts*.[192] A similar approach was taken by the UK Pensions Act 1995, which codified the following standards for plan trustees: a duty of care to exercise skill in the performance of their investment function; regard for the need to diversify portfolios, and the suitability of particular investments as well as the type of investment for a pension scheme; and the procurement of advice on their investments and delegation of investment functions only to fund managers who have appropriate knowledge and experience.[193] Not only has portfolio investment become legalized as the best standard for prudent investment, it is increasingly being demanded. In the New Zealand case of *Re Mulligan* in 1998, the High Court held that by neglecting to use portfolio investment so as to diversify a fund and avoid financial loss, a trustee could be in breach of trust.[194]

Consequences for RI

The foregoing changes in the duty of care have important consequences for RI practitioners. The traditional formulation of the duty effectively precluded any RI that posed unusual risk, as a fiduciary had to assess and justify each investment individually.[195] A fiduciary could not dilute or offset that specific risk by evaluating it in the context of the entire investment portfolio. Today,

---

188 Section 1104.
189 NCCUSL, *Uniform Prudent Investor Act*, 7 B ULA 18, supplement 1997.
190 Ibid., s. 2(ff).
191 See especially s. 404.
192 ALI, *Restatement of the Law Third, Trusts: Prudent Investor Rule*, ALI, 1992.
193 Sections 33–36.
194 *Re Mulligan (Deceased)*, [1998] 1 NZLR 481.
195 Ali and Yano, op. cit., 131.

owing to the influence of MPT, an individual ethical investment – for example a new green technology business – that might seem, in isolation, too risky may in light of other investments constitute a prudent choice. In other words, inclusion of investments selected for their social benefit might be easier to justify within a large portfolio than on a case-by-case basis.

Secondly, misapprehension about an alleged duty to maximize financial returns has been the source of much controversy in the financial industry and a major barrier to RI.[196] Contemporary legal commentators emphasize the overriding responsibility of trustees, particularly in the context of governing a financial institution, to 'maximise the return to members'.[197] Institutional investors, even social ones, habitually acknowledge that their 'overriding duty in law has to be making best returns on behalf of beneficiaries'.[198] Apart from legislative prescription, such a duty has little legal precedent. In the much maligned *Cowan* case, Megarry ruled that '[s]ubject to such matters, under a trust for the provision of financial benefits, the paramount duty of the trustees is to provide the *greatest* financial benefits for the present and future beneficiaries' (emphasis added).[199] By contrast, the influential American *Third Restatement of the Law of Trusts*' modern prudent investor rule doesn't prescribe a duty to 'maximize returns' on an investment-by-investment basis but rather obliges fiduciaries to apply an overall investment strategy for a diversified portfolio that is rational and appropriate to the fund. Nonetheless, the Uniform Prudent Investor Act, which has been adopted by nearly all US states, declares:

> No form of so-called 'social investing' is consistent with the duty of loyalty if the investment activity entails sacrificing the interests of trust beneficiaries – for example, by accepting below-market returns – in favor of the interests of the persons supposedly benefitted by pursuing the particular social cause.[200]

Yet even this statement does not mandate maximization of returns; rather, its focus is on the avoidance of financial loss. Subsequent Anglo-American trusts case law departs from the *Cowan* ruling on this point. In *Martin v. Edinburgh District Council*, which concerned a municipal pension fund's strategy to divest from South African-based assets,[201] Lord Murray stated:

> I cannot conceive that trustees have an unqualified duty simply to invest trust funds in the most profitable investment available. To accept that

---

196 W. Ransome and C. Sampford, *Ethics and Socially Responsible Investment: A Philosophical Approach*, Ashgate, 2011, 125–6.
197 M.S. David and N. Taylor, 'Does "sustainable" investing compromise the obligations owed by superannuation trustees', *Australian Business Law Review* 36, 2008, 47–61, 49.
198 N. White, 'The church as an ethical investor', *Bulletin of ECCR* 66, 2007, 3–5, 4.
199 [1985] Ch. 270, 289.
200 Section 5.
201 [1988] SLT 329.

without qualification would, in my view, involve substituting the discretion of financial advisers for the discretion of trustees.²⁰²

In the *City of Baltimore* case, the Maryland Court of Appeal considered a challenge to Baltimore ordinances requiring municipal employee pension funds to divest from companies operating in South Africa.²⁰³ The funds' trustees argued that the ordinances inhibited their duty of prudence by substantially reducing the universe of eligible investments. While the Court agreed,²⁰⁴ it believed the reduced returns expected from divestment in South Africa would amount to only about ten basis points, or 0.10 per cent annually (despite the need to divest from 47 per cent of the funds' stock portfolios and 10 per cent of their fixed income portfolios), and 'if . . . social investment yields economically competitive returns at a comparable level of risk, the investment should not be deemed imprudent'.²⁰⁵ In finding no imprudent investing, the Court explained that a trustee's duty is not to maximize return on investments but to secure a 'just' and 'reasonable' return while avoiding undue risk. While the Maryland court noted that 'trustees may properly consider the social performance of the corporation',²⁰⁶ the specific facts of the litigation perhaps limit its wider application. (The trustees managed a state-owned pension fund with some defined benefit plan characteristics that limited beneficiaries' potential losses.)

The *City of Baltimore* case also stands for the 'tie-breaker' principle, which allows fiduciaries to practise RI if it would offer comparable risk-adjusted returns to conventional investment. In *Cowan*, the judge also suggested trustees could discriminate between two investments of equal financial suitability on ethical criteria: 'if the investment in fact made is equally beneficial to the beneficiaries, then criticism would be difficult to sustain in practice, whatever the position in theory'.²⁰⁷ Further support for the principle is the US Department of Labor's Advisory Opinion, issued in 1998 to Calvert funds regarding the legality of offering RI options in pension plans governed by ERISA.²⁰⁸

In 2008 the Department of Labor's Employee Benefits Security Administration (EBSA) issued a further ERISA interpretation bulletin, on 'economically targeted investment', which appeared to narrow this opportunity. The EBSA advised that only when two alternative investments 'are of equal economic value to a plan' may fiduciaries 'choose between the investment alternatives on the basis of a factor other than the economic interest of

---

202 Ibid., 334.
203 *Board of Trustees of Employee Retirement System of the City of Baltimore v. City of Baltimore*, (1989) 317 Md. 72; 562 A.2d 720.
204 Ibid., 103.
205 Ibid., 107.
206 Ibid., 106.
207 [1985] Ch. 270, 287.
208 Doyle, op. cit., 143.

the plan'.[209] It defined 'economically targeted investments' as 'investments selected for the economic benefits they create apart from their investment return to the employee benefit plan'.[210] The problem for the tie-breaker principle posed by the EBSA bulletin is its caution that fiduciaries 'will rarely be able to demonstrate compliance with ERISA absent a written record demonstrating that a contemporaneous economic analysis showed that the investment alternatives were of equal value'.[211] That 'contemporaneous economic analysis' would involve 'examin[ing] the level of diversification, degree of liquidity, and the potential risk/return in comparison with available alternative investments'.[212] In the four examples of transactions that the EBSA believes would violate its interpretation of ERISA, one is 'an investment policy that favors plan investment in companies meeting certain environmental criteria (so-called "green" companies)', since applying such a policy would violate the fiduciaries' duty 'to consider all investments that meet the plan's prudent financial criteria'.[213] In light of this example, it appears that EBSA has a broader intent than simply restricting economically targeted investments.

Apart from these legal uncertainties, the tie-breaker principle, as a practical consideration, cannot be easily applied, at least in the US, because trustees typically manage investments on a portfolio-wide basis rather than administering investments on a case-by-case basis. As Thornton explains, in criticizing the tie-breaker standard as impractical, trustees 'are not measuring one given asset against one given alternative, but (in the nature of modern portfolio investment) selecting a range of assets from amongst a very wide pool', and thus 'trustees should be comparing not only the expected return and variance of the two assets themselves, but also the covariance between those assets and the rest of the holdings within the portfolio'.[214]

A growing body of academic research suggests that at a portfolio level, RI can at least match risk-adjusted returns as well as any other investment strategy, although as explained in Chapter 2 this research is possibly unreliable. But certainly the RI industry has increasingly redefined itself as answerable to a business case because of the financial materiality of companies' social and environmental performance.[215] This shift in thinking has implications for fiduciary responsibilities; as Woods explains, 'the

---

209 EBSA, 'Supplemental guidance relating to fiduciary responsibility in considering economically targeted investments', 29 CFR s. 2509.08-1, 73 Federal Register 61735, 17 October 2008.
210 Ibid.
211 Ibid.
212 Ibid.
213 Ibid.
214 R. Thornton, 'Ethical investments: a case of disjointed thinking', *Cambridge Law Journal* 67(2), 2008, 396–422, 405.
215 UNEP-FI, *Show Me the Money: Linking Environmental, Social and Governance Issues to Company Value*, UNEP-FI, 2006, 4; UNEP-FI, *The Materiality of Social, Environmental and Corporate Governance Issues in Equity Pricing*, UNEP-FI, 2004.

fulfilment of the primary mandate . . . is likely to suffer if trustees ignore the long-term consequences of financing environmental degradation'.[216] Gil Yaron, a Canadian lawyer, has commented that 'there is significant legal and empirical support for viewing socially responsible investment practices as a requisite element of prudent and loyal trusteeship'.[217] Climate change has been identified as one example. Mercer Investment Consulting advises:

> Climate risk can have a real impact on portfolio holdings. There is a growing case for trustees to attain some level of knowledge around these issues and to take steps to mitigate any negative consequences of not taking action. . . . [W]e suggest that it is consistent with fiduciary responsibility to address climate change risk.[218]

Similarly, US legal experts have advised that 'fiduciaries not only [are] permitted to consider climate risk but might also have an obligation to consider the issue and act upon it'.[219] But not all commentators agree, and some still fear that overly zealous attention to ESG issues may run afoul of fiduciary responsibility.[220]

A further consequence of the duty of care is the importance of showing benefits accruing *directly* to beneficiaries rather than simply attributing benefits circuitously, such as by virtue of the fact that the beneficiaries are members of society that benefits from a particular investment strategy. Speculative and remote benefits to beneficiaries, such as improved sustainability of the economy, thus might not legally suffice. The universal investor thesis aspires to create a new standard of prudent investment through the wider social and environmental 'returns' offered to beneficiaries, but it has yet to influence lawmakers. In *Cowan*, one argument advanced to justify the RI policy was that by restricting overseas investment, and investment in energy sectors in competition with coal mining, important benefits would accrue to the British economy and thus to the beneficiaries, as members of that society. The court rebuffed that argument, explaining:

> [T]he broad economic arguments of the defendants provide no justification for the restrictions that they wish to impose. Any possible benefits

---

216 C. Woods, 'Funding climate change: how pension fund fiduciary duty masks trustee inertia and short-termism', in J. Hawley, S. Kamath and A.T. Williams (eds), *Corporate Governance Failures: The Role of Institutional Investors in the Global Financial Crisis*, University of Pennsylvania Press, 2011, 242–77, 249.
217 G. Yaron, *The Responsible Pension Trustee: Reinterpreting the Principles of Prudence and Loyalty in the Context of Socially Responsible Institutional Investing*, SHARE, 2001.
218 Mercer Investment Consulting (MIC), *A Climate for Change: A Trustee's Guide to Understanding and Addressing Climate Risk*, MIC, 2005, 18–19.
219 Ceres, *Sustainability and Risk: Climate Change and Fiduciary Duty for the Twenty-First Century Trustee*, Harvard University and Ceres, 2004, 4.
220 R. Copp, M.L. Kremmer and E. Roca, 'Should funds invest in socially responsible investments during downturns? Financial and legal implications of the fund manager's dilemma', *Accounting Research Journal* 23(3), 2010, 254–66.

from imposing the restrictions that would accrue to the beneficiaries under the scheme (as distinct from the general public) are far too speculative and remote. Large though the fund is, I cannot see how the adoption of the restrictions can make any material impact on the national economy, or bring any appreciable benefit to the beneficiaries under the scheme.[221]

There are several further considerations in assessing compliance with the duty of care. Another way the duty of prudence interacts with RI is the requirement that fiduciaries possess adequate skills in investing, which may require soliciting expert advice.[222] This requirement will surely extend increasingly to the education of trustees with regard to RI and to the hiring of expert advisers. In *Martin v. Edinburgh District Council*,[223] the court concluded that one reason the trustees of the municipality's fund acted unlawfully by implementing a policy of divestment against South Africa was their failure to obtain professional advice.

The *methods* of practising RI also weigh on its legality. An RI policy, as for any prudent investment strategy, must be implemented without unduly burdensome and costly administrative procedures. Some RI funds carry higher expenses and charges due to the additional ESG research required.[224] Equally significant, ethical screening and corporate engagement strategies have different financial consequences. Research has predicted that strict exclusionary screens lead to lower risk-adjusted returns over the long term.[225] Portfolio diversification has become easier because RI funds are now available across a broad range of asset classes and economic sectors, as well as due to funds' greater reliance on 'best-in-class' screening, which aims to pick the relative best performers in any sector rather than on absolute categorical exclusions.

RI is most likely to be compatible with the duty of care's expectation of portfolio diversification when implemented through corporate engagement and shareholder activism. In this way, funds can maintain reasonably diversified portfolios in accordance with MPT. However, engagement and activism can be time-consuming and expensive to administer and therefore might undermine compliance with fiduciary standards if undertaken extensively or discriminately. Most major institutional funds such as the Norwegian Government Pension Fund-Global and the New Zealand Superannuation Fund, as discussed later in this book, engage only on a highly selective basis, targeting only the most problematic firms.[226]

---

221 [1985] Ch. 270, 296.
222 Hayton, op. cit., 562–3.
223 (1988) SLT 329.
224 S. Croome-Carther, 'Funds with values', *forbes.com*, 14 November 2007.
225 See analysis in Chapter 2.
226 B.J. Richardson, 'Sovereign wealth funds and the quest for sustainability: cases from Norway and New Zealand', *Nordic Journal of Commercial Law* Fall (2), 2011, 1–27.

Corporate engagement and activism are also more likely to be consistent with fiduciary responsibility, because in some jurisdictions shareholder rights, such as filing resolutions in company meetings, are considered fiduciary assets to be safeguarded and upheld.[227] Traditionally, as Chapter 2 explained, many institutional funds did not see active ownership as a fiduciary responsibility and tended to sell securities rather than speak out if dissatisfied with a portfolio company's performance.[228] This view is gradually changing, although the legal position could be clearer. A number of legal opinions have been given by US regulators, but these have fluctuated in the extent to which they accommodate RI, depending on the political agenda of the administration in power. In 1980, David George Ball, then Assistant Secretary of Labor for the Pension and Welfare Benefits Administration, advised that a fiduciary who 'fails to vote, or casts a vote without considering the impact of the question or votes blindly with management' will violate the rule of prudence.[229] The US Department of Labor issued guidance in 1988 that characterized shareholders' votes as valuable assets of institutional investors[230] and in 1994 advised that shareholder activism is consistent with a fiduciary's obligations where 'there is a reasonable expectation that [it] . . . is likely to enhance the value of the plan's investment in the corporation, after taking into account the costs involved'.[231]

The Department issued further advice on this subject in October 2008, declaring it modified and superseded its earlier bulletins.[232] The 2008 guidance potentially limits the scope for proxy voting and shareholder activism by ERISA-regulated funds for RI purposes. The bulletin amends the previous guidance on when such activism is justified, from '*likely to enhance* the value of the plan's investment in the corporation' to '*will enhance* the economic value of the plan's investment in the corporation' (my emphasis).[233] Because one cannot easily predict the precise effect of shareholder activity, this standard is possibly unworkable, and thus corporate engagement may become exceedingly hard to justify. Yet in language suggesting a more liberal view of active ownership consistent with its earlier advice, the Department's interpretation also refers to fiduciaries' 'reasonable expectation' of enhanced value (implying some

---

227 R. Sparkes, *Socially Responsible Investment: A Global Revolution*, John Wiley and Sons, 2002, 221; Davis, op. cit., 64.
228 K. Peach, 'Shareholder activism "not a fiduciary responsibility"', *Global Pensions*, 8 September 2006, http://globalpensions.com/?id=me/17/news/39/39092/0.
229 'Ball signals continued commitment to proxy voting issues at Department', *Pensions and Benefits Reporter* 17, 29 January 1980, 207.
230 Letter from Deputy Assistant Secretary of Labor, Alan Lebowitz to Helmuth Fandl, Avon Products Inc., reprinted in *Pensions Reporter* (BNA) 15, 29 February 1988, 391.
231 US Department of Labor, 'Interpretative bulletin relating to statements of investment policy, including proxy voting policy or guidelines', Code of Federal Regulations, 29 Ch. s. 2509.94-2 (1994).
232 US Department of Labor, 'Interpretive bulletin relating to the exercise of shareholder rights and written statements of investment policy, including proxy voting policies or guidelines', 29 CFR s. 2509.08-2, 73 Federal Register 61732, 17 October 2008.
233 Ibid.

discretionary judgement in exercising rights to engage firms) and that it is responsible to seek to monitor or influence 'the nature of long-term business plans'.[234] RI groups have criticized the Department's confusing message, which might discourage funds from engaging on ESG issues.[235]

Liability and remedies

Remedies are available to aggrieved beneficiaries or principals for breaches of fiduciary responsibility.[236] However, when such breaches collaterally harm third parties, such as through environmental damage, beneficiaries are unlikely to have an incentive to intervene if their own financial interests are not affected. The available remedies depend on how the breached duties are classified, and the jurisdiction at issue. (The following relates mainly to Anglo-American law.) As the law of trusts and fiduciary law contain some distinct duties, different remedies may flow from breaches of such duties. This distinction, however, is sometimes elided, indeed so often that James Penner, a trusts law expert, has complained: 'If you are able to grasp this difference and bear it in mind when you consider the cases, count yourself as an intellectual of the subject, because far too often judges and commentators make a mess of it.'[237] Penner uses the following example to illustrate the distinction.[238] If the terms of a trust permit a trustee (T) to invest in shares, T is not in breach of trust if he does so. However, if T invests in shares by purchasing his own shares in a company, T is in breach of his fiduciary duty due to the conflict of interest that this scenario creates. The fiduciary relationship between T and the beneficiary makes an otherwise perfectly acceptable act – investing in shares – unlawful, due to conflict of interest.

In most common law jurisdictions, the standard for when a fiduciary is responsible for breach of duty to his/her principal or beneficiary is strict liability, without being mitigated by considerations of honesty or good faith.[239] The strict standard, explains Flannigan, is necessary to protect principals who are in vulnerable positions relative to the fiduciaries and to avoid the evidentiary difficulties resulting from a principal's inability to monitor the fiduciary's activity with respect to her property.[240] However, some statutory-based fiduciary regimes provide defences, as when exercising due diligence and acting with reasonable care and skill.[241] In relation to

---

234 Ibid.
235 Quoted in US-SIF, 'SIF criticizes U.S. Department of Labor employee benefit division for ambiguous recent bulletins on fiduciary duty', Press release, 19 December 2008, http://ussif.org/news/releases/pressrelease.cfm?id=129.
236 L. Ho, 'Attributing losses to a breach of fiduciary duty', *Trust Law International* 12, 1998, 66–76.
237 J.E. Penner, *The Law of Trusts*, Oxford University Press, 2010, 307.
238 Ibid., 308.
239 E.J. Weinrib, *The Idea of Private Law*, Harvard University Press, 1995, 199.
240 Flannigan, 'The boundaries of fiduciary accountability', op. cit., 44.
241 E.g., Canada Business Corporations Act, RSC 1985, s. 123(4).

directors of financial corporations, the business judgement rule may immunize some errors of judgement. There are a number of other general defences, including laches, limitation periods and informed consent by the principal or beneficiary (though such consent may not release a fiduciary from certain statutory breaches).[242]

Another feature of fiduciary liability is its negative operation, though this is not always the approach in all common law jurisdictions. Fiduciaries are strictly liable if they create a conflict of interest or benefit from their position as fiduciary. According to Flannigan, any positive duties that exist between a fiduciary and a principal arise as a function of the specific area of law governing the relationship. In a trustee–beneficiary relationship for example, the positive duty to invest prudently is a duty imposed by trusts law, not fiduciary law. Trustees will not be liable for breach of fiduciary duty unless they breach their negative duty to refrain from using their investment powers for personal gain.[243] However, North American courts have tended to extend fiduciary responsibility from a proscriptive to a prescriptive duty, such as to act in a beneficiary's best interests.[244]

In relation to trusts and writing from a UK perspective, Penner highlights the importance of specifying the type of breach of trust, as it has implications for the applicable liability standard. Where a trust property is misapplied, the trustee is strictly liable.[245] A negligence-type standard tends to apply when the trustee fails to act prudently or with requisite care,[246] though depending on the context and jurisdiction, the care expected may be that of an ordinary prudent person or a prudent professional trustee. It should be recognized that the trust itself, unlike a corporation, has no legal personality, and therefore liability for breaches rests with trustees or other entities assigned responsibility. Where a nominee trustee exists who essentially heeds the beneficiary's direction, the latter may be responsible for any contributory negligence.[247] This situation has relevance to the earlier discussion in this book about strengthening the voice of beneficiaries in the governance of funds.

The remedies available for breach of fiduciary duty are more varied than those available for breach of trust obligations.[248] Depending on the circumstances, these could include an injunction, specific performance, equitable compensation, account for profits or a constructive trust. Even though there may be concurrent claims in contract or trusts law, a plaintiff nonetheless often has a powerful incentive for invoking fiduciary liability in order to obtain more diverse and substantial remedies. Breach of fiduciary duty can

242 E.g., *Forge v. ASIC*, (2004) 52 ACSR 1; [2004] NSWCA 448.
243 Flannigan, 'The boundaries of fiduciary accountability', op. cit., 47.
244 Notably *Guerin v. R*, op. cit.
245 Penner, op. cit., 307.
246 *Learoyd v. Whiteley*, (1886) 33 Ch. D. 347; (1887) 12 AC 727.
247 Penner, op. cit., 322.
248 G. Moffat, *Trust Law: Text and Materials*, Cambridge University Press, 2005, 846.

address both unauthorized gains to the fiduciary and actual losses to the beneficiary, whereas breach of a trustee's duty of care mainly concerns the latter. A fiduciary must thus disgorge any gains from improperly exploiting his position to the person for whose benefit the fiduciary should have acted. A court may also find that financial gains are held on 'constructive trust' for the party to whom the duty is owed. Specific performance (e.g., to compel performance of the terms of the trust) or injunctive relief (to restrain a breach) are other judicial remedies.[249] Breach of fiduciary responsibility may also lead to liability being imposed on a third party, for example, a person who received property while knowing of such a breach or assisting in the breach.[250] In regard to the duty of care in trusts law, common law systems grant monetary compensation for actual losses as the usual remedy. A principal has the potential to receive far greater amounts of compensation where there has been a breach of fiduciary duty than where there has been a breach of the duty of care, because equitable compensation is not subject to the principles of foreseeability, contributory negligence or the duty to mitigate, which often limit the quantum.[251] Personal remedies against a trustee are often not pursued because they are of little utility if the trustee is insolvent. Proprietary remedies involve tracing the specific trust property in order to return to the beneficiaries, such as where there has been misappropriation of trust property.[252]

Penalties for such breaches and other disciplinary proceedings may be imposed, given that most financial institutions operate under a supervised legislative framework to protect the wider public interest. For example, the US Department of Labor may levy a monetary fine against a trustee in an ERISA-regulated pension fund for a statutory breach.[253] Financial corporations are also typically subject to wider-ranging civil penalties and even criminal sanctions for reckless or intentional conduct that breaches statutory duties and regulatory controls.

Measuring compensatory damages for failure to fulfill the ethical preferences of beneficiaries, as in a dedicated RI fund, or in a charitable trust with a philanthropic mandate, would be challenging because the 'loss' is ethical rather than of a quantifiable monetary nature. The law's experience with compensation for non-pecuniary damages suggests difficulties in recognizing ethical and emotional loss,[254] and apart from investors' psychic losses, there are significant methodological challenges to quantifying pure environmental

---

249 G. Moffat, G. Bean and J. Dewar, *Trusts Law: Text and Materials*, Cambridge University Press, 2005, chapter 14.
250 *Barnes v. Addy*, (1873–74) LR 9, Ch. App. 244.
251 Clarke, op. cit., 64.
252 Penner, op. cit., 338–41.
253 J. Youngdahl, 'The time has come for a sustainable theory of fiduciary duty investment', *Hofstra Labor and Employment Law Journal* 29, 2011, 115–39, 117, footnote 20.
254 R. Avraham, 'Putting a price on pain-and-suffering damages', *Northwestern University Law Review* 100(1), 2006, 87–120.

damage, such as the value of ecosystem services.²⁵⁵ But courts have occasionally awarded damages for emotional distress from the loss of a pet animal or mental anguish from fraudulent conduct.²⁵⁶ Israeli courts have also recognized tortious damages for 'the grievance to the individual's integrity or autonomy, manifested in the deliberate disregard of his moral beliefs and preferences'.²⁵⁷ Otherwise, beneficiaries may sue for specific performance, to have their investment policy properly implemented.

A further challenge for providing effective remedies arises from restrictions on legal standing. In a private trust, only the beneficiary or one suing on his or her behalf has standing to enforce a trust. Consequently, individuals or groups who are concerned about the social or environmental performance of an investment fund have no recourse under the general law governing fiduciary relationships. The *Oregon Investment Council* case, discussed earlier, illustrates the obstacles third parties face in trying to ensure RI. Charitable trusts normally lack individual beneficiaries, and consequently, standing to enforce such trusts rests with the state Attorney-General. If the charity is administered by several trustees, one of them may bring enforcement proceedings against the others.

Finally, it should be noted that financial fiduciaries and trustees may also have a responsibility to sue third parties to recover compensation or other appropriate remedy for investment losses from any illegalities. An interesting environmental case is *Oregon Public Employee Retirement Board and State of Oregon v. BP America, et al.*, brought in 2012 by the Oregon Treasury and Oregon Investment Council to recover about US$19 million in losses from investment in BP stock after BP allegedly made materially false statements and omissions regarding safety features and other aspects of their deep-water drilling operations to investors.²⁵⁸

Fiduciary-like responsibilities in civil law systems

While fiduciary and trusts law is a creature of common law systems, in civil law systems, such as in Germany, France and Quebec, somewhat equivalent norms have been legislated, including a concept similar to the trust relationship, involving a separation between control and beneficial use of

---

255 J.C. Dobbins, 'Pain and suffering of environmental loss using contingent valuation to estimate nonuse damages', *Duke Law Journal* 43(4), 1994, 879–946; *British Columbia v. Canadian Forest Products Ltd*, [2004] SCJ No. 33 2004 SCC 38.
256 E.g., *Garland v. White*, (1963) 368 SW 2d 12,16 (Tex. Civ. App.); *Rosener v. Sears, Roebuck and Co.*, (1980) 110 Cal. App. 3d 740, 755, 168 Cal. Rptr. 237, 246; *Brousseau v. Rosenthal*, (1980) 443 NYS 2d 285 (Civ. Ct.).
257 O. Perez, *The New Universe of Green Finance: From Self-Regulation to Multi-Polar Governance*, Working Paper 07-3, Faculty of Law, Bar Ilan University, 2007; citing *Daaka v. Carmel Hospital-Haifa*, (1993) Supreme Court Case 2781/93 and *Tnuva v. Ravi Tufic*, (1997) Supreme Court Case 1338/97.
258 Circuit Crt. of State of Oregon, No. 1204-04955, April 2012.

property.[259] Contract law is also often used to structure the management of assets on behalf of another. The trust concept has spread globally to many different legal systems as a result of international investment and increasing awareness of the business advantages of the trust structure. China, for example, in 2001 adopted a new Trusts Law to promote more professional management of investment funds.[260] Quebec's pension plan legislation utilizes a form of statutory trust and contract law to achieve arrangements similar to common law financial trusts.[261] Consequently, the legality of RI from a 'fiduciary' angle has generated debate in civil law systems. In the Netherlands, for instance, the financial industry has discussed the scope for RI under Dutch financial supervisory regulation that posits 'the equivalent' fiduciary standard of 'acting in the interests of the investor'.[262]

Although the legal responsibilities found in statutes and case law relating to fund managers' relationships with clients and beneficiaries vary widely in civil law jurisdictions, there are several shared legal principles that are similar to the modern prudent investor rule. Foremost among these legal principles is 'a duty to act conscientiously in the interests of beneficiaries', which is consistent with the twin duties of loyalty and care towards beneficiaries found in the common law.[263] The second rule commonly found in civil law statutes regarding institutional funds is the duty to seek profitability, though this rule does not mean maximizing returns regardless of other considerations such as increased risks. Thirdly, in common with fiduciary responsibilities, civil law systems require diversification of investment portfolios. Fourthly, civil law systems generally add various technical managerial requirements, such as maintaining adequate liquidity and allowable asset classes. Most civil law jurisdictions also require investment decision-makers to follow well-established investment processes that reflect professional standards, which increasingly means considering ESG issues in portfolio companies.[264]

Some legal harmonization of fiduciary standards stems from pressures to forge compatible legal standards to facilitate cross-border financial markets. This approach has gone the furthest in the European Community; for instance, the Occupational Pensions Directive of 2003 posits several rules that reflect fiduciary standards, including obligations on pension plan trustees to act in the 'best interests' of beneficiaries and to ensure the security, diversification, liquidity and profitability of investment portfolios.[265] None of these rules,

---

259 The Practical Committee, *The Future has Arrived: Dutch Pension Funds and the Practice of Responsible Investment*, Dutch Association of Industry-wide Pension Funds, 2007, 14.
260 L. Ho, *Trust Law in China*, Sweet and Maxwell Asia, 2003.
261 M. Benoit, 'Trusts in a civil law jurisdiction: a unique Canadian environment for pension fund trustees', *Trusts Law International* 8(1), 1994, 1–9.
262 Dutch Fund and Asset Management Association (DUFMA), *Sustainable Investment Guide*, DUFMA, July 2009, 17.
263 Freshfields, op. cit., 10.
264 Ibid.
265 Directive 2003/41/EC of 3 June 2003, OJ L *235/10*.

however, mention RI considerations. During negotiation of the Directive, the EU Parliamentary Committee on Economic and Monetary Affairs proposed an amendment, which was not adopted, to require each fund to include a statement of its 'ethical and socially responsible investment principles'.[266]

German financial law is worth discussing to illustrate in more detail how fiduciary-like duties manifest in civil law regimes.[267] In Germany, where RI is neither openly prohibited nor mandated, contractual agreements are often relied on to achieve fiduciary management of financial assets. Financial regulations also resemble fiduciary norms found in common law systems, although the standards governing conflicts of interest are not as strict as those imposed under Anglo-American law.[268] One ostensible departure from the exclusive focus on beneficiaries found in Anglo-American law is the stipulation in the German Investment Modernization Act of 2003 that managers of investment funds must act not only 'in the sole interest of its investors' but also for 'the integrity of the market'.[269] While this goal serves to address market abuse, conceivably it might be interpreted more ambitiously to include goals of sustainable, long-term investment, consistent with the objectives of much RI. Regarding legal obligations tailored to specific funds, German insurance companies and pension funds must seek the highest possible profitability and security for their funds, ensure diversification and liquidity of their portfolios and manage investments professionally.[270] For insurance companies and some types of pension funds, this duty is supplemented by the portfolio asset restrictions that cap investment in shares to 35 per cent of a fund's overall portfolio.[271] While other German pension funds are not subject to such asset class restrictions, in practice only about one-fifth of their capital is invested in shares; the majority of assets are held in low-risk assets such as bonds and bank deposits.[272] While German law does not expressly prohibit RI, it is likely permissible only to the extent that it would not have an adverse financial effect, lessen security or reduce the

---

266 European Parliament, Committee on Economic and Monetary Affairs, *Draft Report on the Proposal for a European Parliament and Council Directive on the Activities of Institutions for Occupational Retirement Provision*, PE 295.986/AM/48-134, 8 May 2001, 52.
267 See F.J. Preu and B.J. Richardson, 'German socially responsible investment: barriers and opportunities', *German Law Journal* 12(3), 2011, 865–900.
268 H. Kotz, 'National report for Germany', in D.J. Hayton, S. Kortmann, H. Verhagen (eds), *Principles of European Trust Law*, Kluwer Law, 1999, 85–103, 91.
269 Investment Modernization Act (Investmentmodernisierungsgesetz), 2003, s. 9(2).
270 Law on the Supervision of Insurance Companies (Versicherungsaufsichtsgesetz (VAG)), 17 December 1992, (1993) BGBl. I 2, ss. 54 I, 115 I 3, II; and Pension Fund Investment decree-law (Pensionsfond-Kapitalanlageverordnung (PFKapAV)), 21 December 2001, (2001) BGBl. I 4185.
271 Sections 2–3 and 6, Regulation on the Investment of Assets of Insurance Companies (Verordnung ueber die Anlage des gebundenen Vermoegens von Versicherungsunternehmen (AnlV)), 20 December 2001, (2001) BGBl. I 3913.
272 Deutsches Institut fuer Altersvorsorge, *Wie Pensionsfonds das Geld der Versicherten anlegen* (2010), http://dia-vorsorge.de/files/pensionsfonds_anlagestruktur.pdf; Bundesanstalt fuer Finanzdienstleistungsaufsicht, Jahresbericht 2009, 114.

spread of risks.²⁷³ Such considerations in common law jurisdictions have similarly coloured the interpretation of trustees' fiduciary duties.

French investment companies (*organismes de placement collectif en valeurs mobilières* (OPCVM)) are not subject to any specific legal restrictions against RI.²⁷⁴ But French legislation requires management of OPCVMs to abide by several overarching directives: perform their duties with loyalty, diligence, neutrality and impartiality in the exclusive interest of the unit holders in the company's funds, and with regard to the integrity, transparency and security of the market; endeavour to prevent and resolve conflicts of interest; ensure portfolio diversification to minimize financial risks; comply with their investment policy as approved by the French Financial Market Authority and communicate it to unit holders. The Authority has recommended that OPCVMs act transparently and provide unit holders with information about their chosen definitions of sustainable development and RI, as well as about their 'methods and processes used in the analysis, evaluation and supervision of ESG considerations implemented by management companies and external auditors'.²⁷⁵ The Association Française de la Gestion Financière (AFG, the French asset management association, which represents OPCVMs) has drafted transparency guidelines for voluntary adoption by the funds. The French monetary and financial code requires that if capital investment funds (a type of OPCVM) decide to take ESG considerations into account in their investment and voting policies, they must state in their rules and prospectuses the precise criteria used to analyze such considerations and the methods employed to evaluate them, and also whether their management company consults external specialized valuation agencies.²⁷⁶

Statutory reform of relevance to RI

As already observed in this chapter, fiduciary and trust duties often manifest in a legislative rather than common law format, especially in the context of pension fund regulation. Usually the statutes codify general law standards (albeit usually with different enforcement mechanisms and further remedies), but occasionally they modify those standards in ways that may hinder or facilitate RI.

Particularly influential is the Uniform Trust Code, which has been adopted by many US states. One potentially adverse change for ethical investing engendered by the Code is its provisions that may prevent trust settlors from placing restrictions on investment decision-making that would override the

---

273 J. Scharlau, *Socially Responsible Investment: Die Deutschen und Europarechtlichen Rahmenbedingungen*, De Gruyter Recht, 2009, 120–1.
274 Article L. 214-39, French monetary and financial code (Code Monétaire et Financier), Modifié par Ordonnance 2011-915 du 1er août, art. 3.
275 Freshfields, op. cit., 59.
276 Article 19, Les FCPE déclarés d'investissement socialement responsable *(ISR)* http://www.amf-france.org/documents/general/8103_1.pdf.

pre-eminence given to the duty to act as a prudent investor. The assumption behind the Code, explains Cooper, is that financial prudence dictates what is in beneficiaries' interests.[277] Consequently, in his view this standard could undermine a trust settlor's ability to safeguard his or her beneficiaries' non-monetary ethical values through restraints on trust investments. The Uniform Trust Code is not binding on states, yet some have gone beyond the foregoing approach to attempt to explicitly restrict RI; the Nebraska Investment Council stipulates: 'no assets of the retirement systems . . . shall be invested or reinvested if the sole or primary investment objective is for economic development or social purposes or objectives'.[278] Yet even Nebraska's stance may allow RI if it is an ancillary or secondary consideration.

A modest countervailing legislative trend in some jurisdictions acknowledges RI as a legitimate investment strategy – but usually without actually encouraging it. One shortcoming of trusts law addressed by legislation is with regard to information disclosure to beneficiaries. Trusts law does not require a trustee to disclose to beneficiaries reasons for decisions taken in the administration of the trust.[279] The rule's rationale has been described by a legal commentator as follows:

> First, the disclosure of reasons for a decision is inconsistent with the proposition that the trustee's exercise of a discretionary power cannot be challenged in the absence of *mala fides*. Secondly, on a practical level a requirement to give reasons would add to trustees' already onerous obligations. Thirdly, the beneficiaries' knowledge of the reasons for the trustees' discretion may embitter the relationship between trustees and beneficiaries, and that between beneficiaries inter se, particularly in the case of family settlements.[280]

However, the general law clearly recognizes that trustees must keep accounts of trust property,[281] and beneficiaries have a right to information and inspection of certain trust documents.[282] Historically, beneficiaries' right to inspect trust documents was seen as stemming from their proprietary interest in the trust assets,[283] but more recent British case law rationalizes a beneficiary's right to seek disclosure of trust documents as an incident of the court's inherent jurisdiction to supervise the administration of a trust.[284]

---

277 Cooper, op. cit., 1169.
278 Nebraska Revised Statutes, 2007, s. 72-1239.01.
279 E.E. Gillese, 'Pension plans and the law of trusts', *Canadian Bar Review* 75, 1996, 221–50, 243.
280 G.E. Dal Pont and D. Chalmers, *Equity and Trusts in Australia and New Zealand*, LBC Information Services, 2000, 622.
281 E.g., *Moore v. McGlynn*, [1894] 1 IR 74.
282 *Low v. Bouverie*, [1891] 3 Ch. 82; *O'Rourke v. Darbishire*, [1920] AC 581.
283 *O'Rourke v. Darbishire*, [1920] AC 581.
284 *Schmidt v. Rosewood Trust Ltd*, [2003] 2 AC 709; Law Reform Commission (LRC), *Trust Law: General Proposals*, LRC, 2008, 12.

Pension legislation in most countries now routinely requires plan trustees to disclose their investment policies, procedures and decisions. Some legislation even requires disclosure of any RI policies. Such a reform was introduced in 1999 under the UK Pensions Act,[285] which inspired similar legislation in several other European states and in Australia and New Zealand.[286] Other legislative changes, adopted in the UK and Australia for instance, target the governance of pension funds by prescribing consultation with beneficiaries and appointment of their representatives to the governing boards of trustees.[287] Being a representative of beneficiaries, however, does legally allow a trustee to consider him or herself an *agent* of the beneficiaries, acting only according to instructions given. Trustees remain obliged to respect the purpose of a fund and overriding statutory requirements such as to invest prudently.

Only rarely have governments sought to explicitly modify fiduciary duties to give more latitude for RI. Law reform agencies have occasionally considered the issue, and most would share the view of the Irish Law Reform Commission that 'legislative intervention to allow trustees to follow an ethical investment policy should not be made, and this should remain a matter for the terms of the trust instrument'.[288] But a few exceptions exist.

Two interesting examples are in Canada. In 1993 the Manitoba Law Reform Commission recommended that the province of Manitoba allow trustees to consider non-financial criteria in their investment policies.[289] In 1995 Manitoba's Trustee Act was thus amended to provide:

> Subject to any express provision in the instrument creating the trust, a trustee who uses a non-financial criterion to formulate an investment policy or to make an investment decision does not commit a breach of trust if, in relation to the investment policy or investment decision, the trustee exercises the judgment and care that a person of prudence, discretion and intelligence would exercise in administering the property of others.[290]

In 2005, a similar provision was added to Manitoba's pension fund regulations.[291]

---

285 Occupational Pension Schemes (Investment, and Assignment, Forfeiture, Bankruptcy etc) Amendment Regulations, 1999.
286 B.J. Richardson, 'Pensions law reform and environmental policy: a new role for institutional investors?', *Journal of International Financial Markets: Law and Regulation* 3(5), 2002, 159–69.
287 UK Pensions Act 2004, s. 241(1)(a); Australia's Superannuation Industry (Supervision) Act 1993, ss 52, 58, 89, 101, 107.
288 LRC, op. cit., 141.
289 Manitoba Law Reform Commission (MLRC), *Ethical Investment by Trustees*, MLRC, 1993, 32.
290 Trustee Act, SM 1995, s. 79.1.
291 Pension Benefits Amendment Act, SM 2005, s. 28.1(2.2).

In Ontario, the provincial Financial Services Commission in 1992 issued an advisory bulletin stating that it is not necessarily imprudent for a pension fund to make ethical investments, so long as inter alia the fund's statement of investment policies declares this position, sets out the criteria for investments and notifies plan members.[292] Also interestingly, in 1988 Ontario enacted the South African Trust Investments Act to protect funds taking an ethical investment stance.[293] Where a majority of beneficiaries supported the move, the Act permitted trustees to divest or to reject investments in companies conducting business in South Africa without infringing their fiduciary duty. This reform is notable because it authorized divestments despite any possible *adverse* effect on investment returns.

These two exceptional legislative pronouncements from Canada have significance in the context of comprehending the nature of fiduciary investment standards. The fact that the Manitoban and Ontarian legislatures felt compelled to allow trustees to consider non-financial criteria may imply that those considerations do not otherwise meet prudential investment norms. Conversely, they may be construed simply as measures to clarify and provide trustees with greater certainty regarding the common law position. Both the Manitoban and Ontarian (now repealed) provisions are couched in negative terms, indicating that a trustee will not breach fiduciary duties by considering non-financial factors, and they do not create a positive duty on trustees to invest ethically. Explicit legal duties for RI have so far only been imposed on public financial institutions, notably sovereign wealth funds.[294] These statutory provisions and their implementation are examined in Chapter 5.

Conclusions

Fiduciary law governs how institutional funds manage their assets on behalf of their beneficial owners. In most common law jurisdictions, the traditional rules of equity have been codified or modified by legislation, and as the following chapter will show, their precise manifestation varies somewhat between pension funds, insurance companies, mutual funds and other types of financial institutions. Whereas fiduciary law is traditionally understood to govern a bilateral relationship between fiduciaries and beneficiaries, legislative intervention has in effect introduced into that relationship a third party – the government. As will be seen in more detail in the next chapter, such intervention, including, notably, ERISA, has both given beneficiaries more rights to participate in fund governance and also limited the parameters of finance fiduciary decision-making, requiring heightened levels of trustee

---

292 Financial Services Commission of Ontario, 'Ethical Investments', *Bulletin* 2/4, February 1992.
293 RSO 1990 (repealed in 1997).
294 B.J. Richardson, *Socially Responsible Investment Law: Regulating the Unseen Polluters*, Oxford University Press, 2008, 303–75.

expertise in order to ensure solvency and prudent fund stewardship. The duty of care and prudence has been interpreted as requiring trustees to assess investments not in isolation but by reference to their contribution to whole investment portfolios, to create diverse portfolios and to take professional advice. The duty of loyalty requires fiduciaries to safeguard the interests of beneficiaries and has tended to be interpreted to ensure that they act honestly and exclusively for the beneficiaries, thereby preventing fiduciaries from acting for their own or third-party interests.

The modest, extant case law suggests that courts have not provided a complete enunciation of all relevant considerations on the scope of RI under fiduciary law. Canadian commentator Gil Yaron contends that the case law shows that fiduciary responsibility is 'flexible and open to interpretation', and 'consideration of non-financial criteria does not violate the principles of prudence and loyalty provided that the investment decision adheres to the [fund's] investment policy and independent expert advice'.[295] Anglo-American jurisprudence suggests some modest room for RI, though the practice has not been encouraged or mandated.

The primary obstacle to innovation in fiduciary standards is that their substantive content are informed by prevailing community practices and conventions, which in this case are the investment sector's financial models and goals that are biased toward passive and short-term strategies. Relying on prevailing norms and conventions to guide interpretation of fiduciary responsibility can lead to the dangerous complacency and herd-like behaviour that facilitated the appalling financial losses of the GFC. As is examined in the next chapter, the governance systems in retail and institutional funds generally do not foster the kind of robust debate, interpretation and adaptation of fiduciary responsibility that are necessary to respond to new challenges and circumstances such as new financial risks that inhere in environmental degradation or those emanating from systemic, market failures. The *Cowan* case illustrates the significant challenges that some trustees (in this case, the member-nominated, mining union trustees) encounter in trying to appeal to an alternative set of community norms and conventions, which the presiding judge rebuffed as legally unorthodox. The Freshfields Report of 2005 has been a more successful attempt to alter the prevailing fiduciary paradigm, albeit in a less radical way by appealing to the same financial self-interest of investors through its case for the financial materiality of ESG issues as a legitimate fiduciary concern.

Overall, at present, fiduciary finance law may allow RI in any of the following situations: (i) when ESG issues are financially material to investment performance; (ii) when investment options are comparable in their financial prospects, and the RI option can be the 'tie breaker' that prevails; (iii) when a settlor's trust deed provides a mandate for RI, as in the case of

---

295 Yaron, op. cit., 36.

charitable foundations; and (iv) when beneficiaries consent to RI. Though as already explained in each case, often there are substantial practical difficulties to implementing RI in such situations, such as the difficulty of comparing financial returns under the tie-breaker principle and the unlikelihood that all the beneficiaries in a large fund would agree to RI. A deceptively simple solution, of course, would be for funds seeking to practise RI to have explicit mandates in their governing plans. Trustees exercising fiduciary investment powers must act for the purpose granted. However, pension funds and other kinds of investment institutions are commonly also subject to regulation, which channels their function into providing retirement income for beneficiaries or other prescribed purposes. Thus, there may not be much statutory freedom to manage trusts for other than financial benefits, although trustees may lawfully consider ESG factors that are financially material.

The legal framework for fiduciary finance will continue to evolve incrementally, but probably insufficiently to deal with the intertwined financial market and ecological crises that afflict the global economy, unless there are deeper changes to the governance structures that substantiate the interpretation of fiduciary norms.[296] Reforms in some jurisdictions such as Canada and Britain are already revamping the fiduciary standards of corporate directors and senior managers in an effort to promote greater consideration of environmental and community interests as factors that can shape the prosperity of companies.[297] Parallel legal reforms to this model of 'enlightened shareholder value' might one day be adopted for financial institutions. Fiduciary standards that encourage long-term, sustainable investing might help reduce the harmful myopic and speculative tendencies of financial markets while channelling capital into environmentally beneficial development.

But legislative prescriptions alone may be insufficient to challenge the deeply embedded orthodoxy in the financial sector regarding how fiduciary responsibilities are construed. Because the fiduciary standard of prudent investment hinges substantially on adhering to the prevailing conventionality, a fund that wishes to take the initiative on RI might be legally challenged merely because it is out of step with its conservative peers. Terms such as 'long term', 'responsible investment', 'environmental, social and governance factors' and 'financially material considerations' all derive their meaning through the prevailing conventions of investment and financial economics. In financial markets, these conventions primarily take the form of expectations about future cash flows from companies and other investment entities. The expectations arise from shared understandings of how financial markets

---

296 C. Joly, 'Reality and potential of responsible investment', *Issues in Business Ethics* 31, 2011, 193–210.
297 J. Bone, 'Corporate environmental responsibility in the wake of the Supreme Court decision of BCE Inc. and Bell Canada', *Windsor Review of Legal and Social Issues* 27, 2009, 5–30.

should work, what information is relevant to those expectations and how that information will influence those expectations. Since success in these financial markets is defined by how well prediction and management of expectations is performed, any prudent investor standard that is based on factors that depart from these shared understandings will struggle to receive support. Thus, there is a significant collective action barrier to RI that might be resolvable only through legal intervention that encourages new understandings of what constitutes 'prudent' investment and renders such new understandings essential considerations in fiduciary finance law. This challenge requires reforming the governance of financial institutions and the market as a whole to stimulate a more democratic and critical enquiry that nurtures new investing conventions appropriate to the challenges of environmental sustainability and intergenerational economic justice.

4 Fiduciary law in retail and institutional finance

Introduction

Having considered in the previous chapter the foundational legal principles governing fiduciary finance, we now investigate their application in specific institutional contexts. This chapter is certainly not exhaustive or definitive, because the various subjects it canvasses require their own specialized treatment, each of which would entail a further book. Nonetheless, four specific themes are explored here, allowing for a nuanced comparison of fiduciary finance law in different investment institutions and transactions.

Firstly, we trace how the fiduciary law framework is warped by different institutional and jurisdictional settings. The chapter investigates variations and similarities in the fiduciary and related legal rules governing specific entities in the institutional and retail investment sectors, which the literature about fiduciary law and RI has tended to gloss over. Most writings assess pension fund trusts, while little has been said about financial corporations and retail funds. The prospects for RI may vary depending on the financial institution or transaction. In particular, by highlighting the institutional context, we can better appreciate that fiduciary finance law does not manifest as disembodied legal rules but more expansively resonates as a set of governance arrangements in which fiduciary relations are shaped by an entity's membership, expertise, decision-making procedures and a host of other variables.

Secondly and relatedly, the legal framework for fiduciary finance transcends the traditional fiduciary and trusts law norms outlined in the last chapter. Investing is enveloped by a mosaic of legal and regulatory controls, which commonly include corporate governance, securities regulation and contract law. For example, the relationship between an individual retail investor and a mutual fund is governed by not only a fiduciary duty but also the contractual terms derived from the investment prospectus. While a fund manager may have an underlying fiduciary duty to avoid personal gain at the expense of investors' returns, contract law may modify that stipulation to allow fees and other arrangements to benefit the fund sponsor. Regulatory obligations may also differ from the standards implied by fiduciary duty; obligations to disclose to clients and treat them fairly and honestly, common features of business conduct regulation, tend to be less stringent than the duty of loyalty. The interplay between these areas of law can thus result in a 'mismatch between regulatory requirements and fiduciary obligations' because the regulatory regime may operate 'in addition to the fiduciary obligation' rather than to 'displace it'.[1]

A third theme of this chapter is the prevalence of transparency regulation as a means of disciplining the RI market. A trend affecting both the institutional and the retail sectors, funds are increasingly obliged to publicize their RI policies and practices (in addition to other parameters of their investment activities). Although they are not obliged to invest ethically and responsibly, the policy assumption is that enhanced disclosure will foster a more informed, efficient market, as well as encourage RI, because few funds would wish to declare their indifference to it. The quality of some disclosure in practice remains problematic.

A final theme is the involvement of beneficiaries in fund governance. Traditionally, the fiduciary relationship relegated beneficiaries to a passive role; they were entitled to be informed about the administration of trust assets but lacked rights to be consulted or to instruct trustees. Trustees are not ordinarily legally obliged to consult with beneficiaries; trustees must act in the 'best interests' of their beneficiaries, yet they need not inquire what those best interests are. Consequently, the potential of tying RI practices to the will of beneficiaries has been legally obscured and hindered. Through legislative reform, this traditional picture is beginning to change, especially in the pension fund sector, where beneficiaries are acquiring rights to nominate representatives to trustee boards, be consulted on investment policy and, with the emergence of portable pension plans, direct their retirement savings into their preferred RI options.

Rise of institutional investors

When individuals invest on their own behalf, they can pander to their own ethical values. But institutional funds such as pension plans, which manage large portfolios on behalf of numerous individuals, face practical and legal constraints to investing. Thus, it is not surprising to hear commentators warn that funds' custodians have an 'obligation to achieve growth and income for their fund-holders, who would be unlikely to appreciate the ethics of an investment policy that diminished the quality of their retirement'.[2] Institutional investors include mutual funds, pension plans, endowments, insurance firms, investment banks and sovereign wealth funds. They professionally manage huge portfolios of financial assets, including corporate

---

1 A. Tuch, 'Investment banks as fiduciaries: implications for conflicts of interest', *Melbourne University Law Review* 29(2), 2005, 478–517, 515.
2 J. Hancock, *Ethical Money*, Kogan Page, 2002, 22.

shares, bonds, real estate and fixed-income deposits. A retail investor in contrast is an individual directly participating in financial markets, such as buying shares in her own name. The institutional and retail sectors converge where individuals invest through intermediaries such as mutual funds and commercial banks.

Although this chapter discusses the institutional sector through separate analyses of different organizational types, their dissimilarities are diminishing as deregulated financial markets spur the establishment of omnibus or conglomerate financial companies. In some jurisdictions, insurance firms and banks have restructured to become full-service financial 'supermarkets', offering access to mutual funds, personal pension plans and ancillary financial advisory services, in addition to their respective core business of depositor and creditor services and insurance risk policies. Some banks have morphed into major institutional investors, establishing trading desks in corporate and sovereign securities in search of additional revenue streams in the ever more competitive, global economy.

According to several indicators, institutional investors have become the dominant actor in the financial economy, surging to prominence in the late twentieth century. In major markets, institutions now hold the majority of corporate stocks, as well as significant portfolios of other asset classes such as bonds, private equities and real estate. In 2005, institutional investors held approximately 75 per cent of the stock issued by Fortune 1000 companies[3] and in 2007 owned about 60 per cent of all issued American corporate stock.[4] Investment assets under management by pension funds, mutual funds and insurance companies amounted worldwide to US$79.3 trillion in 2010, up from US$39.6 trillion in 2000.[5] Further, approximately US$52 trillion were amassed in alternative funds such as private equity and private wealth funds.[6] Some have captured a bigger share of this financial bonanza. American depository institutions' portion of these assets plummeted from 54.9 per cent in 1967 to 23.7 per cent in 2007, while over the same four decades pension funds' share rose from 12.8 to 18.5 per cent, and mutual funds' soared from 2.6 to 19.3 per cent.[7] Another measure of these trends is how they compare to GDP: the UK has the highest ratio of investment funds as a percentage of GDP (257 per cent in 2010), followed by the US (224 per cent) and Switzerland (211 per cent).[8] Conversely, institutional equity funds are much smaller in Europe's biggest economy, Germany, with its tradition of

---

3 G.E. Davis, 'The rise and fall of finance and the end of the society of organizations', *Academy of Management Perspectives*, August, 2007, 27–44, 33.
4 Conference Board, *The 2007 Institutional Investment Report*, Conference Board, 2007.
5 CityUK, 'Fund management', CityUK, October 2011, 1.
6 Ibid., 2.
7 J. D'Arista and S. Griffith-Jones, 'Agenda and criteria for financial regulatory reform', in S. Griffith-Jones, et al. (eds), *Time for a Visible Hand: Lessons from the 2008 World Financial Crisis*, Oxford University Press, 2010, 126–49, 133.
8 CityUK, op. cit.

bank-based finance.[9] Changes to German corporate and taxation law, which were introduced in the 1990s and 2000s to attract global investors, are starting to shift the German investment profile closer to the Anglo-American pattern.[10]

The institutional sector's surge, which has been particularly notable in the global financial hubs of London and New York, has been fuelled by several factors.[11] On the supply side, they include market deregulation and technological developments; on the other side, demographic changes, greater household wealth and strains on traditional social security systems have spiked demand. Institutional investment managers can in theory deliver better risk management and return on investment than are generally attainable by individual investors. These economies of scale advantages also lower transactional costs.[12] Such changes have been accompanied by greater consolidation in the financial industry through mergers and takeovers, as well as more market complexity, leading to increasing reliance on specialized financial advisers and managers to whom fiduciaries such as pension plan trustees commonly delegate responsibility.

These institutional intermediaries have given rise to a phenomenon known as 'agency capitalism', whereby the management and 'gains of investment activity go disproportionately to intermediaries rather than underlying owners'.[13] This trend contrasts with previous eras of financial market history (especially in the Anglo-American sphere), which were dominated by individual and family investors. The rise of agency capitalism strains the fiduciary responsibility paradigm when trustees and managers of funds may be very remotely connected to the individuals or organizations in whose name they purport to act, and therefore may have little knowledge of their identity, needs or values. The mechanisms of accountability and oversight fray as the chain of transactions and agents lengthens.

On the other hand, the ascendancy of institutional investors in major public companies around the world might give us confidence that they can wield influence for RI. Individual shareholders face nearly insurmountable barriers to meaningfully impacting any firm's governance, principally owing

---

9 H. Schaefer, 'Ethical investment of German non-profit organizations – conceptual outline and empirical results', *Business Ethics: A European Review* 13(4), (2004), 269–87, 270–1; J. Corbett and T. Jenkinson, 'The financing of industry, 1970–1989: an international comparison', *Journal of Japanese and International Economies* 10, 1996, 71–96.
10 E.g.. Second Financial Market Promotion Act (Gesetz ueber den Wertpapierhandel und zur Aenderung boersenrechtlicher und wertpapierrechtlicher Vorschriften) 1994; Law on the further Reform of Corporation Law and Accounting Law (Gesetz zur weiteren Reform des Aktien- und Bilanzrechts, zu Transparenz und Publizitaet), 2002; Law on the Improvement of Investor Protection (Anlageschutzverbesserungsgesetz), 2004.
11 See G.L. Clark, *European Pensions and Global Finance*, Oxford University Press, 2003, 170–92 (explaining the UK's prominence in world financial markets).
12 Ibid., 191.
13 C. Berry, *Protecting Our Best Interests: Rediscovering Fiduciary Obligation*, FairPensions, 2001, 7.

to the costs of gathering information and coordinating action. But the colossal portfolios of institutional funds, combined with their emerging tendency to collaborate in monitoring companies, may eventually better align business managers' interests with those of shareholders. Such collaboration is becoming more feasible not only because of the funds' economic incentives for more consistent, long-term returns but also because of easier securities regulations that facilitate communication between shareholders, as well as technological changes that lower the transaction costs of monitoring and coordinating responses. The emergence of investor governance networks and coalitions interested in ESG issues may strengthen the market's capacity to stimulate RI without legal changes. These coalitions include the CDP, Institutional Investors for Climate Risk, Coalition for Environmentally Responsible Economies and the Council of Institutional Investors. The presence of such clusters in itself, however, does not illuminate their quality, and opportunities for free-riding can undermine solidarity among investors. The next section builds on the discussion in Chapter 2 about RI's influence and probes more deeply into some of the characteristics of the institutional sector that shape its future contribution to RI and corporate sustainability.

Obstacles to responsible finance

Short-termism

One of the most important forces shaping RI in at least the past decade has been its recasting from a boutique, niche market that follows ethical dogma to a pragmatic business strategy that combines a long-term perspective with active ownership through corporate engagement. The following comments map the principal elements of this trend and their potential, in the face of some fundamental obstacles, to shift institutional investors towards sustainability. Thereby, it sets the context for the subsequent discussion in this chapter about the legal context.

Many commentators increasingly hope that institutional funds will invest responsibly – and hence contribute to sustainability – by taking a longer-term perspective.[14] Because ecological systems function over indefinite time horizons, valuing the future is essential for sustainability. A World Economic Forum report commented:

> Responsible investment requires an orientation towards strategies that optimize long-term returns, both because this delivers better financial returns over the time profile that interests intended beneficiaries, and

---

14 See T. Hebb, *No Small Change: Pension Funds and Corporate Engagement*, Cornell University Press, 2008; M. Staub-Bisang, *Sustainable Investing for Institutional Investors*, John Wiley and Sons, 2012; E.M. Zarbafi, *Responsible Investment and the Claim of Corporate Change*, Gabler Verlag, 2011.

because over these periods social and environmental issues become more material and so can be better considered.[15]

In contrast, the prevailing short-term bias of financial actors is explained by the 2012 *Kay Review of UK Equity Markets and Long-Term Decision-Making* as:

> ...a tendency to under-invest, whether in physical assets or in intangibles such as product development, employee skills and reputation with customers, and as hyperactive behaviour by executives whose corporate strategy focuses on restructuring, financial re-engineering or mergers and acquisitions at the expense of developing the fundamental operational capabilities of the business.[16]

Contrary to the assumptions of corporate governance theory that such problems likely reflect insufficient accountability of companies to shareholders or that shareholders are insufficiently consulted, the corporate behaviours described above 'have been supported or even encouraged by a majority of the company's shareholders'.[17] Any shareholder dissatisfaction is usually displayed by emphasizing exit (selling shares) over voice (exchanging views with the company).

These impatient investors may financially suffer over the long term, to the detriment of fiduciary responsibility. A study by the CFA Centre for Financial Market Integrity and Business Roundtable Institute for Corporate Ethics concluded, 'The obsession with short-term results by investors, asset management firms, and corporate managers collectively leads to the unintended consequences of destroying long-term value, decreasing market efficiency, reducing investment returns, and impeding efforts to strengthen corporate governance.'[18] Researchers have found that firms that reduce advertising, research and development investment and other discretionary spending in order to narrowly beat market quarterly forecasts accrue short-term gains in stock price yet under-perform over the subsequent three years.[19]

Planning over several years or decades defies the normal range of perspective of most investors and indeed is beyond most types of institutions or individuals; but some believe institutional investors should have more patience. Whereas individual investors tend to hold relatively more liquid and shorter-term investments, institutional investors have 'a comparative

---

15 World Economic Forum (WEF), *Mainstreaming Responsible Investment*, WEF and Account Ability, 2005, 10.
16 J. Kay, *Kay Review of UK Equity Markets and Long-Term Decision-Making*, Department of Business, Innovation and Skills, 2012, 10.
17 Ibid., 21.
18 CFA Centre for Financial Market Integrity and Business Roundtable Institute for Corporate Ethics, *Breaking the Short-Term Cycle*, CFA, 2006, 1.
19 S. Bhojraj, et al., 'Making sense of cents: an examination of firms that marginally miss or beat analyst forecasts', *Journal of Finance* 64(5), 2009, 2361–88.

advantage in compensating for the increased risk of long-maturity assets by pooling'.[20] Studies identify a trend towards more interest in long-term investing, mostly among public sector pension funds in Anglo-American markets.[21] One financial group dedicated to this task is the UK-based Marathon Club,[22] formed in 2004 by a cohort of pension funds to draft practical guidance for trustees on long-term investment management.[23] Another example is the Long-Term Investors Club, established in April 2008 by the French state-owned bank Caisse des Dépots et Consignations.[24] With membership open to an array of public and private funds, as well as financial regulators, the Club participants agree to follow seven key investing principles, including taking greater consideration of ESG issues.

For large institutional investors, the imperative of investing responsibly has most fluently been theorized through the concept of the 'universal owner', as discussed in Chapter 2. James Hawley and Andrew Williams hypothesize that institutional investors who invest widely across the market will benefit financially by taking into account the social and environmental externalities in their portfolios.[25] As economy-wide investors, they should 'have no interest in abetting behavior by any one company that yields a short-term boost while threatening harm to the economic system as a whole'.[26] The theory implies that any 'externality' of an individual company may result in a costly 'internality' for an investor's global portfolio. Some interesting research has begun to measure the cost of environmental externalities to universal investors. A report prepared for the UNPRI Secretariat evaluated the price of environmental damage worldwide, and estimated it in 2008 to be US$6.6 trillion, or 11 per cent of global GDP.[27] The report expects such costs by 2050 to grow to US$28.6 trillion (18 per cent of projected global GDP).[28]

But theoretical concepts for sustainable, long-term investing tend to be divorced from prevailing market practices. There is abundant evidence both that short-termism remains rife in global financial markets and that institutional funds contributed to the GFC. The fetishistic focus on short-term performance may involve inflating current profits at the expense of the long-term health of a fund or firm, for example by investing in assets with concealed risks and borrowing excessive debt to deceptively boost short-term

---

20 E.P. Davis and B. Steil, *Institutional Investors*, MIT Press, 2001, 293.
21 Hebb, *No Small Change*, op. cit., 6.
22 See http://www.uss.co.uk/UssInvestments/Responsibleinvestment/marathonclub/Pages/default.aspxhttp.
23 Marathon Club, 'Guidance note for long-term investing', 2007.
24 See http://www.ltic.org.
25 J. Hawley and A. Williams, *The Rise of Fiduciary Capitalism: How Institutional Investors Can Make Corporate America More Democratic*, University of Pennsylvania Press, 2000.
26 S. Davis, J. Lukomnik and D. Pitt-Watson, *The New Capitalists. How Citizen Investors are Reshaping the Corporate Agenda*, Harvard Business Press, 2006, 18.
27 UNEP-FI and the UNPRI Secretariat, *Universal Ownership: Why Externalities Matter to Institutional Investors*, PRI Association and UNEP-FI, 2011, 2.
28 The majority of these costs are attributed to GHG emissions and unsustainable water use.

profits or portfolio returns.[29] It may also include using short-term trading strategies that ignore the underlying value of firms that on average over a longer term lead to investment losses. Additionally, in the lead-up to the GFC, some institutional funds exploited short-term arbitrage opportunities, using voting rights, for example, to pressure firms into providing immediate payback to owners through dividend payouts, share buybacks or selling off assets.[30] Consequently, market prices may fail to reflect the enduring value of companies' sustainability performance.

Many factors contribute to these behaviours, of which a full analysis would require another book. They include informational gaps and deficiencies in financial models about the economic value of long-term performance; technological changes in markets that allow financiers to utilize short-term trading strategies more frequently; structural factors that motivate managers to manipulate financial data and profitability, such as to enhance a company's credibility in capital markets, convey future growth prospects and secure high credit ratings; personal managerial motivations to earn performance bonuses by seeking super profit targets; the competitive organizational culture in investment banking and fund management; and, in terms of individual psychology, behavioural biases, such as the tendency of individuals to heavily discount the future or to be overly optimistic about it.[31]

One powerful indicator of short-termism is the high volume of turnover of corporate securities. The average holding period for shares listed on the New York Stock Exchange has plunged from about seven years in the 1940s to just over five years in 1970 and down to six months in 2009.[32] The average holding period for UK corporate shares has reportedly dropped from five years in the mid-1960s to 7.5 months in 2007.[33] Among emerging markets such as China, similar statistics exist.[34] Asset turnover is common in the retail fund market, with annual turnover rates in the three largest mutual fund groups in the US in 2012 of: American Funds (31 per cent), Fidelity (70 per cent) and Vanguard (35 per cent).[35] Companies with an 'ownership base dominated by transient institutional shareholders are more likely' to

---

29 L.L. Dallas, 'Short-termism, the financial crisis, and corporate governance', *Journal of Corporation Law* 37(2), 2012, 266–362, 267.
30 D. Walker, *A Review of Corporate Governance in UK Banks and Other Financial Industry Entities: Final Recommendations*, UK Treasury, November 2009, 78.
31 Dallas, op. cit., 268–71; K.A. Froot, A.F. Perold and J.C. Stein, 'Shareholder trading practices and corporate investment horizons', *Journal of Applied Corporate Finance* 5(2), 1993, 42–52; CFA, op. cit.
32 H. Blodget, 'You're an investor? How quaint', *Business Insider*, 8 August 2009, http://www.businessinsider.com/henry-blodget-youre-an-investor-how-quaint-2009-8.
33 A. Haldane, 'Patience and finance', Beijing, Oxford China Business Forum, September 2010, 6.
34 Ibid., 17.
35 Statistics by Morningstar, as of 30 June 2012, http://quicktake.morningstar.com/FundFamily/. For a definition of 'asset turnover', see http://www.morningstar.com/InvGlossary/turnoverratio.aspx.

engage in opportunistic strategies to meet short-term earnings targets, such as to trade shares or cut research and development expenses, 'than firms dominated by dedicated and quasi-indexer institutional shareholders'.[36]

Asset turnover and other myopic investment strategies are fostered by the appointment and monitoring of fund managers based on short-term relative performance.[37] To reduce agency problems, fund managers are commonly given short mandates, typically for three years, with regular performance reviews.[38] Their compensation and bonuses are tied to quarterly or other short-interval financial performance metrics relative to market index benchmarks or other asset managers in a similar field.[39] Such performance evaluation affects fund managers' attitudes to risk and time horizons, motivating them to seek the highest returns or at least out-perform their peers within their performance evaluation period.[40] For the market as a whole, however, this is a zero-sum game; competition among fund managers to out-perform one another by anticipating the fluctuating whims of market sentiment is largely at the expense of each other and contributes nothing, collectively, to the absolute performance and value of companies. The time horizons under which asset managers operate are also generally much shorter than the time horizon over which the beneficiaries of funds look to maximize returns, a mismatch that risks a dereliction of fiduciary responsibility.

Among relevant evidence, a 2004 survey in the UK by the National Association of Pension Funds and the Investment Management Association found that fund managers were normally appointed on three-year terms (in 69 per cent of cases surveyed), while 16 per cent were given a term of less than three years, and none longer than five years.[41] Research for the UK's Myners Report on institutional investment found similar evidence: 29 per cent of investment schemes gave fund managers contracts of 12 months or less.[42] By contrast, fund managers of state-sponsored pension plans have much longer tenure, up to ten years.[43] From her survey of 64 UK fund managers, Mae Baker found that the 'performance benchmarking and monitoring system in use for pension fund managers provides a perceived pressure to adopt more

---

36 Dallas, op. cit., 303.
37 P.L. Davies, 'Institutional investors in the United Kingdom', in D.D. Prentice and P.R.J. Holland (eds), *Contemporary Issues in Corporate Governance*, Oxford University Press, 1993, 69–95, 72; M. Baker, 'Fund managers' attitudes to risk and time horizons: the effect of performance benchmarking', *European Journal of Finance* 4, 1998, 257–78.
38 Davis and Steil, op. cit., 136.
39 Hebb, *No Small Change*, op. cit., 95.
40 Innovation Advisory Board, *Innovation: City Attitudes and Practices*, UK Department of Trade and Industry, 1990.
41 National Association of Pension Funds (NAPF) and the Investment Management Association (IMA), *Short-termism Study Report,* NAPF and IMA, 2004, 3.
42 UK Department of Work and Pensions (DWP), *The Myners Principles and Occupational Pension Schemes*, volume 2, DWP, 2004, 114.
43 K. Kjaer, 'The Norwegian Petroleum Fund', A.R. Musalem and R.J. Palacios (eds), *Public Pension Fund Management*, World Bank, 2004, 241–57, 244 (referring to the Irish National Pension Reserve Fund).

short-termist attitudes and shorter holding periods than would otherwise be the case'.[44]

Systemic market risks

The GFC confirmed doubts about the capacity of institutional funds to be an effective influence for active, long-term investment. They largely failed to anticipate, let alone forestall, the crisis. Prior to this financial meltdown, few investors in the RI industry were interested in structural reform of financial markets.[45] Although institutional investors can be attentive to financial risks associated with individual firms, they have largely overlooked sectoral and systemic financial risks.[46] Regulators in the US and Europe were also culpable for this stance because they allowed relatively relaxed supervision of financial markets in order to stimulate market growth and maintain their pre-eminence as global entrepôts.[47] Financial market supervisors failed to identify the nature of the risks posed by the US-sourced mortgage-based securities and thus failed to take pre-emptive action.[48] They also left under-regulated certain risky financial entities such as hedge funds, which in the US were exempt from many disclosure obligations and investor protections (including fiduciary responsibility) provided for under the Investment Advisors Act.[49]

The legal system has also contributed to market practices that create structural barriers to RI. While the emerging popularity of passive investment management, based on tracking the holdings of a stock index, can reduce asset turnover and myopic behaviour, it augments investors' exposure to systemic market risks. As institutional investors increasingly rely on similar investment and risk management strategies, the ensuing herd-like practices amplify investors' exposure to catastrophic market collapses, as occurred in the GFC. James Hawley and others warn that investors' reliance on MPT to limit asset-specific risks 'left unexamined ... the impact of systemic risk, which ... was seen as strictly exogenous' and something that could not be diversified away.[50] In this milieu, broad exposure to the market requires more

---

44 Baker, op. cit., 272.
45 For an exception, see CalPERS, *Financial Market Reform Principles: Returning to the Basics*, CalPERS, 2002.
46 J.P. Hawley, S.J. Kamath and A.T. Williams, 'Introduction', in J.P. Hawley, S.J. Kamath and A.T. Williams (eds), *Corporate Governance Failures: The Role of Institutional Investors in the Global Financial Crisis*, University of Pennsylvania Press, 2011, 1–25, 5.
47 See the UK analysis by Walker, op. cit.
48 For example, only a few months before the spectacular collapse of Northern Rock, the UK's Financial Services Authority allowed the bank to lower its capital reserves and to increase its dividends to its shareholders by 30 per cent: J. Herring, 'The known, the unknown, and the unknowable in financial policy: an application to the subprime crisis', *Yale Journal on Regulation* 26, 2009, 391–404, 400.
49 1940, Pub. L. 76-768; J.S. Taub, 'The sophisticated investor and the global financial crisis', in Hawley, Kamath and Williams, op. cit., 188–216, 200.
50 J. Hawley, K. Johnson and E. Waitzer, 'Reclaiming fiduciary duty balance', *Rotman International Journal of Pension Management* 4(2), 2011, 4–16, 5.

active and systemic investment policies. The ubiquitous reliance on MPT 'worked well to a point, but as MPT became the primary mode of operation in the economy, it created risk and undermined its own effectiveness'.[51] Reliance on 'diversification, securitization, hedging, arbitrage and leverage ... to control risks at the portfolio level while maximizing returns can create market-level risks that threaten financial and economic stability'.[52] The culture of passivity fostered by the comfort of MPT led investors to ignore the rising financial bubble and corporate scandals that eventually led to the 2008 market implosion.

Fiduciary law standards encourage this lemming behaviour. Because trustees and asset managers are behooved by the current view of fiduciary responsibility to invest like their peers, a climate in which short-term decision-making and inadequate assessment of ESG risks is prevalent can flourish. Gordon Clark and Eric Knight believe the 'reluctance to engage [with RI] issues can be explained by a narrow interpretation of fiduciary duty that excludes reference to anything other than the risk-adjusted rate of return'.[53] Fund managers have a legal incentive to imitate investment conventions in order to mitigate any liabilities that might arise should they under-perform their peers, even though herding exposes beneficiaries to collective irrationality and consequential loss. There can thus be palpable disincentives for fiduciary investors to exert leadership and innovate in a manner that is socially responsible but financially unorthodox. Joshua Getzler argues that 'liberalised rules for trust investment played a part in setting the conditions for today's bloated and destabilized capital markets; and that the canons of investment mandated by older equity jurisprudence might provide insights to help build a more durable and stable system'.[54] To combat the legal licence given to commercially aggressive and risky investment, Getzler advocates a return to the more restrictive approach of trusts law that focused on maintenance of capital over the long term and restricted the range of allowable asset classes. The derivatives market and hedge funds, which prior to the GFC attracted large inflows of institutional funds searching for super returns,[55] are examples of investments that might be intrinsically unsuitable for long-term, fiduciary investors.

The GFC exposed another structural barrier to RI, namely investors' misunderstanding of their financial risks in the complex, global market. While the RI literature has focused on investors' imperfect knowledge of the

---

51 J.P. Hawley, S.J. Kamath and A.T. Williams, 'Introduction', in Hawley, Kamath and Williams, op. cit., 1–25, 9.
52 Ibid., 18.
53 G.L. Clark and E. Knight, 'Implications of the UK Companies Act 2006 for institutional investors and the market for corporate social responsibility', *University of Pennsylvania Journal of Business Law* 11(2), 2009, 256–96, 294–5.
54 J. Getzler, 'Fiduciary investment in the shadow of financial crisis: was Lord Eldon right?' *Journal of Equity* 3, 2009, 1–31, 2.
55 Hebb, *No Small Change*, op. cit., 96.

financial materiality and consequences of ESG issues, there are deeper, structural cognition deficits in institutional investors. The problem of 'bounded rationality' is theorized in scholarly literature to describe how organizations and individuals are not wholly knowledgeable and perfectly rational.[56] They make mistakes. Companies led by incompetent managers can commit errors that produce wider social impacts than just for the company, expensive pollution 'accidents' being a case in point.[57] They may also suffer cognitive limitations that reflect the state of academic knowledge about how to incorporate ESG factors into financial analysis.[58] Thus, even where companies or their financiers have incentives not to exploit market failures and where the interests of corporate managers and shareholders, or trustees and beneficiaries, are closely aligned, boundedly rational actors can misunderstand complex environmental problems.

It is well known that 'institutional investors demand standardized disclosure of market-sensitive information such that data are rendered *comparable* between companies, . . . *consistent* in definition and measurement over time, and *comprehensive* in nature and scope'.[59] The RI market doesn't yet have access to such information for the purposes of assessing sustainability performance, as financial reporting and accounting rules do not properly reflect all aspects of companies' environmental and social performance. The International Accounting Standards Board (IASB), an influential standard-setter, lacks metrics for these issues.[60] Likewise, some credit rating agencies have done poorly in furnishing company-specific credit ratings that account for each firm's long-term sustainability performance, and the recent global credit crisis also revealed deficiencies in the agencies' conventional evaluation criteria. In response, some individual states, especially within the EU, have established more comprehensive corporate reporting standards of relevance to social investors, as discussed later in this chapter. The emerging ESG analysis industry, which serves social investors and mainstream funds, is also a new knowledge provider, helping investors to understand how ESG issues can be financially material. Broader access to reliable ESG information and a common metric to analyze such data is important to enable the RI market to capture mainstream institutional investors.

Investors' bounded knowledge is not limited to ESG issues but rather encompasses basic financial risks and issues, ignorance of which contributes to systemic problems in the financial economy. Markets have been regulated

---

56 See H. Simon, *Reason in Human Affairs*, Stanford University Press, 1983; J. Elster, *Sour Grapes: Studies in the Subversion of Rationality*, Cambridge University Press, 1983.
57 C. Mackenzie, 'The scope for investor action on corporate social and environmental impacts', in R. Sullivan and C. MacKenzie (eds), *Responsible Investment*, Greenleaf Publishing, 2005, 20–38.
58 National Round Table on the Environment and the Economy (NRTEE), *Capital Markets and Sustainability: Investing in a Sustainable Future*, NRTEE, 2007, 31.
59 Clark and Knight, op. cit., 284.
60 Ibid.

on the belief that most institutional funds, unlike individual investors, are 'sophisticated' enough to understand the financial risks and opportunities involved.[61] The notion of 'sophisticated investors' (SI) is embedded in securities laws, allowing securities issuers to exempt institutional funds from some legal requirements designed to protect lay retail investors from inadequate disclosures. It was partly US financial regulators' reliance on the SI assumption that unleashed the market in complex financial instruments and derivatives that later precipitated the GFC.[62] Collateralized debt obligations grew far more complex than the cognitive capacity of most market participants, even of many ostensible financial experts. The credit rating industry itself wrongly rated some securities as safe, thereby spurring pension funds and other supposedly cautious investors to buy up toxic subprime mortgage securities. In short, neither the entities that are deemed by law as SIs nor the ultimate investors who put their money at risk had the capacity to understand the complexities of the new finance. Public disclosure is an inadequate regulatory standard when investors lack the cognitive capacity to analyze disclosed information or lack the resources and incentives to act on that information.

This book is not designed to examine in-depth the causes and solutions to global financial instabilities, which has already been taken up in extensive literature.[63] The foregoing limited discussion of this subject does, however, set the context to some of the main structural barriers to institutional investors' capacity for long-term, sustainable investing. The rest of this chapter shifts to consider the fiduciary law position in specific financial institutions, highlighting how the economic function and legal context of different types of institutions can lead to variations in their ability and willingness to practise RI.

Pension funds

Institutional characteristics and fiduciary responsibilities

Pension funds are pools of capital administered by trustees or other custodians for the future benefit of the fund's beneficiaries. A pension plan is established by a business, trade union or government authority, and it invests income contributed by the founding sponsor and by beneficiaries to pay benefits

---

61 The embedding of the SI concept occurred after the Great Depression, around the enactment of the Securities Act of 1933, Pub. L. No. 22, which governs the offering and sale of securities.
62 Taub, op. cit.
63 See R.J. Shiller, *The Subprime Solution*, Princeton University Press, 2008; P. Savona, J. Kirton and C. Oldani, *Global Financial Crisis: Global Impact and Solutions*, Ashgate, 2011; T. Ciro, *The Global Financial Crisis: Triggers, Responses and Aftermath*, Ashgate, 2012.

upon the retirement of the beneficiaries.[64] Pension plans were first created in Europe in the seventeenth century to support war veterans and retiring civil servants,[65] and they have since become widespread in employment relationships, with pension assets surging to become one of the largest sources of capital. Global pension assets at the end of 2011 were US$30.9 trillion, with the US accounting for 58 per cent of this total and the UK 10 per cent.[66] Four types of pension schemes exist: state-sponsored pension plans, associated with national social security systems; public sector pension plans for government employees; private sector occupational pensions; and fourthly, personal pension plans arranged individually through insurance companies and other financial service providers. Some pension funds have been at the forefront of the RI movement, especially public sector varieties under trade union influence. The CalPERS (in the US) and the Universities Superannuation Scheme (in the UK) are among these leaders committed to RI. A 2011 survey of 169 pension funds in Europe found that 66 per cent believed that having a policy on RI was part of their fiduciary duty, though only 56 per cent had adopted such a policy.[67] While the following discussion focuses on occupational pension plans, we should appreciate that workers' retirement savings plans are increasingly structured through contracts with insurance providers that may operate outside the parameters of fiduciary law.[68]

In common law jurisdictions, a pension plan is usually established with a trust structure,[69] functioning in the shadow of regulations and contractual arrangements between the employer and employees that may influence the investment decision-making responsibilities and procedures.[70] In an archetypal trust model, the employer, as settlor, vests the pension fund and its earnings in the custody of one or more trustees to manage on behalf of the employee beneficiaries. The trustees have legal title to the fund's assets (while the beneficiaries hold an equitable interest) and control the investment and management of those assets. The trustees commonly enjoy a plenary power to invest subject to restrictions by the trust deed, in addition to applicable common law rules or government regulations.[71] In practice, the trustees may

---

64 See E.P. Davis, *Pension Funds, Retirement-Income Security and Capital Markets – An International Perspective*, Oxford University Press, 1995.
65 R. Blackburn, *Banking on Death. Or, Investing in Life: the History and Future of Pensions*, Verso, 2002, 34–9.
66 CityUK, 'Pension markets: March 2012', 28 March 2012, http://www.thecityuk.com/research/our-work/reports-list/pension-markets-2012.
67 S. Grene, 'Many pension funds failing to act on SRI', *Financial Times*, 3 October 2011, 2.
68 A.N. Kaplan, *Pension Law*, Irwin Law, 2006, 5.
69 E.g., E.E. Gillese, 'Pension plans and the law of trusts', *Canadian Bar Review* 75, 1996, 221–50; L. Millett, 'Pension schemes and the law of trusts: the tail wagging the dog?', *Trust Law International* 14(2), 2000, 27–35.
70 J.K. Maxton and J. Farrar, 'Social investment and pension scheme trusts', *Law Quarterly Review* 102, 1986, 32–5.
71 OECD, *Survey of Investment Regulations of Pension Funds*, OECD, 2006. A standard trust deed contains details of the rights, powers, and remuneration of the trustee(s), details of benefits of members, winding up provisions, disclosure, record keeping and actuarial review: e.g., Trustee Act, 2000 (UK), ss 3(1) and 6(1)(b); Pensions Act, 1995 (UK), s. 34(1).

be only notional, with the employer exercising real control. In North America and Australia, defined benefit pension plans are often in the custody of trust corporations appointed by the employers. Such an entity acts on instructions from the employer (as administrator) or its nominees, who often are hired investment managers. This structure, lacking an independent board of trustees and without oversight by plan members, can cause a conflict of interest when financial decisions are taken that may affect the sponsoring employer. Another quirk is that sometimes the employer can be categorized as a co-beneficiary, in recognition of its interest in the financial success of the pension plan.[72]

Occasionally, particularly in the public sector, a pension plan and its governance derive from collective bargaining agreements. Representatives appointed by the employer and employees' union jointly sponsor and supervise the pension plan. Commonly, a hired plan administrator manages the scheme,[73] with responsibility to formulate investment procedures, ensure plan solvency and calculate benefits to beneficiaries, while an external fund manager handles the fund's portfolio of assets. Trustees nominated by beneficiary members may face conflicting interests in managing a pension plan because of loyalty to the beneficiaries who supported their nomination.

Pension fund legislation generally clarifies rather than radically alters the fiduciary standards of the common law. The regulatory regime relies on vetting of investment agents, requirements for obtaining professional advice and mandatory disclosure to beneficiaries as the primary means to discipline trustees. Britain's Pensions Act[74] and its subordinate regulations[75] require trustees to exercise their investment powers 'in a manner calculated to ensure the security, quality, liquidity and profitability of the portfolio as a whole',[76] and they must invest assets 'in the best interests of members and beneficiaries'[77] and to ensure portfolio diversification.[78] Trustees must obtain proper advice when preparing their statements of investment principles[79] and follow those principles as far as practicable.[80]

These standards may allow RI that is financially prudent. Australian occupational pension plans (known as 'superannuation funds') are governed primarily by the Superannuation Industry (Supervision) Act of 1993, which incorporates fiduciary investment standards similar to other common law jurisdictions.[81] The Association of Superannuation Funds of Australia

---

72 See e.g. Canada's Pension Benefits Standards Act, 1985, RSC s. 8(3) (requiring an administrator to administer the pension plan as a trustee for the employer and the plan beneficiaries).
73 See Z. Bodie and E.P. Davis (eds), *The Foundations of Pension Finance*, Edward Elgar, 2000.
74 See ss 33–36.
75 Occupational Pension Schemes (Investment) Regulations, 2005 (UK), cl. 4(3).
76 Ibid., cl. 4.
77 Ibid., cl. 4(2)(a).
78 Ibid., cl. 4(7).
79 Ibid., cl. 2(2)(a).
80 Pensions Act, 1995 (UK), s. 36(5).
81 E.g., ss 7, 52(2) and 62.

believes RI is acceptable so long as funds adhere to prudential investment standards, they minimize costly administrative overheads and the investment policy enjoys wide acceptance among fund members.[82]

In an important innovation, South African pension fund law was amended in 2011 to alter the trustee duty of prudent investing by requiring all funds 'before making an investment . . . [to] consider any factor which may materially affect the sustainable long-term performance of the asset including, but not limited to, those of an environmental, social and governance character'.[83] The regulation governs private sector and public pension plans. Its practical effect is yet to be determined, and it is unclear what sanctions would apply if a fund neglected the new standard, but it conveys a clear signal to the South African investment community about the legal legitimacy of ESG considerations.

Fiduciary standards may extend to the fund managers to whom trustees often delegate responsibility, depending on the nature of the investment management relationship.[84] Contrary to the common law prohibition, pension legislation typically authorizes such delegation, so long as the fiduciary retains control over policy decisions, is satisfied of the agent's competency for the job and carefully supervises the delegate. An investment management agreement typically governs the relationship between trustees and their fund managers. The Freshfields Report advised that 'fiduciary duties do not apply directly to fund managers or investment consultants in typical circumstances, because they do not act as custodians of fund assets in the way that trustees do'.[85] Nonetheless, Freshfields concluded that fund managers 'are often effectively subject to the same obligations as trustees regarding their decision-making'[86] through regulation and contract.[87] Some commentators believe that investment managers with discretionary authority may be deemed fiduciaries,[88] and FairPensions contends that 'asset managers exercise control over beneficiaries' interests in circumstances which make the beneficiaries heavily dependent on their skill and good faith'.[89]

In each jurisdiction, it is important to consider how relevant pension fund legislation apportions responsibilities between trustees and their agents.

---

82 Association of Superannuation Funds of Australia, *Development of ASFA Policy on 'Ethical Investment'*, October 2000, 8.
83 Pension Funds Act, 1956: Amendment of Regulation 28, 2011, s. 2(c)(ix).
84 K.P. Ambachtsheer and D. Ezra, *Pension Fund Excellence: Creating Value for Stockholders*, John Wiley and Sons, 1998, 67–71; Kay, op. cit., 68.
85 Freshfields, op. cit., 85.
86 Ibid.
87 E.g., UK's Pensions Act, 1995, s. 36 (duties to assess the suitability of each investment and have regard to the need for diversification); see further J. Franks and C.P. Mayer, *Risk, Regulation and Investor Protection. The Case of Investment Management*, Oxford University Press, 1989.
88 E.g., S. Willey, 'Investment management and fiduciary duties', in D. Frase (ed.), *Law and Regulation of Investment Management,* Sweet and Maxwell, 2004, 237–63.
89 Berry, op. cit., 37.

The UK's Pensions Act of 1995 allows trustees to delegate their powers, but not their fiduciary responsibilities. It stipulates that trustees cannot avoid liability for breach of their duty of care by delegating to asset managers,[90] unless trustees have taken all reasonable steps to satisfy themselves that the manager has the appropriate expertise and is undertaking his or her duties competently.[91] In the US, fiduciary liability under ERISA attaches not only to trustees but also to any person with discretionary authority over pension plan assets. However, trustees can remove their risk of personal liability under ERISA by hiring an investment manager, so long as the trustees act prudently in the appointment and retention of the investment manager.[92] Thus, the investment manager will be responsible for any unlawful acts or omissions in managing ERISA pension plans. Australia's Superannuation Industry (Supervision) Act of 1993 prevents a trustee from entering into an agreement that exempts a fund manager from liability for negligence.[93]

Pension fund investment disclosure rules

The fiduciary law context for pension plans has been coloured in some jurisdictions by obligations to disclose RI policies. While these duties don't alter the underlying fiduciary imperative, they may colour its interpretation. When the UK pioneered this reform, Russell Sparkes, a leading RI commentator, declared:

> It is my belief that history will consider the day the UK's RI pension fund regulations came into effect, 3 July 2000, as a momentous day in the evolution of investment management. It was a date of global rather than of local importance. For the first time ever, the building blocks of the world's capital markets were legally obliged to consider non-financial issues in setting their investment policy.[94]

The British initiative and comparable efforts in other nations aim to counter misguided perceptions among pension fund trustees that practising RI would necessarily breach their fiduciary responsibility. They also aim to raise awareness about ESG issues in order to stimulate demand for more responsible and ethical investments.[95]

Governance of RI relies increasingly on transparency-based regulation. While most legal experts don't consider disclosure to be a fiduciary duty

---

90 Section 33(1).
91 Section 34(4).
92 Section 3(38).
93 Section 116.
94 R. Sparkes, *Socially Responsible Investment: A Global Revolution*, Wiley, 2002, 4.
95 J. Donnan, 'Regulating ethical investment: disclosure under the Financial Services Reform Act', *Journal of Banking and Finance Law and Practice* 13(3), 2002, 155–74, 170 (discussing the equivalent provision in Australian legislation).

per se, fiduciaries are compelled to make disclosures in order 'to obtain their principals' consent to [any] self-interested activity'.[96] Disclosure in the context of investment activities is usually a matter of legislative requirements. In addition to revelation of pension fund investment policies, disclosure may be required of funds' proxy voting policies and voting records, and regular corporations may need to report on aspects of their sustainability performance. The general rationale is to redress information asymmetry and thereby enable a more efficient, informed market. Transparency regulation may encourage financial institutions to consider ESG issues and to ask pertinent questions of the firms in which they invest.[97] Public disclosure may also empower third parties such as NGOs to pressure investors and companies to act more responsibly. While there has been some industry resistance to these regulations, based on cost and perceived lack of utility, the investment community has generally been an advocate of enhanced corporate disclosure – as is evident in their support for the CDP.

The UK precedent was soon followed in several other European countries, as well as in Australia and New Zealand,[98] and similar initiatives have been proposed in some other jurisdictions, including Ontario, Canada. In July 1999, the UK government issued a regulation under the Pensions Act of 1995 requiring trustees to amend their statements of investment principles to declare '[t]he extent (if at all) to which social, environmental or ethical considerations are taken into account in the selection, retention, and realization of investments'.[99] The disclosure obligation extends to each fund's 'policy (if any) directing the exercise of the rights (including voting rights) attaching to investments'.[100] Germany mimicked the UK example in 2001 by requiring disclosure of RI policies in state and private sector pension plans and sellers of life insurance savings products[101] but exceeded the UK precedent by mandating disclosure of *how* any RI policy is implemented. French legislation since 2001 requires companies' pension plans to explain how they address

---

96 See D. Jensen, 'Prescription and proscription in fiduciary obligations', *Kings Law Journal* 21, 2010, 333–54, 339.
97 See D. Hess, 'Social reporting: a reflexive law approach to corporate social responsiveness', *Journal of Corporation Law* 25, 1999, 41–84.
98 B.J. Richardson, 'Pensions law reform and environmental policy: a new role for institutional investors?', *Journal of International Financial Markets: Law and Regulation* 3(5), 2002, 159–69.
99 Occupational Pension Schemes (Investment, and Assignment, Forfeiture, Bankruptcy etc.), Amendment Regulations, 1999, cl. 2(4). Now in the Occupational Pension Schemes (Investment) Regulations, 2005: cl. 2(3)(b)(vi)–(3)(c).
100 Ibid. A similar requirement was imposed on municipal pension funds: Local Government Pension Scheme (Management and Investment of Funds) (Amendment) Regulations, 1999.
101 Section 115, Part 4, VAG; Certification of Retirement Pension Contracts Act (AltZertG), s. 7(4); Versicherungsaufsichtsgesetz, s. 10a, abs. 1, appendix D, ch. III, 2(cc); Altersvorsorgevertraege-Zertifizierungsgesetz, s. 7, abs. 4; Gesetzesentwurf Alterseinkuenftegesetz, art. 5.

social, ethical and environmental issues.[102] Belgium's legislation of 2003 requires pension fund managers to disclose in their annual reports similar information.[103] Likewise, these precedents were soon adopted in Austria in 2005,[104] Italy in 2008[105] and Denmark in 2009.[106] Curiously, despite the spate of reforms in individual EU states, no equivalent provision was included in the EU Occupational Pensions Directive of 2003.[107]

In 2008 the New Zealand Government, acting under pressure from the Green Party, amended the KiwiSaver Act of 2006 to require providers of 'KiwiSaver' financial products to disclose whether or not they have a policy for RI, in order to enable investors to differentiate between funds that invest ethically and those that do not.[108] The KiwiSaver is an employment-based voluntary long-term savings scheme to encourage New Zealander workers to provide for their retirement.

In 2001, Australia mandated RI disclosures by superannuation funds, mutual funds and life insurance investment providers,[109] primarily in order to foster a market for RI products by providing investors with a form of quality assurance.[110] The Australian Conservation Foundation (ACF), one of the country's most important environmental NGOs, was a principal lobbyist for the reform.[111] It obliges funds in their 'product disclosure statements' (PDS) to explain 'the extent to which labour standards or environmental, social or ethical considerations are taken into account in the selection, retention or realization of the investment'.[112] Compliance with the legislation is enhanced by penalties for issuing a misleading PDS[113] and by accompanying regulations

---

102 Projet de loi sur l'épargne salariale, 7 February 2001, no. 2001-152, art. 21; Code monétaire et financier, art. L. 214-39.
103 Loi relative aux pensions complémentaires et au régime fiscal de celles-ci et de certains avantages complémentaires en matière de sécurité sociale, 28 April 2003, art. 42(3), Moniteur Belge, 15 May 2003.
104 Federal Act on the Establishment, Administration and Supervision of Pensionskassen, 1990, as amended in 2005, s. 25(a)1(6).
105 Decreto Legislativo, 5 December 2005, n. 252, art. 16(14).
106 Act amending the Danish Financial Statements Act (Årsregnskabsloven), 8 October 2008. s. 99a(1).
107 Directive 2003/41/EC of 3 June 2003, OJ L 235/10. The matter was considered during its drafting: European Parliament, Committee on Economic and Monetary Affairs, *Draft Report on the Proposal for a European Parliament and Council Directive on the Activities of Institutions for Occupational Retirement Provision*, PE 295.986/AM/48-134, 8 May 2001, 52.
108 Section 205A.
109 The changes were incorporated into the Corporations Act, 2001 (Cth).
110 G. Frost, et al., 'Bringing ethical investment to account', *Australian Accounting Review* 14(3), 2004, 3–9, 7.
111 M. Haigh and J. Guthrie, 'Management practices in Australasian ethical investment products: a role for regulation', *Business Strategy and the Environment* 19(3), 2010, 147–63, 150.
112 Corporations Act, 2001 (Cth), s. 1013D(1)(l); and B.J. Richardson, 'Ethical investment and the Commonwealth's Financial Services Reform Act 2001', *National Environmental Law Review* 2, 2002, 47–60.
113 Sections 1021D, 1021E and 1021F.

that require the PDS issuer to explain which ESG considerations it takes into account and how far it takes them into account in selecting, retaining or realizing an investment.[114] These measures are buttressed by the Australian Securities and Investments Commission (ASIC) regulatory guidelines, which expect an explanation of the criteria for measuring investment standards or considerations, a general description of whether adherence to the methodology is monitored, and an explanation of actions taken when a specific investment no longer adheres to the stated RI policy.[115]

While more transparent RI decision-making should enhance fiduciary accountability, the foregoing reforms have some limitations. First, most focus on disclosure of investment *policies* rather than investment *practices*. Beneficiaries of pension funds are not usually informed of the methodology behind RI-based portfolio selections. A requirement to disclose all steps taken to invest responsibly, as well as independently audited reports and sanctions for misleading statements, would help reduce perfunctory RI policy disclosures. Another deficiency is that the regulations don't define 'responsible investment'. While this omission may be reasonable given that pension funds aren't legally obliged to practise RI, the funds should at the very least justify *why* they view their investment policies as ethically responsible. Only the Australian regime attempts to address this problem. On the other hand, increased disclosure, as in the case of the more expansive Australian reform, has 'resulted in a more confusing state of affairs', as fund members become overwhelmed by the increased complexity of information they must interpret, resulting in their increased reliance on professional advice.[116]

The extent and quality of mandated disclosures to date provide grounds for such concerns. The UK reform has been the most extensively researched. Its effects do not appear to quite fulfill some observers' hope that it would spur a 'marked increase in the size and power of the SRI sector'.[117] While early surveys found a surge in pension fund RI policies,[118] by 2004 one credible study found that 'a gap has emerged between policy and practice'.[119] A 2006 FairPensions study of the 20 largest pension funds concluded: 'Only a handful of pension schemes show evidence of serious attempts to develop and disclose robust policies to tackle specific environmental, human rights, or governance

---

114 Corporations Regulations, 2001 (Cth), reg. 7.9.14C.
115 ASIC, *Section 1013DA Disclosure Guidelines*, ASIC, 2003; and *Policy Statement 168: Product Disclosure Statements*, ASIC, 2005.
116 J. Fear and G. Pace, 'Australia's "choice of fund" legislation: success or failure?', *Rotman International Journal of Pension Management* 2(2), 2009, 26–34, 31.
117 A. Friedman and S. Miles, 'Socially responsible investment and corporate social and environmental reporting in the UK: an exploratory study', *British Accounting Review* 33(4), 2001, 523–48, 523.
118 E. Mathieu, *Response of UK Pension Funds to the SRI Disclosure Regulation*, UKSIF, 2000; EIRIS, *How Responsible is Your Pension?* EIRIS, 2003.
119 C. Gribben and A. Faruk, *Will UK Pension Funds Become More Responsible? A Survey of Trustees – 2004*, UKSIF, 2004, 4.

problems within their investments.'[120] A later UKSIF survey learned that the proportion of respondent funds with a notional RI policy had increased to about 80 per cent in 2009 from 65 per cent in 2007.[121] Its 2010 study to mark the decennial anniversary of the UK reform found further evidence of incremental improvement in the incorporation of ESG analysis into pension plans.[122] Research on the implementation of the German disclosure rules found that approximately half the respondents in a 2008 study were 'taking into account' sustainability issues in their investment decisions and activities,[123] but 'some occupational pension providers still are not reporting on the (non-)use of ethical, social and ecological criteria. There are providers who were unaware of their reporting obligation until contacted to take part in this study.'[124] Research on the Australian disclosure regulation suggests it works best in reporting descriptions of investment selection strategies but not in other aspects of fund management.[125] An empirical study of its implementation from 2004 to 2007 found that most investor managers objected to the prescriptive reporting requirements, which were seen as too detailed and superfluous.[126]

One problem identified by these studies is the lacklustre monitoring of RI policy implementation by some trustees, who commonly delegate portfolio administration to fund managers, granting broad discretion to take RI issues 'into account' as the managers deem appropriate.[127] Many RI policies tend to be uninformative, boilerplate statements, conservatively couched with reference to fiduciary duties understood as demanding the best financial returns.[128] Also, a survey by the Australian Council of Superannuation Investors (ACSI) cautioned that '[m]any funds felt that they did not yet have enough skills or resources to consider ESG issues',[129] and because they

---

120 FairPensions, *UK Pension Scheme Transparency on Social, Environmental and Ethical Issues*, FairPensions, 2006, i.
121 UKSIF, *How the Pension Funds of the UK's Corporate Responsibility Leaders are Approaching Responsible Investment*, UKSIF, 2009.
122 UKSIF, *Focused on the Future: 2000–2010 Celebrating Ten Years of Responsible Investment Disclosure by UK Occupational Pension Funds*, UKSIF, 2010.
123 Fortis Investments and Federal Environmental Ministry of Germany, *Occupational Pensions and Sustainable Investments in Germany*, Federal Environmental Ministry of Germany, 2008, 9.
124 Ibid., 12.
125 E. Banasik, M. Barut and L. Kloot, 'Socially responsible investment: labour standards and environmental, social and ethical disclosures within the SRI industry', *Australian Accounting Review* 20(4), 2010, 387–99.
126 Haigh and Guthrie, op. cit., 158–60.
127 D. Wheeler and J. Thomson, *Comparative Study of U.K. and Canadian Pension Fund Transparency Practices*, NRTEE, 2004, 20.
128 See, e.g., South Yorkshire Pensions Authority (SYPA), *Statement of Investment Principles as at 1 July 2006*, SYPA, 2006, cl. 7; British Broadcasting Corporation (BBC), *Statement of Investment Principles: BBC Pension Scheme*, BBC, 2006, cl. 6.2. But there are exceptions, such as the more detailed and prescriptive RI policy of the Universities Superannuation Scheme: *Statement of Investment Principles*, 2011.
129 Australian Council of Superannuation Investors (ACSI), *The ESG Survey Report*, ACSI, 2007, 1.

commonly pooled their investments into other trust funds managed externally, they felt unable to dictate to those fund managers how they should incorporate ESG considerations.[130] Overall, perhaps the main benefit of disclosure reforms has been to shift investment funds from not doing anything – believing that their fiduciary duties constrain them – to acknowledging that ESG issues can be taken into account. The debate in the pension sector is shifting from 'whether' to 'how' to practise RI.

In addition to legal measures to improve the provision of information to pension plan beneficiaries, in some cases further rights to be consulted or participate in fund governance are available, as examined next.

Involvement of beneficiaries in fund governance

Policy considerations

The appropriate level of involvement that plan members should have in fund governance is contentious. If we expect financial institutions to account for the social and environmental sequelae of their investments, then the ultimate owners of capital should have more say in investment decisions. Because RI can involve complex ethical issues that are characterized by widespread social disagreement, it may benefit from decision-making procedures that foster informed dialogue. Furthermore, intelligent judgements about what is environmentally sustainable conduct sometimes hinge on specific circumstances to which blanket, generic standards alone don't supply answers. Where a case-by-case approach is needed, beneficiaries may have something useful to say about the values at stake. For pension funds, as explained shortly, there are additional reasons for more consultative decision-making. On the other hand, relevant academic research doubts that beneficiary representation in pension plans would improve financial returns, suggesting that good pension fund governance depends on proper motivation and investment management expertise.[131]

'Participation' by beneficiaries may be conceptualized as spanning a ladder of escalating levels of involvement. The lowest rung offers informational rights about investment policies, decisions and other actions – often a necessary precondition to higher levels of engagement. Higher on the ladder are opportunities to be consulted and to advise trustees and fund managers. At the apex is the right to nominate or elect beneficiary representatives to governing boards. Beyond individual financial organizations, participation of representatives of beneficiaries and non-investor stakeholders could occur in various forms in industry networks and supervisory regimes, such as the UNPRI and UNEP-FI, as well as in government regulation-making processes.

130 Ibid., 2.
131 See the articles in 'Effective pension governance: new insights and research findings', *Rotman International Journal of Pension Management* 1, 2008, 1–71.

So far, the RI industry hasn't been enthusiastic about democratizing its own affairs, even though it demands greater openness and accountability from its portfolio companies. It emphasizes that consideration of ESG issues requires 'expert' analysis and dedicated full-time professionals – a stance that marginalizes the views of beneficiaries and other stakeholders, and assumes that ethical dilemmas can be reformulated as merely financial and technical challenges to master. And the tendency of institutional funds to outsource asset management to external providers, often by pooling their assets with many other funds, further removes beneficiaries from investment decisions.

Of all financial entities, occupational pension funds are the most obvious candidate for accommodating the democratic imperative. Because they invest the savings of ordinary workers and because the employment relationship suggests workplace decisions should extend to employees' retirement funds, some commentators argue that pension plan decisions should be democratized as a means to promote development that provides collateral benefits for workers' communities.[132] Because 'exit' from a pension trust isn't an easy option for beneficiaries compared to the flexible position of corporate shareholders, having 'voice' within the pension plan becomes correspondingly more significant. The importance of linking democratic decision-making to RI is recognized in France in the certification given to a range of pension investment products by the Comité intersyndical de l'épargne salariale.[133] The certification criteria include a requirement that employee representatives have a majority of members in the accredited fund's governance structures.

A further reason for enhancing the voice of beneficiaries is that pension plans are increasingly offered only on a defined contribution (DC) rather than defined benefit (DB) basis, which shifts the financial risks to beneficiaries. Between 1979 and 2005, the proportion of retirement plans in the US offered as DB declined from 62 per cent to 10 per cent, while correspondingly DC plans rose from 16 per cent to 63 per cent.[134] (The remaining comprised hybrid plans with a mix of defined benefit and contribution.) Applicable OECD guidelines recommend that beneficiaries of DC plans choose their own investment options.[135] Canadian pension law expert Ron Davis believes that

---

132 J. Gates, *The Ownership Solution: Toward a Shared Capitalism for the 21st Century*, Addison-Wesley Publishing, 1998; A. Fung, T. Hebb, and J. Rogers (eds), *Working Capital: The Power of Labor's Pensions*, Cornell University Press, 2001; T. Ghilarducci, *Labor's Capital: The Economics and Politics of Private Pensions*, MIT Press, 1992; Hebb, *No Small Change*, op. cit.

133 G. Bourque, 'L'épargne salariale en France et l'initiative du Comité intersyndical de l'épargne salariale (CIES)', *Vie economique* 1(2), 2007.

134 US Department of Labor, *Form 5500 Summary Report*, Department of Labor, 2004, quoted by Employee Benefit Research Institute (EBRI), 'Retirement trends in the United States over the past quarter-century', EBRI, June 2007.

135 OECD, *Recommendation on Core Principles of Occupational Pension Regulation*, 21 July 2004, 5.16, 5.24 and 5.27.

plan beneficiaries are entirely capable of making such choices, as well as contributing more generally to RI policy-making:

> [They] are primarily adults [and] ... are clearly capable of listening to reasoned advice and deciding on an appropriate policy. In addition, the types of decisions at issue – the corporate governance policies that should determine how proxy votes attached to the fund's investments should be exercised – are not decisions to which a particular form of specialized expertise is required.[136]

The main countervailing argument to beneficiary activism is the risk of politicizing decisions and hurting investment returns.[137] Jon Entine, perhaps the staunchest of such critics, quips that 'union members and social liberals have been most active in trying to use the pension system to promote pet causes'.[138] In addition, Canadian researchers have observed that beneficiary nominated 'trustees ... face many challenges acquiring the skills, knowledge and networks to assist them in becoming active and integrated participants on the pension board'.[139] A beneficiary representative may have views about ethical investing but lack sufficient expertise about actual investment management.

This debate about the societal function and governance of pension plans dates at least to the 1970s, when Peter Drucker heralded the US as the world's first 'socialist' country because its workers, through their pension plans, were acquiring a dominant stake in American businesses.[140] Through that voice, he reasoned there would be a shift from immediate profit-making to long-term investment of social benefit to workers and their communities. Yet Drucker downplayed several complications of pension fund governance. Corporate management typically appoints the trustees to pension plans.[141] Those managers, explains Davis, 'have little or no interest in encouraging the practice of active intervention by pension fund trustees in corporate governance'.[142] Furthermore, pension plan administration has become outsourced and highly concentrated in the hands of investment banks and insurance companies, creating agency problems for beneficiaries who wish to exercise oversight.[143]

---

136 Davis, op. cit., 67.
137 R. Hannah, 'The control of pensions: a brief history and possibilities for the future', *Management Decision* 40(10), 2002, 938–46, 943; D. Hess, 'Protecting and politicizing public pension fund assets: empirical evidence on the effects of governance structures and practices', *University of California Davis Law Review* 39(1), 2005, 187–224, 199.
138 J. Entine, 'The politicization of public investments' in J. Entine (ed.), *Pension Fund Politics: The Dangers of Socially Responsible Investing*, AEI Press, 1–12, 8.
139 J. Weststar and A. Verma, 'What makes for effective labor representation on pension boards?', *Labor Studies Journal 32(4)*, 2007, 382–410.
140 P. Drucker, *Unseen Revolution: How Pension Fund Socialism Came to America*, Heinemann, 1976.
141 J. Rifkin and R. Barber, *The North will Rise Again: Pensions, Politics and Power in the 1980s*, Beacon Press, 1978, 104–9.
142 R. Davis, *Democratizing Pension Funds: Corporate Governance and Accountability*, UBC Press, 2009, 55.
143 See R. Minns, 'The social ownership of capital', *New Left Review* 21, 1996, 42–61, 48; R. Blackburn, 'The new collectivism: pension reform, grey capitalism and complex socialism', *New Left Review* 233, 1999, 3–65, 5.

In practice, beneficiaries' views often carry scant weight in fund administration,[144] including the consideration of ESG issues.[145] A 2005 survey of UK pension trustees revealed that 53 per cent of respondents attached 'no significance' and only 13 per cent attached 'great significance' to the views of their members when considering ESG issues.[146] Conversely, 39 per cent attached 'great significance' to the views of their investment consultants. Another study of UK pension plan trustees conducted in 2005 found 'about 80% of trustees indicated that they rarely or never sought beneficiaries' views' on RI matters.[147] The most democratically-managed pension plans tend to be in the public sector,[148] especially those managed jointly by workers and employers.[149] Many private funds have boards that include senior executives whose main concerns are bolstering their position in the company and the solvency of the fund. Their investment strategy is largely deferred to consultants, and any interest in ESG issues likely depends on perceptions of their financial, not ethical, significance.[150]

Whether democratizing fund governance engenders RI is debatable on current evidence. Are beneficiaries more likely to demand RI if their voice carries greater weight? The current anecdotal evidence suggests a modest correlation. More democratic funds sometimes appear to be at the forefront of RI. Research on US public pension plans and urban revitalization coordinated by Harvard and Oxford Universities documented many examples of investors partnering with community development associations and local financial intermediaries to promote urban renewal and local economic improvement.[151] Tessa Hebb's study of pension fund engagement in North America found that public sector funds such as CalPERS were more committed than their private counterparts to engage with companies on RI issues, partly because of the greater presence of member-nominated trustees and trade union influence in pension plan governance.[152] Other studies, however, point to the vast majority of public pension funds remaining 'rationally apathetic' and leaving engagement with companies and other RI initiatives in the hands of a few

---

144 G.S. Alexander, 'Pensions and passivity', *Law and Contemporary Problems* 56(1), 1993, 111–39, 113.
145 E. Caerlewy-Smith, G.L Clark and J.C. Marshall, 'Agitation, resistance, and reconciliation with respect to socially responsible investment: the attitudes of UK pension trustees and Oxford undergraduates', *Environment and Planning* 38, 2006, 1585–9.
146 C. Gribben and M. Gitsham, *Will UK Pension Funds Become More Responsible: A Survey of Trustees*, UKSIF, 2006, 14.
147 E. Caerlewy-Smith, et al., op. cit., 1586.
148 S. Waygood, *Capital Market Campaigning: The Impact of NGOs on Companies, Shareholder Value and Reputational Risk*, Risk Books, 2005 (discussing the USS).
149 M. O'Connor, 'Labor's role in the shareholder revolution', in *Working Capital*, op. cit., 67–92, 69.
150 See Clark and Knight, op. cit.
151 Http://urban.ouce.ox.ac.uk/research.php. See especially G. Clark, T. Hebb and L. Hagerman, *U.S. Public Sector Pension Funds and Urban Revitalization: An Overview of Policy and Programs*, Oxford University Centre for the Environment, 2004.
152 Hebb, *No Small Change*, op. cit.

institutional activists.[153] An earlier Canadian study on the impact of union representation in pension funds found 'some evidence that union involvement is facilitative of social investment'.[154] On the other hand, US research suggests that the presence of beneficiary-nominated trustees has not affected the plans' investment returns.[155]

Legal reforms to democratize pension fund governance

From a fiduciary and trusts law perspective, beneficiaries' involvement in fund governance has potential consequences. As already explained in Chapter 3, traditional legal rules in this area generally do not accommodate an active role for beneficiaries – the fiduciary relationship assumes beneficiaries are passive. Furthermore, the fiduciary duty of impartiality limits the scope for practising RI when beneficiaries disagree about investment strategy.

By providing for representation of beneficiaries in fund governance, however, it might no longer be necessary for trustees to find a consensus of opinion among beneficiaries in order to practise RI. Through beneficiaries' representatives, such issues could be considered and ultimately acted upon by the governing board. In an ordinary trust, the trustees cannot make decisions unless they are unanimous, but legislation commonly allows trustees to make decisions by a majority vote. For instance, the UK's Pensions Act of 1995 provides that '[d]ecisions of the trustees of a trust scheme may, unless the scheme provides otherwise, be taken by agreement of a majority of the trustees'.[156] Being a beneficiary representative, however, does not under trusts law allow a trustee to consider herself an *agent* of the beneficiaries, acting only on their instructions. *Cowan v. Scargill* held that trustees who could be considered as having been appointed in a representative capacity would violate their duties if, instead of applying their minds independently to a fiduciary issue that was before them, they submissively followed a policy decision of the body (in this case, the National Union of Mineworkers) that they themselves might be regarded as representing.[157] Robert Megarry V.C. rejected the suggestion that the defendants' impugned investment policy could be justified because it was consistent with the majority views of a representative body of beneficiaries, as expressed by the investment policy adopted by their union at their annual conference.

Several jurisdictions have legislated for beneficiaries' representation on pension fund boards. Britain amended its Pensions Act in 2004 to prescribe

---

153 V. Ho, '"Enlightened shareholder value": corporate governance beyond the shareholder-stakeholder divide', *Journal of Corporation Law* 36(1), 2010, 598–111.
154 J. Quarter, et al., 'Special investment by union-based pension funds and labour-sponsored investment funds in Canada', *Industrial Relations* 56(1), 2001, 92–113, 108.
155 Cited by Davis, op. cit., 72.
156 Section 32(1).
157 (1985) Ch. 270, 293.

that 'at least one third' of the trustees must be 'member-nominated',[158] and the government may enact regulations to raise this number to one half of member-nominated trustees.[159] Australia's Superannuation Industry (Supervision) Act of 1993 mandates 50 per cent member representation on trustee boards of funds that have at least five members.[160] Often their representatives on trustee boards are not, in fact, elected by beneficiaries but rather nominated by third-party organizations such as trade unions, and members in retirement aren't represented at all – a situation that led the 2010 Cooper Review to recommend removing this legislative requirement.[161] Canadian governments have also established some mechanisms for member participation in pension plan governance. Quebec law requires an elected pension committee, separate from the employer-administered plan unit, with some decision-making authority.[162] Another legislative model is the joint, union–employer trusteeship of public sector pension schemes, such as provided for by British Columbia's Public Sector Pension Plan Act.[163] Among other jurisdictions, South African law mandates at least 50 per cent member representation on trustee boards,[164] while Brazilian legislation stipulates mandatory employee representatives to make up between one third and one half of the governing organs of public and private pension funds.[165] In the US, while many public sector funds, especially state and municipal government plans, have various provisions for member representation in governing boards and other functions, corporate sector plans under ERISA do not provide equivalent rights, apart from allowing beneficiaries to be appointed as trustees if the underlying trust or plan instrument allows for such appointment.[166]

Some governments have also enacted legislation that allows beneficiaries to choose the investment portfolio that best matches their ethical and financial preferences. Australia's Superannuation Legislation Amendment (Choice of Superannuation Funds) Act of 2004 gives employees the right to choose the fund into which their compulsory superannuation contributions are paid.[167] The reform aimed to increase market competition in the pension fund sector by allowing members to choose providers offering lower fees and better returns. But the scheme hasn't elicited much response, with only about 10 per cent of Australian workers choosing funds other than their employers' default funds; and most switching has been passive, such as when an employee

---

158 Section 241(1)(a).
159 Section 243(1).
160 Sections 52, 58, 89, 101, 107.
161 J. Cooper, *Super System Review: Final Report*, Commonwealth of Australia, 2010, 31.
162 Supplemental Pension Plans Act, 2001, SQ, s. 147.
163 SBC, 1999.
164 Pension Funds Act, 1956, as amended, s. 7A.
165 Lei Complementar No. 109 (2001), Capítulo III, art. 31; Lei Complementar No. 108 (2001), Capítulo III, art. 9.
166 Section 403(a); Hannah, op. cit., 943.
167 Part 3A.

changes jobs.[168] In the US, most private sector DC plans also offer a variety of investment options, pursuant to the 'section 401(k)' retirement savings plans allowed as a tax benefit under the Internal Revenue Code.[169] Under this arrangement, an employee requests that her employer pay a predetermined portion of the employee's earnings into an individual 'plan' account, which may be matched by the employer. These individual plans, which are usually bundled together and managed by external providers, may be provided to workers covered by ERISA. The plan beneficiaries may choose among the fund options arranged by the employer or its external plan provider.[170] Neither is, however, obliged to offer a specific menu or quantity of investment options beyond the minimum of no less than three investment options with 'materially different risk and return characteristics'. A typical 401(k) plan may offer 20 or more investment choices, including RI portfolios.[171]

Financial trustees may also be subjected to a statutory duty to consult with their beneficiaries when formulating investment policies. In one of the few legislative mandates for RI, Ontario's former South African Trust Investments Act of 1988 provided that in the case of pension funds with at least 100 beneficiaries, the trustees could refuse to acquire or dispose of a South African investment once they had made inquiries and had reasonable grounds for believing that most beneficiaries would consent and that they held a majority of the beneficial interests in the pension fund's assets. In other trusts law contexts, legislation has also sometimes intervened to require consultation with beneficiaries. In Britain, the Trusts of Land and Appointment of Trustees Act of 1996 requires trustees to consult with beneficiaries when exercising specified functions.[172] The concept of a 'duty to consult' in fiduciary law has been most strongly developed by Canadian courts in the context of the government's obligations to Aboriginal peoples. Courts hold the duty arises when the government (federal or provincial) contemplates conduct that might adversely affect Aboriginal rights.[173] A duty to consult, however, is not tantamount to a duty to accommodate; trustees who are required to ascertain the views of beneficiaries do not necessarily have to give effect to their wishes.

How beneficiary participation in fund governance might be strengthened is discussed further in this book's final chapter. At this stage we should note that it is preferable to give beneficiaries more formal opportunities to be heard than to rely on informal, less transparent and unaccountable arrangements. Strengthening their voice by legal rights, either to be consulted or to be represented on boards, provides a concrete mechanism to convey their

168 Fear and Pace, op. cit., 29.
169 (201) 26 USC, s. 401(k).
170 A. Landier and V.B. Nair, *Investing for Change: Profit from Responsible Investment*, Oxford University Press, 2009, 25.
171 S. Morgan, '401(k) plans get responsible', http://www.smartmoney.com/invest/funds/401k-plans-get-responsible-1318458228287.
172 Section 11.
173 D. Newman, *The Duty to Consult: New Relationships with Aboriginal Peoples*, Purich, 2009.

views and to enable trustees to make investment decisions legitimated by the imprimatur of the democratic process. This could even facilitate ethical deliberation to guide RI decisions. Such an approach would herald a significant evolution in the nature of the fiduciary relationship, away from the traditionally subservient role of beneficiaries. However, it would be naïve to expect that democratization of pension plans alone would necessarily be transformative because beneficiaries may be apathetic or feel unqualified to participate. One piece of evidence is that in DC plans that offer participants a range of investment fund options to select, the vast majority of 'selections' tend to be in the default, conventional fund designated by the employer.[174] A proper social debate about the ethics of RI and the sustainability of financial markets might also need to be supported through other institutions, such as revamping multi-stakeholder forums governing the UNPRI, Equator Principles and other RI codes, as well as in government regulatory processes such as ethics councils to oversee investing by public funds such as sovereign wealth funds.

Charitable 'mission-based' investors

A trust structure is often used by charities for investing, and some such charities hold substantial assets to devote to their mandate. Charities may see RI as a means of advancing their philanthropic mandate. 'Mission-based investing', as this RI niche is commonly known, 'means that a charity uses some of its investment assets . . . in ways that accomplish its investment objectives while also supporting its charitable mission'.[175] Charitable funds commonly take the form of foundations managed by boards of trustees, and they may be associated with universities, environmental organizations or community groups. Unlike other forms of RI, which typically have a more multi-dimensional scope, mission-based investing tends to focus narrowly on a few issues connected with the specific charitable purpose at hand. Few charitable investors, however, appear to practise RI. A US study of 72,000 foundations found that less than 1 per cent of their investments were directly aligned with their missions.[176] Indeed, a few years ago the behemoth Gates Foundation allegedly had an estimated US$8.7 billion of its assets invested in companies acting contrary to the foundation's charitable goals or philosophy.[177] Customarily, charities relied on gifting grants as the principal way to support

---

174 Watson Wyatt Worldwide Thinking Ahead Group, 'The default dilemma: when DC members can not or will not choose an investment option', *Watson Wyatt Perspective*, Winter 2009, 37–8.
175 S.N. Gary, 'Is it prudent to be responsible? The legal rules for charities that engage in socially responsible investing and mission investing', *Northwestern Journal of Law and Social Policy* 6(1), 2011, 106–29, 111.
176 M. Kramer, 'Foundation trustees need a new investment approach', *Chronicle of Philanthropy* 18(11), 2006, 43–4, 43.
177 C. Piller, E. Sanders and R. Dixon, 'Dark cloud over good works of Gates Foundation', *Los Angeles Times*, 7 January 2007, A1.

their missions, while regarding their investment portfolios solely as means to finance grants.

The principal quandary for charitable investors is how to reconcile the need to maximize their revenue to support philanthropic aims with selecting investments that ethically dovetail with their mission. The duty to fulfill the charitable purpose reflects the previously discussed duty of obedience to a trust deed, a key constituent of fiduciary responsibility. A charity dedicated to animal welfare might be tempted by lucrative investments in drug testing companies, but following through on such investments could compromise its ethical mission. The latter position is more consistent with the fiduciary duty of loyalty to the purpose of the charitable trust, while the former approach is more aligned with the duty of care to invest prudently. But choosing to focus on the most profitable investments could backfire and hurt the financial standing of the charity if it incurs bad publicity that puts off potential benefactors. Unpalatable examples of this would be a charity that promotes peace investing in a weapons manufacturer, or a cancer-fighting charity holding stock in a tobacco producer. The British Red Cross, to illustrate, was lampooned in the press for allegedly holding stocks in armaments traders.[178]

Little case law addresses investment management by charities. Guidance from the American Law Institute's restatement of trusts law advises that a trustee can consider a charitable purpose as a factor in making investment decisions:

> [S]ocial considerations may be taken into account in investing the funds of charitable trusts to the extent the charitable purposes would justify an expenditure of trust funds for the social issue or cause in question or to the extent the investment decision can be justified on grounds of advancing, financially or operationally, a charitable activity conducted by the trust.[179]

Other guidance on the prudential standard governing charitable investing provided by the Uniform Prudent Investment Act confirms that a trustee may consider a number of factors, including the charitable purpose and the non-financial preferences of a beneficiary.[180] But 'if an investment has a below-market return or carries a high level of risk, the investment may not be prudent'.[181] Donors to a charity may also influence the interplay between these fiduciary duties. Their donation to the charity may be subject to directions about how the charity should invest the donated monies.

---

178 A. Penman, 'Red Cross unloads guns', *Mirror*, 28 February 1997, 11.
179 American Law Institute (ALI), *Restatement of the Law Third, Trusts*, ALI, 2007, s. 90.
180 Section 2(a)–(c); see also R.A. Brand, 'Investment duties of trustees of charitable trusts and directors of nonprofit corporations: applying the law to investments that acknowledge social and moral concerns', *Arizona State Law Journal*, 1986, 631–89.
181 Gary, op. cit., 120.

The state Attorney-General is typically responsible for enforcing the governance of a charity, including its investment activities. Unlike other institutional investors considered in this chapter, charities are legally unique in that they do not have a specific, identifiable class of beneficiaries to whom they are accountable. Instead, the 'beneficiary may be a charitable purpose or an indefinite number of unidentified beneficiaries'.[182] Some US case law suggests private persons having a special interest in the performance of a charitable trust can sue for its enforcement if they can show 'their interest is not merely derived from their status as members of the general public' or if they are 'entitled to preference under the terms of the trust, is a member of a small class of identifiable beneficiaries, or to receive certain trust benefits'.[183]

In the important English case of *Scott v. National Trust*, the High Court dismissed an application brought by several hunters and farmers for judicial review of the National Trust's plans to ban deer hunting with hounds on its trust lands.[184] The Court acknowledged that the National Trust exercised public functions and that its decisions were amenable to judicial review; and also that the applicants had a sufficient interest to seek judicial review. Further, by enacting section 33 of the Charities Act 1993, which allows 'persons interested' to bring proceedings with the permission of the Charity Commissioners, the Court affirmed that Westminster had not intended to allow the Attorney-General to monopolize proceedings for judicial monitoring of charities. However, in this case the Charity Commissioners had not granted permission, and the High Court would not otherwise allow the applicants to circumvent that to bring judicial review.

Donors are also not typically involved in the governance of investments by charitable foundations. However, some jurisdictions such as California 'allow for some donor involvement in the fiduciary oversight process by granting a donor access to the courts to seek the removal of a trustee for breach of fiduciary duty – for example, the social investment of the trust property'.[185] In the American case of *Carl J. Herzog Foundation, Inc. v. University of Bridgeport*, it was found that the Herzog Foundation, having not expressly reserved the right to enforce the terms of a US$250,000 gift to the University, lacked standing to bring suit to recover a portion of the grant that was designated for nursing education scholarships but that, it claimed, the University had used for another purpose.[186] Thus the Supreme Court of Connecticut affirmed that otherwise only the Attorney-General or a person with a special interest in the enforcement of a trust could maintain a suit.

---

182 Ibid., 112.
183 C.E. Rounds Jr, 'Why social investing threatens public pension funds, charitable trusts, and the social security trust fund', in J. Entine (ed.), *Pension Fund Politics: The Dangers of Socially Responsible Investing*, AEI Press, 2005, 56–76, 69.
184 *Scott and others v. National Trust for Places of Historic Interest or Natural Beauty and another*, [1998] 2 All ER 705.
185 Rounds, op. cit., 60, referring to California Pub. Code, s. 15642 (West. 1991).
186 (1997) 243 Conn. 1,699 A.2d 995.

Financial corporations: fiduciary responsibility and enlightened shareholder value

Several types of financial organizations take a corporate form: banks, as well as some insurance firms and mutual funds. Hence, we must enquire how fiduciary responsibility arises specifically in the corporate context. In many jurisdictions there has been increasing convergence between financial and nonfinancial firm governance, though some differences remain – for instance, banks and insurance companies are often restricted from obtaining a substantial equity stake in any other company. There are also salient differences between fiduciary responsibility in corporations, whether financial or nonfinancial, and pension funds. Unlike pension plan trustees, who simply serve a fund's beneficiaries, directors of a company must be cognizant of more interests. Corporations are embedded in a more complex array of relationships involving the workforce, customers, creditors and other third parties. The following discussion canvasses corporate governance generally before looking specifically at banks and insurance companies.

A longstanding academic debate has considered whether and how corporations should accommodate the needs of these other stakeholders, in addition to those of their shareholders.[187] In Anglo-American systems of corporate governance, managers and directors have a fiduciary duty to act in good faith in the best interests of the firm,[188] although in practice courts tend to assume this means the general body of shareholders rather than the company as an entity outside and apart from its investors.[189] Related fiduciary obligations to this core duty are to avoid conflicts of interest and to act for a proper purpose. Directors and managers also have a separate statutory duty of care, which may be owed to a range of parties with whom the corporation interacts with or affects.[190] Corporate bondholders and other lenders are not seen as owed a fiduciary duty, except perhaps when a firm is financially parlous.[191] The standard objection to extending fiduciary responsibility to other stakeholders is that corporate decision-making might become an

---

187 S. Worthington, 'Reforming directors' duties', *Modern Law Review* 64, 2001, 439–58; C. Francis, '*Peoples Department Stores Inc. v. Wise*: the expanded scope of directors' and officers' fiduciary duties and duties of care', *Canadian Business Law Journal* 41, 2005, 175–83; R.E. Freeman, 'The politics of stakeholder theory: some future directions', *Business Ethics Quarterly* 4, 1994, 409–41.
188 See *Peoples Department Stores v. Wise*, [2004] 3 SCR 461; and Australia's Corporations Act 2001 (Cth), ss. 180–1.
189 E.g., *Greenhalgh v. Arderne Cinemas Ltd*, [1951] Ch. 286. The interests of shareholders and the company may conflict when a company's board adopts defences to takeovers: *Unocal Corp. v. Mesa Petroleum Company*, (1985) 493 A.2d 946 (Del.).
190 L.P.Q. Johnson and D. Millon, 'Recalling why corporate officers are fiduciaries', *William and Mary Law Review* 46, 2005, 1597–653.
191 The standard reason given is that creditors have no ownership interest in a debtor-corporation's assets while the corporation is solvent. Instead, they have contractual rights: T.R. Hurst and L.J. McGuiness, 'The corporation, the bondholder and fiduciary duties', *Journal of Law and Commerce* 10, 1991, 187–217.

arbitrary balancing of many interests that could create opportunities for self-interested decisions by directors or senior managers emboldened by greater discretionary power.

Of particular importance to social investors has been the emergence of 'enlightened shareholder value' (ESV) as a doctrinal framework for addressing these challenges. Since the early 1990s, a growing number of developed and emerging market countries have enacted corporate governance codes or legislation that reflect ESV. It has relevance for social investors mostly in relation to the governance component of ESG. It may give some space for non-shareholder constituencies in corporate governance, though with some limitations.[192] The stakeholders that companies are asked to consider generally do not ordinarily have legal standing to have their interests considered and protected.

Europe has been quite receptive of ESV, perhaps because of its tradition of stakeholder corporate governance.[193] In Germany, France and a number of other continental EU member states, companies have tended to be conceived as 'industrial partnerships' in which management accommodates a network of interests, including creditors and workers, with an emphasis on consensus decision-making and long-term economic goals.[194] The EU has also spoken of the need for enlightened corporate governance as part of its efforts to promote sustainable development. The 2003 Communication on Corporate Governance from the European Commission remarked that 'well managed companies, with strong corporate governance records and sensitive social and environmental performance, out-perform their competitors'.[195] These ideas have also inspired some social investor lobbyists and researchers to enshrine ESV as a new legal yardstick for fiduciary responsibility for pension plans and other non-corporate funds.[196]

More stringent legal standards for corporate disclosure of ESG performance have been the main measure adopted in the EU to support CSR. The EU's 2003 Accounts Modernization Directive commits each company to prepare 'a fair review of the development and performance of the company's business and of its position, together with a description of the principal risks and

---

192 C.A. Williams and J.M. Conley, 'An emerging third way? The erosion of the Anglo-American shareholder value construct', *Cornell International Law Journal* 38, 2005, 493–551.
193 K.J. Hopt, 'Common principles of corporate governance in Europe?', in J.A. McCahery, et al. (eds), *Corporate Governance Regimes: Convergence and Diversity*, Oxford University Press, 2002 (discussing German corporations), 175–204.
194 M. Gerlach, *Alliance Capitalism: The Social Organization of Japanese Business*, University of California Press, 1992; J. Edwards, et al., 'Corporate governance in Germany: the role of banks and ownership concentration', *Economic Policy* 15(31), 2000, 237–67.
195 Communication from the Commission to the Council and the European Parliament, *Modernising Company Law and Enhancing Corporate Governance in the European Union: A Plan to Move Forward*, COM (2003) 284 final, 3.
196 FairPensions, *The Enlightened Shareholder: Clarifying Investors' Fiduciary Duties*, FairPensions, 2011.

uncertainties that it faces' in its annual report.[197] Further, it requires that 'to the extent necessary for an understanding of the company's activities' the review 'shall include ... where appropriate, nonfinancial key performance indicators relevant to the particular business, including information relating to environmental and employee matters'.[198]

Among individual EU member states, the UK has codified ESV in its Companies Act of 2006. Section 172(1) provides that '[a] director of a company must act in the way he considers, in good faith, would be most likely to promote the success of the company for the benefit of its members as a whole, and in doing so have regard' to community, environmental and other itemized considerations. As well, the legislation requires directors to report on implementation of this duty in their annual business reviews.[199] Although Cynthia Williams and John Conley herald the UK innovation as 'close to a stakeholder model of director's duties',[200] other commentators caution that it is 'very different from CSR where the company is motivated by responsibilities towards external stakeholders'.[201] While the codified directors' duties explicitly acknowledge factors that had previously been implied for fostering the long-term success of a company, section 172 is drafted in a manner that limits its utility. The opening clause suggests a personal and subjective judgement, despite the subsequent confusing reference to the more objective 'good faith' standard. Both *Re Southern Counties Fresh Foods Ltd*[202] and *People & Planet v. HM Treasury*[203] emphasized this subjective test and thus framed the question as whether the directors acted in a manner they personally believed would promote the companies' success. Also, in *Iesini v. Westrip Holdings*, it was noted that courts were not in the best position to weigh the relevant considerations under section 172 except in unambiguous cases, as those judgements are essentially of a commercial nature best made by directors.[204] These views largely reflect judicial attitude prior to the enactment of section 172.[205] The UK Department for Business, Innovation and Skills in late 2009 commissioned a study to evaluate awareness of and compliance with the Companies Act and found that the new directors' duty was not well understood and hadn't resulted in momentous behavioural

---

197 Directive 2003/51, art. 1, 14(a), 2003 OJ L 178, 18. Member states may exempt small and medium enterprises from these disclosure obligations.
198 Ibid.
199 Section 417.
200 C.A. Williams and J.M. Conley, 'Triumph or tragedy: the curious path of corporate disclosure reform in the UK', *William and Mary Environmental Law and Policy Review* 31(2), 2007, 317–61, 354.
201 Clark and Knight, op. cit., 277.
202 [2008] EWHC 2810.
203 [2009] EWHC 3020.
204 [2009] EWHC 2526; [2010] BCC 420.
205 N. Okoye, 'The BIS review and section 172 of the Companies Act 2006: what manner of clarity is needed?', *Company Lawyer* 33(1), 2012, 15–16, 15.

changes among company directors.²⁰⁶ A 2011 study for the Association of Chartered Certified Accountants (ACCA) also concluded that section 172 has had minimal behavioural impact.²⁰⁷

Conversely, Gordon Clark and Eric Knight contend that the seminal feature of the Companies Act is its enhanced environmental disclosure obligations in the annual business review, which they believe improves market pricing of corporate securities and facilitates institutional investors' capacity to engage with companies on ESG issues.²⁰⁸ Largely adopted to implement the EU Modernisation Directive, section 417(2) of the Companies Act requires directors, not the company, to compile a business review 'to inform members of the company and help them assess how the directors have performed their duty under section 172'. The section elaborates on factors to review, including the impacts of the company's business on the environment, its employees, and social and community issues. Clark and Knight interpret the UK reform as aimed at protecting shareholder rather than stakeholder interests, as the government was 'largely motivated by a conviction that environmental and social information had a clear link to stock market pricing and future financial performance'.²⁰⁹

By contrast, corporate law in the US, which remains heavily wedded to the management-friendly Delaware model, has generally not touched directors' duties. However, many states have enacted so-called 'constituency statutes' that allow directors to take the interests of employees and other specified stakeholders into account when making certain policy decisions, such as during a business takeover.²¹⁰ Since the 1980s, over half of US state governments have passed such laws, which mostly allow but do not mandate consideration of stakeholder interests. Of these permissive statutes, some allow directors to take into account how their decisions 'affect' stakeholders, whilst others authorize directors to consider the 'interests' of stakeholders. Only two states, Connecticut and Arizona, have mandatory statutes that require directors to heed the interests of non-shareholder constituencies.²¹¹ Another innovation comes from Oregon, which in 2007 amended its Business Corporations Act to permit expressly an Oregon company's articles to include a provision 'authorizing or directing the corporation to conduct the business of the corporation in a manner which is environmentally and socially

---

206 ORC International, *Evaluation of the Companies Act 2006: Volume 1*, ORC International, 2010, 67–72.
207 D. Collison, et al., *Shareholder Primacy in UK Corporate Law: An Exploration of the Rationale and Evidence*, ACCA, 2011.
208 Clark and Knight, op. cit., 263.
209 Ibid., 274.
210 S.M. Bainbridge, 'Interpreting nonshareholder constituency statutes', *Pepperdine Law Review* 19, 1992, 991–1025.
211 Connecticut Code 2011 – Title 33, Ch. 601, s. 33-756: Arizona Revised Statutes – Title 10, Ch. 23, art. 1, s. 10-2702.

responsible'.²¹² The Oregon law doesn't oblige companies to have such an objective – rather, they may choose it. In this sense, the Oregon effort incorporates some dimensions of the social enterprise model, as found in the UK's community enterprises and the US's benefit corporations.²¹³

In contrast to these legislative approaches, in Canada the ESV philosophy has taken root judicially. Although the seeds were planted in the 1973 provincial court case of *Teck Corporation Ltd v. Millar*,²¹⁴ it was not until the Supreme Court rulings in *Peoples Department Stores v. Wise*²¹⁵ and *BCE v. 1976 Debentureholders*²¹⁶ that it was firmly established that directors may, consistently with their fiduciary responsibility, consider the interests of parties with whom the company interacts in order to further its business success. In the latter case, the Court said that promoting the corporation's best interests means 'having regard to all relevant considerations, including, but not confined to, the need to treat affected stakeholders in a fair manner, commensurate with the corporation's duties as a responsible corporate citizen'.²¹⁷

In all the aforementioned jurisdictions, the business judgement rule gives boards and managers latitude to make ESV-guided decisions.²¹⁸ It is aptly described in the following passage from the Canadian case of *Maple Leaf Foods Inc. v. Schneider Corp.*:

> The court looks to see that the directors made a reasonable decision not a perfect decision. Provided the decision taken is within a range of reasonableness, the court ought not to substitute its opinion for that of the board even though subsequent events may have cast doubts on the board's determination.... The fact that alternative transactions were rejected by the board is irrelevant unless it can be shown that a particular alternative was definitely available and clearly more beneficial to the company than the chosen transaction.²¹⁹

The business judgement rule has allowed courts to permit corporate philanthropy on the assumption that collateral benefits, such as an enhanced reputation, may accrue to the corporation and its shareholders.²²⁰ The

---

212 Oregon Revised Statutes, 2007 s. 60.047(2)(e).
213 See http://www.bcorporation.net.
214 (1972), 33 DLR (3d) 288 (BCSC), 313–4.
215 [2004] 3 SCR 461.
216 [2008] 3 SCR 560.
217 Ibid., para. 82.
218 K. Davis, 'Discretion of corporate management to do good at the expense of shareholder gain: a survey of, and commentary on, the U.S. corporate law', *Canada–United States Law Journal* 13, 1988, 7–75.
219 (1998) 42 OR (3d) 177, 192.
220 M.A. Blair, 'A contractarian defense of corporate philanthropy', *Stetson Law Review* 28, 1998, 27–50, 42–9. Some governments have also legislated to put beyond doubt the legality of corporate charitable giving.

rule moderates the harshness of any fiduciary norm to seek optimal financial returns, giving additional scope for RI by managers of financial corporations.

ESV is also encroaching on corporate governance in a number of developing countries, of which South Africa has been the pioneer. In 1994 its King Committee on Corporate Governance drafted the King Report/Code (revised in 2002 and 2009), providing voluntary standards for corporate governance that encourage companies to move from an exclusive focus on shareholder-wealth maximization to consider a wider community of stakeholders. Apart from the fact that the King Code is applicable to South African financial corporations directly, some Code provisions speak to issues relevant to social investors in regular corporations, especially development of a stakeholder management strategy and integrated sustainability reporting. The King Report II advises:

> A well-managed company will be aware of, and respond to, social issues, ... [and is] responsible with regard to environmental and human rights issues. A company is likely to experience indirect economic benefits such as improved productivity and corporate reputation by taking those factors into consideration.[221]

Though officially not binding, the King Code may inform the interpretation of companies' statutory duties. In *South African Broadcasting Corporation Ltd and Another v. Mpofu*,[222] the court concluded the board of a state-owned enterprise under the Public Finance Management Act of 1999 must behave with regard to best practice standards expressed in the King Code. A similar position was taken in *Minister of Water Affairs and Forestry v. Stilfontein Gold Mining Company Ltd*.[223] Furthermore, the JSE obliges listed companies to report on their compliance with the King Code and provide reasons for any non-compliance. Empirical research suggests that the poor quality of corporate governance systems has triggered suspension of some firms from the JSE.[224]

Like in South Africa, the corporate governance reform movement in India began in the late 1990s with a voluntary code, framed by the Confederation of Indian Industry.[225] In 2011 the government tabled new

---

221 Institute of Directors in Southern Africa (IDSA), *King Report on Corporate Governance for South Africa*, IDSA, 2002, 12, para. 18.7.
222 [2009] 4 All SA 169.
223 [2006] ZAGPHC 47, para. 16.7.
224 M. Mangena and E. Chamisa, 'Corporate governance and incidences of listing suspension by the JSE Securities Exchange of South Africa: an empirical analysis', *International Journal of Accounting* 43, 2008, 28–44.
225 S. Mutyala and H. Dasaraju, 'Corporate governance in developing economies – a study of emerging issues in India', *2nd International Conference on Corporate Governance*, Institute of Public Enterprise, 2011.

companies legislation that institutionalizes CSR as a mandatory goal of companies. The Indian Companies Act, which would replace 1950s-era legislation, alters directors' core duties to include acting 'in the best interests of the company, its employees, the shareholders, the community and for the protection of environment'.[226] The Bill also requires any large public company to establish a Stakeholder Relationship Committee,[227] draft a CSR policy to address issues such as 'ensuring environmental sustainability'[228] and earmark at least 2 per cent of the firm's net profits for implementing it.[229]

In financial corporations, which often are more economically salient than non-financial firms, ESV may facilitate a more expansive view of the interests that should be addressed by fiduciary law. Failure of a financial institution can ripple through the economy, decimating the entrusted life savings of people. Financial corporations also face greater risks, being highly leveraged and holding illiquid assets, which amplifies their vulnerability to unexpected adverse events. Traditionally, these considerations have tended to be addressed through additional prudential regulation, such as capital adequacy standards, rather than by redefining core fiduciary duties. However, as a *permissive* legal mandate, the ESV standard presently fails to impose a sustainability obligation on corporate actors and extends little 'protection to corporations acting with the environment in mind beyond what is already allowed under the business judgement rule'.[230]

The following sections assess the status of fiduciary responsibility in banks and insurance companies and the scope for enlightened and responsible finance.

Fiduciary law and governance of banks

Regulation of banks for responsible finance

Some banks and other credit institutions (e.g., credit unions) have shown increasing interest in environmentally responsible lending and in supporting local communities, as evident in the establishment of the Equator Principles for global project financing. While many lenders increasingly incorporate environmental risk appraisal into due diligence procedures, such as assessing the credit risks of a project finance borrower, a small minority have gone beyond 'defensive' banking to the active financing of sustainable

---

226 Clause 166(2).
227 Clause 178(5)(6).
228 Clause 135(1); schedule VII.
229 Clause 135(5). The Bill also obliges a company to explain any non-compliance with this expectation.
230 J.C. Jones, 'Environmental disclosure: toward an investor based corporate environmentalism norm?', *Boston University Public Interest Law Journal* 20, 2010–2011, 207–39, 227.

development.²³¹ As in the RI industry generally, a mix of ethical and business factors have influenced banks' commitment to such financing.

There are ample grounds to impress on banks some social responsibility objectives and for governments to harness banks as means of furthering sustainable development. The complexity of bank business, their vulnerability to market shocks and their capacity to amplify initial, small shocks throughout the economy are among the conventional rationales to discipline banks more closely than other industry sectors.²³² The failure of a major bank may precipitate collateral economic damage and the collapse of associated businesses. Already, governments worldwide mobilize banks to further specific policy objectives, such as money-laundering controls. For RI purposes, governments could require banks to undertake some environmental due diligence before making loans and mandating preferential lending to projects or companies that meet sustainability criteria.

Governments subject banks to additional prudential and business conduct regulation to address financial risks and consumer protection, but little effort has been made to stimulate socially responsible lending. Prudential supervision typically addresses both the financial conditions of individual banks and the stability of the banking sector generally, such as through capital adequacy and liquidity requirements.²³³ Business conduct regulations accommodate investor protection and consumer service standards through risk management systems, deposit guarantee systems and payment systems controls.²³⁴ Unfortunately, the adequacy of many of these regulatory regimes was revealed as severely deficient in some jurisdictions in the wake of the GFC. Moreover, none of this banking regulation directly addresses RI issues, except incidentally. Financial due diligence procedures may prompt banks to scrutinize any environmental hazards associated with a borrower's project to ensure that loan collateral remains valuable and the borrower's solvency and ability to meet loan repayments is not jeopardized. A bank may also be motivated to protect its reputational value from any adverse environmental publicity. Banking regulation may even inhibit collaboration among lenders to set ethical lending standards, as any collusive practice to control the market 'could be deemed to breach monopoly or competition regulations'.²³⁵

In the so-called 'bank-based economies', notably Germany, banks have traditionally assumed special economic significance. German companies'

---

231 See J.J. Bouma, M. Jeucken, and L. Klinkers (eds), *Sustainable Banking: the Greening of Finance*, Greenleaf Publishing, 2001; O. Weber and S. Remer (eds), *Social Banks and the Future of Sustainable Finance*, Routledge, 2011.
232 D. Heremans, *Corporate Governance Issues for Banks. A Financial Stability Perspective*, Katholieke Universiteit, 2006; J.R. Macey and M. O'Hara, 'The corporate governance of banks', *Economic Policy Review* 9(1), 2003, 91–107.
233 R. Lastra, *Central Banking and Banking Regulation*, London School of Economics, 1996.
234 J.R. Macey, et al., *Banking Law and Regulation*, Aspen Publishers, 2001.
235 A.B. Coulson, 'How should banks govern the environment? Challenging the construction of action versus veto', *Business Strategy and the Environment* 19, 2009, 149–61, 153.

capital needs are mainly met through debt financing provided by banks.[236] The ensuing intimate relationship between banks and companies can lead to loans being secured by a bank holding shares in a firm (a relationship known as the *Hausbank*).[237] For small and medium-sized firms (*Mittelstand*) whose shares are not publicly traded, an even more intimate relationship with lenders can exist.[238] The ties between banks and companies often last for decades, in theory ameliorating pressures for short-term financial return and encouraging long-term growth strategies. In the US and UK, by contrast, such relationships are more at arm's length, with banks generally distancing themselves from corporate governance and operational affairs.

Presently, there is no general legal obligation on German banks to promote RI. They are structured into three groups: commercial banks, cooperatives and public sector banks.[239] The primary focus of the latter, by law, is to foster regional economic development and not profit-maximization per se.[240] Cooperative banks are owned by their members and legally must support their financial needs.[241] While commercial banks lack this quasi-social mandate, a few such as UmweltBank have moved into the ethical lending niche. Some cooperative banks, such as EthikBank and GLS-Gemeinschaftsbank, have done likewise. A 2003 study by the Wuppertal Institute on commercial banks found that very few promoted products or services for socially responsible financing.[242] Furthermore, corporate environmental performance was rarely considered a major criterion in project financing or other forms of corporate lending.[243] Only the environmental-branded banks comprehensively took account of good environmental practices.[244]

An interesting American precedent for responsible banking is the Community Reinvestment Act (CRA) of 1977.[245] It obliges banks to alleviate the financial plight of the local communities in which they are chartered, by ensuring public access to credit and low-cost banking services, especially to low-income and minority communities.[246] A bank's record on

---

236 Schaefer, op. cit., 271.
237 A. Hackethal, 'German banks and banking structure', in J.P. Krahnen and R.H. Schmidt (eds), *The German Financial System*, Oxford University Press, 2004, 71–105, 71.
238 J.W. Cioffi, 'Corporate governance reform, regulatory politics, and the foundations of finance capitalism in the United States and Germany', *German Law Journal* 7, 2006, 533–62, 551.
239 A. Brunner, et al., *Germany's Three-Pillar Banking System: Cross Country Perspectives in Europe*, IMF, 2004, 2.
240 *Law on Savings Banks of the State of North Rhine-Westphalia (Sparkassengesetz* (SpkG)), 2008, s. 2 I-III.
241 Law on Cooperatives (Genossenschaftsgesetz (GenG)), 2006, s. 1 I.
242 T. Busch and T. Orbach, *Zukunftsfaehiger Finanzsektor: Die Nachhaltigkeitsleistung von Banken und Versicherungen*, Wuppertal Institute, 2003, 35–6.
243 Ibid., 40.
244 Ibid., 41–2.
245 Pub. L. No. 95-128.
246 J.T. Campen, 'Banks, communities and public policy', in G.A. Dymski, et al. (eds), *Transforming the U.S. Financial System: Equity and Efficiency for the 21st Century*, M.E. Sharpe, 1993, 221–52.

such matters is periodically reviewed and taken into account when considering a lender's application for deposit facilities and institutional mergers. Unsurprisingly, banks have generally been unenthusiastic about the CRA, seeing it as an unjustified regulatory burden that offers little financial reward for servicing seemingly high-risk, low-income communities.[247] Yet CRA-governed lenders were less exposed to the follies of the subprime mortgage crisis that began in late 2007. The CRA was not substantially responsible for encouraging the subprime lending boom and the ensuing housing market bust; the Act only applies to depositories and doesn't cover most of the major subprime lenders.[248] The Board of Governors of the Federal Reserve System also 'determined that the CRA does not require excessive risk-taking or lending that would undermine the safety and soundness of covered institutions'.[249]

An alternative approach to encourage socially responsible lending is financial incentives. The Netherlands has gone the furthest in this regard. Its 1995 Green Project Directive and 2004 Regulation on Social and Ethical Projects were initiated to provide tax concessions to approved environmental and social project funding.[250] The law exempts taxes on interest and dividend income from qualifying environmental funds established by banks and other financial intermediaries.[251] Funded project proponents must also obtain a 'green certificate' from the government to verify compliance with the scheme's sustainable development criteria.[252] It facilitates eligible projects – typically involving organic agriculture, renewable energy and sustainable housing – that otherwise might not generate a sufficient return on investment without the tax advantage. Both boutique and mainstream financiers have taken advantage of the scheme. The Dutch Association of Investors for Sustainable Development attributed about 50 per cent of the growth in Dutch RI from 1996 to 2004 to the Green Project Directive.[253] A 2002 KPMG study found

---

247 Ibid., 223.
248 L. Ellis, 'The housing meltdown: why did it happen in the United States?' Working Paper No. 259, Bank for International Settlements, 2008. Only about 20 per cent of subprime loans were made by lending institutions covered by the CRA: Testimony of Professor M.S. Barr, Before the Committee on Financial Services US House of Representatives Hearing on 'The Community Reinvestment Act: thirty years of accomplishments, but challenges remain', 13 February 2008, 1–11, 4.
249 Board of Governors of the Federal Reserve System, *The Performance and Profitability of CRA-Related Lending*, report submitted to the Congress pursuant to section 713 of the Gramm-Leach-Bliley Act of 1999, 17 July 2000.
250 Regeling groenprojecten buitenland, Staatscourant 1 (2 January 2002): 31; Regeling sociaal-ethische projecten, Staatscourant, 44 (4 March 2004), 10; Regeling groenprojecten, Staatscourant 131 (11 July 2005): 13.
251 Jeucken, op. cit., 94.
252 T. van Bellegem, 'The green and social funds system in the Netherlands', in *Solidarity-based Choices in the Market-place: A Vital Contribution to Social Cohesion*, Council of Europe, 2005, 157–69, 161.
253 Vereniging van Beleggers voor Duurzame Ontwikkeling (VBDO), *Socially Responsible Savings and Investments in the Netherlands: Developments in Volume and Growth of Socially-responsible Savings and Investments in Retail Funds*, VBDO, 2005, 11.

that since 1996 the Directive had delivered €2.8 billion of investment from 140,000 individual investors in over 2,100 projects.[254] Despite such a positive impact, which has been corroborated by research by the Dutch government,[255] the scheme will be phased out by 2014.[256]

Fiduciary responsibility of banks

Fiduciary law governs some aspects of banking business, notably between banks and their customers, and between senior managers or directors and their bank. Thus, in addition to banks' regulatory envelope, the directors owe a fiduciary duty to act in the best interests of their institution and a separate tortious duty to take reasonable care. While the former responsibility is owed exclusively to the bank (and derivatively perhaps to its shareholders), the latter may extend to other stakeholders affected by the bank's operations. The following discussion focuses on the fiduciary relationship in the retail business of banks.

In most countries, the core banking activities of deposit taking and lending aren't considered fiduciary in nature, since these relationships are viewed as largely governed by contract.[257] Once money is deposited, it simply becomes a debt due by the bank to the account holder. In the classic 1848 English case of *Foley v. Hill*, the House of Lords explained:

> [T]he money placed in the custody of a banker is, to all intents and purposes, the money of the banker, to do with it as he pleases; he is guilty of no breach of trust in employing it; he is not answerable to the principal if he puts it in jeopardy [or] if he engages in hazardous speculation.[258]

In the bank–borrower relationship, where the roles of debtor and creditor are reversed, it is also well established doctrinally that the relationship between a bank and its borrower is also that of debtor and creditor, without any fiduciary responsibilities normally.[259] This relationship thus should entail no special duties beyond those in contract, though minority US case law suggests the debtor–creditor relationship can sometimes be 'quasi-fiduciary'.[260]

---

254 KPMG, *Sustainable Profit. An Overview of the Environmental Benefits Generated by the Green Funds Scheme*, KPMG, 2002, 6.
255 Netherlands Ministry of Finance, *The Green Funds Scheme: A Success Story in the Making*, Ministry of Finance, 2006, 5.
256 Personal communication, Dutch Ministry of Finance, 5 February 2012.
257 See generally J. Glover, 'Banks and fiduciary relationships', *Bond Law Review* 7(1), 1995, 50–66.
258 (1848) 2 HLC 28, 36.
259 See C.J. Hunt, 'The price of trust: an examination of fiduciary duty and the lender-borrower relationship', *Wake Forest Law Review*, 29, 1994, 719–80.
260 *Commercial Cotton Co. v. United Cal. Bank*, (1985) 209 Cal. Rptr. 551; see also R. Plato-Shinar, 'The bank's fiduciary duty: an Israeli-Canadian comparison', *Banking and Finance*

Absence other legal constraints, banks may thus invest and loan funds regardless of any ethical preferences expressed by depositors. Several RI campaigns have targeted banks, such as those operating in South Africa in the 1980s and more recently against financiers of environmentally destructive projects.[261] But no breach of fiduciary law arises here. Conversely, banks have no fiduciary duty to advise borrowers of any special environmental risks associated with how they might use the funds.

The business of banks today, however, has changed dramatically since the mid-nineteenth-century case of *Foley*, and many other activities of banks may attract fiduciary obligations.[262] The 1937 US case of *Stewart v. Phoenix National Bank*[263] was one of the earliest to recognize that the bank–customer relationship can be more than just a debtor–creditor or bank–borrower contract. Fiduciary principles can apply when the relationship involves expert financial advice that is relied upon by a less sophisticated client.[264] The US case of *Klein v. First Edina National Bank* held that 'special circumstances' between parties, such as when a bank knows the customer is putting his trust and confidence in the lender, may attract fiduciary standards.[265] As well, banks have been regarded as fiduciaries in 'control creditor' cases, when a lender becomes so immersed in a borrower's affairs that the borrower has lost its separate identity under the domination of the bank.[266] Depending on the relationship and circumstances, the fiduciary obligation may be owed by the bank itself or by individual bankers.

The presence of a fiduciary duty requires the bank to avoid conflicts of interest and, in some US case law, to more actively advance the client's best interests.[267] Improper conflicts of interest may arise where a bank advises two or more clients on a single transaction or provides advice that is motivated to advance the bank's financial position at a client's expense. In the English case of *Woods v. Martins Bank*,[268] a court found a fiduciary relationship when a banker advised a customer without business experience to buy shares in another corporate customer, although the bank was aware of the latter's

---

Law Review 22, 2006, 1–22 (explaining how Israeli law imposes a fiduciary duty on banks towards their customers).

261 J. Nerys, 'The campaign against British bank involvement in apartheid South Africa', *African Affairs* 99, 2000, 415–33; M. Chan-Fishel, *Time to Go Green: Environmental Responsibility in the Chinese Banking Sector*, Friends of the Earth and BankTrack, 2007.
262 N.B. Schaumann, 'The lender as unconventional fiduciary', *Seton Hall Law Review* 23, 1992, 21–66.
263 (1937) 64 P.2d 101 (Ariz).
264 E.g., E.F. Mannino, *Lender Liability and Banking Litigation*, Law Journals Seminars-Press, 2006, 3–34.3; *CBA v. Smith* (1991) 42 FCR 390, 391.
265 (1972) 196 NW 2d 619.
266 *Taylor v. Standard Gas and Electric Co.*, (1939) 306 US 307.
267 K.M. Lodge and T.J. Cunningham, 'The banker as inadvertent fiduciary: beware a borrower's special trust and confidence', *Commercial Law Journal* 98(3), 1993, 277–303, 301.
268 (1959) 1 QB 55.

financial troubles.[269] Australian case law suggests that the client need not be financially unsophisticated to benefit from a fiduciary relationship;[270] such a relationship may therefore exist when an investment bank advises a savvy corporate client, so long as there is still an element of vulnerability in the sense of reliance on the superior financial expertise and experience of the bank.[271]

Informed disclosure is one way to mitigate the stringency of fiduciary responsibility. The Australian court in *Commonwealth Trading Bank of Australia v. Smith*[272] suggested that a banker can be absolved from fiduciary liability by obtaining informed consent from the aggrieved customer. A bank may also exclude or modify its fiduciary obligations through contractual techniques, subject to two important limitations. Such contractual terms, especially if used against unsophisticated investors, might be struck down as 'unreasonable' or 'unconscionable'.[273] Further, it is unlikely that contractual techniques will give the bank the unlimited right to act for opposing parties in the same transaction when the customers' respective interests are in conflict or exclude liability where the deliberate suppression of information has deceived a customer.

There are thus several situations in which a bank may encounter legal problems in relation to its handling of social and environmental considerations. One is where a bank provides inappropriate investment advice that is relied on by a client, such as a recommendation that is wrongly dismissive of financial risks associated with the environmental dimensions of a venture.[274] Also, if a bank makes public representations that it is a socially responsible lender but makes loans to the contrary, 'a customer who did business with the bank in reliance on that policy might assert a claim against the bank for fraud, false advertising, or on some other grounds'.[275] Furthermore, the fiduciary obligation that a bank's directors and senior officers owe toward their corporation and shareholders may require being attentive to environmental risks that financially threaten the bank.

A special fiduciary situation of environmental significance for banks is when they foreclose on the property of a defaulting mortgagor and become trustee of that asset pending its disposal. In some jurisdictions banks have incurred expensive liability for cleanup of contaminated properties on which they have foreclosed.[276] Lender environmental liability was a major hazard for American banks pursuant to the Comprehensive Environmental Response

269 Ibid., 73.
270 *Aequitas v. AEFC*, (2001) 19 ACLC 1006, 1063.
271 Tuch, op. cit., 504.
272 (1991) 102 ALR 453.
273 M.H. Ogilvie, *Bank and Customer Law in Canada*, Irwin, 2007, 196.
274 Glover, op. cit., 51–61.
275 J.A. Snyder and A.B. Muir, 'Green wave or greenwash?', *The Secured Lender* 61(6), 2005, 32–70, 35.
276 D.R. Berz, 'Lender liability under CERCLA: in search of a new deep pocket', *Journal of Banking Law* 108(1), 1991, 4–29.

Compensation and Liability Act (CERCLA) of 1980,[277] when banks were sued for their deep pockets to pay for the remediation of thousands of brownfield sites across the US. Legislative amendments in 1996 greatly abated this risk, and CERCLA includes an explicit fiduciary exemption that precludes legal action against the bank that merely holds a security interest or is a bare trustee of a tainted property.[278] Most other major jurisdictions seem to protect lender trustees in such situations so long as their conduct doesn't give rise to any other causes of legal action, such as for negligence.

Banks' duty of care

Although not all jurisdictions conceive of a fiduciary duty of care and skill that infuses more positive responsibilities towards beneficiaries, a separate duty of care in regulation or the common law may to some extent fulfill this purpose (though the triggers of liability and remedies can differ). Establishing such a duty requires a close and direct relationship between the parties, and it must be reasonably foreseeable that carelessness by one party could harm the other. The duty's presence in the banking industry has been acknowledged judicially for over a century,[279] with authority noting that bank directors 'must keep in mind that a national bank is not a private corporation in which stockholders alone are interested'.[280] But the lodestar UK case of *JP Morgan Chase Bank v. Springwell Navigation Corporation*[281] affirms that the courts will not readily impute such an additional duty within a banking relationship already contractually defined. US courts also stress that a bank doesn't owe a duty of care to a borrower when the lender's role in the transaction is within its conventional role as a mere money-lender.[282] Banking law usually leaves it undefined when the duty of care may arise; for example, Canada's Bank Act of 1991 obliges bank directors and officers to '(a) act honestly and in good faith with a view to the best interests of the bank; and (b) exercise the care, diligence and skill that a reasonably prudent person would exercise in comparable circumstances'.[283] The common law approach is illustrated by *Selangor United Rubber Estates v. Cradock*,[284] where Judge Ungoed-Thomas explained:

> The standard of that reasonable care and skill is an objective standard applicable to bankers. . . . [R]elevant considerations include the prima facie assumption that men are honest, the practice of bankers, . . . and the

---

277 Pub. L. 95-510.
278 Asset Conservation, Lender Liability and Deposit Insurance Protection Act, 1996, HR 3610, Title II, subtitle E, ss. 2501–2504.
279 *Briggs v. Spaulding*, (1891) 141 US 132.
280 *Atherton et al. v. Anderson*, (1938) No. 7298, 99 F.2d 883.
281 [2008] EWHC 1186.
282 E.g., *Plata v. Long Beach Mortgage Co.*, [2005] US Dist. LEXIS 38807 (ND Cal.).
283 SC 1991, s. 158(1).
284 (1968) 2 All ER 1073.

extent to which an operation is unusual or out of the ordinary course of business.[285]

A duty of care is most likely to be found in a bank's investment management and advisory services when there is an assumption of responsibility coupled with reliance by the client.[286] It may arise either by accepting a customer's request for advice or if giving advice is within the scope of the bank's business.[287] Banks increasingly advise customers about RI products and services, such as 'green' mortgages and ethical mutual funds, situations that may give rise to these legal obligations.

In assuming this responsibility, however, a bank doesn't necessarily have a continuing duty to keep its advice under review and possibly correct it in light of new market conditions.[288] The bank is also not liable when the information or advice it supplies to its customer is passed on without its knowledge to third parties who rely on it. In *Caparo Industries v. Dickman*,[289] a leading English case on auditors, the House of Lords held there must be a proximate relationship between an adviser and the recipient who acts in reliance on it. For such a proximate relationship to exist, the adviser must know both the purpose for which the recipient is supplied with advice or information and that the recipient is likely to rely on the communicated information or advice for the known purpose.[290] Also, the bank's duty to take reasonable care doesn't imply a duty to warn clients against or advise on the risks inherent in following their instructions. Thus, the bank would not necessarily be obliged to offer advice about the possible financial imprudence of an RI product that explicitly prioritized ethical over financial considerations. In *Suriya and Douglas v. Midland Bank*[291] the English Court of Appeal affirmed that the bank–customer relationship itself did not engender a duty of disclosure on the part of the bank as a matter of general law.[292]

We should distinguish between providing information and giving advice, which can be important in an RI context. When a bank informs, it aims to enable the recipient to decide upon a course of action. In such circumstances the bank is liable only for the consequences of information being factually wrong. But when a bank recommends to a client a course of action, the bank is potentially liable for all the foreseeable consequences of the client relying on its advice.[293] However, a bank is not considered a financial adviser to a

285 Ibid., 1118–9.
286 P.J. Cresswell, et al. (eds), *Encyclopaedia of Banking Law*, Butterworths, division c, 49.
287 Cresswell, op. cit., 61.
288 *Fennoscandia Ltd v. Clarke*, (1999) 1 All ER 365.
289 [1990] BCC 164.
290 Ibid., 184.
291 (1999) 1 All ER 612.
292 Ibid., 618.
293 Cresswell, op. cit., 81.2.

customer who merely approaches it for a loan or some other form of financial accommodation. In *Lloyd's Bank v. Cobb*, the court held:

> [T]he ordinary relationship of customer and banker does not place on the bank any contractual or tortious duty to advise the customer on the wisdom of commercial projects for the purpose of which the bank is asked to lend money. If the bank is to be placed under such a duty, there must be a request from the customer, accepted by the bank, or some other arrangement between the customer and the bank, under which the advice is to be given.[294]

There may be situations in which a bank, lending to a customer, also assumes a fiduciary advisory role, as in *Verity and Spindler v. Lloyds Bank*,[295] where a bank manager gave bad advice to the plaintiffs, who lost money in buying a specific property that wasn't viable for re-development.[296] Factors that influenced the court's finding of a duty to warn the client included: the plaintiffs' financial inexperience, the business nature of the proposed project, the bank's advertisement about free financial advice and the inspection of the property by the bank manager.[297]

In conclusion, several observations can be made about the ambit of banks' fiduciary and tortious obligations. First, the level of experience of the customer with whom a bank is dealing can be relevant. A highly sophisticated customer who holds himself out as capable of understanding complex business and financial issues, including ethical or environmental matters, faces more difficulties in proving that the bank breached a duty of care.[298] Second, the nature of a transaction makes a difference. Courts are not inclined to imply a broad duty of care into a speculative or highly risky transaction, such as foreign exchange derivatives or commodities trading.[299] Some ethical financial products might be construed as more financially risky. Third, the content and wording of a bank's advertisement is relevant, and a bank is likely to be held liable against the promises that it makes in its promotional literature, especially when dealing with unsophisticated customers.[300] Fourth, when a bank offers an explanation for a financial transaction, it should do so in a fair and reasonable manner; but if it fails to inform customers proactively about RI products and services, as research has found occurs,[301] no legal lia-

---

294 18 December 1991, unreported, CA. It was applied in *Barclays Bank v. Green and Challis* (17 November 1995), unreported: quoted in Cresswell, ibid., 91.
295 [1995] CLC 1557.
296 Ibid., 1588.
297 Ibid., 1580–1.
298 *Bankers Trust International v. P.T. Dharmala Sakti Sejahtera*, [1996] CLC 518.
299 *Lloyd v. Citigroup Australia*, (1986) 11 NSWLR 286.
300 Ellinger, op. cit., 160.
301 U. Schrader, 'Ignorant advice – customer advisory service for ethical investment funds', *Business Strategy and the Environment* 15, 2006, 200–14, 200.

bility arises. Finally, since banks are corporations, their directors may be able to avail the business judgement rule to defend discretionary decisions made on an informed basis, honestly and in good faith. The rule, found in Anglo-American jurisdictions, tends to shield decisions involving simple negligence in contrast to situations involving a stricter duty of care or fiduciary responsibility. Further discussion about the legal responsibilities of banks as financial advisers is provided in the penultimate section of this chapter, which is dedicated to financial advisers per se.

Insurance companies

Insurers are major institutional investors, with global assets that rival pension funds.[302] This sector principally comprises life insurers and providers of property and casualty insurance. At end of 2010, insurers worldwide held assets worth US$24.6 trillion, of some US$79.3 trillion assets under institutional management from all financial sectors.[303] Extended financial liabilities maturing over several decades should cause life insurance companies (like pension funds) to have long-term investment horizons.[304] Insurers' business also exposes them to specific environmental risks that might motivate them to take an interest in sustainability. One distinctive risk is climate change. The prospect of greater weather-related losses financially threatens insurers, which they have to address eventually in their investment portfolios and insurance underwriting policies.

The insurance industry has only recently embraced RI after a long history of limited engagement with corporate governance and sustainability in their portfolio investments.[305] Several global collaborative mechanisms to promote responsible finance in this sector have been launched, which may lead to a new prudential investing convention to inform applicable legal standards. In 2006, UNEP-FI established an Insurance Working Group (now known as the Insurance Commission) to assess and promote ESG issues in insurance business. In 2012 the Commission launched the Principles for Sustainable Insurance, a code that aims to provide insurance tools for environmental risk management.[306] These risks to insurers' business range from climate change and natural disasters to water scarcity and food insecurity. Its initial 30 signatories include heavyweight insurance companies such as AXA, Munich Re and Swiss Re. In 2007, the sector also issued the ClimateWise Principles to help companies report how they incorporate climate change issues into the management of their business, including investment

---

302 See OECD Statistics on Institutional Investors: http://www.oecd.org.
303 CityUK, 'Fund management', October 2011, 1.
304 Davies, op. cit., 79. However, life insurers also need some short term liquidity to meet early surrender of insurance policies.
305 A.M. Abdalyan, 'The corporate governance role of life insurance companies as institutional investors', *Assurances* 65(1), 1997, 17–37.
306 Http://www.unepfi.org/psi.

portfolios.³⁰⁷ So far, however, most insurers have viewed any commitment to environmental responsibility as largely confined to the direct ecological footprint of their physical operations rather than as indirect effects from their investments.³⁰⁸ An independent review of implementation of the ClimateWise Principles in 2011 identified major failings by signatories in achieving Principle 4 ('to incorporate climate change into our investment decisions').³⁰⁹ An example of better practice is Aviva, a leading UK insurer, which in 2011 offered insurance products that 'support commercial development of low-carbon products including wind farms and biomass energy conversion plants'.³¹⁰

Relatedly, due to deregulation of financial markets, many insurance firms have restructured into omnibus financial 'supermarkets', offering a range of financial services, including pension plans, in addition to traditional insurance products. Life insurers often sell long-term saving vehicles such as annuities.³¹¹ Life insurance companies also sometimes act as external asset managers for pension plans, further expanding their presence in financial markets. While the property and casualty insurance sectors also manage substantial assets to invest, derived from insurance premiums, they don't sell savings products.

This incipient trend to RI is not yet reflected in the legal framework governing insurance business. Its legal context depends somewhat on whether the insurer takes the form of a mutual or stock company (these being the principal options, in addition to reciprocals and Lloyd's associations).³¹² Mutual insurers are owned by the policy-holders, while insurance companies are held by shareholders (who may or may not hold insurance policies).³¹³ This institutional distinction is gradually disappearing as market competition drives insurers to demutualize and become public stock companies, which may enjoy better operational efficiency, access to capital and tax savings. From 1986 to 2004, 60 per cent of American mutual life insurers converted to the stock structure.³¹⁴ But the mutual sector is still significant in some countries.³¹⁵ The International Cooperative and Mutual Insurance Federation

---

307 Http://www.climatewise.org.uk.
308 E.g., Standard Life's analysis of its carbon footprint: *Annual Report and Accounts 2010*, Standard Life, 2011, 45.
309 PriceWaterhouseCoopers, *ClimateWise Principles: Fourth Independent Review*, ClimateWise Secretariat, 2011, 10.
310 Aviva, *Annual Report and Accounts 2010*, 2011, 78.
311 E.P. Davis, *Portfolio Regulation of Life Insurance Companies and Pension Funds*, OECD, 2001, 10.
312 D. Mayers and C.W. Smith, 'Organizational forms within the insurance industry: theory and evidence', in G. Dionne (ed.), *Handbook of Insurance*, Springer, 2000, 689–707.
313 J. Hansmann, 'The organization of insurance companies: mutual versus stock', *Journal of Law, Economics and Organization* 1(1), 1985, 125–53.
314 O. Erhemjamts and J.T. Leverty, 'The demise of the mutual organizational form: an investigation of the life insurance industry', Working Paper, Bentley College, 2007, 1.
315 M.J. Keneley, 'The demise of the mutual life insurer: an analysis of the impact of regulatory change on the performance of Australian life insurers in the 1990s', *Accounting History* 15(1), 2010, 65–91.

(ICMIF) currently has 221 members in 71 countries, with this individual membership representing over 600 distinct insurance mutual organizations.[316] A further 1,500 mutual insurers are indirect members of ICMIF.

A mix of contract law, fiduciary law, prudential regulation and business conduct regulation governs the investment activities of insurers.[317] The companies legislation under which insurers are incorporated may restrict the scope of their activities; for example, Canada's Insurance Companies Act limits an insurer to 'the business of providing financial services', a mandate that might conceivably restrict some forms of RI.[318] By contrast, a non-financial corporation normally may carry on any business except to the extent restricted by its articles. Company law also imposes a fiduciary duty on the directors of an insurer to act in its best interest, which is commonly understood to be preserving its financial security.

Regulation serves to protect policy-holders, mainly through solvency criteria to ensure that claims can be met and through consumer protection standards, which govern the selling of financial products and the administering of claims. Insurance policies and savings plans are also legal contracts between the insurer and its policy-holders. Regulation of insurers' investing activities draws on both quantitative portfolio regulation and prudent investment standards in order to ensure the insurers quarantine sufficient reserves to cover their liabilities and maintain a healthy solvency margin. Some jurisdictions also tightly regulate the investment choices of insurance companies (the so-called 'laundry list' of allowable, safe investments).[319]

Insurance companies increasingly offer pension plan services and products that encroach upon the traditional trustee-administered occupational pension funds. Insurers may be contracted to provide workplace pension plans or sell personal pension products to individual, self-employed workers. This trend gives rise to important legal issues, yet 'little consideration has been given to the legal duties owed by insurance companies to their policy-holders, or to the potential accountability gap that arises with the absence of trustees'.[320] In the UK and Australia, where this trend is particularly pronounced, the 'contract-based pension providers do not have fiduciary duties, either directly or indirectly'.[321] In general, neither insurance regulation nor companies legislation gives policy-holders (whether they be holders of insurance risk or investment policies) any rights to participate in the

---

316 Http://www.icmif.org/member-organisations.
317 See generally, OECD, *Policy Issues in Insurance – Investment, Taxation and Insolvency*, OECD, 1996; G.M. Dickinson, 'Issues in the effective regulation of the asset allocation of life insurance companies', in H. Blommestein and N. Funke (eds), *Institutional Investors in the New Financial Landscape*, OECD, 1998, 422–32.
318 SC 1991, s. 440(1).
319 S. Randall, 'Insurance regulation in the United States', *Florida State University Law Review* 26, 1999, 625–99.
320 C. Berry, *Protecting Our Best Interests: Rediscovering Fiduciary Obligation*, FairPensions, 2011, 4.
321 FairPensions, *The Enlightened Shareholder*, op. cit., 47 (referring to UK pensions).

governance of an insurance business operated as a stock company. Therefore, any democratic input regarding RI policies is limited to shareholders. Unusually, Canadian legislation gives policy-holders in an insurance company some of the rights usually reserved to shareholders, such as to requisition a meeting, to file proposals and to vote on such proposals, as well as on the election of directors at an annual meeting of the company's shareholders and policy-holders (subject to certain procedural requirements).[322] In theory, such participatory rights could be used to address ESG aspects of an insurer's investing policies. One difference to shareholder rights in the Canadian scheme is that 'an individual policy-holder can only have one vote ... regardless of the number of policies held'.[323] In the minority of insurance businesses organized as mutuals, policy-holders enjoy similar participatory rights.[324]

Financial services regulation and contract law provide the principal legal framework governing pension provision through insurers, but it may be inferior to trustee-based supervision. An OECD report notes that 'contract-based DC plans and personal pension arrangements are not usually run by a governing board that caters exclusively to the interest of members and beneficiaries'.[325] The insurance company typically has no contractual relationship with the trustees, through whom fiduciary responsibilities could arise indirectly, even though the employer chooses the provider and selects the fund options offered to members. The contractual relationships are directly between the insurer and individual employees.

In relation to personally-arranged pension plans, where there is no employer at all, different legal issues arise. As these individuals can freely choose their pension providers and savings products, there should be less need for fiduciary-like legal protections. Yet the lack of governance structures to represent and defend their interests may make them vulnerable, 'particularly given the information imbalances between consumers of complex financial products and their providers'.[326] Commentators have suggested that additional public regulation or policy-holder advocates should be appointed by regulators to provide better legal protection for individual retail customers of pension products.[327]

Where insurance companies have fiduciary responsibilities, they function somewhat differently to pension trusts. In life insurers, the beneficiary of the fiduciary duty depends on whether the business is organized as a mutual

---

322 Insurance Companies Act, SC 1991, ss 147(1.1)(c), 159(1)–(2) and 175.
323 G.W. Gee, 'Policyholder proposals: the ultimate in consumer protection?', *Canadian Financial Services* 5(3), 1992, 17–24, 19.
324 B. Crawford, 'The nature, source and extent of participation rights in mutual insurance companies', *Canadian Business Law Journal* 25(3), 1995, 337–55, 338.
325 F. Stewart and J. Yermo, *Pension Fund Governance: Challenges and Potential Solutions*, OECD, 2008, 28.
326 FairPensions, *The Enlightened Shareholder*, op. cit., 49–50.
327 Ibid., 50.

company or a stock company. A mutual insurer is owned by and managed for the benefit of its policy-holders. Thus, directors have fiduciary duties to those policyholder-owners, analogous to the duties the directors of a stock company owe to the company and its stockholders. In regard to an insurer organized as a stock company, typically governments have not imposed a separate fiduciary obligation to their insured policy-holders, although a separate duty of care to them may exist.[328] Thus, in the *Fidelity and Casualty* case in the US, the court stated that 'the policyholder acquires certain specified proprietary interests [in the company] but, apart from these, the relationship is not of a fiduciary nature and is essentially . . . measured by the contractual terms of the policy'.[329]

Courts in some jurisdictions have recognized that some functions of insurance businesses are trustee-like and have thus imposed a fiduciary duty on the management of insurance companies when insurers offer pension plans and savings products. In the landmark American case of *John Hancock Mutual Life Insurance Co. v. Harris Trust and Savings Bank*,[330] the US Supreme Court extended ERISA's fiduciary responsibilities to some aspects of insurance companies' business. It held that general account assets of a guaranteed annuity contract are 'plan assets' and must therefore be managed according to ERISA's fiduciary standards. This litigation arose when an insurance provider used certain plan assets for its own cash flow needs, in breach of fiduciary responsibilities. Thus, as for pension fund trustees, a life insurance company is required under ERISA to manage its general account assets 'solely in the interest of participants and beneficiaries' of such annuity contracts and 'for the exclusive purpose of providing benefits to such participants and beneficiaries'.[331] Therefore, queries about the legality of RI may arise in this context. On the other hand, *John Hancock* confirms that exempt from ERISA's fiduciary law purview are insurance products that 'guarantee benefits' to policy-holders[332] because such products allocate investment risk to the insurer.[333] Moreover, in the US, an insurer 'ordinarily is not a fiduciary to its insureds' in relation to the administration of insurance risk policies and the handling of compensation claims made pursuant to such policies.[334] Commentators argue that while an insurer's obligations to its insured include an 'implied obligation of good faith and fair dealing that includes certain elements of fiduciary duty', the duty of good faith is different than the duty

---

328 T. Allegaert, 'Derivative actions by policyholders on behalf of mutual insurance companies', *University of Chicago Law Review* 63, 1996, 1063–97, 1071–2.
329 *Fidelity and Casualty Co. of New York v. Metropolitan Life Insurance Company*, (1963) 42 Misc. 2d 616; 248 NYS 2d 559, 623.
330 (1993) No. 92-1074, 510 US 86.
331 Section 404(a).
332 ERISA, s. 1101(b)(2)(B).
333 A subsequent legislative amendment to ERISA clarified and affirmed this position.
334 W.T. Baker, P. Glad and S.M. Levy, 'Is an insurer a fiduciary to its insured?', *Tort and Insurance Law Journal* 25, 1989, 1–14, 1 (focusing on Californian law).

of a fiduciary in several respects.[335] Whereas 'a fiduciary owes his principal a duty of undivided loyalty ... an insurer engaged in determining and performing its contractual obligations may give [equal] consideration to its own interests'.[336]

Overall, the insurance industry is a pivotal sector in the global economy for sustainability, potentially able to reduce and share environmental-related risks by insuring corporate pollution liabilities, as well as able to foster innovation and underpin sustainable development by deployment of vast pools of investment capital. The industry should also have considerable financial self-interest in ESG issues. The fiduciary law framework governing insurers is particularly complex because of their diverse organizational forms and widening array of financial activities beyond the traditional business of insuring risks. Unlike other financial actors considered in this chapter such as pension plans or mutual funds, the beneficiaries to whom insurers are accountable in their investing activities are less visible and less clearly recognized.

Retail funds

RI's fungible and cosmetic standards

In the retail market, individuals may channel their money towards socially and environmentally responsible choices by joining collective investment funds marketed to the general public. The first RI fund, the Pioneer Fund, was established in the US in 1928, and since the 1980s a vast mutual fund sector catering to ethical investors has spread globally. They are commonly established by investment companies, which may oversee a family of different funds, each with its own investment policy and individual fund manager. Depending on the jurisdiction, the funds are known by diverse names, such as mutual funds, income trusts or investment trusts. In this book, for convenience, they will generally be referred to as 'retail funds' or 'mutual funds'. They have been popular for social investors, as fund providers can readily tailor investment portfolios to meet diverse and changing market demands. At the close of 2010, worldwide mutual fund assets totalled US$24.7 trillion, of which just over half were in American funds.[337] Unlike occupational pension funds, which do not 'sell' investment products, mutual funds allow investors to shop around for the fund best tailored to their ethical and financial preferences. While the retail fund market has fewer assets than pension or insurance sector assets, it is significant for its contribution to the RI industry's philosophies and methods.

---

335 Ibid., 2.
336 Ibid., 2–3.
337 Investment Company Institute (ICI), *2011 Investment Company Fact Book*, ICI, 2011, 1.

Mutual funds may take the form of a corporation, a trust or a purely contractual relationship.[338] The trust is commonly used in Commonwealth countries such as Canada and the UK.[339] Investors in a trust hold 'units' that represent a proportionate beneficial interest of the trust's assets. Because retail funds are often established by investment companies, as in the US under the Investment Company Act of 1940,[340] an additional corporate governance paradigm can apply. Additional regulatory controls may apply to safeguard the market. For example, German funds are obliged by the Investment Modernization Act of 2003 to act not only 'in the sole interest of its investors' but also for 'the integrity of the market'.[341]

The legal framework for retail funds facilitates a flexible approach to investing that may accommodate various RI practices. The articles of incorporation, the prospectus issued by the fund, or its governing trust instrument, as the case may be, will establish the basic constitution of the fund and its investment objectives. These need not be exclusively financial objectives. The Australian Corporations Act of 2001 doesn't require an investment fund to act in the best *financial* interests of its members[342] – rather, 'the members are left to determine for themselves, through their [fund's] constitution, what the best interests of the fund are to be'.[343] The UK's Financial Services and Markets Act of 2000 is less open-ended in this regard, specifying that investment companies be managed 'with the aim of (a) spreading investment risk; and (b) giving its members the benefit of the results of the management of those funds'.[344] All funds, regardless of their RI policy, have a statutory duty to manage their investments with care and diligence.[345] In addition, funds are subject to a 'corporate-like oversight structure to minimize the opportunities for abuses',[346] with disclosure standards that aim to ensure that investors are informed about the financial condition, service fees and investment policies of each fund.

While mutual funds have the flexibility to tailor investment portfolios to the ethical or financial needs of individual investors without the same degree of fiduciary law constraint as in the institutional sector, their capacity to

---

338 J.K. Thompson and S.M. Choi, *Governance Systems for Collective Investment Schemes in OECD Countries*, OECD, 2001.
339 See especially K.F. Sin, *The Legal Nature of the Unit Trust*, Clarendon Press, 1998; J. Thompson, *Corporate Governance and Collective Investment Schemes*, OECD, 2001, 24–30.
340 Pub. L. 76-768.
341 Investment Modernization Act (Investmentmodernisierungsgesetz), 2003, s. 9(2).
342 Section 601FC(1)(c).
343 Parliamentary Joint Committee on Corporations and Financial Services, *Corporate Responsibility: Managing Risk and Creating Value*, Commonwealth of Australia, 2006, 73.
344 Section 236.
345 Section 601FC(1)(b); see also P. Ali, 'Investing in the environment: some thoughts on the new breed of green hedge funds', *Derivatives Use, Trading and Regulation* 12(4), 2007, 351–7 (arguing for the importance for prudential investment duties).
346 W.J. Baumol, et al., *The Economics of Mutual Fund Markets: Competition versus Regulation*, Kluwer Academic, 1990, 52.

promote credible RI has been undermined by an organizational culture concerned with short-term returns and competitive advantage.[347] Indeed, major mutual funds groups in the US, notably Fidelity and Vanguard, have been accused of some unethically problematic investments.[348] An NGO campaign against Fidelity eventually led it to dump its shares in PetroChina, supposedly because of its controversial ties to Sudan.[349] In an industry where funds choose their own criteria for ethical or social responsibility, it shouldn't surprise us that much of the sector's parlance is vague, broad and indiscriminate. Commonly used marketing terms such as 'innovator' or 'best-in-class' may confuse rather than educate investors. Lacking baseline regulatory standards over funds' investment criteria and practices, the retail industry is vulnerable to cheap talk and salesmanship.[350]

Some of the RI industry's foremost associations are similarly complicit in this laissez-faire approach. By obfuscating as to whom, why and how social or environmental factors are considered, they are able to rationalize much investing as 'socially responsible'. Table 4.1 lists examples of vague or overly broad definitions of RI.

Investors shopping for a better world face innumerable choices across a bewildering array of philosophies, from evangelical Christian ethics to deep ecology. One assumption behind such offerings is that RI is a personal values choice, 'render[ing] ethics into a subjective realm incapable of any thoughtful discussion or analysis'.[351] But in this supermarket of funds, unsophisticated investors may be duped. They likely 'do not have access to the methodology, the screening, the ranking criteria, or any other data that would inform them about how or why a particular company is included in a portfolio'.[352]

RI funds typically offer predetermined investment prospectuses, in which statements of investment philosophy and objectives are disclosed in general parlance. For example, the Winslow Green Funds' 2011 prospectus outlines over 24 pages of its investment policies, practices, procedures, fees and other information that may enable social investors to make an informed choice about whether to join. However, only two pages explain the fund's environmental and sustainability criteria, and the statements are sufficiently broad to encompass many investments. The basic criteria are that the company

---

347 M. Haigh, 'Camouflage play: making moral claims in managed investment', *Accounting Forum* 30(3), 2006, 267–83.
348 Accusations by Investors Against Genocide: http://www.investorsagainstgenocide.org.
349 A. Paternack, 'Fidelity divests from Sudan-linked PetroChina', *Treehugger*, 16 May 2007, http://www.treehugger.com/corporate-responsibility/fidelity-divests-from-sudan-linked-petrochina.html.
350 D.H. Schepers and S.P. Sethi, 'Do socially responsible funds actually deliver what they promise? Bridging the gap between the promise and performance of socially responsible funds', *Business and Society Review* 108(1), 2003, 11–32; G. Frost, et al., 'Bringing ethical investment to account', *Australian Accounting Review* 14(3), 2004, 3–9.
351 M.S. Schwartz, 'The "ethics" of ethical investing', *Journal of Business Ethics* 43(3), 2003, 195–213, 208.
352 P. Hawken, *Socially Responsible Investing*, Natural Capital Institute, 2004, 22.

Table 4.1 Industry definitions of RI

RI Group / Association	Description of What Constitutes RI
Association for Sustainable and Responsible Investment in Asia	'Investment which allows investors to take into account wider concerns, such as social justice, economic development, peace or a healthy environment, as well as conventional financial considerations.'
Canadian Social Investment Organisation	'The integration of environmental, social and governance factors in the selection and management of investments.'
European Social Investment Forum	'Combines investors' financial objectives with their concerns about social, environmental, ethical (SEE) and corporate governance issues. . . . SRI is based on a growing awareness among investors, companies and governments about the impact that these risks may have on long-term issues ranging from sustainable development to long-term corporate performance.'
French Forum for Responsible Investment	'SRI is the application of sustainable development to financial investment. In other words, it is a form of investment which takes into account environmental, social and governance criteria in addition to traditional financial criteria.'
Responsible Investment Association of Australasia	'An umbrella term to describe an investment process which takes environmental, social, governance (ESG) or ethical considerations into account. This process stands in addition to or is incorporated into the usual fundamental investment selection and management process.'
UN Principles for Responsible Investment	'Integrate the consideration of environmental, social and governance (ESG) issues into investment decision-making and ownership practices, and thereby improve long-term returns to beneficiaries.'
US Forum for Sustainable and Responsible Investment	'The consideration of environmental, social and corporate governance criteria in addition to standard financial analysis.'

Source: RI associations' websites, as of October 2012.

in question 'utilizes clean, efficient, environmentally responsible business practices and seeks to reduce its environmental impact' or 'provides products or services that offer effective solutions to the world's environmental challenges'.[353] Though each of these goals is elaborated with a list of examples, in each case the relevant fund manager or adviser, who is not necessarily recruited for such expertise, has discretion to interpret these criteria and assess companies' performance against them. More informatively, the Calvert Social Index Fund provides quite useful statements of its policy on indigenous peoples, human rights, product safety and corporate governance,

353 Winslow Green Mutual Funds, *Winslow Green Growth Fund: Prospectus*, 2011, 5.

among other RI issues.³⁵⁴ So too does Domini Social Investments, which published a weighty 50-page guide to its policies.³⁵⁵

Some of the most confusing and disingenuous practices are associated with funds' portfolio screens. Application of seemingly morally absolute and rigid criteria can obstruct the nuanced, case-by-case analysis that may be required by the circumstances. Further, many RI funds set ambiguous thresholds for determining whether to exclude a company. For example, the Desjardins Ethical Canadian Balanced Fund explains that it does 'not invest in companies that generate a significant proportion of their income from tobacco products'.³⁵⁶ What does 'significant' mean, and why was that threshold chosen? Even an insignificant amount of such activity can be substantial for a large company in absolute terms.³⁵⁷ Should a paper producer that supplies cigarette wrappings to a tobacco retailer be excluded? Simplistic screens also can fail to fully capture firms operating through extended franchises, subsidiaries and contractors that might ostensibly be viewed as independent businesses.

Because of their sometimes irresolute and abstruse standards, RI portfolios may be little different from 'conventional' retail funds. The Natural Capital Institute's study in 2004 found 'the screening methodologies and exceptions employed by most SRI funds allow practically any publicly-held corporation to be considered as an SRI portfolio company'.³⁵⁸ Over 90 per cent of the Fortune 500 index is included in the RI mutual fund portfolios reviewed by the Institute.³⁵⁹ The growth of corporate engagement methods of RI, at the expense of exclusionary screens, signals a further blurring of the distinction between RI and non-RI portfolios.³⁶⁰ While some RI funds may justify a 'mainstream' portfolio on the basis of their reliance on shareholder activism and engagement in investee companies in order to leverage change, as Chapter 2 explained, most funds are not active owners.

Fiduciary law in retail funds

Whether structured as trusts or as corporations, the controllers of investment funds owe fiduciary responsibilities to their unit-holders or shareholders respectively to pursue stated investment objectives in a loyal and competent manner.³⁶¹ The applicable duties fall on custodial trustees or corporate directors, as well as on the fund managers to whom they delegate responsibilities. Financial planners and advisers who substantially control the selling of

---

354 Http://www.calvert.com.
355 Domini Social Investments (DSI), *Global Investment Standards*, 2006.
356 See http://www.fondsdesjardins.com/en/gammefonds/35ethicalcanbalanced.pdf.
357 Schepers and Sethi, op. cit., 17.
358 Hawken, op. cit., 16.
359 Ibid., 3.
360 G.J. MacDonald, 'A rethink of shunning sin', *Christian Science Monitor*, 23 October 2006.
361 R.C. Pozen, *The Mutual Fund Business*, MIT Press, 1998, 22.

mutual fund investments and other financial products may also have separate fiduciary and regulatory obligations towards clients.[362] The fiduciary parameters are also informed by the contractual terms of the fund's relationship with investors, as reflected in the fund's prospectus.[363]

Retail funds may, within the parameters of securities and investment company laws, manage their portfolio as sold to shareholder or unit-holder investors. Fund managers have authority to select and manage assets within an agreed investment policy, but normally the beneficiary investors must approve any alteration of investment policies. Further, in an investment company, fund managers must fulfill their fiduciary duty to act in the best interests of the firm, as is the case for senior officers and directors of ordinary business corporations. While many institutional investors such as pension plans delegate their portfolio management to external providers, the chain of fiduciary responsibility may still attach to the institutional principal.[364] Thus, a fund trustee who delegates all or a major part of its powers and responsibilities to an external manager may be liable for derelictions of fiduciary responsibility.

A fund manager's implicit duty in fiduciary, trusts or regulatory law to maximize profits can be modified by disclosing investment policies such as ethical criteria that might affect profitability and, in the case of investment companies, by operating within the protection offered by the business judgement rule. The latter is a common law standard of judicial review that protects directors and managers from liability for lost profits when they make informed, good-faith decisions about the operation of a company.[365] Appropriate disclosure, as required by securities regulations, provides further protection to fund managers on the assumption that once relevant information about a fund or company is made public, investors assume the financial risks based on their assessment of that information. Disclosure of risks could involve an RI fund that deliberately prioritizes ethical considerations.

Fund managers can obtain legal protection by seeking shareholder approval for changes in investment policies, since shareholder approval bars claims for breach of fiduciary duty if managers act within the policy parameters. In most jurisdictions, a fund manager must obtain shareholder approval to depart materially from the investment policy outlined in the fund's prospectus.[366] Materiality depends on the specific portfolio and purpose of each fund. If the fund is marketed as environmentally responsible, acquisition of investments in major polluting companies may amount to a

---

362 G. McMeel and J. Virgo, *Financial Advice and Financial Products: Law and Liability*, Oxford University Press, 2002.
363 C.Z. Qu, 'Australia's managed investment schemes: the nature of relationships among scheme participants', *Asia Pacific Law Review* 12(1), 2004, 69–94, 84–5.
364 *Froese v. Montreal Trust Company of Canada*, (1996) 137 DLR (4th) 725.
365 D. Branson, 'The rule that isn't a rule – the business judgment rule', *Valparaiso University Law Review* 36(3), 2002, 631–54.
366 Under US law, see Investment Company Act, 1940, Pub. L. 76-768, 15 USC, s. 80A–13.

material change to a fund's investment composition, requiring shareholder approval.

Sometimes regulation modifies the basic fiduciary responsibility in a manner that facilitates RI. Thus, America's Sudan Accountability and Divestment Act of 2007[367] shields fund managers who divest or avoid companies operating in Sudan in the targeted sectors of oil, mineral extraction, power production or production of weapons, so long as the practice is disclosed in periodic reports. But the legislation doesn't alter the ongoing obligation of fund managers to seek shareholder approval for changes to the fund's investment policies, nor does it apply to other types of social investment decisions. In practice, shareholders readily acquiesce to managers' investment recommendations. Alternatively, if fund managers make investment decisions not specifically prohibited by the prospectus that would not materially affect its investment portfolio, they are likely protected by the business judgement rule.

Mutual fund governance and investor passivity

In practice, investors have little input into investment decisions, even strategic ones. Mutual fund managers' main incentive is to enlarge the quantum of assets under their auspices, thereby boosting their fees. They have no interest in encouraging investor control over fund governance, though they are usually willing to create new mutual funds to fill every conceivable niche, including an ethical one, in order to grow the portfolio domain.[368] Mutual fund governance assumes most investors aren't interested in getting involved in investment decisions, as they're presumably too busy or unqualified. The funds cater to people who apparently don't wish to invest in the stock market themselves but prefer to delegate responsibility to specialists who offer the advantages of portfolio diversification, economies of scale and other risk-management strategies. Even among ostensible RI funds, generally no special emphasis is placed on the participation of members. A few funds, such as Ethical Funds (Canada) and Domini Social Investments (US), consult formally or informally with investors, such as through annual member surveys to gauge investors' views on ESG issues, but mainly for information gathering rather than fostering dialogue.[369] Many fund operators 'have focused on fund proliferation and marketing' and 'salesmanship' rather than meaningful engagement with their investors.[370]

Investors in mutual funds are thus considered to be customers buying financial products rather than active owners of investment assets. Traditionally,

---

367 Pub. L. 110-174.
368 J.C. Bogle, *Battle for the Soul of Capitalism*, Yale University Press, 2005.
369 C.J. Cowton, 'Playing by the rules: ethical criteria at an ethical investment fund', *Business Ethics* 8(1), 1999, 60–9, 64.
370 Bogle, op. cit., 139–41.

fiduciary law has fostered this democratic deficit in fund management by assuming that beneficiaries play a passive role. Instead of the ideal of an active and participatory investor fraternity that integrates social values with the market, a 'retail ethics' prevails. The practice of RI is not anchored in a process of participatory ethical deliberation, but rather investors are the purchasers of 'ethical' portfolios managed by financial experts under the auspices of mutual fund sponsors. In the US, which has by far the world's largest mutual fund market, 53 per cent of assets in its fund industry in 2010 were concentrated in just 10 mutual fund groups, dominated by the triumvirate of Vanguard, Fidelity and American Funds.[371] They are also known for relatively deferential attitudes towards their portfolios companies; for example, regarding shareholder campaigns against high executive compensation, studies allege that the big funds exhibit 'the most management-friendly voting patterns on the shareholder proposals and director voting broad categories'.[372] The notion of 'mutual' therefore seemingly has little relevance to the reality of the mutual fund business.

On paper, however, investors enjoy a range of rights to participate in fund governance.[373] In the US, where mutual funds predominantly take the form of corporations, the Investment Company Act of 1940 allows shareholders to vote on proposed changes to a fund's investment policy objectives; to file resolutions; to receive certain information, including the fund's prospectus; and to vote on the appointment of directors of the fund and changes in the investment adviser (i.e., fund manager).[374] In the UK, where retail funds are structured as trusts or investment corporations, pursuant to the Financial Services and Markets Act of 2000, the unit-holders or shareholders respectively enjoy some similar rights in voting on major changes to the fund, filing resolutions and accessing key information.[375] Likewise, Australian investors in funds structured as corporations possess comparable rights by virtue of the Managed Investments Act of 1998 and Corporations Act of 2001. In particular, unit-holders can change the constitution and investment mandate of an investment company by special resolution.[376] Similar fund governance arrangements and participation rights exist in most other jurisdictions.

In all these cases, however, investors typically exert little influence on fund governance, and the exercise of those rights is generally not encouraged by their managers or trustees. It is highly unlikely that unit-holders or

371 American Federation of State, County and Municipal Employees, *Tipping the Balance? Large Mutual Funds' Influence Upon Executive Compensation*, 2011, 10.
372 Ibid., 4.
373 J.S. Taub, 'Able but not willing: the failure of mutual fund advisers to advocate for shareholders' rights', *Journal of Corporation Law* 34(3), 2009, 844–73.
374 J.A. Haslem (ed.), *Mutual Funds Portfolio. Structures, Analysis, Management, and Stewardship*, John Wiley and Sons, 2010.
375 Financial Services Authority (FSA), *Collective Investment Schemes*, FSA Handbook, 2008, s. 4.3.
376 Corporations Act 2001 (Cth), s. 601GA–GC.

shareholders would spend the time and effort required to change an investment policy when they can simply move their money to another mutual fund that seemingly better caters to their needs. In relation to electing the directors of the fund's board, for example, the practice in the US has been described as 'nothing more than a ritualistic ratification of nominees either by the external manager of the incumbent independent directors'.[377] Further, because mutual funds are intermediaries and voting decisions in their portfolio companies are made by funds' agents, shareholders or unit-holders do not receive direct voting rights in the securities the mutual fund holds. Within the fund itself, investors' voice is weighted to the wealthiest. Their shares or units represent the prorated market value of the assets held by the fund. Voting – and thus voice – is not on the basis of 'one member, one vote' but is based on the aggregate size of one's shareholding. Thus, the holders of the majority of the stock in a meeting of shareholders or unit-holders have little need to consult their peers. This governance regime systematically allows proprietary interest to trump any reasoned discussion, which is discouraging for social investors with relatively small holdings. And of course those without any shares or units have no formal voice.

Disclosure of RI policies and practices

Disclosure standards

The dominant method of regulation of retail funds is to require disclosure. Rather than dictate how funds should invest, disclosure regulations aim to ensure that fund investors are given information to make rational decisions, thereby facilitating market efficiency. However, effective disclosure requires not only the identification of relevant information and its timely communication but also a clarity and precision of expression that will ensure its *comprehension*.[378] As Glorianne Stromberg explains, 'If consumers do not have the fundamental ability to understand and make use of the information that is communicated to them, then none of the other consumer protection remedies (particularly those based on disclosure) will work effectively.'[379] Pursuant to securities and financial regulation and contractual law, funds and their advisers must inform investors about many issues, including selected investments, as well as the considerations or strategies for risk management, profitability, growth, portfolio diversity, fees charged and investors' legal rights. This information is disclosed when a fund issues its initial prospectus

---

377 R.M. Phillips, 'Deregulation under the Investment Company Act – a reevaluation of the corporate paraphernalia of shareholder voting and boards of directors', *Business Lawyer* 37, 1982, 903–13, 910–11.
378 G. Stromberg, *Investment Funds in Canada and Consumer Protection: Strategies for the Millennium*, Industry Canada, 1998, 89.
379 Ibid., 8.

and thereafter through periodic disclosures of performance and any material changes.

The prospectus is the main form of disclosure to investors.[380] A prospectus may contain several pieces of information to help inform social investors about the suitability of the fund for their ethical preferences, including its fundamental investment objectives and philosophy (e.g., ethical, industry sector or geographic scope) and investment risks. Continuous disclosure by investment funds encompasses annual financial statements, management reports of fund performance, material change performance, and proxy solicitation and information circulars. Together, these disclosures may help prevent fraudulent activities and deter questionable business practices, maintain the public's confidence in the securities markets, as well as improve the efficiency of capital markets. It is the legal responsibility of a mutual fund to deliver a prospectus that does not contain any material misrepresentations, fraudulent statements or omissions, since 'a solid majority of fund investors consult this material more than any other source for information about their investment decisions'.[381]

Disclosure standards across national jurisdictions are broadly similar, though some contain additional measures of particular value to RI. Notably, Canadian and US law requires mutual funds to disclose their shareholding proxy voting policies and voting records,[382] a reform motivated to discourage fund managers from passively colluding with corporate management and to improve the quality of corporate governance through a more active proxy process. Peter Kinder heralded the intervention as pioneering, a message that proxy voting is a fiduciary responsibility of fund managers.[383]

Australia has gone the furthest to legislate disclosure standards for RI-related information. Product Disclosure Statements (PDSs) have replaced prospectuses for financial products sold by mutual funds and other managed investment schemes. PDSs must include 'all such information as investors and their professional advisors would reasonably require and reasonably expect to find in the prospectus, for the purpose of making an informed assessment' of the financial product.[384] Since 2001, all funds governed by the PDS requirements, which includes pension fund investments as explained earlier in this chapter, must provide a PDS explaining the extent to which

---

380 R.A. Robertson, 'In search of the perfect mutual fund prospectus', *Business Lawyer* 54, 1998–99, 461–532.
381 Ibid., 467.
382 Securities Exchange Commission, *Disclosure of Proxy Voting Policies and Proxy Voting Records by Registered Management Investment Companies*, SEC, 31 January 2003; Canadian Securities Administrators, *National Instrument 81-106 Investment Fund Continuous Disclosure and Companion Policy 81-106 CP*, 2005.
383 P. Kinder, 'New fiduciary duties in a changing social environment', *Journal of Investing*, Fall, 2005, 24–38, 26.
384 Austrade, 'Managed funds in Australia 2008', 37, http://www.austrade.gov.au/financialservices.

Fiduciary law in retail and institutional finance 215

ESG-related considerations are taken into account in investment decisions.[385] These measures are buttressed by the ASIC's regulatory guidelines[386] that aim to facilitate the 'quantity, format and accuracy of SRI disclosure'.[387] If a fund claims to invest responsibly, the ASIC expects its PDS to explain the criteria for measuring investment standards or considerations, a general description of whether adherence to the methodology is monitored and an explanation of actions taken when an investment no longer adheres to the stated investment policy. The ASIC's guidance is remarkably detailed and attentive to the problems of misleading RI claims:

> [I]f a claim is made that no investment is made in companies associated with product X, the disclosure should clarify what associations this negative screen captures. For example, is the negative screen limited to companies that are directly associated with product X (e.g. they manufacture, mine or grow it) or does it extend to companies that have indirect associations with it (e.g. they transport or retail it)?[388]

EU law in this area, including the Prospectus Directive of 2003,[389] does not contain any comparable provisions directly relevant to RI, but some useful reforms have been enacted by individual EU member states. French investment regulations have recently been modernized to promote sustainability reporting by financial institutions. Investment trusts and fund management companies, as well as insurance companies and credit institutions, must report how they deal with ESG criteria.[390] They must also specify 'how voting rights attaching to financial instruments resulting from these "sustainable" investment policy choices are exercised'.[391] Thus, the route is opened to more socially responsible investments. The reforms stem from a wider overhaul of French environmental legislation initiated in 2007, known as the 'Grenelle de l'environnement', which arose from a negotiation process involving government, business and trade unions.[392] The first piece of legislation (known as the 'Grenelle I' Act) was intended to be a framework for the state's future action, setting broad environmental performance targets.[393] The

---

385 Corporations Act, 2001 (Cth), s. 1013D(1)(l).
386 ASIC, *Section 1013DA Disclosure Guidelines*, ASIC, 2003; and *Policy Statement 168: Product Disclosure Statements*, ASIC, 2005.
387 A. George, N. Edgerton and T. Berry, 'Mainstreaming socially responsible investment (SRI): a role for government–policy recommendations from the investment community', Institute for Sustainable Futures, University of Technology, 2005, 11.
388 ASIC, op. cit., 11.
389 Directive 2003/71/EC, OJ L. 345/64, 31 December 2003.
390 Ordinance no. 2011-915, 1 August 2011, art. L. 523-22-1; Monetary and Financial Code, art. L. 214-12.
391 Art. L. 114-17 Mutual Insurance Code; Art. L. 322-26-2-2 Insurance Code.
392 K. Tetzlaff and F. Malet-Deraedt, 'France', *Yearbook of International Environmental Law* 20(1), 2012, http://yielaw.oxfordjournals.org/content/early/2012/05/10/yiel.yvr012.
393 Loi no. 2009-967 3 August 2009, de programmation relative à la mise en œuvre du Grenelle de l'environnement.

second reform, the 'Grenelle II' Act, amends a swathe of corporate governance and financial regulation to inter alia extend environmental reporting.[394]

While transparency regulation may be theoretically attractive, in practice disclosure can fail to achieve its goal. Information provided may be presented superficially, fragmented among several documents, or generic rather than tailored to a specific audience. As well, novice investors may not recognize the importance of a prospectus or may place excessive trust in their advisers to exercise due diligence on their behalf.[395] Meaningful disclosure should fulfill three key aims: identify relevant information, communicate it to the client and enable the client to comprehend it.[396] To meet those standards, securities regulators may require a simplified prospectus to accompany the full version.[397] The simplified prospectus should contain plain language, in which mutual funds use 'common everyday words' and 'short sentences and paragraphs', while avoiding 'unnecessary technical, legal and business jargon' or 'excessive detail'.[398]

Any financial institution or adviser who misrepresents the characteristics of a fund or other financial product or service it or he sells to the public risks legal liability. A fund that advertises an RI policy has a fiduciary and contractual obligation to its investors to follow that policy. The following section considers the legal controls on deceptive information.

Controlling misrepresentation

The lack of authoritative regulation on what qualifies as 'responsible investment' leaves lay investors vulnerable to vague, unsubstantiated or false marketing. The adequacy of disclosure controls for financial markets generally was rocked by the massive losses precipitated by the GFC, which led to many lawsuits alleging misrepresentation relating to the sale of mortgage-backed securities.[399] Although there are few legal precedents of retail funds being prosecuted for misleading practices in relation to RI, complacency is unjustified. Investors have been known to complain to securities regulators about self-styled RI funds that act contrary to their own policies,[400] and the media has reported on banks investing contrary to their avowed ethical policies.[401] Securities regulation typically authorizes

---

394 Loi no. 2010-788, 12 July 2010, portant engagement national pour l'environnement.
395 Stromberg, *Investment Funds in Canada*, op. cit., 92.
396 Ibid., 89.
397 M.R. Gillen, *Securities Regulation in Canada*, Carswell, 2007, 532.
398 On Canada's approach, see Companion Policy 81-101 CP, s. 3.
399 K. Maerker, 'Fehlerhafte Anlageberatung beim Verkauf von Lehman–Zertifikaten–eine Zwischenbilanz', *Neue Juristische Online-Zeitschrift* 10, 2010, 524–8; *Yu v. State Street Corporation*, (2011) no. 08 Civ. 8235 (SDNY).
400 G. Djurasovic, 'The regulation of socially responsible mutual funds', *Journal of Corporation Law* 22, 1997, 257–94, 276.
401 Several German church-owned banks were ensnared in such a scandal. Pax Bank and Liga Bank, owned by the Catholic Church, had bought shares in tobacco businesses, weapon

regulators or private parties to bring causes of action for fraudulent or deceptive disclosure.

The case of Pax World exemplifies the legal problems that may arise from deceptive RI practices.[402] Pax World Management Corporation (PWMC), one of the biggest players in the American RI retail market, oversees a family of investment funds. It purported to exclude investments in companies involved in military weapons, alcohol, tobacco or gambling, and serviced its funds by developing RI screening policies and procedures, and monitoring portfolios for ongoing RI compliance. Also, PWMC authorized its fund managers to buy only securities that were approved by its Social Research Department. Although PWMC represented to investors that it adhered to these ethical restrictions and policies, from 2001 to 2005 its funds acted contrarily, and PWMC failed to monitor funds' holdings for compliance. In 2005 the SEC initiated an investigation, which resulted in administrative sanctions against Pax World pursuant to the Investment Advisers Act and the Investment Company Act, resulting in a US$500,000 civil penalty.[403] Subsequently, PWMC purported to alter its RI policies and procedures, including lifting its no-tolerance policy against 'sin stocks' – specifically, alcohol and gambling – in favour of a more nuanced approach to assessing corporate social responsibility.[404]

Securities regulation typically imposes liability for a 'material' misrepresentation that would affect the value of the security being sold. There are nuanced differences in how this materiality standard is interpreted in different jurisdictions. Both Canadian and US regulators essentially follow the materiality test outlined by the US Supreme Court in *TSC Industries Inc. v. Northway Inc*,[405] which states that 'proof of materiality involves whether, objectively, a statement would have misled a *reasonably prudent investor* about the nature of the investment in a given situation'.[406] As well, for nondisclosure to be legally actionable, 'there must be a substantial likelihood that a reasonable investor would have viewed disclosing the omitted fact as having

---

industries, and nuclear power utilities. Ironically, for a Catholic bank, they had also invested in a US pharmaceutical company (Wyeth) that produces birth control pills: V.M. Oppong and P. Wensierski, 'Banken: sündige rendite', *Spiegel* 12 September 2010, 82–3.

402 This discussion of the Pax World case draws upon the SEC's report, http://www.sec.gov/litigation/admin/2008/ia-2761.pdf.
403 SEC, 'In the matter of Pax World Management Corporation', Administrative Proceeding No. 3-13107, July 2008; B. Sanders, 'SEC launches inquiry into Pax World funds', *New Hampshire Business Review* 27(21), 2005, 1.
404 J. Hechinger, 'Pax Funds strayed from its mission: "socially responsible" firm broke rules against investing in certain companies', *Wall Street Journal* (eastern edn.), 31 July 2008, C1. See also Pax World's statement, http://www.paxworld.com/homepage/2008/07/30/a-letter-from-the-president-and-ceo-of-pax-world-funds.
405 (1976) 426 US 438. On the Canadian standard, see e.g., CSA, National Instrument 51-102, Continuous Disclosure Obligations Part 1, Definitions and Interpretation, 1.
406 D. Monsma and J. Buckley, 'Non-financial corporate performance: the material edges of social and environmental disclosure', *University of Baltimore Journal of Environmental Law* 11, 2004, 151–203, 186.

significantly altered the total mix of information made available'.[407] Reliance must also be reasonable; 'a sophisticated plaintiff or investor with superior access to the truth is not justified in relying on the misstatement or omission'.[408]

In the UK, common law rulings also suggest a materiality standard that would require an investor to show that he or she relied on the misleading advice by the professional adviser.[409] The Financial Services and Markets Act of 2000 provides for slightly different standards regarding initial and ongoing disclosure by security issuers to investors.[410] In general, a material misrepresentation to social investors could arise in several situations: at the level of a fund's overall portfolio if it fails to fulfill the broad ESG criteria it advertises, such as to 'invest in the greenest and most sustainable companies'. Unlawful misrepresentation may ensue because of deficiencies in the fund's prospectus. Alternatively, a material deception could be traceable to a specific investment decision, such as acquisition of securities in an individual business with a woeful environmental record. More difficult to judge are qualitative actions, such as concerning the adequacy of corporate engagement on ESG issues.

'Materiality' is a broad, ambiguous notion that can be hard to enforce. The materiality standard may fail to provide investors with essential information about corporate ESG performance. Although courts stress that materiality is an 'objective' standard, and thus companies may not rely on their own arbitrary judgements as to whether ESG matters are 'material', in practice investors rely on the company to ascertain and disclose material risks. A substantial ESG research industry has grown to service the RI sector, which may help social investors to verify the materiality of ESG performance, but it is a service that must be paid for when companies should perform their own due diligence. Further, the materiality standard focuses on financial risks to the issuer – the company – rather than on the many stakeholders potentially affected by corporate activities.

Consequently, companies do not generally consider climate change or species extinctions, for instance, as 'material', unless they believe they may present a risk to the issuer. A 2008 study by the Ontario Securities Commission on corporate environmental disclosures found that material information regarding environmental matters was often segregated into voluntary reports and was not included in securities regulatory filings; the information provided was not necessarily complete and was of a boilerplate character that did not provide meaningful information to investors; it was not provided in a timely

---

407 *TSC Industries Inc.*, op. cit., 449. See also *Wilson v. Bernstock*, (2002) 195 F. Supp. 2d 619.
408 J.W. Bagby, et al., 'How green was my balance sheet? Corporate liability and environmental disclosure', *Virginia Environmental Law Journal* 14, 1995, 225–342, 323.
409 This conclusion follows from the *Hedley Byrne and Co. Ltd v. Heller and Partners Ltd* (1963) 2 All ER 575.
410 Sections 90–90A.

manner; and the information was not integrated into financial reporting.[411] The Ontario study led to issuance of new Canadian guidance on when environmental issues may be considered 'material'.[412] Likewise, in the US market in 2010 the SEC released interpretative guidance on disclosure of climate change risks in response to lobbying of investor and environmental groups.[413]

Common law remedies for misleading business communications are also available under contract law and tort law.[414] These remedies are advantageous as they often have longer limitation periods than statutory actions under securities regulation and can provide claimants with greater damages and different types of relief, such as injunctions. Nevertheless, despite these advantages, common law remedies are expensive to litigate and potentially hard to prove. It is challenging for investors to prove the tort of intentional or negligent misrepresentation, and they must further demonstrate they relied on the defendant's statements when deciding to invest in a fund and incurred consequential damages. Investors might have more success finding relief from contractual remedies, such as breach of the warranties about responsible investing promised in a fund's prospectus.

In conclusion, disclosure has become the key legal mechanism worldwide for aligning the behaviour of financial fiduciaries with their investors in the retail market. Its effectiveness remains highly debatable. Not only are there problems in ensuring the quality of information provided by financial institutions, but the companies they invest in also have their own environmental and financial disclosure obligations that may not be honoured. These reporting standards are typically limited by the need to tie information to the financial position of the company and don't take account of very long-term risks and performance. Furthermore, the underlying accounting standards, such as the International Financial Reporting Standards issued by the International Accounting Standards Board, which are widely used for securities reporting, are not well adapted to capturing ESG information of a qualitative nature.[415] There is also a range of extra-legal disclosure that comes not from direct reporting by market participants but by scrutiny from environmental NGOs or human rights groups. Such disclosure can lead to adverse media publicity that disciplines investors and companies, compelling them to improve their sustainability performance. An example is the Pembina Institute's investigation of environmental disclosure by Canadian oil sands

---

411 Ontario Securities Commission, *Staff Notice 51-716 – Environmental Reporting*, 2008, 31 OSCB 2228.
412 Canadian Securities Administrators, Staff Notice 51-333, October 2010.
413 SEC, 'Commission guidance regarding disclosure related to climate change', Interpretation, 2 February 2010.
414 In relation to disciplining deceptive CSR, see T. Spencer, 'Talking about social responsibility: liability for misleading and deceptive statements in corporate codes of conduct', *Monash Law Review* 29(2), 2003, 297–315.
415 See http://www.ifrs.org/Home.htm.

businesses.[416] Disclosure is also used for such purposes in the relationships between financial advisers and clients, as the next section discusses.

Financial advisers

Because some investors lack in-depth finance expertise, they turn to professionals for assistance. A financial adviser is an individual or firm (including banks) that provides investment advice and associated financial advisory services, and increasingly such advisers assist clients who wish to invest ethically.[417] A financial adviser may also be a key intermediary in accessing mutual funds, for often investors do not buy directly into those funds but rather use the services of a specialist adviser. Financial advisers and investment consultants are also widely relied upon by large institutional funds for their expertise.[418] Indeed, they may be legally obliged to do so; British pension trustees must obtain and consider the advice of investment experts when drafting their investment policies.[419] An emerging hallmark of fiduciary responsibility in this area includes enquiring into clients' investment values and preferences, and making known available RI options where appropriate. According to Meir Statman, a Santa Clara University academic who researches investors' behaviour, investment advice that ignores clients' non-monetary interests is 'fundamentally flawed'.[420] However, because financial advisers often earn 'remuneration from [the funds] via commissions, rather than directly from their clients, significant conflicts of interest can arise and arguably compromise much of the financial advice that is provided'.[421] That advice may not be formulated in clients' best interest.

The extent to which fiduciary responsibility applies to this link in the investment chain is sometimes uncertain, and the 2012 *Kay Review of UK Equity Markets and Long-Term Decision-Making* recommended legal clarification to confirm its application.[422] Legal commentators disagree about 'the legal elements in any factual context that may suffice to constitute a fiduciary relationship'.[423] Fiduciary law can offer benefits in addressing situations where investment advisers and consultants have conflicting roles, such as

---

416 N. Lemphers, *Full Disclosure, Environmental Liabilities in Canada's Oil Sands*, Pembina Institute, 2011.
417 M. Statman, 'Socially responsible investors and their advisors', *Journal of Investment Consulting* 9(1), 2008, 14–25.
418 The notion of financial or investment 'adviser' used in this section is not intended to mean a fund manager, as the term implies in US mutual fund law, but rather professionals who deal directly with individual investors in providing financial planning services or selling financial products.
419 Occupational Pension Schemes (Investment) Regulations 2005, cl. 2(2).
420 M. Statman, 'Why you're not a rational investor', *Fortune Magazine*, 7 November 2007, 154.
421 Fear and Pace, op. cit., 31.
422 Kay, op. cit., 69.
423 Ibid.

acting as advisers to both investors and companies.[424] In most jurisdictions the financial adviser industry is only lightly regulated, as complemented by various industry-based codes.[425] The legal landscape also includes private law rules in tort and contract, and fiduciary responsibility itself, as modulated by regulation. If the relationship between an adviser and her client is fiduciary in character, the obligation may simply be proscriptive, such as to eschew conflicts of interest or, as in some countries, include positive duties to provide the best advice and promote the client's financial or ethical preferences.[426] Fiduciary principles can apply when intermediaries possess and handle client assets or provide professional advice that the parties expect will be relied upon.[427] Where the financial adviser offers services that are expected to be comprehensive or continuous, fiduciary responsibility is more likely to arise.[428]

British investment advisers and consultants do not generally appear to regard themselves as fiduciaries,[429] though when advising on complex or risky investments that might benefit themselves through higher service fees, they can attract fiduciary responsibility.[430] Australian case law has imposed fiduciary standards when any stockbroker 'who holds himself out as having expertise in advising on investments is approached for advice on investments and undertakes to give it'.[431] Another landmark Australian case, dealing with one aftermath of the financial losses associated with the GFC, held that the investment firm was conflicted in its fiduciary duty to give sound financial advice to the municipal councils and its own interest 'to earn very significant fees' in its sales of investments that later became known as 'toxic assets'.[432] American financial advisers may incur fiduciary responsibility by virtue of the Investment Advisers Act, which the US Supreme Court interprets as reflecting 'the delicate fiduciary nature of an investment advisory relationship' and which aims to 'eliminate, or at least to expose, all conflicts of interest which might incline an investment adviser – consciously or unconsciously – to render advice which was not disinterested'.[433] The recent Dodd-Frank Act

---

424 E. Knight and A.D. Dixon, 'The role of investment consultants in transforming pension fund decision-making: the integration of environmental, social and governance considerations into corporate valuation', in Hawley, Kamath and Williams, op. cit., 217–41.
425 See I.H.Y. Chiu, 'The nature of a financial investment intermediary's duty to his client', *Legal Studies* 28(2), 2008, 254–80.
426 Tuch, op. cit., 493.
427 Ibid., 257; and L.S. Sealy, 'Fiduciary relationships', *Cambridge Law Journal* 1962, 69–81.
428 S. Ober, 'Fiduciary responsibility: liability and consequences', *Journal of Financial Planning* 18(11), 2005, 50–63.
429 FairPensions, op. cit., 43.
430 Ibid.
431 *Daly v. Sydney Stock Exchange*, (1986) 160 CLR 371, 385.
432 *Wingecarribee Shire Council v. Lehman Brothers Australia Ltd (in liq.)*, [2012] FCA 1028, para. 300.
433 *SEC v. Capital Gains Research Bureau, Inc.*, (1963) 375 US 180, 191–2.

empowers the SEC to extend fiduciary duties to broker-dealers when they furnish investment advice that is personalized to clients.[434]

The general common law of negligence also governs investment intermediaries. Historically, a financial adviser wasn't liable for any careless advice in the absence of an underlying contractual relationship.[435] The law of negligence was transformed by *Donoghue v. Stevenson*[436] and has since evolved to encompass negligent advice that occasions economic losses.[437] British law obliges financial intermediaries to exercise care and skill in discharging their functions to clients.[438] Some legal commentators believe the standard of care imposed under general law is higher than normal, in order 'to countervail the discretionary power that an investment intermediary may be able to exercise over investors, who are likely to be in a position of information asymmetry vis-à-vis the investment intermediary'.[439] As well, investment advisers are subject to regulatory controls on fraud, misrepresentation and conflicts of interest, which is vital given the difficulties of relying wholly on fiduciary principles when conflicts of interest may arise where an intermediary's business serves numerous investors and clients. Legislation in major markets governing financial advisers typically addresses several broad categories of investor protection: disclosure of material facts relating to the financial product, registration of the product, prohibition of transactions involving conflicts of interest, prohibition of misleading advertising, product suitability requirements, and redress mechanisms.[440] Regulatory rules can be considered as equivalent to contractual terms that modify the underlying nature and scope of any fiduciary or tortious duties.[441]

Not only must financial intermediaries act transparently towards clients; they should request from clients 'information on financial standing, investment appetite, knowledge and experience' to ensure the suitability of any advice.[442] EU law requires a financial intermediary to assess the suitability of a transaction for a client if it comes within portfolio management or investment advice.[443] Germany's 'Bond' case illustrates the potential liability of banks' financial advisers for not considering the suitability of rec-

---

434 Dodd–Frank Wall Street Reform and Consumer Protection Act, 2010, Pub. L. No. 111-203, s. 913(g).
435 See *Banbury v. Bank of Montreal*, [1918] AC 626.
436 [1932] AC 562.
437 *Hedley Byrne v. Heller & Partners Ltd*, (1963) 2 All ER 575.
438 *Lloyd Cheyham and Co. Ltd v. Eversheds*, (1985) 2 Lloyds PN 154.
439 Chiu, op. cit., 268.
440 O.O. Cherednychenko, 'The regulation of retail investment services in the EU: towards the improvement of investor rights?', *Journal of Consumer Policy* 33, 2010, 403–24.
441 Law Commission, *Fiduciary Duties and Regulatory Rules*, Cm 3049, Law Commission, 1995; C. Harpum, 'Fiduciary obligations and fiduciary powers', in P. Birks (ed.), *Privacy and Loyalty*, Clarendon Press, 1997, 145–68.
442 Chiu, op. cit., 263.
443 Notably, Directive 2004/39/EC of the European Parliament and of the Council of 21 April 2004 on markets in financial instruments amending Council Directives 85/611/EEC and 93/6/EEC.

ommendations to clients. According to the German Supreme Court, investment advice to clients should be geared to their personal circumstances, and if a bank lacks information concerning a client's needs or situation, it must obtain it.[444] In contrast to the 'suitability' standard, a 'best interest' standard is imposed in some other countries, such as the US.[445] The difference between a 'suitability' and 'best interest' standard can be crucial to social investors. An adviser may recommend an investment portfolio that is generally suitable for the client's ethical needs and earns the adviser a higher sales commission, while another portfolio that is better tailored to the clients' specific ethical preferences offers a lower commission and may thus be 'overlooked' by the adviser. If a fund misleads investors, such as by not practising the ethical policies promised in the fund's prospectus, the landmark case of *Janus Capital Group v. First Derivative Traders*[446] suggests that investment advisers will not be liable because they are not considered to be the 'maker' of the underlying investment policies in question, though they may be liable for associated regulatory offences, such as aiding and abetting.

Australian regulatory guidance is unusually attentive to clients' possible RI preferences. The ASIC's guidance to financial advisers explains that 'as a matter of good practice (and irrespective of any current legal requirement)', advisers 'should seek to ascertain whether environmental, social or ethical considerations are important to the client and, if they are, conduct reasonable inquiries about them'.[447] The Australian approach suggests that the general client suitability rule pertains to such situations, but it actually empowers advisers to determine the importance of ESG considerations for any given client. Advisers are encouraged to engage with their clients on ESG issues rather than merely regard ESG matters as a discrete checkbox compliance requirement.

When determining whether financial advisers stand in fiduciary relationships with or owe special duties of care to their clients, it is also important to consider professional codes of conduct.[448] A key component of the governance framework for financial intermediaries is provided by their own industry associations, which commonly issue self-regulatory codes and business practice standards. In Canada, to illustrate, three bodies set such standards for professional investment advisers: the Investment Industry Regulatory Organization of Canada (IIROC), the Mutual Fund Dealers Association of Canada and the Financial Advisors Association of Canada. The IIROC, which oversees all investment dealers in debt and equity markets in Canada, aspires to set business conduct standards, protect investors and

---

444 German Supreme Court, 6 July 1993, BGHZ 123, 126.
445 E. Waitzer, 'Make advisors work for investors', *Financial Post*, 14 February 2011, 11.
446 [2011] US 564.
447 ASIC, *Regulatory Guide 175, Financial Product Advisors – Conduct and Disclosure*, 2011, 38.
448 Dolden Wallace Follck (DWF) LLP, 'Legal liability for financial advisors in Canada', 2011, 34.

strengthen market integrity while maintaining efficient and competitive capital markets.[449] In 2011, the IIROC published proposed reforms to its codes of professional conduct between clients and advisers, which avoids obliging advisers to act in their clients' best interests; instead, IIROC focuses on 'knowing your client's needs' and improving compliance with the existing 'suitability' standard of advising and improving disclosure with respect to conflicts of interest and performance reporting.[450] When looking to what is considered the prevailing best practice convention, for the purpose of informing the fiduciary duty or duty of care, these industry codes of conduct can be influential.

Conclusions

Financial institutions, from insurance companies to pension trusts, are bound in fiduciary relationships with their clients and members. Characterizing the relationship as fiduciary, however, doesn't adequately describe it: the scope and content depends on the parties' own circumstances, as well as synergistic effects from other legal norms in regulation, contracts, common law principles and even business codes of conduct, which may modify the parameters of fiduciary accountability. The regulatory framework is particularly influential, as their standards typically emphasize enhanced disclosure, business conduct rules and sometimes restrictions on certain investments and maintenance of adequate reserves to meet liabilities and buffer risks. The precise enunciation of these standards varies somewhat from institution to institution, and across different jurisdictions. But the underlying fiduciary framework informs how investment decision-makers should act and for whose benefit. In any institution, the fiduciary standard ultimately performs a similar function: to align financial decision-making with the interests of beneficiaries.

Formally, RI has been subjugated by this model. Yet RI has grown in recent years in diverse financial sectors. Banks increasingly take into account the environmental impacts of project financing, mutual funds sell ethical portfolios to eager lay investors, and some 'universal' pension funds acknowledge ESG risks in their portfolios. Can we thus sanguinely conclude that fiduciary law is trivial? Not really. RI has prospered because it hardly challenges the economic values and private interests protected by fiduciary norms. Despite earlier legal skirmishes, the prevailing RI market sits quite comfortably with fiduciary law because it doesn't seek radical change. The composition of many mutual funds' RI portfolios is remarkably similar to regular portfolios; their investment goals make similar promises of prosperity. For pension funds and banks, RI is mainly a means to manage another type of

---

449 IIROC: http://www.iiroc.ca/English/About/OurRole.
450 Waitzer, 'Make advisors work for investors', op. cit.

business risk. Ethical imperatives get downplayed unless they fit within a business case.

If there were a cultural shift in the financial sector, the current formulations of fiduciary law and related legal norms would struggle to accommodate an unadulterated style of ethical investment. The trust governing a pension fund could be redrafted to define beneficiaries' 'interests' more ethically, but overriding prudential regulation tends to frame those interests as being of a financial character. Mutual funds have more flexibility to meet diverse investment goals, including ethical ones, and investors can shop for funds that best meet their ethical or financial needs. But current fiduciary standards do not *require* explicit consideration of social and environmental matters. They remain discretionary concerns, to be weighed by the very market forces that have traditionally marginalized them.

5 Sovereign wealth funds

The ethical and financial mandates of SWFs

Sovereign wealth funds (SWFs) might be one of the best candidates for leading the financial sector towards sustainability because of their relatively long-term investment horizons, large size and potential market leverage, and public sector accountability. SWFs also display the hallmarks of true fiduciary investors, in that they manage large pools of assets on behalf of the state to meet its citizens' future economic needs. SWFs have become a major presence in global financial markets since the late twentieth century, and several purport to invest ethically. Their engagement with RI issues has the potential to precipitate widespread change beyond SWFs' own portfolios, by setting best practice for private sector counterparts. Already, the ethical investment practices of Norway's SWF are copied by a number of Norwegian financial institutions, including KLP (a municipal pension fund) and DNB (a private financial group).[1] Yet like private investors, SWFs also prioritize profitability. A tension therefore simmers between the ethical and financial expectations of SWFs.

This chapter investigates how this tension is managed in three contrasting case studies, the Norwegian Government Pension Fund-Global (NGPF-G), the New Zealand Superannuation Fund (NZSF) and the French Pension Reserve Funds (FRR). They all have legislative mandates to invest ethically and have been hailed for their progressive approaches to RI.[2] Already, the NGPF-G is the world's largest investor to apply RI criteria. These case studies will help us understand how fiduciary investing may accommodate environmental considerations in entities legally mandated to invest responsibly. So far this book has examined the limitations of fiduciary finance law without affirmative duties to invest responsibly. Although the SWFs studied here are not strictly speaking 'fiduciary' actors, as a matter of legal doctrine, they function at least in a political sense as quasi-fiduciaries, and

---

1 E. Bengtsson, 'A history of Scandinavian socially responsible investing', *Journal of Business Ethics* 82, 2008, 969–83, 978.
2 UNEP-FI Asset Management Working Group and UKSIF, *Responsible Investment in Focus: How Leading Public Pension Funds are Meeting the Challenge*, UNEP-FI, 2007, 7.

their performance can provide insight into the reforms proposed in the final chapter about enlisting SWFs as public fiduciaries for RI.

While there is no international authoritative definition of SWFs, several salient characteristics have been identified. The IMF's criteria describe a SWF as controlled by a national government, managing financial assets on a long-term basis and investing to achieve specific macro-economic objectives.[3] The Sovereign Wealth Fund Institute (SWFI) defines a SWF as: 'a state-owned investment fund or entity that is commonly established from balance of payments surpluses, official foreign currency operations, the proceeds of privatizations, governmental transfer payments, fiscal surpluses, and/or receipts resulting from resource exports'.[4] Of the examples considered in this chapter, only the NGPF-G and NZSF are commonly identified as SWFs. However, the FRR should also be included because it meets the aforementioned core indicia and others discussed in the literature.[5]

The spread of SWFs seemingly defies an era in which many governments have sought to deregulate or otherwise limit their hand in the market.[6] SWFs are typically created as separate legal entities with full capacity to act and be governed by a specific constitutive law, but some take the form of state-owned enterprise or are constituted by a pool of assets without a separate legal identity under the control of the state's central bank.[7] Yet, while SWFs are formally public institutions, functionally they are generally expected to behave like private investors. Their dyadic character means that while participating in global financial markets, SWFs are harnessed to meet states' macro-economic policy objectives,[8] such as to buffer government budgets against swings in international markets or to build savings to meet intergenerational commitments. SWFs are typically funded either through commodity-based earnings, such as from a country's natural resources sector, or through non-commodity-based resources, such as foreign exchange reserves and general taxation revenue.[9] The NGPF-G is a commodity-based fund,

---

3 IMF, 'Sovereign wealth funds – a work agenda', 29 February 2008, 4–5.
4 SWFI, 'What is an SWF?', http://www.swfinstitute.org/what-is-a-swf.
5 Government-employee pension funds or social security reserve funds are not ordinarily defined as SWFs, because they are established within the overall social security system and funded by surpluses of employee/employer contributions. However, some pension funds deemed to be SWFs are financed mainly from fiscal transfers from the state to meet future deficits of the social security system, as is the case for the FRR: A. Blundell-Wignall, Y.-W. Hu and J. Yermo, 'Sovereign wealth and pension fund issues', *OECD Working Papers on Insurance and Private Pensions*, No. 14, OECD, 2008, 5.
6 A. Monk, *Sovereignty in the Era of Global Capitalism: The Rise of Sovereign Wealth Funds and the Power of Finance*, School of Geography and the Environment, Oxford University, 2010; R. Beck and M. Fidora, 'The impact of sovereign wealth funds on global financial markets', *Intereconomics* 43(6), 2008, 349–58.
7 E.L. van der Zee, *In Between Two Societal Actors: The Responsibilities of SWFs Towards Human Rights and Climate Change*, Masters thesis, Utrecht University 2012, 12.
8 Blundell-Wignall, Hu and Yermo, op. cit., 4.
9 R. Sarkar, 'Sovereign wealth funds as a development tool for ASEAN nations: from social wealth to social responsibility', *Georgetown Journal of International Law* 41, 2010, 621–46, 623.

built on Norway's large oil reserves, while the NZSF and FRR are supported by non-commodity financing.

Such concentration of wealth has made SWFs, an institutional phenomenon dating from the mid-1950s, potentially influential actors in the global economy.[10] According to the SWFI, as of May 2012 there were at least 61 SWFs worldwide, with assets totalling US$5.004 trillion.[11] At that time, Norway's SWF ranked the second largest, with US$661 billion in assets, while New Zealand's much smaller SWF had US$15.9 billion.[12] France's FRR had €35.6 billion as of June 2011.[13] As a proportion of global financial securities, in 2008 SWFs' share was only about 3 per cent, still dwarfed by private sector funds, such as those held by insurance companies (17 per cent) and mutual funds (18 per cent).[14] However, the assets of any SWF typically greatly exceed that of any individual private investment fund, and the latter are less likely than SWFs to coordinate their activities on RI issues.

As SWFs' assets have soared, and that wealth has been invested beyond national borders, the economic clout and capacity of SWFs to project state political power globally has raised concerns.[15] Their ownership or control by states can enmesh them in the machinery of government and thereby render them instruments of public policy. Concern is rising about the alleged lack of transparency and accountability in the management of some SWFs.[16] Their financial performance might also suffer under such conditions. Ashby Monk and Gordon Clark, who co-direct the Oxford University SWF Project, contend that some SWF governance is 'subject to partisan interests and bureaucratic encroachment such that its functional performance would be fundamentally compromised'.[17] For instance, during the GFC in 2009, the Irish government dubiously directed the national pension reserve fund to invest in two ailing Irish banks.[18] Also in that year, the Swedish government directed its public pension 'AP funds' to use their ownership rights in Swedish companies to help align the companies' executive compensation practices

---

10 Ibid., 631.
11 SWFI, 'Sovereign wealth funds cross 5 trillion dollar barrier', 2 May 2012, http://www.swfinstitute.org/swf-news/sovereign-wealth-funds-cross-5-trillion-dollar-barrier/. The list of SWFs is at http://www.swfinstitute.org/fund-rankings/.
12 Ibid.
13 FRR, Press release, 9 August 2011, http://www.fondsdereserve.fr/IMG/pdf/Assets performancesasof30June2011-3.pdf.
14 'Asset-backed insecurity', *The Economist* 386(8563), 17 January 2008, 71–3.
15 L.C. Backer, 'Sovereign investing in times of crisis: global regulation of sovereign wealth funds, state-owned enterprises, and the Chinese experience', *Transnational Law and Contemporary Problems* 19, 2010–11, 3–144, 11.
16 E.M. Truman, *Sovereign Wealth Funds: The Need for Greater Transparency and Accountability*, Peterson Institute for International Economics, 2007.
17 G.L. Clark and A. Monk, 'Partisan politics and bureaucratic encroachment: the principles and policies of pension reserve fund design and governance', working paper, SSRN, 2011, 1.
18 'Wasting wealth in Ireland', Oxford SWF Project, 31 March 2010, http://oxfordswfproject.com/2010/03.

with the government's policy.[19] Furthermore, the ethical goals of some SWFs have stirred debate about the wisdom of mixing non-financial criteria with wealth maximization, as well as the appropriateness of attempting to influence corporate social and environmental behaviour.[20]

Although SWFs do not formally become parties to international law treaties in the same manner that states at large do, they may use such treaties as a moral compass for their RI practices, and some commentators query whether, as a matter of state responsibility under international law, an SWF could be considered an organ of the state to whom such responsibilities extend.[21] Some SWFs have signed up to international soft law codes such as the UNPRI and UN Global Compact. The international community has also drafted a code exclusively for SWFs – the Santiago Principles of 2008.[22] However, the motivating idea behind the Santiago Principles 'seems to be to avoid political interference by SWFs, which also may include ethics and human rights'.[23] The Principles emphasize transparency, clarity and equivalent treatment to private funds. They do not contain any expectations about RI practices, instead stressing that the core focus of an SWF should be to 'maximize risk-adjusted financial returns in a manner consistent with its investment policy, and based on economic and financial grounds'.[24] However, SWFs may exclude certain investments on other grounds, including social, environmental or ethical reasons, so long as such considerations are clearly explained and publicly disclosed.[25]

SWFs share several characteristics that might make them more inclined to invest in sustainable development than private sector financiers. Firstly, the public visibility of SWFs potentially exposes sponsoring states to political damage from any unethical investment. Secondly, given their sheer size and government backing, SWFs should have higher risk tolerances and might therefore experiment with investment strategies eschewed by private financiers. Further, because of their economic goals, including the meeting of future financial liabilities, SWFs tend to have longer-term financial

---

19 C. Severinson and F. Stewart, 'Review of the Swedish National Pension Funds', OECD Working Papers on Finance, Insurance and Private Pensions, No. 17, 2012, 16.
20 G.L. Clark and A. Monk, 'The Norwegian government pension fund: ethics over efficiency', *Rotman International Journal of Pension Management* 3(1), 2010, 14–19, 17; L.C. Backer, 'Sovereign wealth funds as regulatory chameleons: the Norwegian sovereign wealth funds and public global governance through private global investment', *Georgetown Journal of International Law* 41(2), 2010, 425–500, 453.
21 van der Zee, op. cit.
22 International Working Group of Sovereign Wealth Funds, *Generally Accepted Principles and Practices: Santiago Principles*, October 2008, http://www.iwg-swf.org/pubs/gapplist.htm.
23 G. Nystuen, A. Follesdal and O. Mestad, 'Introduction', in G. Nystuen, A. Follesdal and O. Mestad (eds), *Human Rights Corporate Complicity and Disinvestment*, Cambridge University Press, 2011, 1–15, 5.
24 Principle 19.
25 Principle 19.1.

considerations than the private sector.[26] This may encourage investing that is mindful of climate change and other sustainability concerns. Referring to the FRR, William Baue described its mandate as 'a perfect marriage with RI, which looks beyond the quarterly earnings statements that mainstream investors fixate on to assess how long-term social and environmental factors will inevitably impact financial returns, positively and negatively'.[27]

Though regulations to encourage RI in the private sector are emerging, explicit duties to practise RI have so far been imposed only on public financial institutions, including SWFs.[28] The first precedents arose in the 1980s in some US states and municipalities, restricting government pension funds from investing in firms operating in South Africa[29] or Northern Ireland.[30] Since 2000, the SWFs of Norway, New Zealand and France have been subject to legislative direction to invest ethically, with more comprehensive and ambitious obligations than the American precedents. None of these legal mandates amount to fiduciary responsibilities in the sense discussed earlier in this book. These SWFs lack a specific class of beneficiaries to whom they are accountable, as in the case of an occupational pension plan. Instead, legal standards and directions that govern SWFs can be construed as a form of administrative law, subject in some situations to judicial review for compliance. The substantive merits of SWFs' investment decisions are probably beyond legal reproach. But the SWFs may still be viewed as *political fiduciaries*, accountable to the government of the day and indirectly to the general public on whose behalf they act.

Ethical investment by SWFs is controversial. Apart from the traditional belief that any investment should serve only financial purposes, there is further concern with SWFs that RI could be a means for sponsoring states to insinuate their social and environmental policies globally.[31] The RI legislative mandates attract controversy, as they can be perceived as making it difficult to hold SWF managers accountable for optimal financial

---

26 J. Yermo, *Governance and Investment of Public Pension Reserve Funds in Selected OECD Countries*, Working Papers on Insurance and Private Pensions, No. 15, OECD, 2008, 4.
27 W. Baue, 'French pension reserve fund commits 600 million euros to responsible investment', *Social Funds News*, 5 July 2008, http://www.socialfunds.com/news/article.cgi/1750.html.
28 B.J. Richardson, *Socially Responsible Investment Law: Regulating the Unseen Polluters*, Oxford University Press, 2008, 303–75.
29 P. McCarroll, 'Socially responsible investment of public pension funds: the South Africa issue and state law', *Review of Law and Social Change* 10, 1980–81, 407–34; G. Jubinsky, 'State and municipal governments react against South African apartheid', *University of Cincinnati Law Review* 54, 1985, 453–78.
30 See C. McCrudden, 'Human rights codes for transnational corporations: what can the Sullivan and MacBride Principles tell us?', *Oxford Journal of Legal Studies* 19(2), 1999, 167–201; N.J. Conway, 'Investment responsibility in Northern Ireland: the MacBride Principles of fair employment', *Loyola of Los Angeles International and Comparative Law Review* 24, 2002, 1–17.
31 Clark and Monk, 'Partisan politics and bureaucratic encroachment', op. cit., 10; Backer, 'Regulatory chameleons', op. cit.

returns.³² Proposals to include an RI mandate in Ireland's National Pensions Reserve Fund Act of 2000 were rejected in Parliament on the grounds it would 'politicize' the Fund's investment mandate and cause significant difficulties in its interpretation and implementation.³³ A 2009 survey of 146 asset managers having routine dealings with SWFs reported that most 'did not think governments should have any influence over investment decisions, despite the fact that SWFs are managing governments' money'.³⁴ But such concerns misunderstand the changing rationale and aims of RI, which, as already discussed in this book, is geared increasingly to a financial rather than ethical analysis of social and environmental behaviour.

This chapter takes up these themes by examining the RI legal mandates, policies and practices of the Norwegian, New Zealand and French SWFs. In comparing how they attempt to reconcile their ethical and financial aspirations, the chapter highlights the important influence of the governance frameworks. While there are some salient differences in how each SWF is governed and the breadth and rigour of their RI practices, they have somewhat shared a focus on avoiding complicity in unethical conduct or social and environmental harm. This stance represents a narrow approach to RI, limiting the capacity of these SWFs to promote sustainable development. More recently, all three funds have begun to accept the business case for RI and have reconceptualized RI as a means of promoting long-term financial returns. But no SWF is mandated to actively *promote* sustainable development or to seek improvements in corporations' sustainability performance. In the future evolution of SWFs, the creation of explicit duties to invest in sustainability is perhaps the next logical step if they are to be RI leaders in the global economy.

Before looking at the SWF case studies from France, Norway and New Zealand, a brief discussion about some other SWFs and public sector funds with RI mandates or practices is worthwhile, in order to illustrate the range of legal and institutional approaches.

Responsible investment by public financial institutions

US state and municipal funds

The US was the first country to legislate RI restrictions, imposing on some state and municipal pension plans bans on certain investment activities. Their trustees are often political appointees or are elected by plan members. Unlike the RI mandates for SWFs examined later in this chapter, the

---

32 R. Pozen, 'Arm yourself for the coming battle over social security', *Harvard Business Review* 80(11), 2002, 52–62.
33 Select Committee on Finance and the Public Service, *Parliamentary Debates* 44, 23 February 2006, 5. Yet, subsequently the reserve fund adopted a mild RI policy, without legislative change.
34 G.L. Clark and A. Monk, *The Oxford Survey of Sovereign Wealth Funds' Asset Managers*, School of Geography and the Environment, University of Oxford, 2009, 1.

American precedents have focused narrowly on specific ethical issues and adopt a more negative or passive stance, merely avoiding unethical investment. An interesting feature of the US reforms is their link to voluntary RI codes that have developed independently of the state.

Apartheid in South Africa galvanized the first wave of such reforms. During the 1980s, various US states and city governments began to prohibit their pension funds from investing in companies conducting business in South Africa unless a company adhered to the Sullivan Principles[35] and had been rated a good performer under its scoring system.[36] Massachusetts also directed its pension funds to avoid investment in banks that had outstanding loans to South Africa.[37] The validity of these measures from a fiduciary law perspective was upheld in the *City of Baltimore* case (as discussed in Chapter 3).[38] Also, the federal government in 1986 enacted the Comprehensive Anti-Apartheid Act[39] to restrict foreign investment in South Africa.

Investment restrictions were also adopted to address religious discrimination in Northern Ireland and, more recently, human rights abuses in Sudan. Several US states and the federal Congress legislated adoption of the MacBride Principles,[40] which forbid public pension funds from investing in businesses in Northern Ireland that fail to promote equal hiring practices or ensure the security and safety of employees.[41] The federal Sudan Accountability and Divestment Act of 2007 was enacted to allow (but not oblige) state and local governments as well as private fund managers to divest lawfully from businesses dealing with Sudan, thereby overriding any fiduciary duty to act in clients' financial and legal interests to the exclusion of social concerns.[42]

Beyond adherence to these legislative controls, US public funds have tended to be more active in corporate governance than their private sector counterparts.[43] They are more likely to manage their portfolios internally and vote their own shares. Even when they use external managers, they retain voting authority more frequently than private funds.[44] Some public funds have also strongly supported community investment. Large public employee pension plans such as CalPERS are among the most progressive practitioners

---

35 H.J. Richardson, 'Leon Sullivan's principles, race and international law: a comment', *Temple International and Comparative Law Journal* 15, 2001, 55–80.
36 Carroll, op. cit.
37 Massachusetts Ann. Laws, ch. 32, (Supp. 1984), s. 23(1)(d)(ii).
38 (1989) 317 Md. 72; 562 A.2d 720.
39 Pub. L. No. 99-440.
40 The MacBride Principles, written by Seán MacBride, an international human rights activist, are a US corporate code of conduct drafted in 1984 to address religious discrimination in Northern Ireland: K.A. Bertsch and H.E. Booth, *The MacBride Principles and U.S. Companies in Northern Ireland*, Investor Responsibility Research Centre, 1991.
41 See McCrudden, op. cit.; Conway, op. cit.
42 Pub. L. 110-174; see L.A. Patey, 'Against the Asian tide: the Sudan divestment campaign', *Journal of Modern African Studies* 47(4), 2009, 551–73.
43 R. Romano, 'Public pension fund activism in corporate governance reconsidered', *Columbia Law Review* 94, 1993, 795–853, 820–1.
44 Ibid., 832.

of RI, with extensive policies on corporate engagement and portfolio screening.[45] CalPERS has dedicated US$500 million to investment in asset portfolios that use environmental screens, and a further US$200 million for clean environmental technology development, although these commitments represent minute portions of its portfolio, which is worth US$241.9 billion as at 27 September 2012.[46] But it would be misleading to deduce that all US public pension funds are pioneering RI; some go no further than exclusionary screening on the limited set of issues mandated by legislation.[47]

Swedish AP funds

The early 2000s saw the rise of RI in Sweden, spearheaded by a new legislative mandate for Swedish public pension funds that was promoted by trade unions and NGOs.[48] On 1 January 2001, the largest state-controlled pension funds became legally obliged to include consideration of environmental and ethical issues in their investment policies and to report annually to the government on implementation. The Swedish public pension system centres on five 'AP funds' that serve to buffer intergenerational fluctuations in demand for retirement income.[49] Although the funds operate under similar legislative standards with a common RI mandate, each is managed separately. The National Pension Insurance Funds (AP-Funds) Act of 2000, as amended in 2001,[50] obliges the AP funds to take 'environmental and social considerations ... into account without relinquishing the overall goal of a high return on capital'.[51] However, there is no legal guidance on how the AP funds should fulfill this duty. Each must formulate an annual business plan, describing how it accounts for such factors in its investment activities, while the Swedish Finance Department is responsible for monitoring funds' compliance. External RI service providers such as GES Investment Services are used by some of the AP funds.

Four AP funds cooperate through an advisory Ethical Council established in 2007 to assess the ethical conduct of non-Swedish companies in their portfolios.[52] They choose to collaborate because they recognize that they deal

---

45 Http://www.calpers.ca.gov.
46 CalPERS, 'Current investment fund values', 27 September 2012, http://www.calpers.ca.gov/index.jsp?bc=/investments/assets/mvs.xml.
47 D. Hess, *Public Pensions and the Promise of Shareholder Activism for the Next Frontier of Corporate Governance: Sustainable Economic Development*, Ross School of Business, University of Michigan, 2007, 23–4.
48 Bengtsson, op. cit., 976.
49 E.g., http://www.ap1.se.
50 AP-fonden i det reformerade pensionssystemet, 1999/2000, 46, 76.
51 Oxford Business Knowledge, *Recent Trends and Regulatory Implications of Socially Responsible Investment for Pension Funds*, OECD Roundtable on Corporate Responsibility, 2007, 21. The Swedish text states: 'Hänsyn till miljö och etik skall tas i placeringsverksamheten utan att avkall görs på det övergripande målet om hög avkastning'.
52 'AP Funds team up to put foreign firms under ethical microscope', *European Pension and Investment News*, 28 February 2007. The fifth AP fund (known as AP6) has its own legislative charter and invests in Swedish private equity.

with common ESG issues in the same companies, and it is advantageous to speak with a common voice.[53] The five-person Ethical Council comprises one representative from each of the four participating AP funds, who then appoint a fifth member as Secretary-General. But the Council, which has no official legal framework, lacks formal representation from outside interest groups, and it does not consult the general public. It relies on international treaties ratified by Sweden to guide RI assessments,[54] though any divestment decisions are ultimately made by each fund separately, as the Council only makes recommendations. The Ethical Council monitors ESG performance in over 4,000 companies in the AP funds' portfolios but annually engages closely with far fewer; in 2011 it reportedly had dialogue with 126 companies on ESG and sustainability issues.[55]

Despite the homogenizing influence of the Ethical Council, the AP funds retain somewhat different strategies to meet their RI legislative obligations.[56] AP-1 has relied on a norms-based approach to screening but divests as a last resort. AP-2 focuses heavily on corporate governance issues and screens on a limited basis through a 'best-in-class' standard. Corporate engagement and governance issues are also a priority of the AP-3 fund. AP-4 has taken a relatively low-key approach to RI. Companies divested from one or more of the AP funds in recent years include nine associated with production of cluster munitions or anti-personnel mines (e.g., Alliant Techsystems, GenCorp and Textron).[57]

Australian Future Fund

The legislative framework governing Australia's principal SWF omits any explicit reference to RI. The national Future Fund, established in 2006 by the Future Fund Act, is designed to meet unfunded superannuation liabilities forecast to arise from the demographic bulge of the retiring 'boomer' generation.[58] The Future Fund Board of Guardians aims to 'maximize the return earned on the Fund over the long term, consistent with international best practice for institutional investment' and subject to any directions given by the responsible Ministers.[59] The Australian Government has issued investment policy directions to the Future Fund.[60] In language redolent of the New Zealand legislation, to be discussed later in this chapter, these

---

53 Personal correspondence, John Howchin, Secretary-General Ethical Council, 12 June 2012.
54 UNEP-FI and UKSIF, op. cit., 14–15.
55 Ethical Council, *Annual Report 2011*, Ethical Council, 2012, 3.
56 I. Hamilton and J. Eriksson, 'Influence strategies in shareholder engagement: a case study of five Swedish national pension funds', *2010 PRI Academic Conference: Mainstreaming Responsible Investment*, Copenhagen, 5–7 May 2010.
57 Ethical Council, op. cit., 25.
58 Http://www.futurefund.gov.au.
59 Future Fund Act, 2006 (Cth) s. 18(1).
60 P.H. Costello and N.H. Minchin, *Future Fund Investment Mandate Directions*, Commonwealth Government, 3 May 2006.

directions state that 'the Board must act in a way that . . . is unlikely to cause any diminution of the Australian Government's reputation in Australian and international financial markets'.[61] Further, the Board must 'have regard to international best practice for institutional investment in determining its approach to corporate governance principles, including in relation to its voting policy'.[62] In 2006, a parliamentary inquiry recommended that the Fund become a signatory to the UNPRI, but as of October 2012, this has not happened.[63]

Other provisions in the Future Fund investment policy that could have some RI ramifications include acknowledgement that:

> Australia has ratified a number of international conventions and treaties that limit certain activities. Where the Board becomes aware that the activities of an entity or funding activity may contravene such a convention or treaty, the Board will consider the exclusion or removal of the investment from the portfolio generally having regard to the nature of the limitations.[64]

Also, there seems to be some indication that ESG issues will be considered when the Board 'believes that it can play a role in advancing good practice for institutional investment, contributing to system integrity, protecting investor rights and building new markets'.[65] This includes, explains the Board, 'to encourage the proper use of ownership rights and to enhance governance arrangements'.[66]

In an attempt to strengthen the Future Fund's mandate for RI, the Green Party in 2011 tabled the Government Investment Funds Amendment (Ethical Investments) Bill. It proposes to amend the Future Fund Act (and the Nation-building Funds Act 2008) to require the responsible Ministers to issue, by regulations, RI guidelines for each fund and to direct the Future Fund Board to have regard to the guidelines when investing.[67] Additionally, the Future Fund Ethical Investment Guidelines would be required to specify financial assets that the Fund can't hold, and these exclusions would have to include manufacturers of tobacco products, components of cluster munitions and nuclear weapons. Whatever the fate of this proposal, it has at least helped stimulate greater public debate in Australia about the social and environmental impacts of public investment funds.

---

61 Ibid., cl. 1(b).
62 Ibid., cl. 1(c).
63 Parliamentary Joint Committee on Corporations and Financial Services, *Corporate Responsibility: Managing Risk and Creating Value*, Commonwealth of Australia, 2006, 77.
64 Future Fund Management Agency, *Future Fund Statement of Investment Policies*, Commonwealth of Australia, 2012, 25.
65 Ibid.
66 Ibid.
67 See http://www.austlii.edu.au/au/legis/cth/bill/gifaib2011624.

Other examples

The Canada Pension Plan (CPP) has incorporated a modest RI stance, albeit without an explicit legislative mandate. The CPP is a contributory, earnings-related social insurance program, managed by the CPP Investment Board (CPPIB) in accordance with the Canada Pension Plan Investment Board Act of 1997.[68] It operates at arm's length from government, and no change to the legislation or the CPPIB's mandate can happen without agreement from the federal government and two thirds of the provinces (representing two thirds of Canada's population), a feat that is not easy to achieve. The CPPIB is not required to submit its investment strategy to government for approval. In a political sense, the CPPIB could be regarded as a fiduciary, acting on behalf of its approximately 18 million members.

While the CPPIB is thus highly insulated from political interference, it hasn't been able to insulate itself from public debate and criticism about some of its investment policies. Having once attracted derision for investing in tobacco stocks and armaments companies,[69] the Board issued its first RI policy in 2004. The current policy, from August 2010, recognizes that ESG issues can be financially material. The CPPIB says it incorporates ESG issues into its investment analysis and corporate engagement, but it generally does not practise exclusionary ethical screening or divestment.[70] Its stated 'overriding' responsibility remains to 'maximize investment returns without undue risk'.[71] According to Donald Raymond of the CPPIB, 'Engagement is a more effective approach to bring about positive change and enhance long-term financial performance.'[72] However, of some 3,100 firms currently in its portfolio, the CPPIB engages with only some 10 to 15 companies annually and therefore alone cannot possibly exert a wide-ranging or sustained influence on the ESG performance of its portfolio companies.

An alternative model that allows beneficiaries to have some choice regarding RI, albeit while not obliging a comprehensive change of approach by a fund, is to offer a menu of portfolio options. An example is the UK Government's National Employment Savings Trust (NEST), launched in 2012 to provide pension coverage for all UK workers who otherwise lack access to occupational pension plans. Funded by compulsory contributions from the employers and employees, the NEST offers beneficiaries a menu of at least five fund options to choose if they do not like the default fund. One of these options is the NEST Ethical Fund, whose policy purports to cater to members 'concerned

---

68 1997, SO.
69 S. Cordon, 'Critics call for halt to CPP investments in tobacco companies', *Canadian Press Newswire*, 5 December 2002; P. Gillespie, 'Your pension contributions at work?', *Toronto Star*, 22 December 2005, A23; T. Flynn, 'War and weapons funded by Canada Pension Plan', *Alternatives Journal* 30(4), 2004, 16.
70 CPPIB, *Policy on Responsible Investing*, 2010, 2.
71 Ibid.
72 D.M. Raymond, 'Mainstreaming responsible investment: our approach', *GLOBE 2006*, Vancouver, 30 March 2006, 5.

about the impact that organisations have on the environment and on society, in areas such as human rights and fair trade'.[73] At the time of writing, at an early stage of the NEST, it is unknown what proportion of workers will choose the ethical fund option. Sweden's public pension system also earmarks 2.5 per cent of workers' salary into individual pension accounts, which allow beneficiaries to choose from a large menu of investment portfolios that include RI.[74] When the scheme began, in 2000, two thirds of contributors made an active fund choice, but by 2004 only about 10 per cent of new entrants made such a choice.[75]

Norwegian Government Pension Fund-Global (NGPF-G)

Institutional and legal structure

The NGPF-G is a sovereign fund that invests proceeds from Norway's petroleum industry, which has prospered since oil was discovered in the North Sea in 1969. Originally incarnated as the Petroleum Fund through the 1990 Act of the Government Petroleum Fund (Lov om Statens petroleumsfond), the Fund's statutory framework was overhauled in 2005,[76] and it was renamed the 'Government Pension Fund-Global' (*Statens pensjonsfond-Utland*) to reflect its envisioned role in meeting future pension financing costs. While the government mandates the NGPF-G to operate like a private investor, it expects it to fulfill two broad policy goals of the state: to build long-term savings to ensure that a reasonable share of the country's petroleum wealth benefits future generations of Norwegians; and to eschew investments that would make it complicit in unethical practices. Ethical investment regulations for the NGPF-G were adopted in 2004 and revised in 2010.[77] Investing only in foreign assets so as to avoid overheating the domestic economy, the NGPF-G has grown immensely to reach almost NOK 3,300 billion at the beginning of 2012[78] and now holds about 1 per cent of the value of the world's listed corporate stock.[79] Its sister fund,

---

73 'NEST Ethical Fund', http://www.nestpensions.org.uk/schemeweb/NestWeb/includes/public/docs/NEST-Ethical-Fund-information-sheet,PDF.pdf.
74 For a description of this model, see http://www.ap2.se/en/about-ap2/Our-mission/A-unique-pension-system.
75 K.R. Weaver, 'Design and Implementation Issues in Swedish Individual Pension Accounts', US Social Security Office, 2004, http://www.ssa.gov/policy/docs/ssb/v65n4/v65n4p38.html. It is unknown how many of those choosing their fund selected an explicit RI option, although the default fund evidently includes some RI.
76 Act of the Government Pension Fund (Lov om Statens pensjonsfond), no. 123, 2005.
77 The regulations are consolidated as the *Management Mandate for the Government Pension Fund*, http://www.regjeringen.no/Upload/FIN/Statens%20pensjonsfond/mandatspueng.pdf.
78 Norwegian Ministry of Finance, *The Management of the Government Pension Fund in 2011*, Report to the Storting, 2012, 9.
79 Nystuen, Follesdal and Mestad, op. cit., 7.

the Government Pension Fund Norway, invests just in Norway and other Scandinavian countries.

Unlike some SWFs, the NGPF-G's operations are closely tied to the machinery of the state. Its administration is divided among three governmental entities. The Ministry of Finance retains ultimate responsibility for the policy and management of the NGPF-G, including RI decisions to exclude any company. The Norges Bank (Norway's central bank) has operational control of the funds, and through its ownership rights in companies, it handles corporate engagement. The Bank has devolved many of its responsibilities to Norges Bank Investment Management (NBIM)[80] and external fund managers. The third entity, the Council on Ethics, advises on RI decisions relating primarily to the exclusion of companies. The activities of all these entities are overseen by the Norwegian Parliament (Storting), which approves the NGPF-G's investment strategy and scrutinizes annual reports of the Ministry of Finance and its ethical investment guidelines.

While the NGPF-G functions under a legal framework that reflects a 'public commitment to procedural democracy'[81] and encourages practices that are broadly reflective of Norwegian values, the general public itself has negligible opportunity to participate directly in the fund's governance. Nonetheless, the NGPF-G's decision-making, at least, is highly transparent. All recommendations of the Council are publicly disclosed, with detailed reasons.[82] The Norges Bank consults with the public before submitting to the Ministry its plans for active ownership in the NGPF-G's portfolio companies,[83] and it informs the public about its practices and treatment of ESG issues.[84] Another transparency mechanism is the Ministry of Finance's annual reporting to the Storting on the performance of the NGPF-G.[85] While no citizen may easily judicially challenge a decision of the Council or the Ministry, these procedures allow for some public input into their decisions. The Council meets annually with NGOs to discuss its policies and practices; attendance is on an invitational basis but is routinely granted to groups that have been in recent contact with the Council. Informal channels of complaint

---

80 Http://www.nbim.no.
81 Clark and Monk, 'The Norwegian government pension fund', op. cit., 15.
82 The Council's Guidelines oblige it to justify its recommendations, including 'the Council's assessment of the specific basis for exclusion and any comments on the case from the company', and it shall, insofar as possible, rely on evidence that 'can be verified': *Guidelines for Observation and Exclusion from the Government Pension Fund Global's Investment Universe* (2010), s. 5(4), http://www.regjeringen.no/en/sub/styrer-rad-utvalg/ethicscouncil/ethical-guidelines.html?id=425277.
83 *Guidelines for Norges Bank's Work on Responsible Management and Active Ownership of the Government Pension Fund Global* (2010), s. 2(3), http://www.regjeringen.no/en/dep/fin/Selected-topics/the-government-pension-fund/responsible-investments/Guidelines-for-Norges-Banks-work-on-responsible-management-and-active-ownership-of-the-Government-Pension-Fund-Global-GPFG.html?id=594253.
84 Ibid., s. 4.
85 See, e.g., Norwegian Ministry of Finance, *The Management of the Government Pension Fund in 2009*, Report No. 10 (2009–2010) to the Storting, 2010.

also exist; for example, any individual or group may write to the Council or the Ministry to voice concerns.[86]

An ethical investment mission

The NGPF-G has an RI mission that combines deontological and teleological ethical approaches. It lacked any such mandate until 2001, when the Norwegian Government established on a three-year trial a dedicated 'Environment Fund' within the larger Petroleum Fund (as it was then known) for investing in companies in emerging economies that met environmental performance criteria.[87] Concomitantly, because the NGPF-G's decisions or omissions may be attributed to Norway as a matter of state responsibility under international law, or at least politically, the Fund would sometimes consider issues of human rights or environmental protection in any context of its portfolio. The Fund's first ethical screenings were guided by an Advisory Commission on International Law, appointed by the Ministry of Finance in 2001.[88] The Commission responded to enquiries from the Ministry regarding whether specific investments might conflict with Norway's international legal obligations. For example, in April 2002 the Ministry directed the Fund to divest from Singapore Technologies Engineering because of its links to production of anti-personnel mines, contrary to Norway's obligations under the Ottawa Convention on Anti-Personnel Mines.[89]

In 2002 Norway moved to develop regulations to create a normatively and procedurally clearer approach to ethical investment by the Fund. It appointed a committee chaired by Professor Hans Peter Graver for this purpose.[90] While the Graver Committee did not believe the Fund should have an overriding mission to leverage its resources to improve corporate social and environmental behaviour, it concluded: 'The requirement for a long-term return gives rise to ethical obligations in relation to the requirement for sustainable development in a longer-term perspective. Sustainable development is a precondition for return on . . . financial investments in the long term.'[91]

---

86 One example is when the Rainforest Action Group lobbied the NGPF-G to exclude some extractive industries.
87 In 2004, the Environment Fund was integrated into its parent Fund, whose entire investment portfolio became subject to an ethical mandate.
88 The Advisory Commission was replaced by the Council on Ethics in 2004.
89 The Petroleum Fund Advisory Commission on International Law, *Memorandum to the Ministry of Finance: Question of Whether Investments in Singapore Technologies Engineering Can Imply a Violation of Norway's International Obligations* (22 March 2002), citing the Ottawa Convention, which stipulates that States Parties should not 'assist, encourage or induce, in any way, anyone to engage in any activity prohibited to a State Party under this Convention'. The Ottawa Convention is officially known as the Convention on the Prohibition of the Use, Stockpiling, Production and Transfer of Anti-Personnel Mines and Their Destruction, I.L.M. 1997, 36, 1507.
90 I. Bay, *Valueless Money? The Petroleum Fund – the Road Towards Ethical Guidelines*, Report 1/2001, Framtiden I Våre Henders Forskningsinstitutt, 2002.
91 Ibid., s. 3.1.

In addition, the Graver Committee rationalized ethical investment on the ground that the Fund should avoid *complicity* in gross or systematic breaches of ethical norms relating to human rights and the environment:

> Even though the issue of complicity raises difficult questions, the Committee considers, in principle, that owning shares or bonds in a company that can be expected to commit gross unethical actions may be regarded as complicity in these actions. The reason for this is that such investments are directly intended to achieve returns from the company, that a permanent connection is thus established between the . . . Fund and the company, and that the question of whether or not to invest in a company is a matter of free choice.[92]

In identifying a broad, democratic basis to support RI decisions, the Graver Committee sought to rely on international agreements on environmental protection and human rights that Norway supports, rather than to define a separate basis rooted in Norwegian culture or national policy.[93] The Committee reasoned that while most international legal obligations apply only to states, companies may aggravate or facilitate human rights and environmental violations committed by states, and the NGPF-G might contribute to companies' misdeeds through its stock ownership. While excluding companies from the NGPF-G might influence their behaviour, in addition to any influence achieved by corporate engagement, the Graver Committee focused on exclusion as a means of *avoiding* the Fund's own complicity in ethically problematic activities. By contrast, the former Environment Fund was conceived as a mechanism to promote sustainable development and leverage environmental improvements in the targeted economies.

Regulations inspired by the Graver Committee were adopted in November 2004, and a Council on Ethics took charge to evaluate potential investments for compliance.[94] The five members of the Council, each appointed by the Ministry of Finance, blend practical and theoretical expertise. Presently, it comprises two academics, a former government diplomat, a professional scientist and an investment manager. The Council, which typically meets monthly, is serviced by a secretariat of eight staff, who are responsible for collecting information about companies from public sources (e.g., media reports and websites) and making field trips to obtain direct knowledge about specific companies.

---

92 Ibid., s. 2.2.
93 Norwegian Ministry of Finance, *The Report from the Graver Committee*, 11 July 2003, http://www.regjeringen.no/en/dep/fin/Selected-topics/the-government-pension-fund/responsible-investments/The-Graver-Committee---documents/The-Graver-Committee-and-Ethical-Guideli.html?id=434926.
94 Regulations on the Management of the Government Pension Fund – Global (Forskrift om forvaltning av Statens pensjonsfond utland) (2006), s 8(1).

The Council submits its recommendations to the Ministry of Finance, which makes final decisions on exclusion of companies. The Council usually makes its recommendations on a consensual basis. It has wide discretion in passing judgement on serious human rights violations, gross corruption, severe environmental damage and general violations of fundamental ethical norms. The Council's recommendations to exclude or divest are divided into two sub-categories: 'exclusion on the basis of certain products and exclusion of companies on the basis of corporate conduct'.[95] In assessing investments on these grounds, it relies not only on international treaties ratified by Norway but also on soft law standards approved by Norway, such as the UN Global Compact and the OECD Guidelines for Multinational Enterprises.[96]

Reflecting a deontological impulse, the Council on Ethics applies a negative screening mandate that excludes specific companies or classes of investment based on its conception of ethical duties, as emanating from fundamental international norms. Deontological ethics is rule-based ethics, analyzing the rightness of an action based on a specific moral rule, such as respect for human rights. By contrast, the Norges Bank, which administers the Fund, employs a teleological approach through its corporate engagement strategies, which aim to change the behaviour of targeted firms. Investment exclusion may sometimes influence the behaviour of companies, but the exclusionary recommendations of the Council on Ethics are driven primarily by a desire to avoid complicity in ethically problematic activity rather than to exert influence on purged companies.

NGPF-G's revised ethical guidelines

The NGPF-G's current ethical guidelines were adopted in 2010 following a major review in 2008 of the legal mandate and practices of the Council on Ethics conducted by the Ministry of Finance. The review included a separate commissioned report written by the Albright Group and Professor Simon Chesterman.[97] The results of the review were mainly procedural rather than normative. It concluded that the ethical guidelines had proven to be generally robust but recommended more engagement with companies, particularly firms under scrutiny.[98] It also recommended that tobacco production be singled out as a new criterion for investment exclusion. The Albright and Chesterman Report advocated greater collaboration between the Council and

---

95 Nystuen, Follesdal and Mestad, op. cit., 8.
96 UN Global Compact: http://www.unglobalcompact.org. OECD Guidelines for Corporate Governance and for Multinational Enterprises: http://www.oecd.org/dataoecd/56/36/1922428.pdf.
97 Albright Group and S. Chesterman, *Assessment of Implementation of Articles 3 and 4 of the Ethical Guidelines for the Government Pension Fund – Global*, Report for Norwegian Ministry of Finance, May 2008.
98 Norwegian Ministry of Finance, *On the Management of the Government Pension Fund in 2008*, Report no. 20 (2008–2009) to the Storting, 2009.

NBIM, more attention to climate change, more opportunities for public submissions and dialogue with companies and improved disclosure of implementation of the ethical guidelines.[99]

Consequently, in March 2010 the Ministry of Finance issued two standards that were accepted by the Storting: the Guidelines for Observation and Exclusion from the Government Pension Fund Global's Investment Universe[100] (hereafter referred to as Guidelines I) and the Guidelines for Norges Bank's Work on Responsible Management and Active Ownership (hereafter Guidelines II).[101] The Ministry of Finance also initiated a complementary program for active environmental-related investment, focusing on firms that pioneer climate-friendly energy efficiency, carbon capture and storage, water technology, and waste and pollution management. The program is worth about NOK 20 billion, to be invested between 2010 and 2015 (equivalent to less than 1 per cent of the value of the NGPF-G portfolio).[102] Many of these targeted investments are in environmental bonds for financing eco-friendly projects, such as the World Bank's Green Bonds.

The Guidelines continue the exclusion mechanism for companies that engage in unethical activities and strengthen the NGPF-G's use of active shareholding and exertion of responsible influence in its portfolio companies with a view to promoting sustainable development. The Guidelines I require, on the advice of the Council, exclusion of companies related to specific products, namely those that produce tobacco, produce certain types of weapons that are deemed to violate fundamental humanitarian principles, or sell weapons or military material to pariah states.[103] The Guidelines also allow for exclusion in a secondary category relating to corporate conduct that the Ministry, on the advice of the Council on Ethics, believes is 'an unacceptable risk that the company contributes to or is responsible for'.[104] Such conduct includes:

a) serious or systematic human rights violations, such as murder, torture, deprivation of liberty, forced labour, the worst forms of child labour and other child exploitation;
b) serious violations of the rights of individuals in situations of war or conflict;
c) severe environmental damage;

---

99 Albright Group and Chesterman, op. cit., 5–7.
100 Http://www.regjeringen.no/en/sub/styrer-rad-utvalg/ethicscouncil/ethical-guidelines.html?id=425277.
101 Http://www.regjeringen.no/en/dep/fin/Selected-topics/the-government-pension-fund/responsible-investments/Guidelines-for-Norges-Banks-work-on-responsible-management-and-active-ownership-of-the-Government-Pension-Fund-Global-GPFG.html?id=594253.
102 Norwegian Ministry of Finance, *On the Management of the Government Pension Fund in 2008*, op. cit., 11.
103 Section 2(1)–(2).
104 Guideline I, s. 2(3).

d) gross corruption;
e) other particularly serious violations of fundamental ethical norms.[105]

Within these categories, which already pitch a high threshold for offending conduct, the Council's 'aim is to target [the] worst case[s]'.[106] Consequently, some unethical behaviour will not be targeted by the NGPF-G. From the yardstick of sustainable development, for example, the Guidelines' threshold of 'severe environmental damage' is too high to capture a lot of environmental degradation such as climate change that is piecemeal and only significant cumulatively. Consequently, the NGPF-G must rely on other mechanisms if it wishes to address environmental issues more comprehensively.

The Guidelines I elaborate factors that the Ministry may take into consideration, which include 'the probability of future violations of ethical norms, the severity and extent of the norm violations, the connection between the norm violations and the company in which the Fund is invested, and whether the company does what may reasonably be expected to reduce the risk of future violations of norms within a reasonable time frame'.[107] Positive actions taken by a company to safeguard the environment may also be taken into account,[108] and companies excluded may be re-admitted to the NGPF-G if their behaviour improves. Importantly, the Ministry may use other measures before excluding a company, such as active engagement or close observation of a firm.[109] Companies proposed for exclusion must be warned and given reasons, with opportunity to respond.[110] The revised Guidelines also contain provisions to improve communications between the Council on Ethics and the Norges Bank to ensure any contact with companies is coordinated.[111]

The Guidelines II, which are directed to the work of the Norges Bank, reflect assumptions of the 'universal investor' thesis, in which long-term financial returns are postulated to hinge on maintenance of healthy social and environmental returns.[112] Thus, while the Guidelines II require Norges Bank to manage the NGPF-G in order to achieve the 'highest possible return',[113] this objective is qualified as 'dependent on sustainable development in economic, environmental and social terms [and] well-functioning, legitimate and effective markets'.[114] Relatedly, the Guidelines II oblige the Bank to integrate good corporate governance, environmental and social issues

---

105 Ibid.
106 Nystuen, Follesdal and Mestad, op. cit., 9.
107 Guideline I, s. 2(4).
108 Ibid., s. 2(5).
109 Ibid., s. 3.
110 Ibid., s. 5(3).
111 Ibid., s. 6.
112 The Norwegian Ministry of Finance has explicitly endorsed this thesis: *The Management of the Government Pension Fund in 2009*, op. cit., 133–6.
113 Guideline II, s. 1(1).
114 Ibid.

in its investments,[115] and to contribute actively to robust international standards in responsible management and active ownership.[116]

Despite the 2010 revisions to the NGPF-G's governance, with more emphasis on the economic rationale for RI, some commentators have criticized that 'the process supporting the ethical mandate actually constrains the fund's functional efficiency' and that it 'may pay a high price for its ethical policies over the long-term'.[117] However, these criticisms are perhaps less valid now than they ever were. The NGPF-G achieved average annual returns in the decade since January 2000 of 3.02 per cent, above the government's expected benchmark investment performance of 2.40 per cent each year.[118] While many RI practitioners believe that engagement is preferable to exclusionary policies, by allowing a more diversified portfolio and to retain influence within targeted companies,[119] the NGPF-G's experience shows that these strategies are not mutually exclusive. Corporate engagement can occur in the lead-up to exclusion, as well as afterwards; for example, after Rio Tinto was excluded, it sought re-admission and began dialogue with the NGPF-G about how it could redeem itself.

Norwegian RI practices

Traditionally, the primary strength of the NGPF-G's approach to RI was its scrutiny of individual companies before choosing to inflict, if necessary, investment sanctions. But targeting individual firms is highly selective in a portfolio of over 8,000 companies and thus does not ensure a systematic approach. The NGPF-G has recently refined its approach as a result of several initiatives, including: changes to the Fund's governing regulations; its new program for positive environmental investment; more systematic incorporation of ESG analysis into its entire investment portfolio; publication of its 'expectations' documents on climate change, water management and other concerns; and greater collaboration with other institutional investors.[120] The NGPF-G therefore has in theory become better positioned to take a more comprehensive approach to sustainable development.

In making recommendations to the Ministry, the Council on Ethics follows a sequence of procedures for gathering information, reviewing evidence and applying ethical guidelines. In considering specific cases, the Council

---

115 Ibid., s. 1(2).
116 Ibid., s. 3.
117 Clark and Monk, 'The Norwegian government pension fund', op cit., 14, 17.
118 NBIM, *NBIM Performance Results*, Norges Bank, 2010, 8.
119 D. Watt, 'Why RI funds aren't a monolithic group', *Morningstar*, 23 April 2009, http://www.morningstar.ca/globalhome/Industry/News.asp?Articleid=288065 (referring to the policy of Ethical Funds).
120 T. Myklebust, 'The Norwegian Government Pension Fund: moving forward on responsible investing and governance', *Rotman Journal of International Pension Management* 3(1), 2010, 20–23, 21.

may act on its own volition or at the request of the Ministry. The Council is not a legal tribunal and is not bound by rules of evidence or other judicial-like formalities, although its recommendations resemble rudimentary court judgements in their evaluation of evidence and justification of decisions.[121] It uses a 'quasi-legal' process, following its precedents and allowing companies to hear allegations and respond to them.[122] But the Council is not obliged to prove occurrence of an environmental violation or other wrong in order to recommend exclusion of a company. Indeed, much of its work addresses the 'unacceptable risk of breaches taking place in the future', which has a speculative quality, rather than responding to documented ongoing or past breaches.[123]

The Council's advice is generally persuasive, as nearly always the Minister for Finance accepts its recommendations.[124] The Ministry of Finance typically consults with other government ministries, depending on the subject matter, before reaching a decision. As of September 2012, the Minister had rejected the Council's advice in only four known instances. One involved the German company Siemens, suspected of corruption and subsequently placed on the Council's watch list. The second was Monsanto, which through its subsidiaries has been implicated in exploitation of child labour in India's cottonseed industry. The Ministry and the Norges Bank opposed singling out Monsanto for exclusion, favouring instead an engagement process that involved many companies in this troubled economic sector.[125] In 2011 the Ministry decided to place the French company Alstom SA under observation rather than exclude it as recommended by the Council for alleged risks of gross corruption.[126] The other 2011 example concerned the Chinese behemoth PetroChina, which the Council recommended be excluded 'because of the risk of human rights violations in connection with the construction of two oil and gas pipelines in Burma'. The Ministry believed PetroChina wasn't sufficiently complicit, because other companies were more directly responsible for the violations.[127] EarthRights International, an environmental NGO, had earlier censured the NGPF-G for its investments in the problematic Burmese oil and gas sector.[128]

---

121 S. Chesterman, 'The turn to ethics: divestment from multinational corporations for human rights violations – the case of Norway's Sovereign Wealth Fund', *American University International Law Review* 23, 2008, 577–615, 605.
122 Ibid., 594.
123 Recommendation from the Norwegian Ministry of Finance, *The Petroleum Fund's Council on Ethics on Total S.A.*, 14 November 2005, s. 3.3.
124 Clark and Monk, 'The Norwegian government pension fund', op. cit., 16.
125 J. Acher, 'Norway fund drops Rio Tinto on ethical grounds', *Reuters*, 9 September 2008, http://www.reuters.com/article/2008/09/09/us-norway-fund-riotinto-idUSL8728522 20080909.
126 Council on Ethics for the Government Pension Fund Global, *Annual Report 2011*, Council on Ethics, 2012, 7.
127 Ibid., 6.
128 EarthRights International (ERI), *Broken Ethics: The Norwegian Government's Investments in Oil and Gas Companies Operating in Burma (Myanmar)*, ERI, 2010.

With a support staff of eight and an annual budget of NOK 11.6 million (at the beginning of 2012),[129] the Council can scrutinize closely just a small fraction of the NGPF-G's investment portfolio. Such 'resource constraint', suggest some critics, 'forces it to make subjective decisions about ethical targets'.[130] To overcome such hindrances, the Council increasingly relies on external consultants to monitor companies and provide it with monthly reports.[131] The NBIM also plays a key role in discharging the NGPF-G's ethical investment policy, as it exercises the Fund's ownership rights through sponsoring and supporting shareholder resolutions, proxy voting and informal corporate engagement. In 2007, for example, the NBIM voted on more than 38,000 shareholder proposals in about 4,200 companies.[132] But, as with the Council, the NBIM has limited institutional capacity and has elected to engage mainly with the largest (but not necessarily the most problematic) companies.

The NGPF-G investment regulations do not instruct how to resolve any trade-offs between ethical and financial considerations, although they postulate a long-term synergy between financial returns and sustainable development.[133] In practice, the NGPF-G is increasingly governed on the premise that it can be both ethical and financially prosperous.[134] The Ministry of Finance affirmed in its 2010 annual report that '[s]olid financial returns over time depend on a sustainable development in economic, environmental and social terms',[135] and it regards the NGPF-G as a 'universal owner' exposed to environmental and social externalities that it should address.[136] Nonetheless, the Ministry of Finance acknowledges:

> In some cases, the concerns of ensuring long-term financial returns and taking widely shared values into account will coincide, but not always. For example, the Fund will not invest in companies that are in gross breach of fundamental ethical norms, regardless of the effect this will have on returns.[137]

---

129 Council on Ethics, op. cit., 10.
130 Clark and Monk, 'The Norwegian government pension fund', op cit., 17.
131 Ibid., 7.
132 A.M. Halvorssen, *Addressing Climate Change Through the Norwegian Sovereign Wealth Fund (SWF)*, Legal Studies Research Paper Series, No. 2010-06, Faculty of Law, University of Oslo, 2010, 29; also A.M. Halvorssen, 'The Norwegian sovereign wealth fund's ethical guidelines: a model for investors', *European Company Law* 8(2–3), 2011, 88–93.
133 Guidelines II, s. 1.
134 Norwegian Ministry of Finance, *On the Management of the Government Pension Fund in 2009*, op. cit., 11, 16; also Secretary General T. Eriksen, 'The Norwegian Petroleum Sector and the Government Pension Fund – Global', Ministry of Finance, June 2006, 23.
135 Norwegian Ministry of Finance, *The Management of the Government Pension Fund in 2010*, Report No. 15 (2010–2011) to the Storting, 2011, 3.
136 Ibid., 12.
137 Norwegian Ministry of Finance, *The Management of the Government Pension Fund in 2009*, op. cit., 15.

The NGPF-G presently screens companies using the services of several consultancy firms. Using the information provided by them, the Council on Ethics short-lists some 200 to 300 companies for greater scrutiny. It pays close regard to international law in judging companies, although its ethical guidelines mandate it to go beyond international law. A company thus does not have to breach any international treaty to be recommended for exclusion; indeed, companies are not true international legal personalities who can be prosecuted in an international court. Thus, the Council routinely sifts for other evidence of ethical violations, including breaches of national law or soft law standards such as the UN Global Compact.

Based on the Council's recommendations, the NGPF-G has divested from companies producing cluster bombs (e.g., Lockheed Martin) and nuclear weapons components (e.g., Boeing), breaching human rights and labour standards (e.g., Walmart) and causing severe environmental damage (e.g., Freeport McMoRan Copper & Gold). One of its most publicized divestments was US$400 million of Walmart shares in March 2006, which led to protests from the US Ambassador to Norway.[138] As of September 2012, the NGPF-G had divested from or excluded 55 companies, a tiny number compared to the some 8,300 companies in its portfolio.[139] The Fund has also excluded one state, Myanmar (Burma), by refusing to buy its government bonds. Divestment has usually occurred after dialogue with the targeted firm has failed.[140] The NGPF-G has also occasionally re-admitted excluded companies following new evidence presented by the Council of improved behaviour.[141]

Whereas the mandate of the Council on Ethics is to recommend exclusion of companies, the Norges Bank handles *engagement* with companies whose behaviour needs improvement and who are considered redeemable. The NGPF-G presently has an average ownership stake of about 1 per cent in its 8,300 companies[142] and only engages with a handful of firms at any one time. Engagement may occur as a prelude to recommending exclusion. When the Council envisions recommending exclusion, it sends a draft recommendation to the company's management for response.[143] This process may trigger some dialogue with the firm and persuade it to make changes (e.g., to sell off part of the business or to cancel a project) in order to avoid exclusion.[144]

---

138 M. Landler, 'Norway keeps nest egg from some U.S. companies', *New York Times*, 4 May 2007, C1.
139 Norwegian Ministry of Finance, 'Companies excluded from investment universe', http://www.regjeringen.no/en/dep/fin/Selected-topics/the-government-pension-fund/responsible-investments/companies-excluded-from-the-investment-u.html?id=447122.
140 NBIM, *Annual Report 2006*, Norges Bank, 2007, s. 4.2.
141 Norwegian Ministry of Finance, *The Management of the Government Pension Fund in 2009*, op. cit., 75.
142 Ibid., 65.
143 G. Nystuen, 'Etikk og kritikk', *Dagens Naeringsliv*, 11 September 2006, 4.
144 This option isn't available for companies liable to be excluded because of the very *nature* of their business (e.g., producing tobacco), as against the *way* they operate.

In 2009, the Norges Bank picked six strategic priority areas for corporate engagement and other forms of active ownership, of which two are explicit environmental issues: climate change and water management.[145] The former presents a moral dilemma for NGPF-G managers: blacklisting companies that contribute to global warming would put Norway in an awkward position, as the NGPF-G is financed from proceeds of the country's fossil fuels. The Council on Ethics believes that since we all pollute the climate in a world ubiquitously dependent on fossil fuels, excluding any specific entity on this basis cannot be justified. Therefore, instead of excluding oil and coal businesses as demanded by some environmental groups, the NBIM has released an 'expectations' document on companies' management of risk factors relating to climate change.[146] The expectations include having:

> strategies for managing both physical and economic climate effects, to measure its emissions and set targets for reducing them, to explore and exploit opportunities to develop new products and services that will help the transition to a low-carbon economy, and to develop a strategy for dealing with climate change risk in the supply chain.[147]

Such measures, in turn, should enable the NGPF-G to manage its own climate change risks, which the Ministry of Finance recognizes as 'a long-term investor with a broad portfolio'.[148]

The Ministry has also collaborated in an international research project with other major institutional investors to foster a deeper understanding of the financial risks of climate change.[149] Unusually, the Norges Bank has also written to some US companies to express its concerns about how they campaigned against the imposition of carbon caps.[150] Together, these strategies to address companies and issues on a portfolio-wide basis could provide important means for the NGPF-G to act as an ethical, universal owner.[151]

---

145 Norwegian Ministry of Finance, *The Management of the Government Pension Fund in 2009*, op. cit., 125.
146 NBIM, *NBIM Investor Expectations: Climate Change Management*, Norges Bank, 2008.
147 As summarized by the Norwegian Ministry of Finance, *The Management of the Government Pension Fund in 2009*, op. cit., 126.
148 Ibid.
149 Ibid., 15.
150 Norges Bank Investment Management, *Government Pension Fund – Global Annual Report 2008*, Norges Bank, 2009, 54.
151 Scholars have advocated such measures: e.g., O.P.K. Gjessing and H. Syse, 'Norwegian petroleum wealth and universal ownership', *Corporate Governance: An International Review* 15(3), 2007, 427–37.

New Zealand Superannuation Fund (NZSF)

Legislative and institutional framework

New Zealand is renowned for some of the most progressive environmental and social legislation in the world,[152] and it has, like Norway, begun to consider whether and how to use public financial bodies to promote sustainable development and ethical practices. The NZSF is the country's first major step towards this goal. It was established in 2001 to ease the future financing burden of the country's pension payments. Because the country's population is ageing, there is mounting pressure on public revenue to sustain NZ superannuation.[153] The Fund was created by the New Zealand Superannuation and Retirement Income Act of 2001 to invest government contributions to address this growth in demand for pensions. Since the Fund began operations in September 2003 it has grown rapidly to about US$15.9 billion of assets, as of early 2012,[154] with investments principally in shares in global and New Zealand companies, real estate, commodities and fixed interest.

The legislative framework prescribes arrangements for the management and operation of the NZSF in order to limit political interference. The Fund is administered by a separate entity called the Guardians of New Zealand Superannuation,[155] which enjoys broad plenary power to invest, subject only to specified statutory restrictions.[156] While the Guardians hold assets belonging to the New Zealand government, the legislation declares that they 'are not a trustee'.[157] The effect of this rider presumably is to avoid implying any common law fiduciary standards in the management of the Fund and to limit its governance strictly to the terms of the enabling legislation. However, the Guardians are presumably still subject to judicial review, which would enable courts to issue remedies to ensure that the NZSF is administered in line with its legislative schema.

The Guardians' Board consists of between five to seven members, appointed by the Cabinet on the recommendation of the Minister of Finance, after nominations from an independent nominating committee and consultation with representatives of other political parties.[158] Only persons with 'substantial

---

152 Notable examples include Environment Act, 1987 and the Resource Management Act, 1991.
153 K. Dunstan and N. Thomas, *Demographic Aspects of New Zealand's Ageing Population*, Statistics New Zealand, 2006.
154 SWFI, 'Sovereign wealth funds cross 5 trillion dollar barrier', 2 May 2012, http://www.swfinstitute.org/swf-news/sovereign-wealth-funds-cross-5-trillion-dollar-barrier/. The list of SWFs is at http://www.swfinstitute.org/fund-rankings/.
155 Section 48(1).
156 Section 49(4), with specified restrictions in ss. 58, 59 and 64. While the Minister of Finance can give directions to the Guardians in regard to the Government's expectations to the Fund's performance, the Minister cannot give any direction that is 'inconsistent with the duty to invest the Fund on a prudent, commercial basis' (s. 64(1)).
157 Section 51(2).
158 Section 54(1), 56.

experience, training, and expertise in the management of financial investments' may be Board members.[159] While the Guardians exercise overall control over the Fund, they have, like the NGPF-G, outsourced much work to external fund managers.[160]

The Superannuation and Retirement Income Act includes a qualified obligation to invest ethically, which is considerably less prescriptive than Norway's regulations. The Guardians' primary duty is to:

> invest the Fund on a prudent, commercial basis . . . in a manner consistent with (a) best-practice portfolio management; and (b) maximising return without undue risk to the Fund as a whole; and (c) avoiding prejudice to New Zealand's reputation as a responsible member of the world community.[161]

The legislation does not define any of this terminology and offers no guidance on reconciling any conflicts between these goals. While the Guardians therefore have ample discretion to implement their mandate, they must prepare a statement of investment standards and procedures that covers, inter alia, 'ethical investment, including policies, standards, or procedures for avoiding prejudice to New Zealand's reputation as a responsible member of the world community',[162] as well as the 'retention, exercise, or delegation of voting rights acquired through investments'.[163] The Fund must report annually to the New Zealand government on its performance.[164]

In governance arrangements, the New Zealand approach to RI diverges from Norway's in several interesting ways. Firstly, the ethical investment duty is comingled with other legislative goals relating to financial considerations. By contrast, Norway's ethical screening Guidelines are placed in a separate instrument, to which compliance is not constrained by or conditional on the NGPF-G adhering to other legal norms. While the Guidelines II relating to the Norges Bank's active ownership oblige it to seek 'the highest possible return', this objective is stated as 'dependent on sustainable development in economic, environmental and social terms'.[165] Secondly, the NZSF lacks an ethics council to provide advice; decisions about ethical investment are ultimately the responsibility of the Guardians' Board, a body without special expertise in such matters. Thirdly, while the NZSF must avoid prejudicing New Zealand's reputation internationally, active

---

159 Section 55(1)(a).
160 Controller and Auditor-General, *Guardians of New Zealand Superannuation: Governance and Management of the New Zealand Superannuation Fund*, NZ Government, May 2008, para. 5.8.
161 Section 58(2)(c).
162 Section 61(d).
163 Section 61(1).
164 Section 68(e)–(f).
165 Section 1(1).

consideration of social and environmental issues and promotion of improved corporate behaviour are not explicitly required. Indeed, the legislation has been interpreted by New Zealand Treasury staff as simply requiring the NZSF 'to have a policy regarding ethical investment: it does not prescribe any particular approach to or emphasis on ethical investment'.[166] This laissez-faire approach contrasts with other NZ legislation relating to natural resources management and environmental protection[167] that is much more prescriptive regarding sustainable development and related goals.

Guardians' ethical investment policies and practices

The Guardians' broad discretion to determine the NZSF's ethical investment has enabled it to establish a range of processes and policies. A Responsible Investment Committee was appointed to draft ethical policies, to monitor their implementation and generally to advise the Guardians on RI matters. But it was dissolved in October 2009 when the Board assumed direct oversight of ethical policies as part of an avowed commitment to embed RI considerations throughout its decision-making.[168] Its current RI policy is a relatively brief document that sketches the NZSF's main ethical standards and methods.[169] The Guardians rely on external agencies such as Innovest Strategic Value Advisors and Institutional Shareholder Services to monitor the majority of the NZSF's portfolio for compliance with its ethical policy.

As in the Norwegian approach, the Guardians undertake RI through voting, engagement and divestment.[170] Lately, they have also incorporated environmental and social risk analysis into their due diligence procedures and, like the NGPF-G, have initiated positive investment measures to deliver 'strong environmental or social returns in addition to sufficient investment returns'.[171] In practice, however, there are some differences between the approaches of these two SWFs. The Guardians were slow to fulfill their ethical mandate; they went two years with neither in-house RI experts nor a formal policy. Their current policy of exclusion is mainly determined on the basis of a company's economic sector rather than its individual practices. While the NGPF-G also excludes sectors, such as tobacco producers, its ethical mandate also requires evaluation of firms' specific conduct. The Guardians

---

166 B. McCulloch and J. Frances, 'Governance of public pension funds: New Zealand Superannuation Fund', in A.R. Musalem and R.J. Palacios (eds), *Public Pension Fund Management: Governance, Accountability, and Investment Policies*, World Bank, 2004, 157–210, 189.
167 E.g., Resource Management Act, 1991, s. 5.
168 Guardians of New Zealand Superannuation (GNZS), *Annual Report 2010*, NZSF, 2010, 133.
169 GNZS, *Statement of Responsible Investment Policies, Standards and Procedures*, NZSF, October 2009.
170 GNZS, *How We Invest*, NZSF, 2012, 27–9.
171 Ibid.

have adopted policies since 2006 to exclude entities involved in whaling, the manufacture of tobacco, cluster mines or anti-personnel mines, and the production and testing of nuclear explosives.[172] As of January 2012, it had ousted 13 companies that manufacture such weapons and excluded one whale meat processor and 125 tobacco businesses.[173] The Guardians purport to rationalize exclusions on considerations of international law, voluntary codes and NZ law and government policy. For instance, the Guardians' exclusion of producers of cluster mines was triggered by the New Zealand government's pending ratification of the Convention on Cluster Munitions.[174] The UNPRI and the UN Global Compact are also influential standards for the Guardians.

Another ostensible difference between Norway and New Zealand is that the Guardians focus on 'acting as a responsible shareholder and fostering transparent corporate governance rather than necessarily excluding shares or securities'.[175] In the 12 months leading up to 30 June 2010, the Guardians had engaged on 345 occasions with companies concerning various social and environmental issues.[176] Share exclusion is considered 'a last resort for the Guardians', to be employed only if they 'cannot bring about a positive outcome through exercising their shareholder rights'.[177] However, in practice, the Guardians have used exclusion only for entities in a few designated economic sectors and not as a 'last resort'. Engagement is also used infrequently because it is time-consuming and expensive. The NZSF relies on its external research providers to identify for its 'red list' companies suitable for engagement, with priority depending on whether firms' breaches of international standards are long-term or short-term, historic or ongoing, and isolated or endemic.[178]

Although environmental matters are encompassed in its RI policy, in April 2009 the Guardians released a separate environmental statement and action plan that champions four issues: minimization of waste, efficient use of energy, green procurement and reduction of GHG emissions.[179] Much of this effort centres on reducing the environmental footprint of the NZSF's in-house operations (e.g., use of physical offices and staff travel), in addition to addressing any environmental impacts and risks from its portfolio companies.[180] As for the NGPF-G, the economic threat posed by climate change has galvanized some action. In the 12 months leading up to 30 June 2010, the Guardians engaged on 250 occasions with companies on climate

---

172 Ibid., 138.
173 GNZS, 'Exclusion decisions', http://www.nzsuperfund.co.nz/index.asp?pageID=2145883153.
174 GNZS, *Responsible Investment in Practice Report*, NZSF, 2009, 10. The text of the convention is at *ILM* 48, 2009, 354.
175 Controller and Auditor-General, op. cit., para. 3.62.
176 GNZS, *Annual Report 2010*, op. cit., 134.
177 Controller and Auditor-General, op. cit., para. 3.67.
178 GNZS, *How We Invest*, op. cit., 29.
179 GNZS, *Responsible Investment in Practice Report*, NZSF, 2009, 12.
180 GNZS, *Statement of Responsible Investment Policies*, op. cit., 140.

change issues, representing the substantial majority of its corporate engagement activity.[181] As a signatory to the CDP, the NZSF is able to collaborate with institutional investors, including the NGPF-G, to advocate corporate disclosure of climate-related impacts and policies. In 2008 the Guardians wrote to every company in the NZX 50 Index (New Zealand's premier stock market index) to encourage replies to CDP disclosure requests. According to the Guardians, the response rate increased to 50 per cent from 38 per cent in the previous year, partly due to the Fund's presence.[182] Furthermore, the Guardians see their participation in the CDP as 'important in raising awareness amongst NZ companies that investors globally are interested in the economic impacts of climate change and its potential effect on long-term shareholder value'.[183] The NZSF is also a member of the Investor Group on Climate Change, a club of 20 Australian and New Zealand investors ostensibly concerned about global warming.[184]

While the NZSF has made great strides in its ethical investment policy and practices since 2006, it still tends to trail its Norwegian counterpart and has been dogged by criticisms for alleged complicity in some unethical or unsustainable businesses, including some companies blacklisted by Norway.[185] Some of the most vituperative objections have come from Investment Watch Aotearoa, a national network campaigning for ethical investment to be a duty of all New Zealand public funds. It once brazenly accused the NZSF of 'invest[ing] large amounts of our taxpayer money in companies who ... prop up murderous regimes and commit mass environmental destruction',[186] and it has excoriated NZSF for allegedly investing in corporations that are 'complicit in the Israeli occupation' of asserted Palestinian territories.[187] In August 2011, the NZSF was accused of investing in a Chinese tobacco producer, contrary to the Fund's policies.[188] Also, the NZSF's reluctance to divest more widely has troubled the Green Party,[189] a growing political force in New Zealand politics. When the Green Party denigrated the NZSF for investing in ExxonMobil, a company derided by some as a 'climate change sceptic',[190] then NZSF Chief Executive Paul Costello retorted that his Fund's

---

181 Ibid., 133.
182 GNZS, *Responsible Investment in Practice Report*, op. cit., 9.
183 Ibid.
184 Ibid., 9–10.
185 R. Norman, *Betting the Bank on the Bomb*, Green Party of New Zealand, 2007, 3.
186 Investment Watch, 'NZ Super Fund invests our money in mass murder', 18 March 2007, http://www.indymedia.org.nz/article/73329/nz-super-fund-invests-our-money-mass-mur.
187 Investment Watch, 'NZ NGOs call for Superfund divestment from Israeli war crimes', 3 December 2009, http://investmentwatch.wordpress.com.
188 D. Brooksbank, 'NZ Super Fund facing questions over stake in tobacco-linked Chinese conglomerate', *Responsible-Investor.Com*, 12 August 2011.
189 Green Party of New Zealand, 'Super Fund must stop investing our taxes in nuclear bombs', 9 February 2007.
190 D. Adam, 'ExxonMobil continuing to fund climate sceptic groups, records show', *The Guardian*, 1 July 2009.

policy was to divest only from those firms whose products or activities are illegal in New Zealand.[191] Robert Howell, associated with the NZ Council for Socially Responsible Investment (NZCSRI), has also criticized the ambiguity of the world reputation statutory clause as failing to prevent the NZSF from investing in 'companies with unacceptable or questionable human rights behaviour or environmental impacts, such as Nike, Walmart, BJ Services (operating in Myanmar), and Exxon Mobil'.[192]

The New Zealand government's own Auditor-General has weighed in on the debate, with its 2008 report concluding that 'overall, the Guardians have taken an appropriate and pragmatic approach to responsible investment', but 'a number of challenges still face the Guardians in managing their responsible investment risk'.[193] These include the facts that 'the Fund is not a substantial shareholder in any entity in its own right' and that the Guardians depend on collaboration from other investors whose decisions 'are consistent with their "avoid prejudice" requirement'.[194] The Auditor-General further cautioned that '[i]dentifying which companies to exclude can present challenges and requires a specialist screening agency (for example, checking for a company's involvement in landmine manufacture)', and 'it is not always possible for the Fund to identify all activities in pooled investment structures such as unit trusts'.[195] The Auditor-General also found that the Guardians' investment screening process is limited to equity positions and sovereign securities held by the Fund, thus exposing it to ties to excluded entities through other financial relationships, such as by holding corporate bonds.[196]

French Pension Reserve Funds (FRR)

Establishment and legal framework

A vibrant RI movement emerged in France in the late 1990s, and the widespread support of trade unions and NGOs helped foster a political climate in which RI was increasingly institutionalized as a legal responsibility of financial institutions.[197] This led to the inclusion of RI responsibilities in the governance mandate of the French Pension Reserve Funds (Fonds de

---

191 'Greens urge Super Fund to dump Exxon', *New Zealand Herald*, 6 October 2006, http://www.nzherald.co.nz/nz/news/article.cfm?c_id=1&objectid=10404575.
192 R. Howell, 'The New Zealand Crown financial institutions' non-financial investment criteria', NZCSRI Conference, *Reward, Risk and Reputation – Rethinking the Investment Role of Crown Financial Institutions in New Zealand's Growth*, 2 December 2005, 1.
193 Controller and Auditor-General, op. cit., paras. 3.68 and 3.73.
194 Ibid.
195 Ibid.
196 Ibid., para. 3.74.
197 D.L. Arjaliès-de la Lande, 'A social movement perspective on finance: how socially responsible investment mattered', PRI Academic Network Conference, Ottawa, October 2009, 11–12; F. Déjean, 'L'émergence de l'investissement socialement responsable en France: le rôle des sociétés de gestion', *Revue de l'organisation responsable* 1, 2006, 18–29.

réserve pour les retraites),[198] as well as cognate reforms to company and pension fund laws. The FRR was created in 2001 and became operational in 2003, with a mandate to manage sums entrusted to it by public authorities to finance, from 2020, the old age insurance plan and affiliated pension schemes.[199] The FRR is thus a system of sovereign pension reserve funds, owned by the French state to improve the solvency of its social security system – in particular, to meet a predicted shortfall in the country's pay-as-you-go state pension scheme. The financial crisis of 2008 caused the government to move the date of the first payout from the pension reserve fund from 2020 to 2011.[200]

Importantly, the FRR is obliged by its enabling legislation to disclose how it takes into account environmental and social matters in its investment decisions.[201] While it is not explicitly required to practise RI and lacks the detailed ethical investment regulations of the NGPF-G, the FRR decision-makers have developed a number of policies for RI. The fund defines its overall approach to RI as the promotion of 'long-term sustainability' to 'reinforce intergenerational solidarity',[202] and it has been a UNPRI signatory since April 2006. The FRR's stance towards RI has been coloured by the Fund's primary legal mandate to invest over the long term: 'established for the purpose of managing the sums that are allocated to it in order to build up reserves intended to contribute to the long-term sustainability of pay-as-you-go pension plans'.[203]

The FRR's Supervisory Board, constituted more democratically and broadly than other SWFs by having members from parliament and representatives of employer and employee groups, as well as a minority of members appointed by the Ministers of Social Security, Economy and the Budget,[204] determines the general investment policy of the FRR. The Board is obliged to ensure the policy focuses on the principles of profitability, prudence and adequate spread of risks.[205] The FRR has thus striven to implement a general investment policy that takes into account ESG issues primarily because of their salience in influencing long-term financial returns and to a lesser extent as a means to address the stakeholder-oriented tradition of economic governance in

---

198 Http://www.fondsdereserve.fr.
199 The law no. 2001-624 of 17 July 2001, amended by law no. 2003-775, 21 August 2003, on the reform of pensions, codified in the Social Security Code, in chapter V bis, entitled Fonds de réserve pour les retraites, arts L135-6 to L135-15.
200 FRR, 'Letters from the chairmen', http://www.fondsdereserve.fr/spip.php?article511.
201 The operative provision states: 'Il en rend compte régulièrement au conseil de surveillance et retrace notamment, à cet effet, la manière dont les orientations générales de la politique de placement du fonds ont pris en compte des considérations sociales, environnementales et éthiques': art. L.135-8.
202 FRR, *Annual Report 2007*, 2008, 3.
203 Art. L.135-6.
204 Decree No. 2001-1214, Fonds de réserve pour les retraites, 19 December 2001, art. R.135-19.
205 Ibid., L. 135-8.

France. The FRR's efforts have earned it plaudits for providing RI 'leadership'[206] and being a 'catalyst for change' that has 'increased interest of the mainstream investment community in ESG information'.[207] There has been a surge in the French RI market coinciding with the emergence of the FRR.[208]

A series of legislative and institutional reforms played a seminal role in stimulating the efforts of the FRR and the local RI market.[209] The French government enacted two important laws in 2001: the New Economic Regulations, which oblige public companies to report annually on the social and environmental aspects of their activities,[210] and the so-called Fabius Law, which requires employee saving plans to report on how they take ESG issues into account.[211] Subsequently, in 2010 the so-called 'Grenelle II' Act was promulgated, which widens the corporate reporting requirements to include not only 'information concerning the way in which the company takes the social and environmental consequences of its activities into account' but also 'societal commitments undertaken in favour of sustainable development'.[212] Crucially, Grenelle II extends both reporting requirements to financial institutions, including insurance companies and retail funds. Another important milestone during this decade was the establishment in 2002 of the Comité intersyndical de l'épargne salariale (CIES) in order to provide a trade union-endorsed 'RI label' to a range of pension investment products available to employee saving funds.[213] By certifying the ESG criteria applied by pension fund management products, the CIES sought to become an influential actor in the French RI market. Also important were the creation in 2001 of two 'mobilizing structures', the Forum pour l'Investissement Responsable and the Société Française des Analystes Financiers, which sponsor research, exchange of best practices and public

---

206 Eurosif, *European RI Study*, 2006, 7.
207 H. Jemel-Fornetty, C. Louche and D. Bourghelle, 'Changing the dominant convention: the role of emerging initiatives in mainstreaming ESG', in W. Sun, C. Louche and R. Pérez (eds), *Finance and Sustainability: Towards a New Paradigm? A Post-Crisis Agenda*, Emerald Group, 2011, 85–117, 100.
208 V. Le Sourd and N. Amenc, 'Socially responsible investment performance in France', EDHEC Risk and Asset Management Research Centre, 2008, 22.
209 D.L. Arjaliès, 'A social movement perspective on finance: how socially responsible investment mattered', *Journal of Business Ethics* 92, 2010, 57–78, 67. See also S. Giamporcaro-Sauniere, *Socially Responsible Investment Amongst Supply and Demand: Analysis and Issues of the Social Construction of a Savings Policy*, PhD thesis, University of Rene Descartes Paris V, 2006.
210 Law No. 2001-420, relative aux nouvelles régulations économiques, 15 May 2001, art. 225-102-1.
211 Loi no. 2001-152, sur l'épargne salariale, 19 February 2001, art. 214-39.
212 Loi no. 2010-788, portant engagement national pour l'environnement, 13 July 2010, as discussed by C. Malecki, 'Societal corporate governance and extra-financial information: spearhead or Achilles' heel of corporate governance?', Legal Studies Research Paper Series No. 2011-26, Faculty of Law, University of Oslo, 2011.
213 G. Bourque, 'L'épargne salariale en France et l'initiative du Comité intersyndical de l'épargne salariale (CIES)', *Vie économique* 1(2), 2007.

debate on RI.[214] Unlike most RI associations, which are industry-based, the Forum has a multi-stakeholder membership, including representatives from trade unions and academia.[215]

Responsible investment policies and practices

The FRR Board claims its interest in RI stems from its mandate to serve the 'general interest'. Consequently, its investment strategy explains:

> [T]he FRR's investment policy has a dual aim. On the one hand, it seeks to maximize investment returns over the long term and under the best possible conditions of security. Its investment policy must also be consistent with certain shared values that promote economically, socially and environmentally sustainable development.[216]

In reconciling these aims, the FRR's policy framework for RI has evolved considerably over the past decade. In April 2003, the Supervisory Board formulated its first RI policy, the principal features of which were an active policy for proxy voting at shareholder meetings of FRR portfolio corporations, ESG research and analysis and their inclusion in asset selection and management, and transparency and reporting on application of extra-financial criteria.[217] In February 2005, the FRR published broad proxy voting guidelines for managers under its mandate. Much of the FRR's policy on RI at this early stage was directed towards its European equities holdings rather than applied to all its global assets because of perceived difficulties in assessing ESG information in all markets.

Unlike the NGPF-G or NZSF, the FRR's policy framework for RI has focused more on thematic principles than prospective criteria. In June 2005, the FRR called for tenders for external fund managers to invest €600 million for dedicated RI mandates, over a five-year period until 2011.[218] Fund managers were chosen based on their technical expertise, ability to follow the FRR's stated RI objectives and their competitive management costs. The FRR priorities for the tender were structured around five principles: (i) respect for basic human and worker rights; (ii) promotion of employment through improving the quality of human resource management; (iii) responsibility for the environment; (iv) respect for consumer and fair trade practices; and (v) good corporate governance. Each of these principles was elaborated with several useful examples; in regard to principle (iii), reference was made to the

---

214 Arjaliès, op. cit., 67.
215 See http://www.frenchsif.org/isr/fir/.
216 FRR, 'The FRR's SRI investment strategy and SRI mandate philosophy', June 2005, http://www.fondsdereserve.fr.
217 FRR, Press release, April 2003, http://www.fondsdereserve.fr/spip.php?rubrique127.
218 L. Delain, 'Les fonds éthiques sont en plein essor', Le Monde, 21 May 2006.

development of environmentally friendly and eco-efficiency technologies, reduction of GHG emissions, and the minimization of environmental pollution and biodiversity impairment. This is an inclusive, multi-faceted approach that doesn't aim to exclude certain economic sectors but rather prioritizes FRR's investments into companies that have the best profile combining financial and ESG criteria.

During the 2005 tender, the FRR also explained that its investment approach is to address multiple criteria, and it doesn't apply ethical screens to exclude *a priori* certain economic sectors.[219] Instead, it prefers to advance RI through a 'best-in-class' method of stock selection, guided by international standards such as the UN Global Compact, in order to achieve its social economy vision of SRI as reflected in its five priority themes.[220] Corporate engagement has also been utilized to allow fund managers to take a nuanced approach. The exercise of voting rights is to be done pragmatically, taking into account both the concrete conditions existing in each market or between companies according to their relative size, and also any significant differences that exist between the corporate governance practices of the countries involved.

In 2008, the FRR Supervisory Board adopted a new five-year RI strategy for 2008–12, which aimed to apply ESG screening to all asset classes in which the Fund invests rather than just to niche portfolios.[221] This strategy centered on routine integration of ESG issues into investment decision-making and portfolio management; prevention of financial risks associated with ESG issues; corporate engagement and active shareholding; and participation in RI research efforts in France and abroad.[222] The FRR has used several ESG research providers to help it 'measure the environmental, social and governance quality of its portfolio; assess the extent to which its investment approach contributes to sustainable development, and identify financial threats and opportunities to which the Fund may be exposed'.[223] Although the FRR doesn't rely on exclusionary screens as its primary means of RI, occasionally it will use them, as it did regarding companies implicated in producing cluster bombs.

Significantly, in its 2008–12 strategy the FRR elaborated on its justification for investing responsibly and offered the following three reasons:

> – The first reason is related to its fundamental mission and its objective, which is to optimize the return on the funds entrusted to it for investment under the best possible conditions of security. To this end, it is necessary to incorporate ESG criteria into asset management in order

---

219 FRR, 'The FRR's SRI investment strategy and SRI mandate philosophy', op. cit.
220 UNEP-FI and UKSIF, op. cit., 44.
221 FRR, 'Responsible investment strategy', http://www.fondsdereserve.fr/IMG/pdf/FRRsSRI_investment_strategy_2008_2012.pdf.
222 Ibid.; UNEP-FI and UKSIF, op. cit., 42–3.
223 UNEP-FI and UKSIF, ibid., 45.

to fully apprehend the risks and opportunities attached to the businesses in which the FRR invests and will invest in. . . .

– The second reason is economic in nature: The long-term performance of investments does not depend only on the impact of the financial and extra-financial strategy of the companies, but also on the impacts that they generate for the industry in which they operate or for the whole economy. An analysis of these externalities, positive or negative, and therefore of the environmental and social sustainability of corporate strategies and their implications for the community, is necessary, in particular for an investor whose resources are provided by the public and intended for investment over the long term in a vast number of companies.

– The third is related to the role of the FRR as a public, long-term investor. As such, the FRR is expected to identify and track the risks that some of these investments may pose to its own reputation. . . .[224]

These candid reasons display several standard rationales for RI associated with the business case (first rationale), universal investor thesis (second rational) and reputational standing (the third). While none of these prioritizes sustainability as a priority or valuable goal in its own right, together the FRR's rationale provides a reasonably broad basis to practise RI in comparison with other SWFs. It offers a much wider rationale than the 'complicity' standards behind the NGPF-G's ethical investment guidelines.

To help implement the strategy initiated in 2008, a Responsible Investment Committee of the Supervisory Board was created. The Committee, composed of FRR staff and externally recruited experts, was created out of concern for the reputational risks tied to investing in companies that do not respect the principles of the UN Global Compact, conventions banning biological/chemical weapons, landmines and other controversial weapons and, particularly, the core conventions of the ILO. The Committee is tasked to oversee implementation of the RI guidelines defined in the 2008–12 strategy and to prevent and control the non-financial risks of the Fund's portfolios. The strategy also reaffirms that the Fund will continue to exercise a policy of active voting at general meetings of companies in which the FRR is a shareholder, in order to improve corporate governance.

Within its approach to RI, the FRR launched procedures for the selection of external investment researchers to report on the extra-financial aspects of the Fund's active investment portfolio. The objective of this reporting is to permit the FRR's executive bodies to measure the quality of its portfolio in ESG terms; to determine the extent to which this approach contributes to sustainable development; and to identify extra-financial risks and opportunities to which the Fund could be exposed. Since November 2006 the FRR has sought to routinely assess its entire portfolio for ESG-related financial risks

---

224 FRR, 'Responsible investment strategy', op. cit.

and opportunities.[225] In reviewing corporate stocks for investment, it relies on EIRIS to assess compliance with international standards on basic human and labour rights, and retains Trucost, an environmental research organization, to assess the environmental grounds.[226]

In recent years the FRR has sought to collaborate through a number of global business codes and regimes. It actively participates in the UNPRI, having been a signatory since 2006. Because combatting corruption and promoting good governance are part of the RI strategy adopted by the Supervisory Board in 2008, the FRR announced its support for the Extractive Industries Transparency Initiative (EITI) in 2009. This Initiative is the result of a global coalition of stakeholders, and its aim is to strengthen transparency and responsibility of actors in the mining sector through verification and full disclosure of payments made by companies and income received by governments through the exploitation of resources. The FRR pledged to take an active role in the implementation of the EITI and invites all affected companies and sectors to do the same.[227] The FRR has also supported the CDP and the affiliated Water Disclosure Project, which solicit environmental performance information from major companies in investors' portfolios.[228]

Another important feature of the RI strategy for 2008–12 is to improve analysis of the impact of environmental issues on the FRR's investment portfolio. The Fund conducted a study in 2009 with the help of APREC (Association pour la Promotion de la Recherche en Economie de carbon), entitled 'How Should the Environment be Taken into Account in Defining an Investment Policy?'.[229] It concluded that climate change, decline of natural resources, depletion of water and the loss of biodiversity globally are the environmental issues of most relevance to long-term investors; and they must be considered in terms of both financial risks and opportunities. The study also showed that an investor could attempt to integrate environmental issues at different levels in its investment policy: strategic allocation, choice among asset classes, administration/management, reporting and evaluation. In light of this study and in the context of preparations for the UN Climate Change Conference in Copenhagen in December 2009, the FRR signed a declaration of investors in favour of a robust international agreement at Copenhagen.[230]

Overall, the FRR has one of the most sophisticated repertoires of RI policies and strategies of any SWF. Its record also demonstrates the considerable

---

225 FRR, Press release, November 2006, http://www.fondsdereserve.fr/spip.php?rubrique127.
226 UNEP-FI and UKSIF, op. cit., 45.
227 See http://www.fondsdereserve.fr/IMG/pdf/ITIE7septembre2009.pdf.
228 FRR, 'The FRR supports the CDP Water Disclosure Project', Press release, 12 October 2010.
229 See http://www.developpementdurable.com/annuaire/boutique/29638/association-pour-la-promotion-de-la-recherche-sur-leconomie-du-carbone-aprec.html.
230 J. Murray, 'World's largest investors demand global climate deal', *BusinessGreen*, 17 September 2009, http://www.businessgreen.com/bg/news/1803671/worlds-largest-investors-demand-global-climate-deal.

progress that sometimes can be made through policy-making without a detailed legislative mandate for RI. Another distinguishing feature of the FRR is its 'social economy' approach to RI, with greater emphasis on economic democracy and social equality outcomes than the NGPF-G and NZSF. But there are contradictory views of the FRR's commitment to RI in practice. Some observers believe the Fund is a 'beacon' for RI,[231] while others are critical of its tendency to engage in short-term investments.[232] One impediment to the FRR's aspirations regarding RI is that the Fund believes relatively few investment managers offer suitable RI products; thus, it sees that greater maturity in the marketplace is needed before the RI policy can be advanced across the FRR's entire portfolio.

SWFs as proponents of sustainability

The SWFs considered in this chapter resemble institutional chameleons in their conflicting expectations. They operate like *private* investment vehicles for maximizing shareholder value, while encumbered with *public*, fiduciary-like responsibilities to fulfill state policies that incorporate non-financial considerations. Some commentators thus see tension between these dyadic ambitions and fear that adulterating their financial mandate might cause SWFs to 'serve as a covert mechanism for extending state power'.[233] This book has already explained that RI does not necessarily entail any irresolvable trade-offs between public and private interests, or between financial and ethical goals. While commercial considerations often do not coincide with ethical ones, over the very long term, they should.

To become marathon investors, SWFs must not only avoid companies that harm the environment or violate human rights, but also actively promote sustainable development. Traditionally, the notion of complicity has been a touchstone for their RI policies. The review of the NGPF-G by the Albright Group and Chesterman observed that a 'central tension within the Guidelines is the question of whether they are intended simply to avoid Norwegian complicity or influence the behaviour of others. The former is closer to the truth'.[234] Some of the Council on Ethics' recommendations view divestment as necessary to avoid the complicity of the Fund (and thus Norway) in scandalous behaviour by companies.[235] Somewhat similarly, the NZSF legislation, which obliges the Guardians to avoid 'prejudice to New Zealand's

---

231 P. Skypala, 'French pension fund leads the way on RI', *Financial Times* 25 July 2005, 3.
232 C. Ducourtieux, 'Inquiétudes sur l'avenir du Fonds de réserve des retraites, par', *Le Monde* 2 December 2005, 18.
233 Backer, 'Regulatory chameleons', op. cit., 176.
234 Albright Group and Chesterman, op. cit., 11. The NBIM denies such tension exists, believing both goals are equally valid and achievable simultaneously through divestment and engagement strategies: NBIM, 'Comments on the report by the Albright Group and Simon Chesterman on the implementation of the Ethical Guidelines', 6 June 2008.
235 Chesterman, op. cit., 607.

reputation',[236] implies avoiding the stigma of profiting from the unethical.[237] And commentators and activists who have scrutinized the NZSF's investments often couch their concerns in this language.[238] Neither SWF, however, relies on a strict legal conception of complicity; instead, they view it in a moral and practical sense. By contrast, the FRR has a rather open-ended legislative mandate to address ESG issues, offering it wider scope to promote RI as a means of encouraging companies to improve their sustainability performance (but potentially also more latitude to be lax). As the next chapter discusses, 'complicity' isn't a sufficient yardstick for promoting sustainability, for several reasons. For one, it places overly high thresholds for divestment, such as the cause of severe environmental damage. Moreover, as an ethical and legal concept, complicity is conceptually confusing and imprecise.

While a commitment to sustainability sanctions divestment from the worst businesses, it requires more. SWFs need more *positive* investment in environmental leaders, broad portfolio-wide policies on key sustainability issues such as climate change mitigation and biodiversity conservation, and public policy advocacy to promote better sustainability regulation at both national and global levels. While the NGPF-G and NZSF undertake some of these measures, they are not done comprehensively; for example, less than 1 per cent of the NGPF-G's portfolio is earmarked for positive environmental investment, and both only engage with a miniscule fraction of their investee companies. Fundamentally, both funds are biased to seeing how sustainability contributes to investment value, rather than how investment value may contribute to sustainability. The FRR and Swedish AP funds have declared a quite active approach to encouraging corporate sustainability. The Ethical Council servicing the AP funds publicizes that not only does it react against companies breaching basic international environmental and human rights norms, but its 'mission [is] encouraging companies . . . to address relevant sustainability issues, [and] . . . to enable the business to be operated in as responsible a way as possible'.[239] But, potentially incongruously, these funds are also mandated to prioritise high investment returns.

Conceivably, if each SWF made sustainability a priority, they would be justified in divesting from vast swathes of the global economy. Very few companies in the world presently meet rigorous sustainability standards,[240] and such an approach would be unworkable and undermine the core purpose of

---

236 New Zealand Superannuation and Retirement Income Act, 2001, s. 58(2)(c).
237 While the Fund's legislation and policies do not refer to 'complicity', as a supporter of the UN Global Compact which does, the NZSF has indirectly endorsed this stance: Principle 2 of the Global Compact expects signatories to 'make sure they are not complicit in human rights abuses'.
238 E.g., Auckland University Students for Justice in Palestine and Global Peace and Justice Auckland, 'NZ taxpayer funded murder results in protests at Rakon AGM', Media Release, 31 August 2006.
239 Ethical Council, op. cit., 2.
240 P. Shrivastava and S. Hart, 'Creating sustainable corporations', *Business Strategy and the Environment* 4, 1995, 154–65, 163.

the SWFs. Therefore, in the interim, they would need to rely mainly on corporate engagement and positive investment in environmental programs. Such strategies allow maintenance of broadly diversified portfolios without compromising financial returns so long as the additional administrative costs are carefully controlled. But they will be influential only if undertaken on a much larger scale and if SWFs act in concert, including with other investment institutions, to achieve a critical mass of influence.

Legislative change is likely needed to spur such progress, and additional resources are needed to allow screening, risk assessment, engagement and positive investment on a much greater scale. Legislation could minimize fund managers' discretion to deviate from sustainability goals and to promote a cultural shift in their decision-making. Such reform has already been proposed in New Zealand, but without success. In 2006 and 2010, the New Zealand Parliament debated a Private Member's Bill that sought to strengthen the ethical investment framework of the NZSF and apply similar standards to other NZ Crown financial institutions.[241] The Bill included a duty on the NZSF Guardians 'to promote socially responsible and environmentally sustainable development',[242] and investment policies would have to take into account international norms and conventions supported or ratified by the New Zealand government.[243] Such an ambitious duty would need supplementary rules to provide meaningful direction regarding sustainability indicators and investment time-frames, as well as more administrative resources. New Zealand already displays similar ambition in its environmental and planning legislation, and a substantial body of judicial case law and administrative practice would help to elaborate sustainability goals for investment purposes.[244]

Reforming the legislative basis of SWFs alone is unlikely to be sufficient to propel them into being public fiduciaries for sustainability. Their international governance framework also needs adjusting. Anita Halvorssen argues that 'sustainable development needs to be incorporated into the . . . Santiago Principles'.[245] Presently, principle 19 declares, 'The SWF's investment decisions should aim to maximize risk-adjusted returns in a manner consistent with economic policy.' In recognition that some SWFs' investments are coloured by other policy preferences, sub-principle 19.1 states that other considerations 'should be clearly set out in the investment policy and be publicly disclosed'. Although her proposal presently would lack support from most SWFs, Halvorssen recommends that the Principles should explicitly require SWFs to take into account climate change as a key investment

---

241 Ethical Investment (Crown Financial Institutions) Bill, 2006. It was reintroduced to the NZ Parliament in 2010, but was voted down.
242 Ibid., cl. 9.
243 Ibid., cl. 10.
244 C. Freeman, 'Sustainable development from rhetoric to practice? A New Zealand perspective', *International Planning Studies* 9(4), 2004, 307–26.
245 Halvorssen, op. cit., 80.

variable. Such a reform would render the Santiago Principles ahead of most RI codes such as the UNPRI. A formal international treaty for SWFs that prioritizes sustainability would be even more beneficial, but of course it would face greater political hurdles.

Until then, the NGPF-G will likely remain the lead SWF promoting RI, owing to several distinguishing institutional and structural characteristics. The NZSF is managed solely by the Guardians, who enjoy broad discretion in interpreting and implementing their ethical mandate. The FRR lacks a duty to invest ethically, but its duty to disclose how it takes ESG issues into account has been interpreted as implying a broader mandate. The French funds are managed by a Supervisory Board that somewhat resembles a tripartite stakeholder model of governance, giving representation to the state, business and workers, but environmental issues are yet without an exclusive champion.

By contrast, the NGPF-G is supported by a Council on Ethics, whose institutional separation from the Norges Bank and Ministry allows the Council to focus purely on ethical issues without being distracted about the financial implications of its recommendations or being captured by any stakeholder pressures. In administering the NGPF-G, the Ministry and Norges Bank are subject to ethical guidelines that are much more extensive and detailed than those of the NZSF. The latter faces greater political pressure to meet financial returns,[246] as it must provide for the future funding of pension payments, which are forecast to grow substantially. Likewise, the FRR's primary mandate is to enlarge the reserve funds to sustain pension income support from 2020. (In fact, in the wake of the GFC, the FRR has been mobilized since 2011 to underwrite French pensions.) Although the Norwegian fund is also a 'pension fund', it lacks the same underpinning financial liabilities, and its role in building national savings is less explicitly tied to future pension income. The NGPF-G is also considerably larger than the NZSF and FRR, giving it greater leeway to 'indulge' its ethical mandate alongside its pursuit of financial returns. Finally, the NGPF-G invests only outside its national borders, while the NZSF and FRR invest both abroad and domestically. Because it would be problematic for the NZSF or FRR to exclude domestic companies on the basis of their social and environmental practices, which are already subject to home state regulation, they presumably face greater constraints when making their own judgements regarding unethical behaviour locally.

The NGPF-G, FRR and NZSF have much to gain by engaging with one another, and by collaborating with other socially conscientious SWFs and

---

246 The NZSF is expected to *exceed* the risk-free rate of return (the interest rate on NZ Treasury bills) by at least 2.5% per year over rolling 20-year periods: NZSF, 'Our Expected Rate of Return', http://www.nzsuperfund.co.nz/index.asp? PageID=2145855927. The NGPF-G is expected over the long term to achieve an annual real return of 2.7% on its bond investment, 3.5% on real estate and 5.0% of equities: Norwegian Ministry of Finance, *The Management of the Government Pension Fund in 2009*, op. cit., s. 8.

institutional investors. In recent years there have been periodic meetings and consultations among SWFs and other major institutional investors such as CalPERS and the Dutch pension funds to promote RI. As one of the world's pre-eminent SWFs, and with the resources on the ground to check how companies behave, the NGPF-G is best placed to exert leadership here. Companies excluded or engaged by the NGPF-G are more likely to subsequently be treated similarly by other funds interested in RI.

The following chapter continues the discussion about options for promoting RI, especially through SWFs. The ancient public trust doctrine could be refashioned to underpin legal reform, and SWFs could take the lead as public fiduciaries in implementing environmentally responsible investing.

6 The public fiduciary: in nature's trust

A new direction

Responsible investing both impeaches and enjoins financial markets: it indicts long-standing investment practices that impair ecological health, while inviting reform to safeguard environmental and social values indispensable to the long-term health of the economy. Despite effusive publicity about RI's benefits, most financiers remain unchanged, and any evaluation of environmental impact, even by avowed social investors, tends to be made narrowly for immediate financial advantage. Emptied of its more radical impulse, RI has become a bit of a platitude, serving meekly as either a client-driven ethical 'preference' or a financial risk management tool, rather than an integral strategy for long-term, sustainable finance. Of course, that environmental care and financial prosperity can go hand-in-hand isn't objectionable, in principle; financiers should benefit from companies that lighten their ecological footprint. The unease arises when some masquerading as responsible investors tinker with the status quo rather than embrace 'a financial paradigm shift towards a broad sense of sustainability'.[1]

The principal argument for this 'shift', in the institutional sector, has related to reconceptualizing these actors as 'universal investors' for whom ESG issues are financially salient.[2] The gist of it is that institutional funds have self-interest to reduce their environmental cost externalities because they hold economy-wide portfolios that expose them to such externalities, and that with time such costs diminish portfolio values. The universal owner thesis has been increasingly acknowledged by the RI industry, including the UNPRI and UNEP-FI. A report by the UN advises that the portfolio of universal owners:

> makes it difficult for them to avoid systemic risks of the kind that unmitigated climate change will impose on them. As a result, prudent

---

1 W. Sun, C. Louche and R. Pérez, 'Finance and sustainability: exploring the reality we are making', in W. Sun, C. Louche and R. Pérez (eds), *Finance and Sustainability: Towards a New Paradigm? A Post-Crisis Agenda*, Emerald Group, 2011, 3–15, 14.
2 J. Youngdahl, 'The time has come for a sustainable theory of fiduciary duty investment', *Hofstra Labor and Employment Law Journal* 29, 2011, 115–39, 134–9.

pension funds have good reason to pursue cost effective strategies to support climate change mitigation and adaptation. Arguably, this may even be part of their fiduciary duty.³

I have already distilled, in Chapter 3, the frailties of this thesis and, more generally, the barriers institutional funds face to embracing RI. The unidimensional 'financial materiality' test hardly impels one to prioritize sustainability. In fact, a countervailing business case for intensifying unsustainable practices may be evaluated. Moreover, the competitive RI market stymies coordination of efforts for sustainability. And from a legal standpoint, the universal owner thesis suffers from the problems of 'remoteness' and 'causality'. An RI decision cannot be easily defended as assisting beneficiaries when benefits are potentially deferred for several decades and the benefit may be one that arises from the interventions of many actors, rather than being attributable to a specific investment fund. In other words, acting as a universal investor may not satisfy prevailing interpretations of fiduciary and trusts law that imply more immediate and exclusive benefits for investors. Even if the law were otherwise, it would be difficult to provide beneficiaries with an effective right given that any ethical or financial loss for uncertain, potential harms may not accrue for many years.

While this book has identified some innovations in the RI industry, such as improved ESG analysis and its integration into stock valuations and investment decisions, daunting impediments remain owing to the dominant models of financial decision-making, as well as intransigent organizational cultures and governance models. Hager Jemel-Fornetty and others suggest:

> [f]ocusing on developing tools and methods or attempting to prove a positive link between ESG issues and share price will not be sufficient to make ESG issues part of mainstream investment. It is also important to understand how conventions evolve to create the necessary mechanisms that can lead to change.⁴

Anne Simpson, CalPERS's Director of Corporate Governance, puts the challenges more sternly:

> The scale of the financial crisis has illustrated that investors are no longer simply challenged on long-standing issues of concern, such as the despoiling of the environment. . . . To compound the problem, the basic

---

3 United Nations, 'Investor leadership on climate change', UN Global Compact Office, 2009, 10.
4 H. Jemel-Fornetty, C. Louche and D. Bourghelle, 'Changing the dominant convention: the role of emerging initiatives in mainstreaming ESG', in Sun, Louche and Pérez, op. cit., 85–117, 95.

architecture of the financial system is creaking. . . . The governance systems for regulating the markets are based on nineteenth century designs. The truth is that those concerned with Responsible Investment will not make progress unless these wider issues related to the soundness of the capital markets are addressed.[5]

The systemic woes that manifested in the GFC transcend the cognitive boundaries of typical fiduciary finance relationships. Most RI managers and trustees failed to foresee and did not react in time to the crisis of 2008. The crash bled losses of about US$5 trillion from private pension portfolios that year, according to the OECD.[6] Fiduciary law anchored on prudential investor standards overlooks this systemic risk and encourages myopic, herd-like behaviour. Jemel-Fornetty and others describe investors' tendency to 'mimetic behaviour' as driven by their 'pre-emption assessment' of how they believe others will evaluate financial information, leading to a convergence of stock valuations and investment decisions.[7]

Law can ameliorate such conventions by providing alternative norms and decision-making procedures. Reforming fiduciary law isn't simply about altering specific doctrinal rules; it must also encompass governance systems within and among financial institutions so that the prevailing substantive investment conventions can be critiqued, debated and innovatively redefined. Much of this book has unveiled how legal acts and omissions fuelled financial market instabilities of recent years and created barriers to RI. This final chapter examines how law might redeem itself. It discusses three areas of potential reform: (i) the decision-making procedures of financial organizations, including collaborative, sector-wide decision-making; (ii) an accompanying new prudential investment duty on fiduciary investors; and (iii) a parallel public trust duty on the state, in its supervisory role of financial markets. This isn't an exhaustive list, and the chapter doesn't address the financial governance challenges needed at an international level. Yet, this chapter will explain why and how these measures should help.

The concept of fiduciary responsibility is old, but its content is potentially adaptable. It has been described as 'an area of law susceptible to flexible and expansive interpretation'.[8] In the *Mulligan* case, the New Zealand High Court held that a trustee's duty of prudent investment 'is a flexible standard . . . which will change with economic conditions and in the light of contemporary thinking'.[9] Fiduciary and trust laws are not inert, nor are

---

5 A. Simpson, 'In the wake of the financial crisis: rethinking responsible investment', *Notre Dame Journal of Law, Ethics and Public Policy* 26, 2012, 73–80, 76.
6 H. Stewart and R. Sunderland, 'Credit crunch costs pension funds $5trn', *The Observer*, 14 December 2008, B2.
7 Jemel-Fornetty, Louche and Bourghelle , op. cit., 92.
8 Law Reform Commission (LRC), *Trust Law: General Proposals*, LRC, 2008, 12.
9 *Re Mulligan (Deceased)*, (1998) 1 NZLR 481, 500.

they intrinsically wedded to any specific investment doctrine. In theory, they should be sufficiently malleable to evolve in interpretation over time. The quaint rulings of British courts in the last century, prohibiting municipal authorities (with a fiduciary responsibility to their rate-payers) from offering fair wages to employees or subsidizing public transport, wouldn't be supported today.[10] The American Law Institute's authoritative restatements on trusts law, in rejecting prior interpretations of the duty of care, enjoined: '[t]rust investment law should reflect and accommodate current knowledge and concepts. It should *avoid* repeating the mistake of *freezing its rules against future learning and developments*'.[11]

While enlightened judicial interpretation of existing rules might nudge things along, coupled with greater education of trustees, so far no legal action has disciplined fiduciaries for failure to invest responsibly, even in the narrow sense of ignoring financially material ESG information. Most public debate about enlightening fiduciary finance law has tinkered with the challenges outlined in this book. The main proposals have been for legal clarification that consideration of financially material ESG issues should not be unlawful, but without extending positive duties to invest sustainably or ethically.[12]

Apart from fiduciary law, RI reforms should be nested within a larger program of regulatory reform of financial markets and the economy generally. As Carlos Joly explains, 'the deeper problem of what to invest in is not primarily what RI should exclude from its investment universe; but rather the fact that we do not have enough good investment objects on offer. We need a better investment universe. We invest in the corporate and economic realities that are given, and this is our most severe limitation'.[13] Creating a sustainable economy is a multi-dimensional task. For the financial economy – our focus – the self-regulatory route has only limited potential in engendering fundamental change. The paradoxical notion that 'the more liberalized the financial system is, the greater the need for more effective regulation, to avoid massive and costly crises' has recently given rise to a smorgasbord of policy proposals in the wake of the GFC.[14] These have largely evaded issues of market structure and scale, focusing instead on

---

10 See *Roberts v. Hopwood*, [1925] AC 578; *Prescott v. Birmingham Corporation*, [1955] Ch. 210.
11 American Law Institute (ALI), *Restatement of the Law Third, Trusts*, ALI, 1992, s. 227 (my emphasis).
12 FairPensions, *The Enlightened Shareholder: Clarifying Investors' Fiduciary Duties*, FairPensions, 2011; R.A.G. Monks, 'A review of corporate governance in UK banks and other financial industry entities: the role of institutional shareholders', in W. Sunn, et al. (eds), *Corporate Governance and the Global Financial Crisis: International Perspectives*, Cambridge University Press, 2011, 134–43, 140–1.
13 C. Joly, 'Reality and potential of responsible investment', in W. Vandekerckhove, et al. (eds), *Responsible Investment in Times of Turmoil*, Springer, 2011, 194–210, 197.
14 S. Griffith-Jones, J.A. Ocampo and J.E. Stiglitz, 'Introduction', in S. Griffith-Jones, et al. (eds), *Time for a Visible Hand: Lessons from the 2008 World Financial Crisis*, Oxford University Press, 2010, 1–16, 7.

detailed and often prescriptive rules governing business conduct. Reform must more comprehensively address the 'growing scale and complexity of the financial sector, the emergence of new and unregulated actors and instruments, as well as the increased globalization of financial markets'.[15] In other words, we must somehow tame financial institutions that have become not only 'too big to fail' but also seemingly too big to govern.

Briefly, most commentators and policy-makers seek more transparent financial transactions and risks, stronger capital adequacy standards for lenders to buffer against potential crises, better incentives for bankers and fund managers to act for the long term, and equivalent regulation of all financial institutions and instruments in order to close regulatory lacunae in the 'shadow' financial markets.[16] This last category includes hedge funds and other private pools of capital, and complex and opaque financial products such as over-the-counter derivatives, whose regulation is necessary because of the heightened risk pumped into the financial sector by potentially 'toxic' assets.[17] Many commentators identify 'increased transparency, specifically with respect to corporate reporting' as the key enabling measure.[18] John Nesbitt explains, '[i]mportantly, this is not necessarily about the frequency of reporting, but the quality and the focus of the reporting, preferably focusing more on long-term value preservation and creation'.[19] Such disclosures can reduce the imperfections and asymmetries of financial information that allow inefficient and overly risky investments.[20] And many have stressed more tightly coordinated international regulation, coupled with a supranational institution mandated to require remedial intervention when risks pollinate across jurisdictions.[21]

These and other measures, while not directly designed for RI, would likely help it at both the national and international levels. But the proposals that have garnered the most serious attention, even if implemented, may be insufficient to forestall future crises. The efficacy of enhanced disclosure is undermined by the sheer complexity of many financial products and transactions that even supposedly sophisticated investors do not fully comprehend. Requiring greater disclosure of individual actors and instruments may also do little to mitigate the potential for systemic risk to the market

---

15 J. D'Arista and S. Griffith-Jones, 'Agenda and criteria for financial regulatory reform', in ibid., 126–49, 126.
16 See Sunn, et al., op. cit.; K. Alexander and N. Moloney (eds), *Law Reform and Financial Markets*, Edward Elgar, 2012.
17 L.L. Dallas, 'Short-termism, the financial crisis, and corporate governance', *Journal of Corporation Law* 37(2), 2012, 266–362; M. Dewatripont, et al., *Balancing the Banks: Global Lessons from the Financial Crisis*, Princeton University Press, 2010.
18 J. Nesbitt, 'The role of short-termism in financial market crises', *Australian Accounting Review* 19(4), 2009, 314–18, 317.
19 Ibid.
20 G. Caprio Jr., 'Subprime finance: yes, we still are in Kansas', Griffith-Jones, et al., op. cit., 50–60.
21 M. Williams, 'Governing the global regulatory system', in Griffith-Jones, ibid., 200–17.

generally.²² Some commentators thus emphasize the urgency also to address corporate governance failures, especially in banks and other financial corporations, as well as impose tougher disincentives to short-termism such as through a financial transaction tax.²³ It is beyond the scope of this book to further canvass and critique these wider debates about financial markets reform, but it is an essential perspective to have in addition to legal measures that specifically target RI.

The purpose of RI should be to build not only financial capital, but also to protect natural capital over the long term. Investing in socially responsible companies alone does not help greatly, so long as the share of RI investors doing so remains at its present modest level. We need mechanisms to foster collaboration among many investors. It is unrealistic to expect that individual investors – whether they are retail or institutional – will forgo immediate financial self-interest in favour of an environmentally sustainable and socially optimal return, even though collectively that might be in their long-term interests. Furthermore, the RI sector's codes to promote an esprit de corps, such as the UNPRI, haven't proven to be a credible surrogate market regulator even though they have raised some awareness and facilitated networking.

Several options are canvassed in this chapter to promote RI. One is to extend fiduciary responsibility to the state itself, building on the traditions of the public trust doctrine, so that financial regulators are impressed with overarching responsibilities to safeguard sustainability as a precondition to long-term, prosperous investment. A green economy requires a comprehensive approach that becomes the commitment of all regulators and stakeholders, not just government environmental departments. But because of structural obstacles to engendering change solely through government oversight, additional measures should be implemented within investment entities.

One option is to redefine the notion of prudent investment, requiring fiduciaries to pay attention to the environmental conditions that underpin a prosperous investment portfolio over the long term. In essence, this duty could oblige fiduciaries to focus on long-term investment returns, thereby fostering a new prudential investment convention more compatible with sustainability. Alternatively or in addition, this goal might be furthered by codifying the common law duty of care into a statutory duty of environmental care that gives third parties enforceable rights against financial institutions that pollute or degrade nature.

---

22 S.L. Schwarcz, 'Systemic risk and markets', in R.W. Kolb (ed.), *Lessons from the Financial Crisis: Causes, Consequences, and Our Economic Future*, John Wiley & Sons, 2010, 495–500, 497.
23 J.P. Hawley, S.J. Kamath and A.T. Williams, 'Introduction', in J.P. Hawley, S.J. Kamath and A.T. Williams (eds), *Corporate Governance Failures: The Role of Institutional Investors in the Global Financial Crisis*, University of Pennsylvania Press, 2011, 1–25, 1; 'European Commission financial tax opposed by UK', *BBC News*, 28 September 2011, http://www.bbc.co.uk/news/business-15090761.

Another reform canvassed in this chapter is more democratic and transparent decision-making processes within and among financial institutions so that complex and contentious issues about RI can, where required, be properly debated on a case-by-case basis. So far the interpretation of fiduciary responsibility has been dominated by interests 'largely antagonistic to innovation in investment management'.[24] The notion of prudential investing – a seminal element of fiduciary responsibility – should be understood to include appropriate consultation with and disclosure to beneficiaries about investment policy that raises important ethical and sustainability issues. Because of the difficulty in motivating active participation by lay investors, involvement of civil society groups and other stakeholders should be encouraged in regulatory processes as well as in industry-based RI codes.

We must recognize that fiduciary responsibility is very much about *process* rather than just outcome. Courts have examined whether trustees solicited professional advice, took into account relevant considerations and followed other procedural steps. It is therefore not a question of whether, in hindsight, trustees garnered the best investment returns. The following section summarizes the existing legal measures for RI – some of which were considered earlier in this book – which also resonate this focus on process rather than outcomes. The reforms canvassed in this final chapter, while also acknowledging the role of good process, go farther by defining the parameters of financial decision-making within more substantive environmental performance cues.

Existing legal reforms for RI

A new legal architecture for RI has been emerging in a few countries over the past decade, although it hasn't remedied the structural problems of the financial economy just outlined. The reforms leave largely unaltered the core parameters of fiduciary responsibility. Several interwoven factors have fed this incipient trend. Many Western nations are experiencing a realignment of the roles of the state and market, with a shift towards regulatory *governance* that cedes greater responsibilities to market actors and, to a lesser extent, civil society.[25] Legal commentators have labelled these changes with fancy terms such as 'mutual regulation',[26] 'responsive regulation',[27] 'smart regulation',[28]

---

24 G. Clark, 'Fiduciary duty, statute, and pension fund governance: the search for a shared conception of sustainable investment', Working Paper, SSRN, 2012, 24.
25 See generally J. Black, 'Critical reflections on regulation', *Australian Journal of Legal Philosophy* 1, 2002, 1–35.
26 See P. Simmons and B. Wynne, *State, Market and Mutual Regulation*, Working Paper, Lancaster University, 1992.
27 I. Ayres and J. Braithwaite, *Responsive Regulation: Transcending the Deregulation Debate*, Oxford University Press, 1992.
28 N. Gunningham and P. Grabosky, *Smart Regulation: Designing Environmental Policy*, Clarendon Press, 1998.

274 *Fiduciary law and responsible investing*

and 'post-regulatory governance',[29] among others. Paradoxically, there has also been some modest, countervailing expansion of state authority to correct market abuses and recent financial crises.[30]

The current RI reforms favour economic incentive and informational policy instruments that allow investment funds much discretion to make the ultimate decisions. These RI standards don't require policy consensus concerning definitions of 'ethical' or 'socially responsible'. Instead, they procedurally shape the selection and implementation of investments, thereby ostensibly providing more transparency and accountability. By modifying financiers' incentives and knowledge, reflexive law theory implies that such process-based standards may stimulate changes in actors' social values that contribute to sustainability.[31]

Among these policy instruments are requirements for investment institutions to disclose their policies for RI, and policies for exercising their shareholder proxy votes. As already explained in Chapter 4, these transparency reforms were introduced in several EU states, as well as Australia and New Zealand, and target pension funds.[32] Australian superannuation legislation also allows beneficiaries to choose where their monies are invested, thereby enabling social investors to switch to one of the burgeoning RI funds.[33] Another reform, adopted in Canada and the US, requires mutual funds to disclose their shareholding proxy voting policies and voting records.[34] Its purpose is to discourage fund managers from colluding with corporate management, and through a more active proxy process to improve the quality of corporate governance. As canvassed in Chapter 4, implementation of some of these standards, however, reveals shortcomings.[35] Mandated disclosures sometimes entail vague, perfunctory statements that do not illuminate how RI decisions are effected or their impacts. Process standards have rarely

---

29 C. Scott, 'Regulation in the age of governance: the rise of the post regulatory state', in J. Jordana and D. Levi-Faur (eds), *The Politics of Regulation: Institutions and Regulatory Reforms for the Age of Governance*, Edward Elgar, 2004, 145–74.
30 J. Cioffi, *Corporate Governance Reform, Regulatory Politics, and the Foundations of Finance Capitalism in the United States and Germany*, Comparative Research in Law and Political Economy Research Paper 1/2005, York University, 2005, 1–2.
31 E.W. Orts, 'Reflexive environmental law', *Northwestern University Law Review* 89, 1995, 1127–340; G. Teubner, L. Farmer and D. Murphy (eds), *Environmental Law and Ecological Responsibility: The Concept and Practice of Ecological Self-regulation*, Ashgate, 1994.
32 E.g., UK's Occupational Pension Schemes (Investment) Regulations, 2005: cl. 2(3)(b)(vi)–(3)(c); Australia's Corporations Act, 2001 (Cth), s. 1013D(1)(l); France's Projet de loi sur l'épargne salariale, 7 February 2001, No. 2001-152, arts 21, 23; and New Zealand's KiwiSaver Act, 2006, s. 205A.
33 Superannuation Legislation Amendment (Choice of Superannuation Funds) Act, 2005 (Cth).
34 SEC, 'Disclosure of proxy voting policies and proxy voting records by registered management investment companies', 31 January 2003; Canadian Securities Administrators, *National Instrument 81-106 Investment Fund Continuous Disclosure and Companion Policy 81-106CP*, 2005.
35 FairPensions, *UK Pension Scheme Transparency on Social, Environmental and Ethical Issues*, FairPensions, 2006; UKSIF, *Focused on the Future: 2000–2010 Celebrating Ten Years of Responsible Investment Disclosure by UK Occupational Pension Funds*, UKSIF, 2010.

extended to democratizing investment policy-making, which remains dominated by fund managers, investment consultants and other experts.[36] Modern corporate and investment regulation has long been premised on investors' playing the role of 'passive capital', which is 'excluded from management of the business'.[37]

Economic incentives to alter the cost-benefit calculations of financiers in favour of sustainable development are also on the menu. The leading example is the Netherlands' Green Project Directive,[38] which several studies credit as having materially boosted that country's RI market.[39] The scheme allows taxation deductions for investments in environmentally approved projects, such as renewable energy and sustainable agriculture. Another pioneering example is the New Markets Tax Credit Program, established by the US Congress in 2000 to spur investment into operating businesses and property projects in low-income communities. The program attracts investment capital to these communities by offering federal tax credits to individual and corporate investors who make equity investments in specialized financial institutions called Community Development Entities.[40] Another US example is the Healthy Food Financing Initiative – a collaboration of several federal departments – that provides a mix of tax credits, loan guarantees and subsidies, and grants to encourage investment in various entities that are working to address the lack of healthy foods in deprived American communities.[41] Conversely, economic incentives can be introduced to discourage environmentally unsound projects. Imposing liability on lenders for pollution problems connected to their borrowers was once upheld by US courts under the Superfund legislation,[42] and its drastic effects in dampening lending to the chemical industry contributed to modification of the scheme in 1996 to curb lenders' potential liability.[43]

36 J. Bogle, *The Battle for the Soul of Capitalism*, Yale University Press, 2005, 178–9.
37 R. Flannigan, 'The political imposture of passive capital', *Journal of Corporate Law Studies* 9, 2009, 139–69, 141.
38 The scheme was revamped and extended in 2002 and 2005: *Regeling groenprojecten buitenland*, Staatscourant 1, 2 January, 2002, 31; *Regeling groenprojecten, Staatscourant* 131, 11 July, 2005, 13. The Dutch 'green investment' taxation privileges will be phased out by 2014.
39 Vereniging van Beleggers voor Duurzame Ontwikkeling (VBDO), *Socially Responsible Savings and Investments in the Netherlands: Developments in Volume and Growth of Socially-responsible Savings and Investments in Retail Funds*, VBDO, 2005, 11; KPMG, *Sustainable Profit. An Overview of the Environmental Benefits Generated by the Green Funds Scheme*, KPMG, 2002, 6.
40 US Department of Treasury, 'New Market Tax Credit Program', http://cdfifund.gov/what_we_do/programs_id.asp?programID=5.
41 US Department of Health and Human Services, http://www.acf.hhs.gov/programs/ocs/ocs_food.html.
42 Comprehensive Environmental Response, Compensation and Liability Act, 1980, Pub. L. No. 96-510.
43 M. Greenberg and D. Shaw, 'To lend or not to lend – that should not be the question: the uncertainties of lender liability under CERCLA', *Duke Law Journal* 41(4), 1992, 1211–66; and, on the 1996 amendments: O. de S. Domis, 'New law finally limits environmental liability', *American Banker* 161(189), 1996, 3.

Mandatory performance standards are rare. Some states ban specific undesirable investments; Belgium, for example, prohibits investing in companies that produce or distribute cluster bombs.[44] Some US states ban investing in Sudan because of its poor human rights record.[45] But as the previous chapter explained, obligations to practise RI are largely confined to some SWFs. Owing to its special circumstances, South Africa has obliged its financial industry to support black economic justice. The Black Economic Empowerment Act of 2003 incorporates a Financial Sector Charter to facilitate accessible banking and other financial services to black people and by channelling investment into targeted sectors of the economy. The Charter enjoins financial institutions to provide empowerment financing in black communities, such as for transformational infrastructure, low-income housing and agricultural development, and it expects financiers to allocate annually at least 0.5 per cent of their post-tax operating profits towards such initiatives.[46]

There have been some parallel reforms at the corporate level, as canvassed in Chapter 4, of benefit to social investors. There is a vast literature on CSR and corporate governance of relevance to reorienting business corporations towards sustainability that need not be reviewed here. But briefly, notions of enlightened shareholder value or stakeholder capitalism for revamping corporate governance have guided these reforms. They range from the nuanced reformulation of directors' duties in the UK Companies Act 2006 to the more prescriptive CSR provisions in India's proposed Companies Act 2012. Enhanced transparency measures have also been applied extensively in company law, such as requirements for firms to report their environmental impacts and performance.[47] These measures can help social investors differentiate between corporate laggards and leaders. They could also directly benefit financial institutions structured as corporations, such as banks and insurance companies. Some proponents of RI have even suggested that the 'enlightened shareholder' approach to corporate governance, as exemplified in UK legislation, could serve as the touchstone for a new fiduciary standard for trustee funds. According to FairPensions:

> Section 172 of the Companies Act 2006, which requires company directors to 'have regard' to the longer-term and wider consequences of their decisions, provides a useful model. This model preserves the

---

44 Netwerk Vlaanderen, 'Belgium bans investments in cluster munitions', Press release, 2 March 2007.
45 L. Dhooge, 'Condemning Khartoum: the Illinois Divestment Act and foreign relations', *American Business Law Journal* 43, 2006, 245–316.
46 B.J. Richardson, 'Africa: from object to agent of socially responsible investment', in F. Botchway (ed.), *Natural Resource Investment and African Development*, Edward Elgar, 2011, 247–90, 269.
47 D.W. Case, 'Corporate environmental reporting as informational regulation: a law and economics perspective', *University of Colorado Law Review* 76, 2005, 379–442.

primacy of fiduciaries' duty to their beneficiaries, but recognises that beneficiaries' long-term interests may often be best served by an enlightened approach.[48]

In addition to the plethora of non-state measures manifesting as CSR or RI codes of conduct, such as the UNPRI and Equator Principles, as previously discussed, there are some interesting public–private hybrid initiatives that may help stimulate RI. One recent example is the German Sustainability Code of 2012, developed by the German Council for Sustainable Development (GCSD) to provide voluntary standards 'for promoting credible sustainable development actions in politics, business and especially on capital markets'.[49] The Code comprises 20 criteria, each of which has a few key performance indicators relating to ESG issues. The GCSD itself was established by the German government in 2001, and consists of 15 members drawn from representative stakeholders.

Overall, RI governance reforms have been modest and yet to engineer systemic changes to financial markets to prioritize environmentally sustainable development. Isolated success stories contrast to the more prevalent attitude of business-as-usual. Canadian academic Susanne Soederberg describes the limited agenda of RI activism as cast in 'superficial, market-based terms . . . devoid of any considerations of class and capitalist state relations'.[50] Instead, she wants to see the power of labour unleashed, particularly through its unions, to repoliticize corporate governance and financial markets to achieve structural legal and political change that challenges corporate power and neo-liberal markets.[51] Most RI regulation is far removed from her inventory of reform or that outlined in this book, being designed to avoid imposing burdensome regulatory costs on financial markets. Indeed, as noted earlier, the financial industry has even sought to thwart some reforms.

Redefining the parameters of investor legal accountability

Moving beyond the current menu of legal and policy reforms for RI includes redefining the parameters of investor accountability for sustainable development. This task requires tackling the conceptual question of why the financial sector should be legally accountable for environmental problems associated with the companies or projects it funds. In particular, why should

---

48 C. Berry, *Protecting Our Best Interests: Rediscovering Fiduciary Obligation*, FairPensions, 2011, 6.
49 German Council for Sustainable Development, *The German Sustainability Code*, GCSD, 2012, 2.
50 S. Soederberg, 'Cannibalistic capitalism: securitized pension funds and the social reproduction of neoliberalization', 2010 Meeting of the Standing Group on International Relations of the ECPR, Stockholm, 9–11 September 2010, 10.
51 S. Soederberg, *Corporate Power and Ownership in Contemporary Capitalism: The Politics of Resistance and Domination*, Routledge, 2009.

financiers ever be accountable to a higher standard than the firms they fund, especially if the company's activities, such as a mine or pulp mill, already comply with government environmental regulation?

If these front-line industries in the productive, 'real' economy were perfectly regulated, we could presumably ignore financiers' behaviour because all environmental costs and benefits would be accounted for. The cost of money would wholly reflect environmental performance, with polluters incurring higher operational costs, and thereby competitive disadvantages in raising finance. And consequently, RI would revert to its traditional role of religious- or personal-values investment that shuns morally objectionable activities, such as intoxicants or casinos. Such pristine regulation, we know, hardly exists. As detailed at the outset of this book, the past half-century of environmental regulation has only mitigated, but far from ended, unsustainable living. Even countries with advanced environmental laws are challenged by the growing cross-border investment into jurisdictions with less rigorous legal standards. Given that investors in one country can profit from projects in another, it is imperative to environmentally regulate wholesale decisions about future development. Those decisions emerge when raising finance. Bringing financial institutions to account could moderate pressure on environmental regulation, by decreasing initiation of polluting or other potentially harmful developments. Ideally, they would never receive finance or would be redesigned to meet green benchmarks.

Moreover, owing to deficiencies in the social and environmental regulation of front-line businesses, investors cannot merely set their moral compass by the law of the land, as though a company abiding by its pollution permit is deemed to fulfill all legal and ethical responsibilities. The tobacco industry is a pertinent example: just because an economic activity is licensed doesn't mean it is ethical or without social costs that may give rise to challenges. Courts in a variety of jurisdictions have affirmed that environmental and planning regulation itself doesn't necessarily exhaust the legal claims that may be brought against a business; for example, development permissions issued by municipal authorities may not shield a defendant from a common law action in nuisance.[52] Fiduciary responsibility is also not synonymous with simply avoiding legal transgressions, as asset managers and financial advisers must consider the ethical preferences of their clients or beneficiaries, which may require favouring investments in companies that exceed environmental legal standards.

Institutionalizing environmental responsibility within investment law (and concomitantly in corporate law) would help mitigate the current conflicting legal messages that market participants face between, on the one hand, expectations to seek profitability for themselves and, on the other,

---

52 From Canada, see *Portage La Prairie v. (B.C.) Pea Growers Ltd.* [1966] SCR 150; from UK, *Wheeler v. Saunders*, [1994] EWCA Civ 32; From NZ, *Ports of Auckland v. Auckland City Council*, [2000] NZCA 190.

regulatory restraints to profit-making in order to safeguard the planet. Such dichotomous legal messages have resulted in financial regulators' ignoring the environmental performance of investment entities – unless it has a material impact on profitability – on the assumption that such matters are tasked to specialist environmental agencies. These regulatory silos increase legal complexity through disparate and often conflicting standards, and perversely incentivize businesses to engage in 'creative compliance' in an effort to shirk responsibilities.[53]

A second reason to target financiers relates to their strategic economic position, and potential to be harnessed by governments as a surrogate regulator. The source of this rationale is systems theory, which implies that society's diverse and numerous environmental dilemmas cannot be resolved effectively through sweeping government regulation.[54] This theory depicts modern society as polycentric, centrifugal and acephalous: an assemblage of semi-autonomous subsystems, such as the market or religion, each with its own norms, goals and operations. The implication is that under such conditions it is difficult for a society to coalesce coherently towards shared objectives, such as environmental sustainability. There are assumed to be no universal norms or supreme institutions – even the state itself – that can easily control and integrate these subsystems.

Talcott Parsons and Niklas Luhmann, leading systems theorists, have traced this trend. They conceive these various subsystems as 'autopoietic', implying that each has evolved its own operational codes and protocols, and therefore can respond to problems defined only in their own terms.[55] The economic subsystem, in particular, has become substantially detached from its traditional roots within society.[56] With money as its lingua franca, the economy has forged its own values and goals around competition, acquisition, growth and profitability – in contrast to the legal subsystem's emphasis on rights, duties and rules. For society to regulate the market, it must increasingly rely on economic language and criteria, such as we have seen in how fiduciary law frames the duty of prudent investing around prevailing business conventions. The cost-benefit approach is central to the economic system, and ethical or other norms not congruent with it struggle to resonate. We have observed this trend in relation to the ascending 'business case' rationale for RI. Consequently, a regulatory prescription to the corporate sector to protect biological diversity, for instance, will likely

---

53 F. Haines, 'A ponzi scheme on the environment? Failures of fiduciary duty and the challenges of climate governance', in K. Coghill, C. Sampford and T. Smith (eds), *Fiduciary Duty and the Atmospheric Trust*, Ashgate, 2012, 235–52, 242–3.
54 See N. Luhmann, *Ecological Communication*, University of Chicago Press, 1989; N. Luhmann, *The Differentiation of Society*, Columbia University Press, 1982.
55 N. Luhmann, *Social Systems*, Stanford University Press, 1995.
56 T. Parsons, *The Social System*, Free Press of Glencoe, 1951. Concurrently globalization pushes to reconnect subsystems and to view ourselves as part of an interconnected global community, but it remains very much an incomplete effort.

be interpreted primarily from a cost-benefit perspective congruent with market imperatives.

This conception of social systems has led 'reflexive law' theorists such as Gunther Teubner to call for a less ambitious legal system that works with, rather than against, the market. This involves jettisoning unwieldy command-and-control regulation in favour of more business self-regulation or collaborative governance between the state and the market.[57] Such collaboration might involve the financial sector, which occupies a strategic market position that can be harnessed by government regulators to convey and amplify their demands. Already, lenders help transmit government monetary policy on interest rates, and authorities' money-laundering controls enlist banks to report suspicious transactions.[58] Financiers could also be vehicles for transmitting information about correct corporate environmental behaviour, such as by exposing lenders to liability for any pollution damage caused by their borrowers. That risk would, in turn, encourage lenders to impress upon borrowers the need to be more environmentally diligent. Bob Jessop suggests that organizations straddling the boundaries of different subsystems – such as the financial sector – are potentially well placed to 'enhance mutual understanding' and 'play a role in linking sub-systems'.[59] In other words, by virtue of their strategic, intermediate position between the state and the corporate sector, financial organizations could be harnessed as a means of promoting corporate environmental responsibility.[60]

The financial sector's economic significance and strategic position provide another reason to discipline it and hold it to higher environmental standards than those applicable to the companies it funds. The banking and debt crises in North America and Europe since 2008 show how failings in the financial sector can ripple through the global economy, causing enormous collateral damage.[61] Apart from any environmental effects attributable to the financial economy, many commentators have long argued that traditional economic policy grounds justify controlling financiers more closely.[62] The sector contains propagation mechanisms that can amplify initial, small shocks throughout the real economy; insolvency of a bank usually has far greater ramifications for the economy than the implosion of a non-financial

57 G. Teubner, *Law as an Autopoietic System*, Blackwell, 1993.
58 A. Brown, 'Money laundering: a European and UK perspective', *Journal of International Banking Law* 12, 1997, 307–10.
59 B. Jessop, *State Theory: Putting the Capitalist State in its Place*, Polity, 1990, 329.
60 B.J. Richardson, *Environmental Regulation through Financial Organisations*, Kluwer Law, 2002.
61 R.C. Whalen, 'The subprime crisis: cause, effect and consequences', Networks Financial Institute Policy Brief No. 2008-PB, 2008; G. Soros, *The New Paradigm for Financial Markets: The Credit Crisis of 2008 and What It Means*, PublicAffairs, 2008.
62 D. Heremans, *Corporate Governance Issues for Banks. A Financial Stability Perspective*, Katholieke Universiteit, 2006; J. Macey and M. O'Hara, 'The corporate governance of banks', *Economic Policy Review* 9(1), 2003, 91–107.

company.⁶³ Thus, regulators need to impose measures that reduce systemic risks posed by the financial economy, such as heightened disclosures, higher capital reserves and greater ESG analysis and long-term investment planning. As well, this book began by showing the considerable ecological footprint of the financial sector, through its ability to ramp up economic growth and displace environmental externalities through time and space at great distance from investors. As this rationale for investor accountability was earlier canvassed in detail in Chapter 1, it needs no further elaboration at this point.

Ultimately, the most basic reason for targeting financiers is simply that in deriving profits from companies engaged in environmentally degrading and socially harmful activities, financiers are complicit and should share accountability. These 'unseen' polluters should be unmasked for their contribution to unsustainable development. Capital financing is instrumental to development choices; thus, those who enable, and benefit from, those choices through financial investment must also share in the responsibility. Financial institutions evolved to mobilize capital and to facilitate financial returns for investors. Money has to be actively managed and be reinvested to generate profit for financiers. This pervasive drive to put capital to use, to make more capital, creates a process that fuels social and environmental changes. So even though the financial sector may lack operational control of polluting developments, it cannot be construed as an unknowing, helpless or passive bystander to such impacts.

'Complicity' is often cited as the touchstone for attributing responsibility to investors or companies for social harm, and it informs the NGPF-G's ethical investing policy.⁶⁴ While the notion of complicity has considerable legal and ethical pedigree, it hinges on notions of 'impact' and 'influence' that aren't easily measurable. Complicity essentially means indirect involvement by actors in environmental or human rights abuses – where another party commits the actual harm. The legal meaning of complicity has been spelled out most clearly in the area of aiding and abetting international crimes, as discussed in some of John Ruggie's work.⁶⁵

But complicity alone cannot comprehensively define the parameters of investor responsibility for sustainability. Firstly, it is a negative responsibility, focusing on avoiding association with specific actors who are perpetrating harms, rather than encouraging a portfolio-wide approach to sustainable investing. Secondly, complicity places the threshold for divestment or other sanctions too high, such as *gross* violation of human rights or *severe*

---

63 Some non-financial corporations of course are extremely economically significant, and whose collapse would produce wide-ranging economic effects. The motor vehicle industry is an example.
64 See G. Nystuen, A. Follesdal and O. Mestad (eds), *Human Rights, Corporate Complicity and Disinvestment*, Cambridge University Press, 2011.
65 J. Ruggie, 'Business and human rights: mapping international standards of responsibility and accountability for corporate acts', A/HRC/4/35, UN General Assembly, 19 February 2007.

environmental damage; however, much social injustice or ecological damage stems from incremental actions or omissions that, viewed in isolation, might seem trivial. Thirdly, complicity is conceptually confusing and imprecise regarding the degree of knowledge or assistance necessary to trigger consequences.[66] At one extreme, an actor might be condemned as 'complicit' for practical assistance or encouragement of others to commit the harm; at another pole, merely deriving a benefit from another's human rights abuse or environmental crime might suffice. Some scholars of criminal law thus increasingly advocate abandoning complicity,[67] with James Stewart arguing that complicity is so thoroughly imprecise that it 'should collapse along with all other modes of liability into a single broad notion of perpetration' of crimes.[68]

In mapping a clearer standard for investors' legal accountability, at one level we can say that their clearest responsibility arises where they have an impact on corporate social and environmental behaviour as established by a causal connection, as when a bank provides a substantial loan for a major development project. Here the connection between the actions of the financier and the resulting project is clear and direct, and responsibility for the harm should be proportionate with the financiers' degree of contribution. Yet, much incremental and occasional environmental harm may occur that cannot be captured by an impact-based standard of responsibility because individual contributions to consequences aren't easily ascertained or quantified. An individual company may have thousands of different shareholders, bondholders and ties to many lenders, and the company's own environmental impacts may subtly arise through extended business relationships with contractors, suppliers or franchisees. Such circumstances require more nuanced judgements of culpability. Commentators such as Stepan Wood[69] and Lene Bomann-Larsen and Oddny Wiggen[70] suggest that 'leverage-based' responsibility might allow these kinds of nuanced distinctions to be made in an entity's web of activities and relationships. As Wood explains, '[t]he kernel of a leverage-based approach is the proposition that, in some circumstances where a company is making no causal or other contribution to a state of

---

66 Complicity, as a legal principle, can be defined in various ways in order to attribute liability to actors, such as direct complicity (where an actor knowingly assists another to commit a legal violation) and beneficial complicity (where an actor benefits directly from the violation committed by someone else): see S.H. Kadish, 'Complicity, cause and blame: a study in the interpretation of doctrine', *California Law Review* 73, 1985, 323–410.
67 M.S. Moore, *Causation and Responsibility: An Essay in Law, Morals, and Metaphysics*, Oxford University Press, 2010.
68 J. Stewart, 'The end of "modes of liability" for international crimes', *Leiden Journal of International Law* 25, 2012, 1–74, 3.
69 S. Wood, *An Argument for Leverage-based Business Responsibility for Human Rights*, Working Paper, Robert Schuman Centre for Advanced Studies, European University Institute, 2011.
70 L. Bomann-Larsen and O. Wiggen (eds), *Responsibility in World Business: Managing Harmful Side-effects of Corporate Activity*, UN University Press, 2004.

affairs, it has a responsibility to exercise its leverage over actors with whom it has relationships in an effort to improve that state of affairs'.[71] In other words, a financier might share responsibility not because of any specific contributory behaviour, but for its omissions and failure to exercise leverage over others when it should have and could have made a difference.

This leverage-based responsibility is rooted in the notion of 'sphere of influence' advanced in the CSR literature and norms. The concept appears in the preamble of the UN Global Compact of 2000,[72] and the subsequent draft 'Norms on the responsibilities of transnational corporations and other business enterprises with regard to human rights', proposed by a UN body in 2003.[73] However, the sphere-of-influence yardstick was rejected by John Ruggie, Special Representative of the UN Secretary-General for business and human rights,[74] who argued it represents 'a useful metaphor for companies in thinking about their human rights impacts' outside their own organizational boundaries, but 'a more rigorous approach is required to define the specific parameters of [their] responsibility' to respect human rights[75] and it might lead to companies' performing roles that should be played by states. By contrast, the sphere-of-influence norm is a seminal feature of the ISO's 26000 regime for CSR.[76] While ISO doesn't suggest that having such leverage necessarily always implies a responsibility to exert a positive influence, it says there will be situations that 'are determined by the extent to which an organization's relationship is contributing to negative impacts'.[77]

By this approach, fiduciary law could be redefined to oblige financial actors to exert positive influence and leverage to promote sustainability in portfolio companies when a financier has a material connection to a business (e.g., ownership of its securities), the business itself can make a difference to its environmental behaviour through operational changes, and the cost to the financial institution of acting responsibly, such as through corporate engagement, is reasonably affordable. Of course, any legal responsibility to invest sustainably in light of such criteria could not be absolute and

---

71 Wood, op. cit., 13.
72 UN Global Compact, http://www.unglobalcompact.org/AboutTheGC/TheTenPrinciples/index.html.
73 Norms on the Responsibilities of Transnational Corporations and Other Business Enterprises with Regard to Human Rights, U.N. Doc. E/CN.4/Sub.2/2003/12/Rev.2 (2003), Principle 1.
74 *Report of the United Nations High Commissioner on Human Rights on the Responsibilities of Transnational Corporations and Related Business Enterprises with Regard to Human Rights*, UN Doc. E/CN.4/2005/91, para. 38.
75 J. Ruggie, *Promotion and Protection of all Human Rights, Civil, Political, Economic, Social and Cultural Rights including the Rights to Development. Protect, Respect and Remedy: A Framework for Business and Human Rights*, UN Doc. A/HRC/8/5, UN Human Rights Commission, 2008, para. 67.
76 International Organization for Standardization (ISO), *26000: Guidance on Social Responsibility*, ISO, 2010, cl. 2.19.
77 Ibid., cl. 5.2.3.

open-ended, but rather qualified, depending on the specific context and circumstances.[78]

But the foregoing criteria would be unworkable or incomplete in some situations. They don't directly address the long-term financial interests of beneficiaries in sustainability. Even if a fund can't exert leverage over a company, it may still be in its long-term financial interests to take account of climate change or other environmental impacts. Further, in many financial transactions it would be impossible to satisfy the criterion of a 'material connection'; the array of relationships between corporations and the financial sector is immense and diverse. While a material connection obviously arises when a bank provides a major project finance loan, the financial ties are often much weaker, such as in a large pension fund, in which 'the average traded firm . . . [is] just one stock in large diversified portfolios'.[79] Investors participate in financial markets through many layers and chains of intermediaries, and even the very largest funds, such as SWFs, typically own only a tiny fraction of the shares of an individual company. Thus, while investors' collective influence is significant, that of individual funds in relation to any specific company is greatly diluted.

There are also some countervailing economic arguments against overly broad assignment of responsibility to investors or lenders. Many economists argue that limited liability facilitates financing of new developments and efficiently reduces investors' monitoring costs.[80] Without it, there might even be reduced investment in socially valuable initiatives, such as rehabilitation of brownfield sites. The presence of joint and several liability, which may arise when a firm has numerous financial backers, would facilitate environmental compensation by allowing access to a larger pool of financial resources, but it may compromise the deterrent function of the 'polluter pays' principle by encouraging claimants to pursue the deepest pocket rather than the pocket of the person who caused the most harm. For fund beneficiaries, such as members of a pension fund trust, a further concern is whether and how to relocate liability to them. This chapter is not the place to delve into the vast and contentious literature on this subject, but even the more environmentally sympathetic research here tends to caution against open-ended liability to financiers.[81] There may thus be advantages in widening fiduciary responsibility for sustainability not through the potentially unwieldy liability device,

---

78 Drawing on criteria proposed by Wood, ibid., 1.
79 G.L. Clark and E. Knight, 'Implications of the UK Companies Act 2006 for institutional investors and the market for corporate social responsibility', *University of Pennsylvania Journal of Business Law* 11(2), 2009, 256–96, 266.
80 See generally P. Halpern, et al., 'An economic analysis of limited liability in corporation law', *University of Toronto Law Journal* 30, 1980, 117–50; F.H. Easterbrook and D.R. Fischel, 'Limited liability and the corporation', *University of Chicago Law Review* 52, 1985, 89–117.
81 E.g., A. Ulph and L. Valentini, 'Environmental liability and the capital structure of firms', *Resource and Energy Economics* 26(4), 2004, 393–410; R. Pitchford, 'How liable should a lender be? The case of judgement-proof firms and environmental risk', *American Economic Review* 85, 1995, 1171–86.

but via inculcating new procedural standards in financial institutions that emphasize environmental impact assessment, public reporting and consultation, and other mechanisms for more comprehensive due diligence.

Overall, we can see that an array of perspectives of variable relevance and utility can be formulated to rationalize and implement fiduciary responsibility for environmental sustainability. In some cases, financial institutions should act responsibly because they can influence their portfolio companies. In other cases, regardless of the institutions' power, investor accountability could hinge on investors' own long-term financial well-being. While a seemingly minuscule stake might imply very limited influence, it still could expose investors to costly reputational risk from being seen as complicit in the practices of the offending company. And the state has an interest in disciplining financial institutions to control systemic risks to the broader economy and environmental well-being. No single theory or argument can capture fully the parameters of investors' environmental accountability, but together they can provide a mosaic of reasons and methods for much greater commitment to sustainable development than is presently reflected in fiduciary finance law. The following sections outline some options for this task.

Sustainable investing for the public fiduciary

Duty of prudent investing for the long term

We need to modernize fiduciary finance law to embrace the symbiotic relationship between the sustainability of the economy and those who invest in it. A bold step would be to reformulate the duty of prudent investing, to help shift the market towards an enlightened, long-term focus that respects the environmental conditions that underpin a prosperous investment universe. The prevailing prudential standard in trusts law relies on collective market practice to set benchmarks. Consequently, collective practice has egregiously herded investors towards a limited range of unimaginative practices, because the 'experts' wish to avoid appearing unconventional and thereby risk liability. As Keith Johnston and Frank Jan de Graaf explain, 'what functioned as a "prudent expert" fiduciary standard 30 years ago has become more of a "lemming standard" that increases the severity of booms and busts and discourages adoption of improved practices that are not yet used by peers'.[82] Thus, law and markets have etched destructive incentives for investment herding, fixation on short-term performance and wilful blindness to systemic market risks. The global financial meltdown exposed these follies, creating an opportunity to 'recover the public dimension of trust institutions'.[83]

---

82 K. Johnston and F.J. de Graaf, 'Modernizing pension fund legal standards in the 21st century', Network for Sustainable Financial Markets, 2009, 4–5.
83 J. Getzler, 'Fiduciary investment in the shadow of financial crisis: was Lord Eldon right?', *Journal of Equity* 3, 2009, 1–31, 26.

A different investing benchmark, that recognizes the long-term, intergenerational dimension of financial liabilities and the impact of systemic risks, could be developed legislatively. Even mainstream financial authorities concede this imperative: Andrew Haldane, Executive Director of the Bank of England, recommends robust public policy intervention 'to provide incentives for longer-duration asset holdings'.[84] Climate change looms as the gravest long-term environmental issue facing many investors. The UK's Stern Report of 2007 calculated that global warming, if left unabated, will by 2050 cut world GDP by between 5 to 10 per cent, but only 1 to 2 per cent of GDP if we act expeditiously.[85] Other commentators predict even grimmer economic costs if business-as-usual continues.[86]

A revised fiduciary obligation to act primarily in the long-term interests of fund members would help address such concerns, which eventually may become an investing norm internalized in the organizational culture of financial institutions. We would also need a parallel fiduciary obligation on directors of non-financial companies, as some commentators discuss.[87] Implementation could be facilitated by a cognate duty on financial institutions to report periodically on their progress in acting for the long term. Their trustees would report on environmental impacts and performance, including active steps to reduce the risk of harm. This information would not only help regulators to supervise compliance; it could enable more informed ethical dialogue within funds, as explained later in this chapter. This proposal is not so extreme, being reminiscent somewhat of how trusts law once governed investing, as well as dovetailing with the duty of impartiality that arguably requires fiduciaries to treat inter-generational beneficiaries even-handedly. Traditionally, trusts law put constraints on the risking of long-term capital by requiring trustees to avoid rash investing and to conserve capital through purchase of government bonds, blue-chip private securities and other ultra-safe investments.

A duty to invest for the long term would go beyond current approaches or proposals that merely *allow* fiduciaries to consider ESG information. Permissive approaches that legally shield investors against potential fiduciary liability are insufficient to motivate change. The US Sudan Divestment and Accountability Act of 2007 provides legal protection to investors wishing to shun companies doing business in a country shamed by appalling human rights abuses, yet in practice the statute appears hardly to have redeemed American investment practices.[88] Other examples of permissive legislation

---

84 A. Haldane, 'Patience and finance', Beijing, Oxford China Business Forum, September 2010, 22.
85 N. Stern, *Stern Review on the Economics of Climate Change*, H.M. Treasury, 2007.
86 G. Monbiot, *Heat: How to Stop the Planet Burning*, HarperCollins, 2005; T. Flannery, *The Weather Makers*, Atlantic Monthly Press, 2006.
87 N. Grossman, 'Turning a short-term fling into a long-term commitment: board duties in a new era', *University of Michigan Journal of Law Reform* 43, 2010, 905–70.
88 Pub. L. 110-174; L.A. Patey, 'Against the Asian tide: the Sudan divestment campaign', *Journal of Modern African Studies* 47(4) 2009, 551–73, 564–6.

include Connecticut legislation governing the state's retirement plans and trust funds, which lawfully *may* consider the environmental and social implications of investments,[89] and Manitoba's Trustee Act of 1995, which allows trustees to consider non-financial criteria so long as 'the trustee exercises the judgment and care that a person of prudence, discretion and intelligence would exercise in administering the property of others'.[90] Recent proposals by RI lobbyists include amending trustee legislation to affirm that consideration of ESG issues for the purpose of risk minimization and/or long-term value maximization doesn't conflict with established trustee responsibilities.[91] The limitation of these approaches, of course, is that they do not *oblige* consideration of sustainability impacts.

The principal challenges in reformulating the prudent investment duty towards a long-term goal is whether and how any limit should be set to the parameter of 'long term', and the remedies available to aggrieved parties. Defining 'long term' as encompassing time ad infinitum does not appear to create a workable and accountable fiduciary standard. Most conceptions of inter-generational equity evident in modern environmental law and policy have an outer limit of approximately 50 years, such as the long-term carbon emission targets of some countries.[92] In recent US climate change litigation, *Massachusetts v. EPA*,[93] the court considered future harm that the state would experience through to the year 2100.[94] Definitions of 'long term' or 'future generations' thus raise the same kind of murky issues in the debates about sustainability, whose analysis depends heavily on the specific issues, and the aims and values of participants. Whether an investment portfolio is in fact successfully managed for such a time-frame might be known only with the benefit of hindsight, many decades from now, at which point any legal remedy offered might be nugatory.

Therefore, a workable duty of long-term investing would need to be embellished with prophylactic rules that set performance standards for fiduciaries today. These standards could include conducting environmental risk and impact studies, incorporating ESG information into portfolio management and making positive investments in environmental technologies and green businesses, among various possible indicators of a sustainable investment portfolio. Fund managers or trustees acting contrary to such standards would then be subject to the current available remedies that beneficiaries have at their disposal, including specific performance, equitable

---

89 Connecticut General Statutes, 2011, ch. 32, s. 3-13d(a).
90 Trustee Act, 1995, SM s. 79.1.
91 FairPensions, *The Enlightened Shareholder*, op. cit.
92 The UK's Climate Change Act of 2007 has a goal of an 80 per cent reduction from 1990 emissions by 2050.
93 (2007) 549 US 497, 127 S. Ct. 1438.
94 B.C. Mank, 'Standing and future generations: does Massachusetts v. EPA open standing for generations to come', *Columbia Journal of Environmental Law* 34, 2009, 102–88.

damages and injunctions.⁹⁵ Because beneficiaries may be unwilling to sue for breach of such obligations if their fund is presently prosperous, state regulators should concurrently be empowered to act as enforcement watchdogs, a subject we return to later in this chapter when the fiduciary responsibilities of the state itself are explored.

Of course, recasting fiduciary responsibility in this manner would, alone, be insufficient to achieve change. Financial markets have yet to engineer incentives to overcome the mismatch between the long-term horizons over which ESG issues become financially material and the short-term performance benchmarks against which investment managers measure success. A range of collateral measures therefore would need to be adopted. An excise tax on securities transactions and modification of capital gains tax rules, for instance, could help incentivize long-term investing. Another response to short-termism in general concerns the exercise of voting rights by investors, which are sometimes used to pressure firms to engage in expedient decisions. Company law could reward long-term shareholders with weighted voting rights, while excluding from voting the shares acquired through opportunistic borrowing or equity swaps. Regarding informational deficits or deficiencies that contribute to short-termism, a reassessment of financial reporting obligations is necessary to reorient investors and other market participants to long-term value. Requiring disclosure of information to markets relating to long-term values would help mitigate the myopic culture of financial markets.

Duty of environmental care

Whereas the foregoing model implies an obligation to take account of environmental conditions that might affect long-term returns, this prospect could be explicitly articulated through a statutory duty of environmental care. Unlike a duty of long-term investing that keeps fiduciary law focused on beneficiaries' well-being, this approach widens accountability to protect the public at large against environmental harm. The limitation of existing approaches, including the 'enlightened shareholder value' standard emerging in corporate law, is that they don't assist third parties if fiduciary managers choose, in their business judgement, to ignore their interests.

The duty of care is an ancient moral and legal ideal that expresses the ethical norm of nonmaleficence – the responsibility to avoid harm. The extension of this duty to 'require everyone who influences the management of the risks to the environment to take all reasonable steps and practical measures to prevent harm to the environment that could have been reasonably foreseen'⁹⁶ has been accomplished statutorily in several

---

95 G. Moffat, G. Bean and J. Dewar, *Trusts Law: Text and Materials*, Cambridge University Press, 2005, ch. 14.
96 Australian Industry Commission, *Full Repairing Lease: Inquiry into Ecologically Sustainable Land Management*, Australian Government Publishing Service, 1998, 133–4.

jurisdictions.[97] The approach builds on the common law tort of negligence, encapsulating the ethical responsibility of every person to take reasonable and practical measures in their activities to avoid foreseeable harm to another person or their property. In the 1932 seminal case of *Donoghue v. Stevenson*,[98] Lord Atkin declared that 'you must take reasonable care to avoid acts or omissions which you can reasonably foresee would be likely to injure your neighbour'.[99] In the 1990 decision of *Caparo Industries plc v. Dickman*,[100] the House of Lords elaborated that the plaintiff must show that any loss was a reasonably foreseeable consequence of the defendant's conduct; there was a sufficiently proximate relationship between the parties; and it is fair, just and reasonable to impose a duty of care in light of applicable policy considerations. Through such broad criteria, therefore, the duty of care has some plasticity to accommodate changing societal expectations about appropriate environmental behaviour.

The common law approach, however, has several attributes that render it largely unsuitable in its current formula for reorienting financiers towards sustainability. These weaknesses are evident in recent attempts to impose tortious liability for environmental damage, such as the mostly unsuccessful American climate change litigation.[101] The duty of care aims to correct negligent conduct that harms private interests, such as property or personal health; the natural environment and the interests of posterity in its protection are only indirectly addressed. Causation of environmental impacts stemming from numerous sources over long periods is hard to prove. This would be especially prevalent in the case of tracing responsibility to investors in a firm, who may number in the thousands and trade securities frequently. Furthermore, the common law remedies the economic consequences of harm, rather than encouraging pre-emptive actions. And enforcement through courts carries high transaction costs, which may deter plaintiffs.

A duty of environmental care would therefore need to be articulated initially through legislation with provisions to ameliorate the above factors, an approach that is not unprecedented. Such legislation includes England's Environmental Protection Act of 1990, South Africa's National Environmental Management Act (NEMA) of 1998 and legislation adopted in several Australian state jurisdictions such as South Australia (1993), Queensland (1994) and Victoria (1994). The South Australian Environmental Protection Act 1993 provides that '[a] person must not undertake an activity

---

97 M. Shepheard and P. Martin, 'The political discourse of land stewardship reframed as a statutory duty', in B. Jessup and K. Rubenstein (eds), *Environmental Discourses in Public and International Law*, Cambridge University Press, 2012, 71–95.
98 *Donoghue v. Stevenson*, [1932] AC 562.
99 Ibid., 580.
100 [1990] 2 AC 605.
101 See J. Salzman and D. Hunter, 'Negligence in the air: the duty of care in climate change litigation', *University of Pennsylvania Law Review* 156, 2007, 101–54; J. Lin, 'Climate change and the courts', *Legal Studies* 32(1), 2012, 35–57.

that pollutes, or might pollute, the environment unless the person takes all reasonable and practicable measures to prevent or minimise any resulting environmental harm'.[102] Under South African law, 'every person who causes, has caused or may cause significant pollution or degradation of the environment must take reasonable measures to prevent [it] or ... minimise and rectify such pollution or degradation of the environment'.[103] Breaches of these provisions, which do not appear to have been judicially tested against financial institutions, may attract civil and criminal penalties.

There is no insurmountable conceptual barrier to extending such duties to financial fiduciaries. The momentum of business law is already moving towards considering the interests of the community and its environment, in addition to those of market participants.[104] Corporate law often imposes a general duty of care on directors and senior officers of the company, which may be interpreted as owed to various stakeholders affected by its business. Although such an ambitious reform would nonetheless predictably be rejected by the financial industry for being too intrusive, too difficult to implement and sacrificing economic investment for environmental protection, these criticisms overlook the importance of sustainable development for long-term prosperity.

The proposed duty could be imposed on individual fiduciaries, rather than a bank, investment firm or other business entity, to send a clear message to fiduciaries that they are accountable for ensuring that the culture within financial institutions develops and implements systems and policies that are environmentally responsible. The duty would expect fiduciaries to consider the environmental sequelae of their investments, and to take appropriate remedial action such as by divesting from major corporate polluters. While such a duty could preserve the doctrinal simplicity of fiduciary loyalty being owed exclusively to beneficiaries, it would constrain how fiduciaries act for them, similarly to how many existing laws, from human rights to competition law, exert such an effect. The idea does not radically depart from existing law, given that there has never been a legal carte blanche for market participants to act outside the legal norms of a civilized society. To illustrate, if deforestation were illegal but still profitable for fiduciaries given the foreseeable legal penalties, would they have a fiduciary duty to violate the environmental law to obtain the extra financial returns? Clearly not, and indeed they would affirmatively violate one dimension of fiduciary accountability if they chose to act unlawfully.[105] The ultra vires doctrine,

---

102 Section 25.
103 NEMA, s. 28(1).
104 D. Saxe, 'The fiduciary duty corporate directors to protect the environment for future generations', *Environmental Values* 1(3), 1992, 243–52; J. McConvill and M. Joy, 'The interaction of directors' duties and sustainable development in Australia: setting off on the uncharted road', *Melbourne University Law Review* 27(1) 2003, 116–38.
105 American Law Institute (ALI), *Principles of Corporate Governance: Analysis and Recommendations*, ALI, 1994, s. 2.01(B)(1) and s. 4.01.

explains Kent Greenfield, sets off illegal activities as 'beyond the power' of corporations.[106]

The scope of the duty of care could range from responsibility for acts or omissions that cause environmental harm to, more ambitiously, a positive obligation to promote sustainable development through investing. The latter duty would resemble the existing approach of so-called impact investors, such as microfinance supporters, green-tech venture capitalists and community housing lenders.[107] A positive duty would obviously require a greater commitment by investors and be more legally challenging to enforce. Divestment from a polluting company is usually less onerous than having to actively invest and engage with companies to improve their sustainability performance. An open-ended responsibility to 'promote sustainability' could also be too indeterminate and potentially usurped by discretionary interpretations to which financiers could not easily be held accountable. Conversely, this duty might be similarly unworkable if it were rigidly prescriptive, absolute and unconditional, as the parameters of sustainable development often depend heavily on local contexts and specific circumstances. Judicial case law would gradually help to 'settle' the law, but it would be unlikely to settle all situations and thus leave a penumbra of uncertainty outside the core examples. Ex ante standards that can comprehensively determine the constituent elements of a duty to promote sustainability or avoid environmental harm would therefore, at least in the initial stage, need to be supplemented through subsidiary regulations and administrative guidance. Sustainability performance indicators and CSR performance standards have already been designed, which could help inform this work.[108]

A narrower duty to avoid environmental harm from economic investment would also not be straightforward to implement, because the harm is 'essentially aggregative: there is nothing intrinsically harmful to the environment or other people in burning fossil fuels; the harms depend on the joint effects of many people's action'.[109] Negative environmental duties require two elements to be present in order to function effectively: the individual entity's conduct is sufficient, without other entities' acts or involvement, to cause harm; and the harmful effects of an entity's behaviour generally manifest nearby and immediately. These elements are found in the common law doctrine's requirements for 'reasonable foreseeability' and a relationship of

---

106 K. Greenfield, *The Failure of Corporate Law: Fundamental Flaws and Progressive Possibilities*, University of Chicago Press, 2007.
107 A. Bugg-Levine and J. Emerson, *Impact Investing*, John Wiley and Sons, 2011.
108 J. Keeble, S. Topiol and S. Berkeley, 'Using indicators to measure sustainability performance at a corporate and project level', *Journal of Business Ethics* 44(2–3), 2003, 149–58; H. Schäfer, et al., *Who is Who in Corporate Social Responsibility Rating? A Survey of Internationally Established Rating Systems that Measure Corporate Responsibility*, Bertelsmann Foundation, 2006; S. Fowler and C. Hope, 'A critical review of sustainable business indices and their impact', *Journal of Business Ethics* 76(3), 2007, 243–52.
109 J. Lichtenberg, 'Duties, positive duties and the "new harms"', *Ethics* 20(3), 2010, 557–78.

'proximity', and there are no simple alternatives that could be legislated to offer a measurably accountable equivalent. Both elements are unlikely to exist to help assess the harm produced by financial investments, which involve numerous actors in a chain of financial relationships. Only in limited circumstances, such as project financing of major infrastructure, could we identify an individual financier and proximate environmental consequences. Even with reliance on collective attribution of responsibility, as proposed by Gunther Teubner[110] – suggesting that liability could be assigned to a specific economic sector and then reassigned among its members in accordance with their economic significance, size or other indicator – problems would remain. The financial sector is highly dynamic, with shares, bonds and other assets constantly being traded and changing hands, and the financial economy is astronomically vast, with numerous subsectors that would be unmanageable for the kind of collective solution proposed by Teubner.

Existing case law suggests that plaintiffs seeking to uphold statutory duties of environmental care must overcome some significant thresholds. The South African case of *Fuller v. Kendon Eco Estate Ltd and Others* dismissed an action against unauthorized building construction because the plaintiff hadn't established the necessary 'apprehension of irreversible harm' to bring a suit under NEMA.[111] Similarly, the threshold under Queensland's Environmental Protection Act was not satisfied in *Maroochy Shire Council v. Barns*; it concerned clearance of forest from about six hectares of private land, which the court noted had 'no special significance as rare or endangered' and thus did not meet the statutory test of 'material environmental harm'.[112]

A further consideration is that a duty of environmental care might conflict with existing fiduciary and other legal duties. An aggrieved mob of beneficiaries might argue that by investing their money in untried, environmentally focused businesses, the fund failed to focus attention on maximizing investment returns in the short term. Therefore, either the new duty trumps existing legal obligations, or we must create procedures whereby fiduciaries can fulfill the environmental duty without fear of being indicted for contravening other duties. The latter approach is likely to be preferable. Whilst in the longer term, implementation of sustainable development practices should make business sense, initially (such as when environmental externalities are not reflected in market prices) there is a conflict between being environmentally responsible and maximizing investors' returns. During this initial period, the law should not deter fiduciaries from implementing sustainability practices. One effective way of providing them with such a

---

110 G. Teubner, 'The invisible cupola: from causal to collective attribution in environmental liability', in G. Teubner, L. Farmer and D. Murphy (eds), *Environmental Law and Ecological Responsibility: The Concept and Practice of Ecological Self-Organization*, John Wiley and Sons, 1994, 17–48.
111 [2008] ZAECHC 61.
112 [2001] QPEC 031.

legal shield would be to introduce, as proposed by James McConvill and Martin Joy, an 'environmental judgement rule', analogous to the existing business judgement rule in company law.[113] It would relieve fiduciaries of liability under general law or statute for failure to promote the best financial interests of beneficiaries if they make rational investment decisions to comply with the duty of environmental care.

To overcome many of the drawbacks of the common law approach, the focus of the duty would have to be on compliance with subsidiary, prophylactic rules that require financial fiduciaries to adhere to specific procedures, including environmental assessment and reporting on the sustainability of their entire portfolios. Liability would arise for procedural failures rather than necessarily the specific environmental impacts that might flow from such failures (except perhaps for financiers of discrete major development projects or equity investors with a disproportionate influence). The statutory duty would also need to be owed to the environment and community at large, so that anyone, including the government, would have standing to uphold it. Beneficiaries of an investment fund could not be relied on to take enforcement when their own financial interests might be at stake. Whereas private parties through the court system adjudicate the common law duty of care, government regulators could supervise the statutory duty. Charity law offers a useful precedent in its duty on the state Attorney-General to uphold the trust law responsibilities of the charity. Enforcement might involve issuance of an administrative order or notice for which non-compliance is a statutory offence. While a duty of care applied to investors would presumably apply to other actors, and thus the companies they finance, there would sometimes be joint liability situations to resolve. But targeting local financiers under state jurisdiction could offer advantages in several situations, such as where the polluting company they fund is operating abroad, and to provide alternative, deep pockets to support monetary compensation.

In conclusion, challenges in operationalizing an effective environmental duty of care for the financial industry exist, whether it be framed as a positive or negative obligation. Such a duty would most likely be feasible in relation to project financing or equity investors with an influential stake in a company in relation to discrete, immediate and significant environmental impacts. But if the issues outlined here could be satisfactorily addressed, the duty would provide an additional layer of governance to further sustainable development practices instead of reliance only on prescriptive, uniform regulation by the state.[114] As Mark Shepheard explains, 'the essential characteristic (and arguably the appeal) of the civil duty of care process is its capacity to move the boundary of responsibility beyond statute into the field of unwritten social

---

113 McConvill and Joy, op. cit.
114 M. Young, T. Shi and J. Crosthwaite, *Duty of Care: An Instrument for Increasing the Effectiveness of Catchment Management*, Department of Sustainability and the Environment, 2003, 7.

294 *Fiduciary law and responsible investing*

obligations'.[115] The duty could be used in combination with a recast duty of prudential investing for the long term, as the latter is more workable and isomorphic with existing fiduciary finance law.

Democratization of fund governance and the RI industry

Negotiating RI's ethical miasma

The foregoing, proposed changes to fiduciary law and other legal standards would be insufficient to comprehensively or precisely define the role of a public fiduciary, even with the aid of administrative guidance or judicial case law. We lack a clear and comprehensive measure of something as complex as the environmental well-being of the planet and our societal dependence on it. John Elkington, one of the most noteworthy advocates of sustainability from the business community, in the 1990s acknowledged that there were probably about 100 different definitions of the concept.[116]

A space within and among financial institutions (and those who regulate them, as discussed later) is needed to consult, debate and reflect on how to practise long-term investing for sustainability. The hallmarks of good prudential investing should include such consultative processes, in the same manner that investors increasingly see engagement and dialogue with their portfolio companies as best fiduciary practice. The UK government's recent Kay Review, established to examine the lack of long-term investing in British equity markets, recommended that institutional funds 'operate within a culture of open dialogue with beneficiaries – building an agreed understanding of investment objectives and risks'.[117] The need to hear beneficiaries' voice has never been more urgent in global financial markets managed through extended intermediation investment chains that greatly separate the ultimate owners from their portfolio companies. The longer the investment chain becomes, the greater the risk that conflicts of interest and other transgressions of fiduciary loyalty will arise.

While the RI industry increasingly advocates democratic corporate governance, it rarely considers its own governance, within pension plans or mutual funds, in the same manner. Apart from greater disclosure to beneficiaries, the RI industry has not given much thought to more participatory practices within its own ranks. Its nonchalance reflects scepticism that beneficiaries could offer informed opinions or constructively debate the issues.

---

115 M. Shepheard, *Some Legal and Social Expectations for a Farmer's Duty of Care*, Cooperative Research Centre for Irrigation Futures, 2010, 13.
116 J. Elkington, *Cannibals with Forks: The Triple Bottom Line of 21st Century Business*, New Society Publishers, 1998.
117 J. Kay, *Kay Review of UK Equity Markets and Long-Term Decision-Making*, Department of Business, Innovation and Skills, 2012, 57.

The public fiduciary: in nature's trust   295

Responsible investing is viewed as either a matter for specialist financial analysis of ESG information, in the case of institutional funds, or a personal choice, for retail investors. Consequently, there is little support for viewing fund governance as an opportunity for ethical deliberation about the values that might inform RI.

A further industry concern is the perceived unlikelihood that investors could ever agree among themselves on an RI policy. Despite humankind's abundant capacity for moral judgement and ethical behaviour,[118] a shared capacity for moralizing is not the same as shared ethical values. This is reflected in how RI's philosophical dimensions remain poorly elaborated, confusing and divisive. One observer indicts a 'persistent inability on the part of all participants in the debate to develop a simple, coherent definition' of RI.[119] Some bemoan that '[a]lmost any legal business activity will be regarded as ethical by a sufficient group of investors to be included in an ethical fund'.[120] Even regulatory authorities have acknowledged that 'ethical considerations are clearly subjective and impossible to fully define'.[121] Many investors reject ethical investment, and within the RI industry a potpourri of philosophies prevails, ranging from evangelical Christianity to deep ecology. Even if social investors share specific goals, they may differ in how to achieve them; during the anti-apartheid campaign, social investors disagreed on whether to divest entirely, or to retain financial ties and seek change through dialogue and tactical pressure.

The ascendancy of *business case* RI is precisely a response to this ethical miasma.[122] The deficiencies of this approach were critiqued in Chapter 2 and need not be repeated. The belief that the business case provides a clear, measurably accountable standard – maximization of financial returns for beneficiaries – is deceptive. This 'single-value' approach to investment management disguises the considerable uncertainty and complexity inherent in this task. As Ransome and Sampford explain:

> it is notoriously difficult to know exactly *how* to set about maximizing it – the highest possible financial return – actually achieving it in markets is inevitably a manifold, complex and unpredictable task. Companies have to address many issues to be successful – including delivering quality products and services to customers, recruiting and retaining

---

118 See M. Hauser, *Moral Minds*, HarperCollins, 2006.
119 M. O'Brien Hylton, '"Socially responsible" investing: doing good versus doing well in an inefficient market', *American University Law Review* 42, 1992, 1–52, 2.
120 J. Hoggett and M. Nahan, 'Ethical investment – deconstructing the myth', *Perspectives* 36, 2003, 1–2.
121 Australian Securities and Investments Commission (ASIC), *Socially Responsible Investing Disclosure Guidelines*, ASIC, 2002, 22.
122 Deni Greene Consulting (DGC), *Capital Idea: Realising Value from Environmental and Social Performance*, DGC, Standards Australia and Ethical Investment Services, 2001, 1.

staff, good relations with suppliers and local communities and complying with the law.[123]

Disagreements over social values are rife, and a sense of moral and cognitive relativism hinders achieving collective action on financial markets and environmental reform.[124] Concepts such as 'sustainable development' or 'corporate responsibility' may be read differently, depending on the actor, context and time.[125] Some RI issues, such as consumption of alcohol or fertility control, involve deeply contested moral dilemmas for which there is no established ethical custom. Other RI concerns flow from market failures where the problem is not so much that an activity is viewed as intrinsically objectionable, but rather, there is too much of the activity occurring (e.g., emitting GHGs or over-fishing). Disagreement here rages over questions of how and when to take corrective action, and who should take it. Academic research on the psychological and socio-economic characteristics of individual social investors, as well as their opinions on various ethical matters, suggests that any deliberation of RI must bridge some cavernous differences of opinion.[126] Presumably, the heterogeneity of values among conventional investors is even greater.

The problem of moral and cognitive relativism thus looms large over attempts to wield legal solutions to facilitate RI. When the Irish Parliament in 2006 rejected a legislative amendment to require its National Pensions Reserve Fund (NPRF) to invest ethically, one parliamentarian captured the mood with these remarks:

> A major difficulty in deciding on ethical investment policy is where to draw the line in defining the parameters of the policy, given that there will inevitably be different opinions and intense debate on what constitutes ethical and socially responsible investment. . . . Furthermore, the list of what might be considered unacceptable investment is likely to change in light of developments in the political, social and scientific spheres.[127]

---

123 W. Ransome and C. Sampford, *Ethics and Socially Responsible Investment: A Philosophical Approach*, Ashgate, 2010, 32.
124 M. Zimmerman, *Contesting Earth's Future: Radical Ecology and Postmodernity*, University of California Press, 1994.
125 See J.S. Dryzek, *The Politics of the Earth: Environmental Discourses*, 2nd edn, Oxford University Press, 2005.
126 J. McLachlan and J. Gardner, 'A comparison of socially responsible and conventional investors', *Journal of Business Ethics* 52, 2004, 11–25; J. Nilsson, 'Investment with a conscience', *Journal of Business Ethics* 83(2), 2008, 307–25; P. Anand and C. Cowton, 'The ethical investor: exploring dimensions of investment behaviour', *Journal of Economic Psychology* 14(2), 1993, 377–85.
127 Parliament of Ireland, Select Committee on Finance and the Public Service, *Parliamentary Debates* 44, 23 February 2006, 5. Curiously, the NPRF subsequently adopted an RI policy: http://www.nprf.ie/ResponsibleInvesting/responsibleInvesting.htm.

Before examining how law might overcome or mitigate the lack of ethical congruence among market participants through more participatory and informed investment decision-making procedures, we should consider the ethical foundations for building an RI policy.

Ethical foundations of RI

Underpinning the concept of sustainability as a beacon for a new fiduciary responsibility of the financial economy are important ethical issues about humankind's moral relationship to the planet and future generations that need to be debated by investors and other stakeholders. The sustainability paradigm is not simply an anthropocentric, utilitarian device to instrumentally sustain the market's prosperity – though that may be one of its effects – but it also embodies fundamental values about maintenance of ecological integrity and inter-generational justice. It provides a way to address the concern expressed by the UN Economic and Social Council on unsustainable global patterns of resource use: '[t]he value systems reflected in these patterns are among the main driving forces which determine the use of natural resources. Although the changes required for converting societies to sustainable consumption and production patterns are not easy to implement, the shift is imperative'.[128]

A sophisticated theory on ecological ethics has evolved to address this challenge.[129] This ethical paradigm morally behooves us to consider all living creatures and their ecosystems,[130] emphasizing humankind's integral and interdependent role in nature's 'web of life'.[131] A cognate perspective affirms the sanctity of all life forms for their 'intrinsic value', regardless of their contribution to human prosperity.[132] This stance, however, does not deny people's entitlement to utilize nature for their survival; but it recognizes that maintenance of other life forms 'is a condition of our existence as participants in the evolutionary process'.[133] But only a handful of scholars have seriously examined RI's ethical underpinnings in relation to this task.[134]

---

128 UN Economic and Social Council, *Implementing Agenda 21: Report of the Secretary-General*, E/CN.17/PC.2/7, 2002, 5.
129 P. Taylor, *An Ecological Approach to International Law*, Routledge, 1998; K. Bosselmann, *The Principle of Sustainability: Transforming Law and Governance*, Ashgate, 2008.
130 For overviews, see R. Eckersley, *Environmentalism and Political Theory: Towards an Ecocentric Approach*, State University of New York Press, 1992; C. Stone, *Earth and Other Ethics*, Harper and Row, 1987; D. Schmidtz and E. Willott (eds), *Environmental Ethics: What Really Matters*, Oxford University Press, 2002.
131 F. Capra, *The Web of Life. A New Scientific Understanding of Living Systems*, Anchor Books, 1996.
132 L. Vilkka, *The Intrinsic Value of Nature*, Rodopi B.V. Editions, 1997.
133 R. Engel, 'The moral power of the world conservation movement to engage economic globalization', *George Wright Forum* 22(3), 2005, 58–71, 62.
134 Notably, Ransome and Sampford, op. cit., and J.D. Cronin, *From Ethical Investment to Investment Ethics*, PhD, Queensland University of Technology, 2004.

Ethics theory suggests that values such as sustainability can be given an objective basis around which investors and other stakeholders might coalesce to articulate some environmentally acceptable parameters to fiduciary finance. The cultivation of ethical opinions for RI raises questions about whether they have truth value, independent of the preferences or circumstances of specific actors' cultures. In other words, in morally objecting to investment in oil sands companies or mining firms, for instance, is the individual simply expressing a personal emotion, or a value of his or her culture, or conveying some objectively verified truth about the inherent wrongness of such development? The theory that moral judgements simply express personal emotions or attitudes is known as emotivism or subjectivism, and denies that moral judgements can ever reflect any objective truth. Alternatively, morality can be viewed as a manifestation of one's social or cultural context, in which there are no necessarily universal moral values but rather moral variation, depending on religion, ethnicity and country. Judgements about right or wrong in one community might not attract the same verdict in another. Both of these approaches to morality are evident in RI practices, such as the deference to personal taste in the retail market and the role of faith-based investing in the institutional sector.

The problem with moral subjectivism is that it doesn't allow us to determine that ethical investing exists, independent of one's personal preferences or cultural context. Thus it isn't possible for any bystander to judge whether any 'ethical' investment portfolio is in fact morally scrupulous. By denying that moral judgements may have objective truth value, overcoming ethical conflicts in investment choices is difficult; it assumes there is no such thing as *the* ethical investment, just varieties of 'ethical' investments. Indeed, as John Cronin explains, there would be 'no need for a distinct label, as all investment is ethical – at least to someone, somewhere'.[135] Such an approach relegates RI to a smorgasbord of diverse preferences and fashionable causes.

Such morally subjective treatment of ethics undermines humankind's capacity to deal with grave ecological threats such as climate change wrought by unsustainable economic growth. The Interfaith Center on Corporate Responsibility (ICCR), a global champion for ethical investment, notes that 'the Occupy Movement is clear evidence of a fundamental shift in the public consciousness around corporate power and the need to keep it in check'.[136] 'The global nature of modern investment practice dictates that we must be able to identify arguments that incorporate nonrelative claims and that can withstand criticism and scrutiny involving few, if any, personal or cultural vagaries', explains Cronin.[137] In other words, it is important that moral posi-

---

135 Cronin, ibid., 238.
136 Quoted in R. Kropp, 'Occupy Movement focuses on Volcker rule', *Sustainability Investment News*, 14 March 2012, http://dev.socialfunds.com/news/article.cgi/article3475.html.
137 Cronin, op. cit., 259.

tions be determined that transcend individual opinions, in the manner advanced by coalitions such as the Occupy Movement and the ICCR. While we cannot ignore differences of moral judgement among individuals or cultures, we must develop the capacities to allow rational people to adjudicate between conflicting moral claims through disciplined moral deliberation. Financial investments should be judged against ethical criteria for sustainability that transcend individual preferences or cultural contexts, providing criteria to justify our decisions and to judge those of others.

This task, however, is not a recipe to follow some reified theory of natural law, as though right and wrong are laid down by some predetermined values that transcend any time and place. Society is not static, and new issues are constantly arising, such as GMOs or climate change, that require new moral analysis and judgement. The dynamic situation we face requires institutions and processes that allow us to debate, rationalize and reflect on the morality of particular activities and situations in an ever-changing world.

In building a framework for an objective morality to underpin RI, we should distinguish between 'universal and tendentious moral facts', in order to accommodate that not all moral positions can possibly be shared. As Cronin explains:

> Universal moral facts are based in universally moral principles that we would wish everyone to observe, while conversely tendentious moral facts are about personal or collective moral principles which while no doubt marked by a strong implicit point of view, we may like others to observe but would not feel compelled to force them to do so.[138]

Thus, investment prohibitions on tobacco or alcohol may be considered tendentious examples, in which it would be hard to justify compelling everyone to conform. Conversely, prohibitions on companies that are complicit in genocide or gross and deliberate environmental destruction are concerns of much wider, international salience. While both tendentious and universal moral facts can be objective, they differ in their scope and universality. It is of course sometimes hard to distinguish between universal and tendentious moral facts, which would need to be one of the responsibilities of a process of critical ethical deliberation.

One clue to this distinction is to look at international legal principles on the environment and human rights that suggest fundamental ethical norms. Already the NGPF-G uses such international principles as a benchmark for its RI decisions. Widely ratified treaties and declarations are among the best candidates for universal values of global responsibility. Those instruments that are incorporated into global industry standards and that enjoy respect from prominent NGOs, religious groups and other stakeholders

---

138 Ibid., 244.

are particularly good candidates. We can also identify in the category of universal norms issues that are associated with market failures, such as climate change, deforestation and over-fishing – these are activities that most would view as not intrinsically unethical, but rather the problem arises that we indulge in them too much. Henderson Global Investors has declared climate change 'an imperative for investors' because it is 'widely recognized as the most significant issue facing the global economy'.[139] On the other hand, tendentious or 'micro' ethical norms are appropriate choices for individual investors in the retail fund sector.

The foregoing analysis has implications not only for what RI stands for, but how it is practised. In addition to the importance of more deliberative processes within the financial industry, its methods of screening and engaging with companies need refining. In many cases, the application of morally absolutist exclusionary portfolio screens cannot capture the nuanced circumstances about specific products or processes. Corporate engagement can both allow for ethical dialogue, between investors and businesses, while also providing a means of moral education and reflection on specific issues. Moral argument and reflection enable people to learn moral facts and apply them in specific situations. For example, while testing on animals may generally be regarded as cruel and morally unacceptable, in very limited circumstances it might be okay if conducted carefully in order to save human lives. Similarly, while production of military weapons may be morally dubious, it might be justified in order to allow self-defence against unreasonable aggressors. The necessity of such moral reflection and debate means we should not allow trustees, fund managers and ESG research providers to remain the self-appointed arbiters of what is socially responsible.

Governance frameworks for ethical deliberation in RI

The foregoing challenges to operationalizing sustainability as a meta-ethical and practical framework for the public fiduciary impress upon the legal system a role to instil better decision-making processes. Law can help financial institutions to acquire the capacity to engage in moral argument, reflection and analysis. Dialogue facilitates consideration of sustainability and other ethical issues in a local context, and to allow for human agency. Law can structure procedural changes within financial organizations to stimulate more consultative and deliberative decision-making that involves beneficiaries and even other stakeholders. Such participation and ethical deliberation should also infuse the industry's collective forums and codes, such as the UNPRI, Equator Principles and the UNEP-FI, as well as government regulatory processes. Given the plurality of values at stake in RI, processes that promote critical reflection and dialogue may, at best, help promote congruence of

---

139 Henderson Global Investors, 'The Carbon 100', June 2005, 5.

viewpoint or, at the very least, ensure greater accountability and legitimacy for the investment decisions taken.

Historically, the fiduciary relationship has legally been cast as largely paternalistic, wherein trustees in their wisdom decide what best serves beneficiaries' interests without needing to consult them. Yet, modern financial institutions are materially different from private trusts from which such an assumption originated, since the beneficiaries contribute some of the capital to be invested, as against the settlor in the case of a typical family trust. Moreover, in most funds, including pension plans that are increasingly provided under defined contribution arrangements, beneficiaries bear the primary risk of investment performance. There is also a public fiduciary character to financial institutions, in terms of their broad membership and societal impacts. In this setting, it is untenable that decision-making should be elitist.

It would be naïve, of course, to expect that more RI would inevitably ensue from democratization of fund governance. It might stall due to widespread apathy among lay investors. For example, the Australian superannuation choice legislation, which allows workers to choose the fund (including RI options) into which their compulsory pension contributions are invested, has induced little change: most workers remain enrolled in their employer's default fund.[140] Also, consultation and dialogue are time-consuming, and many investors are probably too busy or indifferent to care about investment policy-making. And even if they wish to participate, there is no assurance that they would demand ethical investing; they might behave like their trustees or fund managers and shun RI. Most fund beneficiaries are likely to be just as interested in personal wealth maximization as corporations are in profit maximization. This is not to deny room for beneficiaries' participation in fund governance as an accountability tool, but simply to caution that such participation alone is no assurance of RI. However, introducing a statutory duty of environmental care for long-term investing would likely heighten investors' interest in such issues because practising RI would help ensure legal compliance and minimize liability risks.

One of several tasks for law is thus to ameliorate the problem that investors operate 'in an environment of bounded economic and moral rationality. They are constrained in their ability to discover and process all the economic and morally relevant facts necessary to make their investment decisions'.[141] Legal requirements to collect and disclose ESG information can help address this deficit. Currently, at best, law only requires funds to disclose their RI policies, but not their methods, practices and impacts. Fiduciaries should be obliged to disclose in detail their approach to RI, how they make moral judgements and differentiate the ethical dimensions of specific companies, products and

---

140 J. Cooper, 'Super for members: a new paradigm for Australia's retirement income system', *Rotman International Journal of Pension Management* 3(2), 2010, 8–15, 11.
141 Cronin, op. cit., 261.

processes. Informing beneficiaries and fiduciaries about sustainability is a key building block for democratizing RI decision-making.

Law can also foster the institutional spaces and processes for moral reflection and debate. Given the ethical pluralism confronting RI, coupled with the imperative to *justify* rather than preach its worth, legal mechanisms to promote reasoned ethical deliberation and education are essential to motivate action.[142] RI will be sullied if investors regard it simply as received academic wisdom or rigid regulatory prescription. Giving a voice to beneficiaries and other stakeholders in fund governance may reduce the possibility that the ethics of RI will reflect the views only of a vociferous minority. This agenda requires tailoring decision-making to the circumstances of different financial institutions and transactions. In retail markets, where financial advisers and brokers connect individuals with funds and banks, they have a special responsibility to clients. Financial intermediaries must identify the value preferences of investors and match them to suitable investment options. Within mutual funds, investment policy-making should be more substantively informed by ethical debate among fund members rather than ritualistic ratification of policy changes predetermined by fund managers or trustees. This might be achieved through obligations on fund managers to actively poll investors and solicit their views. In pension plans and insurance companies, giving beneficiaries greater rights to be consulted is insufficient. Thus, complementary reforms, such as obliging financial institutions to take measures not only to inform their members about their RI policies but also to involve them in making such policies through surveys and questionnaires, and having representatives on governing boards, are important.

While in large institutional funds it is impossible to get broad agreement on most RI issues, participants might at least partially concur on some underlying principles and procedures. Law could allow for decisions to be made on a majority basis (so long as they are not oppressive to the minority). Corporation law provides a potential model here in its mechanisms to protect minority shareholders from oppressive behaviour by the majority.[143] These responsibilities must fall on trustees, fund managers and other decision-makers. Fiduciaries are legally obliged to act on behalf of their members and must be accountable for procedural morality in the investment process, and ensure that forums allow for critical ethical deliberation and acting on beneficiaries' wishes.

Beyond individual funds, more consultative and participatory decision-making must be stimulated through the existing industry codes overseen by the UNEP-FI, investment associations and other collectives. Opening these

---

142 M. Hajer, *The Politics of Environmental Discourse: Ecological Modernization and the Policy Process*, Clarendon Press, 1995, 16–21; S. Jasanoff and M. Martello (eds), *Earthly Politics: Local and Global in Environmental Governance*, MIT Press, 2004.
143 R.B. Thompson, 'Shareholder's cause of action for oppression', *Business Lawyer* 48, 1992–93, 699–745.

regimes to non-business stakeholders, such as human rights and environmental NGOs, would be more likely to garner active participation and critical insights to help strengthen investing in sustainability than just involving funds' beneficiaries. A growing number of environmental and social justice groups are campaigning on RI issues, including Amnesty International, BankTrack and the Rainforest Action Network. One often-ignored voice that could be brought to the table is the communities or other parties in whose names social investors purport to act. Catherine Coumans's study of the Canadian RI sector's campaign against Goldcorp's Marlin mine in Guatemala found that the funds failed to consult adequately with the local communities, and their intervention allegedly inflamed the situation.[144]

Civil society and NGO participation in investment governance may conceivably take several forms, including as performance scrutinizers, protesters or norm negotiators.[145] Presently, their opportunities for formal involvement are too sparse and *ad hoc*. Most NGOs are 'involved' as outside protesters, such as the campaigns orchestrated by BankTrack against delinquent Equator banks.[146] Occasionally, NGOs have been consulted through round-table discussions in the development of RI codes, as occurred with the drafting of the UNPRI, but most such codes reflect the inputs of the financial industry. Some piecemeal consultation also occurs between civil society groups and financial signatories on implementation of codes, as well as with UN bodies that participate in some RI codes. In the 1990s, UNEP's International Round-Table Meetings on Finance and the Environment provided a systematic framework for NGO participation.[147] Also, increasingly 'the Equator banks collectively meet NGOs to discuss their position in closed sessions' and individual banks such as ABN AMRO have undertaken private negotiations with the Rainforest Action Network to develop their Forest Investment Policy.[148] Friends of the Earth has been a regular participant in some of these processes with the banking sector. Some structured public consultation processes are also convened by RI groups; the UNPRI Secretariat has used them for developing new initiatives such as its reporting framework.[149] The UNEP-FI and Global Reporting Initiative (GRI) convened a multi-stakeholder working group in 2003 for development of new financial

---

144 C. Coumans, 'Mining, human rights and the socially responsible investment industry', *Journal of Sustainable Finance and Investment* 2(1), 2012, 44–63.
145 E. Sjöström, 'CSOs and business partnerships: strategies for interaction', *Business Strategy and the Environment* 14, 2005, 230–40.
146 Http://www.banktrack.org.
147 E.g., see the participant lists in M. Kelly and T. Stoll, *Profitability and Responsibility in the 21st Century, UNEP Financial Institutions Initiative*, Fourth International Round-Table Meeting on Finance and the Environment, UNEP, 1998.
148 A.B. Coulson, 'How should banks govern the environment? Challenging the construction of action versus veto', *Business Strategy and the Environment* 18, 2009, 149–61, 158.
149 UNPRI, *Reporting Framework*, http://www.unpri.org/consultation/2011_06_16_consultation_tor_technical_committee.pdf.

reporting on environmental criteria.[150] The 2006 revision of the Equator Principles was also preceded by a public consultation process.[151] National-level RI industry associations such as the SIO and UKSIF occasionally use public consultation and outreach in promoting new initiatives.[152]

But non-business sector representation in the official governing boards of RI regimes is rare. To illustrate, the new Principles of Sustainable Insurance initiative is governed by a board of representatives from its insurance industry signatories and UNEP – an arrangement similar to other RI codes that limits public oversight. The governance of the UNPRI includes an Advisory Council of 11 elected representatives from investor signatory organizations and two representatives from the UN. Non-business interests can develop their own collective stance on RI issues, as they did in 2003 by drafting the Collevecchio Declaration on Financial Institutions and Sustainability. But although endorsed by some 200 civil society groups worldwide, it has been shunned by the financial industry. A more promising example of collaboration between business and non-business stakeholders is the 2012 Natural Capital Declaration, whose website states that it was 'convened' by UNEP-FI, the Global Canopy Programme (an alliance of scientific forestry-focused institutions) and the Center for Sustainability Studies (GVces) of the Getulio Vargas Foundation in Italy.[153]

Governments could encourage the more participatory and collaborative efforts by selectively endorsing regimes that best fulfill such attributes. Endorsements could take the form of recognizing performance under approved RI codes as fulfilling certain alternative regulatory requirements relating to information disclosure, member involvement and environmental performance. States can harness private sector codes as surrogate regulatory tools that best fulfill the requirements of the enlightened fiduciary responsibility.

The state as nature's trustee

Public trust doctrine

The ultimate public fiduciary is the state. Governments worldwide already regulate the financial economy to remedy a variety of market failures. Although the appropriate degree and form of this intervention is heavily contested by theorists and policy-makers, it is based on three major rationales: safeguarding market competition and efficiency, protecting consumers and

---

150 'Launch of UNEP FI – GRI Public Consultation on Environmental Performance Indicators', *International Corporate Sustainability Reporting*, September 2003.
151 Equator Principles History, Update 2006, http://www.equator-principles.com/index.php/about-the-equator-principles/38-about/about/17.
152 See generally D. Nitsch and M.C. Baetz, 'Creativity, convergence or confusion: what do socially responsible investment organisations contribute to the governance debate in Canada?', *International Business, Governance and Ethics* 2(1/2), 2006, 23–42.
153 Http://www.naturalcapitaldeclaration.org/conveners.

investors from misconduct, and ensuring market stability.[154] The GFC exposed major failings in this financial governance, particularly with regard to systemic risks and market structure. The crisis generated a swathe of proposals for regulatory reform, and some successes, but hardly any speak to the financial sector's environmental risks and impacts. Responsible investing cannot transform the economy towards sustainability if the state itself doesn't act appropriately, as both a market regulator and a significant investor in its own right through public pension funds and SWFs. While this book has identified a range of regulatory reform initiatives obliging or encouraging market participants to practise RI, states have generally failed to modernize their own practices. During preparation of the UK's Financial Services and Markets Act of 2000, which created the Financial Services Authority, the UKSIF proposed that the Authority's mandate include promoting best practice in environmental risk management and encouraging the provision of environmental investing and lending products.[155] This idea was rejected by parliamentarians as outside the conventional parameters for state supervision of financial markets. The UKSIF's American counterpart proposed to President Obama the creation of an Office for Innovation in CSR to 'enhance and coordinate interagency' CSR and RI-related activities.[156] Only in relation to a few SWFs, as the previous chapter discussed, have some states been adventurous in this direction.

The public trust doctrine, an ancient yet ambitious legal precedent, could be deployed for elevating the environmental responsibilities of the state as a public fiduciary in these contexts. The doctrine could conceptually underpin the overarching fiduciary responsibilities of the state as nature's trustee. Trust principles are not a heretical idea for organizing our relationship with nature. They draw on the deep inclination of human beings to secure prosperity and security for their own survival and that of their progeny. The vulnerability of future generations and the environment, which cannot vote or litigate directly, are strong candidates for benefiting from public fiduciary responsibility. The public trust doctrine also dovetails with many religious and spiritual worldviews that view humans as stewards of the Earth.[157]

The following discussion explains the origins and development of the public trust, its application mainly in US jurisprudence, and recent academic debate about novel applications of the doctrine to environmental and economic decision-making. The doctrine in its current form is not applicable

---

154 G.J. Schinasi, *Safeguarding Financial Stability: Theory and Practice*, IMF, 2005; C. Goodhart, et al., *Financial Regulation: Why, How and Where Now*, Routledge, 1998.
155 UKSIF, 'UK Social Investment Forum tells MPs of need to include environment in framework for financial services regulator', Press release, 19 April 1999.
156 US-SIF, 'New American leadership for environmentally and socially responsible investing and corporate responsibility', 14 January 2009, http://ussif.org/documents/Obama AdministrationFINAL1.14.pdf.
157 R. Foltz, *Worldviews, Religion, and the Environment: A Global Anthology*, Thomson/Wadsworth, 2003.

to the financial economy, but could be made so through legislative and judicial innovation. While environmental legislation, financial regulation and other public laws provide specific standards and decision-making procedures, the public trust doctrine could supply a reservoir of authority underlying their statutory mandates and guide decision-making where agencies wield discretionary authority. The doctrine could most easily be applied to public sector funds, particularly SWFs.

In its traditional formulation, the public trust represents the fiduciary mandate of the state as custodian of proprietary interests in natural resources to be managed wisely for the welfare of beneficiaries, both present and future generations of its citizens.[158] As interpreted by Mary Wood, a leading American academic on this topic, 'the focus of the doctrine is not on some amorphous agency conception of the "public interest", but rather on the measurable abundance of the natural assets themselves'.[159] The doctrine emanated from Roman law, and during the reign of Eastern Roman Emperor Justinian it was codified as: '[b]y the law of nature these things are common to all mankind; the air, running water, the sea, and consequently the shores of the sea'.[160] It was revived when the law of England recognized the public nature of foreshores and navigable waters, and placing them in the custody of the Crown for the benefit of all English subjects. The doctrine has continued to inspire many legal and political theorists, such as Paul Finn, who view it as a fundamental organizing metaphor for the Lockean compact between the community and the state.[161] Though in this more extravagant sense, it has received only parsimonious judicial recognition, such as regarding the Crown's fiduciary obligations to Aboriginal people, notably in Canada,[162] and the responsibilities of local governments to their community constituencies, as in Britain.[163]

The public trust doctrine flourishes in many jurisdictions today, enjoying its richest juridical affirmation in the US.[164] Some scholars, notably Joseph Sax and Mary Wood, venerate it for unifying an overarching set of

---

158 See, e.g., *Arizona Center for Law in the Public Interest v. Hassell*, (1991) 837 P.2d 158, 169 (noting that '[t]he beneficiaries of the public trust are not just present generations but those to come').
159 M.C. Wood, 'Advancing the sovereign trust of government to safeguard the environment for present and future generations (part ii): instilling a fiduciary obligation in governance', *Environmental Law* 39(1), 2009, 91–139, 103.
160 *Justinian Institutes*, 2.1.1, T.C. Sandars trans., Callaghan and Company, 1876.
161 P. Finn, 'The forgotten "trust": the people and the state', in M. Cope (ed.), *Equity Issues and Trends*, Federation Press, 1995, 131–55.
162 *R. v. Guerin*, (1984) 2 SCR 335; see also Law Commission of Canada and Association of Iroquois and Allied Indians, *In Whom We Trust: A Forum on Fiduciary Relationships*, Irwin Law, 2002.
163 *R. v. Hopwood*, [1925] AC 578.
164 J.D. Kearney and T.W. Merrill, 'The origins of the American public trust doctrine: what really happened in Illinois Central', *University of Chicago Law Review* 71, 2004, 799–931.

environmental responsibilities for the state.[165] Taking a global perspective, Edith Brown Weiss has advocated a 'planetary trust' to facilitate intergenerational equity on the environment,[166] while some international legal scholars advance the looser notion of the 'common heritage of humankind'.[167] A number of Australian environmental lawyers have recently championed the trust as a specific tool for climate change governance.[168]

The doctrine's paramount requirement is that natural resources be managed for public benefit rather than private advantage. The Attorney-General can sue, as trustee, for compensatory damages or injunctive relief relating to resources held in public trust. In the influential precedent of *Illinois Central Railroad Co. v. Illinois (Illinois Central)*,[169] the US Supreme Court declared the State of Illinois was the trustee of Lake Michigan's shoreline, and could not transfer it out of the public domain to a private railway company. In *Geer v. Connecticut*,[170] the same court applied the trust doctrine to the taking of wildlife. In *re Water Use Permit Applications for the Waiahole Ditch*, the Hawaii Supreme Court extended it to groundwater resources.[171] In *United States v. State Water Resources Control Board*, the California Supreme Court upheld state water regulators' modification of water rights permits to protect water quality as an application of the public trust doctrine.[172]

But beyond these examples, the doctrine has generally not been interpreted by American courts as extending to the full panoply of natural bounty and ecological services.[173] And it has not yet been invoked to address responsibilities for transboundary concerns such as global warming. Courts tend to conclude that any public trust protections in these contexts are either already codified in state legislation or should be, leaving little room for judicial amplification.[174] The natural resources subject to the public trust doctrine are assets in which present and future citizens hold a beneficial property interest that is protected through the trust. In theory, the American jurisprudence suggests that trustee responsibilities apply to

---

165 J.L. Sax, 'The public trust doctrine in natural resource law: effective judicial intervention', *Michigan Law Review* 68, 1970, 471–566; Wood, 'Advancing the sovereign trust', op. cit.
166 E.B. Weiss, *In Fairness to Future Generations: International Law, Common Patrimony, and Intergenerational Equity*, UN University Press, 1989.
167 K. Baslar, *The Concept of the Common Heritage of Mankind in International Law*, Martinus Nijhoff, 1998.
168 K. Coghill, C. Sampford and T. Smith (eds), *Fiduciary Duty and the Atmospheric Trust*, Ashgate, 2012.
169 (1892) 146 US 387.
170 (1896) 161 US 519.
171 (2000) 9 P.3d 409, 445–47).
172 (1986) 227 Cal. Rptr. 161.
173 R.M. Frank, 'The public trust doctrine: assessing its recent past and charting its future', *UC Davis Law Review* 45, 2012, 665–91, 679–80.
174 See, e.g., *Environmental Protection Information Center (EPIC) v. California Department of Forestry and Fire Protection*, (2008) 187 P.3d 888 (rejecting extension of the public trust doctrine to protect endangered wildlife from logging).

all branches of the state, but it has mainly evolved through the courts and has never infused into the general array of environmental regulation. The legislature can be regarded as the custodian of the trust resources, the executive government its agent and the judiciary its definitive guardian through 'the check and balance of judicial review'.[175] While the public interest is not homogeneous, and thus requires the state to balance competing interests, the doctrine expects the state not to trade off public interests to benefit private parties.

American courts have defined several constituent elements of the public trust.[176] The trustee must recover compensatory damages from third parties that harm public resources in order to restore the asset for future generations. The trustee must also publicly disclose the health of the trust assets, and account for any improvements or losses such as area of forest, wildlife numbers or water quality. Where a government agency has discretionary authority, it should select the alternative that best safeguards the natural assets. Courts have affirmed that 'mere compliance by [agencies] with their legislative authority is not sufficient to determine if their actions comport with the requirements of the public trust doctrine'.[177] The fiduciary obligations also endow the state with a more proactive environmental role, to prevent resources from being idly left to waste. However, the doctrine doesn't clearly establish an affirmative duty to undertake positive measures to facilitate sustainable development.

Relatedly, the Attorney-General can also bring *parens patriae* suits to recover for damages to a state's natural resources. The *parens patriae* ('parent of the country') doctrine allows a state to sue to redress injury to its sovereign and quasi-sovereign interests, such as the welfare of its citizens and their environment.[178] In the US, *parens patriae* can be used by the state only when it has an interest in the litigation, apart from that of its citizens. The advantage of the doctrine of *parens patriae*, explains Allan Kanner, is that it 'may provide states with standing to sue for damage to a broader range of resources than the public trust doctrine, because the former doctrine does not require the resources to be associated with property that is owned by the state'.[179] *Parens patriae* litigation has been used creatively by US authorities in the context of mass tort litigation, as demonstrated by the lawsuits against the tobacco

---

175 *Arizona Center*, op. cit., 169.
176 Wood, op. cit., 102–5.
177 Ibid., 108–9.
178 Note, 'State protection of its economy and environment: parens patriae suits for damages', *Columbia Journal of Law and Social Problems* 6(3), 1970, 411–32. For examples, see *Georgia v. Tennessee Copper Co.*, (1907) 206 US 230; *Maine v. M/V Tamano*, (1973) 357 F. Supp. 1097 (SD Me.).
179 A. Kanner, 'The public trust doctrine, parens patriae, and the Attorney General as the guardian of the state's natural resources', *Duke Environmental Law and Policy Forum* 16, 2005, 57–115, 111.

industry.[180] It has also been considered by courts in Canada[181] and India[182] in environmental cases.

In other jurisdictions the public trust doctrine has gained some judicial or legislative recognition, but generally not to the extent as in the US. With respect to its northern neighbour, '[a] long and dusty trail through Canadian law reports reveals that Canadian courts have recognized a public trust with respect of navigation and fishing as well as highways'.[183] One Australian court declared that 'national parks are held by the State in trust for the enjoyment and benefit of its citizens, including future generations'.[184] In several other countries, trust-like responsibilities to the environment have been constitutionalized in national supreme law.[185] These provisions are usually formulated either as citizenry rights to a healthy environment or a state duty to protect it. Domestic courts in India, the Philippines and several Latin American countries have crafted a generous environmental human rights discourse that draws on the public trust.[186] Indian jurisprudence, which has perhaps gone the farthest, has applied it to protect parks of 'historical importance and environmental necessity'.[187] Unusually, Ecuador's constitution accords nature the 'right to exist, persist, maintain and regenerate its vital cycles, structure, functions and its processes in evolution'.[188]

Public trust and the financial economy

Putting financial markets under the auspices of a public trustee wouldn't be easy, and for many would smack of enlightened despotism. Several doctrinal and practical challenges would have to be overcome, particularly that environmental sustainability, as a fiduciary goal, cannot be neatly condensed into any discrete legal formula (and therefore would rely heavily on unelected judges or bureaucrats to flesh out its contours). Furthermore, a public fiduciary might struggle to reconcile the far more numerous and divided array of

---

180 J. Ratcliff, 'Parens patriae: an overview', *Tulane Law Review* 74, 1999–2000, 1847–58.
181 *British Columbia v. Canadian Forest Products Ltd*, [2004] 2 SCR 74.
182 *M.C. Mehta v. Kamal Nath and Others*, (1997) 1 SCC 338; *Karnatoka Industrial Areas Development Board v. C. Kenchappa*, [2006] AIRSCW 2546.
183 K.P. Smallwood, *Coming Out of Hibernation: the Canadian Public Trust Doctrine*, LLM thesis, University of British Columbia, 1993, abstract.
184 *Willoughby City Council v. Minister for Administering the National Parks and Wildlife Act*, (1992) 78 LGERA 19, 34.
185 M.C. Blumm and R.D. Guthrie, 'Internationalizing the public trust doctrine: natural law and constitutional and statutory approaches to fulfilling the Saxion vision', *University of California Davis Law Review* 22, 2012, 741–808; J. May, 'Constituting fundamental environmental rights worldwide', *Pace Environmental Law Review* 23, 2006, 113–82.
186 S. Atapattu, 'The right to a healthy life or the right to die polluted? The emergence of a human right to a healthy environment under international law', *Tulane Environmental Law Journal* 16, 2002, 65–126.
187 *MI Builders v. Radhey Shyam Sahu AIR*, [1999] SC 2468.
188 See A.C. Revkin, 'Ecuador constitution grants rights to nature', *New York Times*, 29 September 2008, http://dotearth.blogs.nytimes.com/2008/09/29/ecuador-constitution-grants-nature-rights/.

interests than corporate directors or fund trustees confront under their more exclusive fiduciary obligations. The trust doctrine has so far been applied to natural assets under public control, whereas its application to the financial economy would touch a plethora of public and private actors and affect decisions that transcend specific resources or lands. Legislative reformulation of the doctrine, however, could make headway.

Already the public trust's doctrinal footprint can intrude into private property rights.[189] Regarding the American jurisprudence, explains Wood, the 'public trust encumbrance on private title has never been extinguished and remains an antecedent servitude to preserve natural infrastructure'.[190] US courts have upheld controls on private activity to stop damage to a public trust resource as a complete defence to 'taking claims'.[191] Similarly, one might justify environmental controls on private financiers as necessary to curb harmful externalities to entrusted assets such as the atmosphere or biodiversity.

Conceptually, the stewardship obligation of the public fiduciary could be defined in terms of *natural capital*, the essential ecosystem services and resources necessary for economic investment and other societal needs. The financial industry's recently adopted Natural Capital Declaration, as noted earlier in this chapter, speaks in these terms:

> We therefore call upon governments to develop clear, credible, and long-term policy frameworks that support and incentivise organizations – including financial institutions – to value and report on their use of natural capital and thereby work towards internalizing environmental costs.[192]

The aim would be to ensure that natural capital is not depleted and, preferably, is actively sustained and replenished. Under this model, investors would have the benefit of the state to protect their financial assets, while in exchange they must not impair natural capital held in trust for present and future generations of common society. Investor rights are subject to the polity's right to regulate them and the development they finance in order to protect public welfare. Investor rights have never preceded the state as a natural given, but are entitlements defined by governments and subject to ongoing adjustment as societal needs evolve. As the world adjusts to global warming and depleted natural resources, there should be an increasing premium to extend the public trust.

---

189 Wood, op. cit., 82–3.
190 Ibid., 93.
191 Kanner, op. cit., 70.
192 *The Natural Capital Declaration: A Commitment by the Finance Sector for Rio+20 and Beyond*, 2012, 3, http://www.naturalcapitaldeclaration.org/wp-content/uploads/2012/05/NCD_leaflet.pdf.

Affirming the state's fiduciary responsibilities over the financial economy would entail several specific consequences. It would endow legal standing to fund beneficiaries and other persons, as members of the public, to vindicate public trust interests. Secondly, it would behoove state agencies to supervise use of and impacts on public trust resources, requiring new levels of collaboration between financial and environmental regulators. Thirdly, the state would need to create remedies and sanctions to address abuse of nature's trust assets, which might require more extensive investment prohibitions as well as positive incentives to stimulate green investing.

In the academic literature, Brown Weiss illuminates how nature's trust might be fashioned more ambitiously, going beyond stewardship of discrete natural assets such as navigable waterways or parks, as in the US or Indian jurisprudence, to more holistic fiduciary responsibility to protect natural capital at large. She focuses on inter-temporal environmental justice, maintaining that humankind holds the 'natural and cultural patrimony of our planet' in trust for all generations of people.[193] Brown Weiss proposes a 'planetary trust' as the instrument that law-makers should embrace to ensure that posterity will be bequeathed their just share of our global heritage:

> the present generation serves both as a trustee for future generations and as a beneficiary of the trust. In fulfilling our role as planetary trustees, we can draw on the law of trusts, a body of distilled teachings concerning inter-generational cooperation and conflict, to help resolve the challenges confronting our global heritage.[194]

Hence, the whole planet is conceived as an enormous trust resource, under the stewardship of enlightened trustees for the welfare of current and future generations.

The planetary trust is more than just a seductive metaphor for our ethical obligations to the environment, possessing several features that correlate with ordinary trusts, in particular, charitable trusts. Firstly, the planetary trust has custody of property, which 'includes both the natural heritage of the planet and the cultural heritage of the human species'.[195] Secondly, the planetary trust has identifiable trustees; to Brown Weiss, 'each generation acts as trustee for beneficiaries in succeeding generations, just as past generations served as trustees for it'.[196] Thirdly, analogous to a charitable trust, the trustees of the planetary trust must manage the property not on behalf of specific beneficiaries but rather for the benefit of 'all human generations, born and unborn'.[197]

---

193 Brown Weiss, op. cit., 2.
194 E. Brown Weiss, 'The planetary trust: conservation and intergenerational equity', *Ecology Law Quarterly* 11(4), 1984, 495–582, 499.
195 Ibid., 502.
196 Ibid., 504–5.
197 Ibid., 503.

Lastly, the trust is founded on a specific purpose, like a trust deed. Brown Weiss argues that:

> [t]he planetary trust is an *inter vivos* trust between generations of the human species. Its existence is implicit in the nature of the relationship between generations. It derives from an implied declaration by each generation that it holds the resources of the planet in trust for future generations. This intention is universally reflected in diverse human cultural and religious traditions.[198]

Several policy benefits might flow from applying Brown Weiss' proposal to oversight of the financial economy (along with other areas of human endeavour). It enunciates lucidly the inter-temporal problems associated with sustainable use of natural resources. Further, it emphasizes the stewardship responsibilities of the state to safeguard posterity's environmental needs, such as access to clean water and a habitable climate. And the planetary trust offers a conceptual framework to underpin specific practical measures to give effect to sustainable development.

Although no government or international body has formally legislated adoption of Brown Weiss' idea, it has been acknowledged sporadically. The Philippine Supreme Court explained in *Oposa v. Factoran*, when applying the trust concept to halt logging of primeval forest, '[n]eedless to say, every generation has a responsibility to the next to preserve that rhythm and harmony for the full enjoyment of a balanced and healthful ecology'.[199] Israel and Hungary have each created an ombudsman for future generations, with 'advisory authority to review legislation and executive acts to assess their impact on future generations and to make recommendations'.[200]

The planetary trust concept has its detractors, whose principal objections are that it is utopian, politically naïve, and at odds with the innate cognitive short-sightedness of most people and political institutions.[201] Brown Weiss' assumption about the universality of one generation's respect for the next is highly contentious.[202] Practical difficulties also abound; given the dynamic qualities of ecosystems – nature isn't a static resource – how would trustees define the parameters of the property to maintain in perpetuity? And as the concept implies stewardship of the environment over the long term, far into the future, to how many future generations should trustees be accountable? How would inter-generational conflicts between current and future beneficiaries be resolved, given that maintaining natural resources for posterity

---

198 Ibid., 504.
199 *Oposa v. Factoran*, [1993] SC, 30 July (Phil.).
200 International Human Rights Clinic, *Models for Protecting the Environment for Future Generations*, Harvard Law School, 2008, 2.
201 C. Woods and G. Clark, 'Intergenerational equity and long-term water management', School of Geography and the Environment, Oxford University, 2010.
202 Ibid.

requires reducing the current generation's share? The enormous difficulties in negotiating a new climate change treaty to update the Kyoto Protocol illustrate such quandaries on a global scale. Largely unrepresented future generations face difficulties in legally protecting their interests against the political clout of today's voters. Governments might be tempted to satisfy popular demands for resources now at the potential expense of posterity because of the political advantages.

Despite its imperfections, a trust-like structure is relatively well suited to the long-term sustainable management of the environment compared to other conceivable institutions, and complements the proposed fiduciary law changes to private sector institutions canvassed in this chapter. Concerns about the planetary trust's vulnerability to intervention by governments on behalf of current interests ignore the reality that any robust environmental regulation that impinges on economic development and private autonomy is politically controversial. Most environmental protective legislation, such as pollution control or environmental impact assessment requirements, implicitly raise judgements about inter-generational justice because of the trade-offs between economic development now and protection of natural resources for the long term. But to surrender to such objections, and allow environmental degradation to continue, offers only a more unpalatable future.

With some modifications, the public trust could be a viable meta-legal mechanism to promote sustainability and inter-generational equity in the context of the financial economy, along with other economic spheres. The trust institution is best organized at a national rather than an international level, at least for now. Placing the trustees in an independent, constitutionally protected entity should minimize political interference and expedient decisions. While national constitutions may be amended, and examples abound of states with ambitious environmental constitutional statements that are just rhetorical,[203] such a structure would still be more impervious to interference than the amendment of ordinary legislation. The trust could be enforced by injunctive relief to stop continuing or impending environmental harm, and collection of compensatory damages for any damages, in the same manner the public trust doctrine is upheld by domestic courts currently.

One serious challenge to adapting the public trust to fiduciary finance is that the public trust has served essentially as a *check* on governmental authority whereas RI requires a more positive stance by fiduciaries. The public trust serves to restrict agencies' ability to allocate rights to private parties to pollute and harm natural resources. By contrast, RI requires financiers not only to avoid corporate polluters, but also to invest positively in environmentally innovative companies and projects, such as clean-tech firms that may help mitigate climate change. This proactive role might best be undertaken by

---

203 For an excellent study on constitutionalizing environmental rights, see D.R. Boyd, *The Environmental Rights Revolution*, UBC Press, 2011.

public sector funds, especially SWFs. They can take a longer-term perspective that emphasizes conservation and inter-generational transfer of natural capital. SWFs need a legislative framework that prioritizes sustainable development while being obliged to consider advice from an ethics council to deal with sustainability issues in specific circumstances, and in a manner that minimizes opportunities for sitting governments to spend the fund's assets for current political advantage. Germany's GCSD is a rough example of the kind of multi-stakeholder, national advisory body that could fulfill this role.[204] Gordon Clark and Ashby Monk, who have scrutinized the practices of SWFs, emphasize the importance of both institutional design and governance in decision-making to promote long-term investing.[205] Creating advisory or supervisory bodies that have the imprimatur of legitimacy from a multi-stakeholder membership, and are insulated from everyday decision-making in the machinery of the state, may help nurture the long-term fiduciary perspective.

Obliging SWFs to invest over the long term rekindles an earlier discussion in this chapter about quantifying 'long term' in a measurably accountable manner for the purpose of a revised duty of prudent investing. Clearly, geological time-frames over thousands of years are incomprehensible. The upper limits of a workable definition of 'long term' for SWFs' investing might be about 50 years. This is the point by which global climate change impacts are forecast to become noticeable, such as sea-level inundation and hotter weather, if significant cuts to GHG emissions aren't made soon. This time-frame is also within the life expectancy of many people today and certainly their children, thus creating a political constituency to support sustainable investment. The sustainability paradigm, as already explained, offers the best available framework for addressing the cognitive difficulties in decision-making for future environmental integrity. It mitigates the perceptual barriers people face in valuing the future or conceptualizing the needs of posterity, by focusing on pragmatic, contemporary issues such as protecting endangered species or lowering carbon emissions. Decisions about such environmental issues do not depend on any vague, indeterminate time-frame or guessing what posterity's needs are. The focus is maintaining core ecological services and functions *now*, and keeping depletion of renewable resources within sustainable harvest rates.

Beyond state funds, the public trust responsibilities of financial economy regulators and managers could extend to supervision of the new long-term prudential investment standard or duty of environmental care, as previously elaborated in this chapter. The state's fiduciary responsibilities could be embellished through subsidiary powers and rules addressing ESG analysis and disclosure and providing incentives for green investing. Regulators,

---

204 Http://www.nachhaltigkeitsrat.de/en/home.
205 See http://oxfordswfproject.com.

to illustrate, might prohibit any financial transaction that encourages inappropriate environmental risk-taking. Financiers could also be required to conduct environmental assessments of their overall portfolios, and explain how they have used best practical means to promote sustainability.

Innovation in articulating and substantiating new understandings of fiduciary principles of long-term investment for sustainability cannot rely wholly on governmental legal intervention. The track record of environmental law practice, as documented in Chapter 1, reveals the barriers posed by bureaucratic inertia, intra-governmental conflicts, and inefficient and unwieldy decision-making. Through the more arms-length form of meta-regulation outlined in this chapter, states could establish the broad parameters for fiduciary responsibility and kick-start new governance procedures and models to stimulate innovation in partnership with civil society and market participants. The timidity of regulatory responses to the GFC owes partly to the regulatory capture by states of the financial industry they are supposed to regulate and the lack of incorporation of broad societal interests into the reform process.[206] The Occupy Movement is one symptom of their marginalization. Multi-stakeholder forums should be nurtured to help develop best-practice protocols for long-term investing, foster collaborative research (as already exemplified by the PRI Academic Network),[207] and articulate through codes of conduct new industry-wide expectations of appropriate investor behaviour.

States can harness these participants by providing spaces for public debate and advice about RI norms and practices, and by linking official governance to the plethora of private sector regimes in the RI industry. A novel idea, proposed by Saule Omarova, is for a 'Public Interest Council' to represent broad societal interests in safeguarding long-term financial systemic stability, with a mandate to feed public input into financial regulatory processes.[208] Such a body could also channel public input into existing governance regimes for the UNPRI, UNEP-FI and Equator Principles. Already, among possible areas of partnership between the state and the private sector, Denmark's financial reporting standard provides that specified business entities may satisfy government ESG-related reporting obligations if they have signed the UNPRI and undertake reporting regularly under that regime.[209] This hybrid approach, combining state and non-state institutions, points to the kind of governance partnerships that could help steer RI by substantiating innovative interpretations of fiduciary responsibility within industry cultures.

---

206 S.T. Omarova, 'Bankers, bureaucrats, and guardians: toward tripartism in financial services regulation', *Journal of Corporation Law* 37(3), 2012, 621–74, 632.
207 Http://academic.unpri.org.
208 Omarova, op. cit., 659–70.
209 Danish Financial Statements Act (Årsregnskabsloven), 2006, s. 99a.

Conclusions

Some in the RI movement have sought to acknowledge the public impacts of private investors, encouraging them to act more ethically and communally. Others dwell on the reverberations for investors themselves. Richard Burrett, Global Head of Project Finance at ABN AMRO, explains, 'the rapid decline and loss of biodiversity and the degradation of ecosystems that sustain it will impact economic growth and business profitability ... if the industry continues to operate in a business-as-usual mode'.[210] Investment as a means for social change has a long history, but so far its effectiveness, even when appealing to financial self-interest, has been modest. The RI industry's main success has been improving corporate ESG disclosure and analysis. While the industry has attracted a bandwagon of sorts, particularly in response to the UNPRI and evidence of ESG's financial materiality, the financial economy generally remains an impediment to environmental sustainability.

Many factors have shaped the fortunes of the RI market, with the legal system being particularly seminal. The custodial relationships under which financial assets are often managed attract legal responsibilities in fiduciary and trusts law. While the fiduciary prejudice against RI has somewhat abated recently, the consequentially more permissive legal climate for investing responsibly has not yet engendered profound change. The global environmental and financial crises ruptured any comfort about laissez-faire supervision of markets, requiring a rethink of basic assumptions about the governance of the financial economy, including to whom and for what investors are accountable. The vast public monies disgorged to bail out insolvent financiers leave taxpayers with a clear and legitimate interest in their own future. The sustainability paradigm offers a framework to address these crises by shifting investing to a long-term outlook that recognizes how natural capital underpins economic prosperity. The RI community officially acknowledges this paradigm and governments' role in facilitating change; UNEP-FI declared in its position statement for the global Rio+20 conference in 2012 that: 'the governments of the world have a unique opportunity at Rio+20 to create an enabling environment for the financial sector as a whole to fulfil its role in achieving a balanced, inclusive and green economy, as a pathway to sustainable development'.[211] But Rio+20 did not result in revolutionary change. The earlier unprecedented financial bailouts were a band-aid, ignoring most of the structural and systemic problems that foster unsustainable depletion of natural capital. A variety of legal models canvassed in this chapter can help reinvigorate RI, including to redefine the 'prudential investing' standard, more consultative and transparent governance of financial

---

210 R. Burrett, 'Putting a value on the priceless', in I. Cherneva (ed.), *The Business Case for Sustainable Finance*, Routledge, 2012, 79–89, 80.
211 UNEP-FI, *Position Paper on the United Nations Conference on Sustainable Development (Rio+20)*, UNEP-FI, 2012, 2.

institutions, more unified and robust oversight by state authorities under the auspices of the public trust doctrine, and greater multi-stakeholder, public–private partnerships.

These reforms for 'nature's trust' may seem far-fetched to some, but more radical and bitter alternatives to finance capitalism may one day be contemplated if we don't make this sector more environmentally accountable now. And this book has dealt with only one slice of the daunting governance challenges to sustainability; many economic sectors and entities that are less connected to the finance economy require different mechanisms for cultivating environmental responsibility. Until investors become public fiduciaries, RI will likely perambulate uninfluentially, led by a small cadre of steadfast social investors and a larger cohort of those more superficially engaged.

Index

Please note that 'RI' stands for 'responsible investment'. References to Tables are in *italic* print.

Aboriginal peoples, consultation of Canadian state with, 11, 98, 120, 180, 306
absolutist judgements, 8–9
accountability, fiduciary, 106, 281, 282
Accounts Modernization Directive (2003), EU, 185
Act of the Government Petroleum Fund (1990), Norway, 238
Action Plan, Equator Principles, 89–90
activism *see* shareholder activism
ad hoc fiduciary obligations, 111–12
Advisory Commission on International Law, Norway, 240
AFG (French asset management association), 146
agency capitalism, 156
Agreement on Financial Services (1999) (subsidiary GATS agreement), 25
Ahrens, Dan, 55
Albright Group, 242, 262
Amalric, Franck, 80
American Bald Eagle, saving of, 19
American Funds, 71
American Law Institute (ALI), 103; restatement of trust law, 6, 108, 133, 134, 182, 270
Amnesty International (AI), 64, 303
Anova Inc. Employee Retirement Pension Plan (Administrator of) v. Manufacturers Life Insurance Co, 127
anti-globalization movement, 35
apartheid regime (South Africa), divestment campaign against (1970s), 27, 50, 53, 60, 102, 233
APREC (French carbon research association), 261

arbitrage pricing theory, 16, 160
Aristotle, 31–2
Asia, currency collapses (1997), 16
asset management business, 82
asset turnover, 160–1
Associated Students of the University of Oregon v. Oregon Investment Council, 126, 143
Association of Chartered Certified Accountants (ACCA), UK, 187
Association of Superannuation Funds of Australia, 167–8
Australia: fiduciary finance law, 107; public trust doctrine, 309; superannuation funds, 167; *see also specific institutions, legislation and organizations*
Australian and New Zealand (ANZ) Bank, 43–4, 77–8
Australian Business Roundtable on Climate Change, 77
Australian Conservation Foundation (ACF), 171
Australian Council of Superannuation Investors, 173–4
Australian Future Fund, 235–6
Australian Securities and Investments Commission (ASIC), 172, 215, 223
Austria, pension funds, 171

bailouts, financial, 17, 99, 316
Baker, Mae, 161–2
Baku-Tbilisi-Ceyhan pipeline project, 90–1
Ball, David George, 139
Bana Etica, Italy, 55
Bank Act (1991), Canada, 197

Bank for International Settlements, 25
banks: Anglo-American, 77; 'bank-based economies,' 191–2; collapse of subprime mortgage market, US, 17, 110; 'defensive' banking, 190; duty of care, 197–200; Equator Principles *see* Equator Principles (EPs); ethical, 55–6; failures, implications, 17; fiduciary responsibilities, 194–7; and influence of RI, 60–1; information versus advice role, 198–9; lending portfolios, 79; project financing, 89; regulation for responsible finance, 190–4; social responsibility, 48; sustainable development, active financing, 190–1; in United Kingdom, 99; *see also* financial institutions; public financial institutions, RI by
BankTrack (NGO organization), 90, 94, 303
Barclays Bank, UK, 99
Basel Committee on Banking Supervision (BCBS), 100
Baue, William, 231
BCE Inc. v. 1976 Debentureholders, 127, 188
Belgium, pension funds, 171
beneficiaries: acting in 'sole' or 'best interests,' 117, 144; involvement in fund governance, 154, 174–81; *see also* trustees; trusts
Bentham, Jeremy, 30
Berle, Adolf, 65
'best-in-class' portfolio screening, 28
biological diversity, 279–80
biosphere, Earth, 7, 12
Birks, Peter, 106
Bishop of Oxford v. Church Commissioners for England, 115–16, 127
Black Economic Empowerment Act (2003), South Africa, 275
Blankenship v. Boyle, 124
Board of Trustees of Employee Retirement System of the City of Baltimore v. City of Baltimore, 135, 233
Bomann-Larsen, Lene, 282
bondholders, 78
boom and bust cycles, 16
borrowing needs, corporate, 57–8
bounded rationality, 164, 301
Bowman, Megan, 77
breach of fiduciary duty, remedies for, 140–3

Breen v. Williams, 107
Bristol and West Building Society v. Mothew, 112
British Columbia Investment Management Corporation, 99
British Petroleum (BP), 86
Brown Weiss, Edith, 307, 311, 312
Browne-Wilkinson, N. (Lord), 103
BT Pension Scheme, 78
Buren, Harry van, 47
Burrett, Richard, 316
Bursa Malaysia, 59
Business Corporations Act (2001), Canada, 76, 96
Business Corporations Act (2007), Oregon, 187
business judgement rule, 109

Caisse des Dépots et Consignations, 159
CalPERS (socially responsible public sector pension plan), 53, 166, 177, 233–4, 266; Double Bottom Line initiative, 63; and responsible investment, 62, 67, 68, 78, 96, 98
CalSTERS (public sector pension fund), 98
Calvert Social Index Fund, 208
Canada: Aboriginal peoples, consultation of Canadian state with, 11, 98, 120, 180, 306; corporate engagement, 64; Enbridge Northern Gateway Project, 67, 98–9; enlightened shareholder value, 188; fiduciary character of relationship of government to aboriginal citizens, 11; impact financing, 63; Ontario Securities Commission, 99; Ontario Teachers Pension Plan, 73–4; pension fund governance, 113; pension fund legislation, 65, 144; public trust doctrine, 309; repeal of fisheries habitat protection controls, 21; Shareholder Association for Research and Education (SHARE), Vancouver, 71, 95–6, 98; Social Investment Organization, 49; Social Sciences and Humanities Research Council, 41; *see also specific institutions, legislation and organizations*
Canada Pension Plan (CPP), 73, 237
Canadian Securities Administrators (CSA), 99
Cancer Stage of Capitalism, The (McMurtry), 13

Index 321

Cancun climate change conference (2010), 7
Caparo Industries v. Dickman, 198, 289
capital adequacy standards, 271
capital asset pricing model, 16
carbon dioxide, atmospheric, 19
Carbon Disclosure Project (CDP), 72, 254, 261
carbon markets, 16
care and prudence duty *see* prudence duty
Carl J. Herzog Foundation, Inc. v. University of Bridgeport, 183
Center for Sustainability Studies (CVces), 304
Ceres Principles, 84, 97, 98
CFA Centre for Financial Market Integrity and Business Roundtable for Corporate Ethics, 158
charitable 'mission-based' investors, 114, 181–90
Charities Act (1993), UK, 114, 183
Charity Commission, UK, 114
Chesterman, Simon/Chesterman Report, 242–3, 262
China, Trusts Law (2001), 144
Choi, Stephen, 68
CIES (France), 257
City Code on Takeovers and Mergers *see* Takeover Code, UK
civic investor thesis, 79, 80
civic regulation, 88
civil law systems, fiduciary-like responsibilities in, 24; 3s, 143–6
Clark, Gordon, 17, 18, 66, 163, 187, 229, 314
Climate Bonds Standard and Certification Scheme, 53
climate change, 1, 2, 13, 33, 70, 137; Cancun conference (2010), 7; and environmental law, 20–1
Climate Change Conference, Copenhagen (2009), 261
Climate Change Lawyers Network, Canada, 99
Climate Group, 95
Climate Principles: A Framework for the Financial Sector (2008) (UNEP-FI), 94, 95
climate risks, 62
ClimateWise Principles, 200–1
codes of conduct, 47, 72; and investor collaboration, 79–95; RI codes, 83–8; as voluntary mechanisms (RI codes), 86, 87
cognitive relativism, 32–3
collateralized debt obligations, 165
collective action barriers to RI, 79–83
collective bargaining agreements, 167
Collevecchio Declaration on Financial Institutions and Sustainability (2003), 84, 87, 304
'command-and-control' regulation, 22
commodities market boom, international, 55
common heritage of mankind, 307
Commonwealth Trading Bank of Australia v. Smith, 196
Communication on Corporate Governance (2003), European Commission, 185
Community Development Entities, 275
community impact investing, 62–3
Community Reinvestment Act (CRA) (1977), US, 192–3
Companies Act (2006), UK, 186, 187, 275, 276–7
Companies Act (2012), India (proposed), 275
complicity, 3, 30–1, 281–2
'comply or explain' requirement, UK, 76
Comprehensive Anti-Apartheid Act (1986), US, 233
Comprehensive Environmental Response Compensation and Liability Act (CERCLA) (1980), US, 196–7
Confederation of Indian Industry, 189
conflicts of interest, 41, 65, 71, 81, 294; charities, 182; duty of environmental care, 292; fiduciary finance law, 109, 116, 117, 131, 140, 141, 145, 146; profitability, versus environmental costs, 8, 15–16, 20, 55; retail and institutional finance, fiduciary law in, 167, 184, 195, 220, 221, 222, 224; in trusts, 117
Conley, John, 88, 186
Convention on Biological Diversity (1992), 122
Convention on Cluster Munitions (2009), 253
Convention on the Elimination of All Forms of Discrimination against Women (1979), 122–3
Cook, Jackie, 64, 99

Cooper, Jeffery, 116, 147
cooperative banks, Germany, 192
corporate engagement, 28, 38; creditors' engagement, 76–8; current patterns, 67–74; fiduciary finance law, 139; and influence of RI, 63–78, 64; legal context, 74–6
corporate finance theory, 56–8
corporate governance, 23, 65, 74; Anglo-American systems, 184; India, reform in, 189–90; Johannesburg Stock Exchange (JSE) Listings Requirements Relating to Corporate Governance, 59, 189; King Committee on Corporate Governance, South Africa, 189; OECD Principles, 84–5; outsourcing, 71; private influence, 68
corporate securities, turnover, 160–1
corporate social responsibility (CSR), 4, 33, 190, 283; codes of conduct, 84, 85
corporations *see* financial corporations
Corporations Act (2001), Australia, 206, 212
cost-benefit analysis, 30
Costello, Paul, 254–5
cottage cheese, Israeli boycott against (2011), 57
Coulson, Andrea, 77
Coumans, Catherine, 303
Council of Institutional Investors, 72
Council on Ethics, Norway, 239, 241, 242, 243, 245–6, 248, 249, 262
Cowan v Scargill, 117–18, 125, 127, 128, 137, 178
CPP Investment Board (CPPIB), 237
credit market, 61–2
credit rating agencies, 164, 165
creditors' engagement, 76–8
Cronin, John, 298

damages, 142–3
Davis, Ron, 115, 129, 175–6
'decentered' regulation forms, 22
decision-making, ethical considerations, 9, 10
Declaration on Climate Change by the Financial Services Sector (2007) (UNEP-FI), 93–4
Deepwater Horizon explosion (2010), 86
defined benefit (DB) schemes, 175

defined contribution (DC) schemes, 175, 180
Denmark, pension funds, 171
deontological ethics, 29–30, 242
Department for Business, Innovation and Skills, UK, 186
Department of Labor, US, 139, 142; Employee Benefits Security Administration, 135–6
deregulation of financial markets, 23, 61
Desjardins Ethical Canadian Balanced Fund, 209
disclosure: pension fund investment, rules regarding, 169–74; RI policies and practices, 154, 213–20; standards, 213–16
discretionary control, in fiduciary relationships, 110, 130
divestment campaigns: South Africa, 27, 50, 53, 60, 102, 233; Sudan, 53, 211, 233
Dodd-Frank Wall Street Reform and Consumer Protection Act (2010), US, 221–2
Dogwood Initiative, 98
Domini Social Investments, US, 209, 211
Donoghue v. Stevenson, 222, 289
Donovan v. Walton, 123–4
Dow Jones Sustainability Indexes, 58, 86
Drucker, Peter, 176
due diligence: ESG, 53; financial, 28, 191
Dutch Association of Investors for Sustainable Development, 193
duty of care: banks, 197–200; financial intermediaries, 222
duty of prudent investing, 130, 285–8; *see also* prudence duty

EarthRights International, 246
Eccles, Robert, 54
ecological crises, and global financial crisis, 12–18
Eco-Management and Audit Scheme (EMAS), EU, 85, 88
Economic and Social Council, UN, 297
economic growth: as main goal of nations, 12–13; and well-being, 14–15

Edwards, Tony, 45
efficient market hypothesis, 16
Ekobanken (Sweden), 55–6
elasticity concept, 56–7
Elkington, John, 294
Employee Benefits Security Administration (EBSA), Department of Labor, 135–6
Enbridge Northern Gateway Project, Canada, 67, 98–9
Endangered Species Preservation Act (1966), US, 19
Enhanced Analytics Initiative (EAI), 28, 84
enlightened shareholder value (ESV), 185–6, 188, 189, 190
Entine, Jon, 176
Environment Fund, Norway, 240
environmental, social and governance (ESG) *see* ESG (environmental, social and governance) criteria
environmental care, duty of, 288–94
environmental judgement rule, 293
environmental law, 18–26; as 'damp squib', 18–19; France, 215; function, 19; and global financial crisis, 20, 21, 25–6; limitations, 19–20, 21, 26; regulation methods, 21–2
environmental management systems (EMSs), 85
Environmental Protection Act (1990), UK, 289
Environmental Protection Act (1993), South Australia, 289–90
environmental standards, importance, 7–8
environmentally sustainable development, 1
Equator Principles Association, 89
Equator Principles (EPs), 87; ANZ as signatory to, 44; and responsible investment, 28, 84, 88–91
ERISA (Employment Retirement Income Security Act) (1974), US: fiduciary finance law, 112, 121, 124, 132–3, 136, 139, 149; fiduciary standards, 204; pension funds, 169
ESG (environmental, social and governance) criteria, 3, 4, 5, 91; and fiduciary finance law, 104, 137, 138; and history of RI, 27–8; and influence of RI, 51, 53, 54, 57, 66, 71; retail and institutional finance, 159, 164, 170, 173, 174, 177, 185, 218, 223; sovereign wealth funds, 236
Essay on Population (Malthus), 13
ethical complicity, 31
Ethical Council, Sweden, 234, 235
Ethical Funds, Canada, 67, 96, 98, 211
ethical investment, 4, 40; *see also* responsible investment (RI)
ethical relativism, 32
ethics: decision-making, ethical considerations, 9, 10; deontological, 29–30, 242; ethical foundations of RI, 297–300; ethical investment, 4, 40; governance frameworks for ethical deliberation in RI, 300–4; Guardians' ethical investment policies and practices (New Zealand), 252–5; NGPF-G ethical investment mission/revised ethical guidelines, 240–5; philosophical approaches to RI, 29–33; RI's ethical miasma, negotiating, 294–7; SWFs, ethical and financial mandates, 227–32; theory, 298; virtue ethics, 31–2
Ethics Council, Norwegian Government Pension Fund - Global, 12
European Commission, 65, 68
Evans v. London Cooperative Society, 123
externalities, 14, 79; failure to control, 55
Extractive Industries Transparency Initiative (EITI), 72, 85, 261
ExxonMobil, 254

'facts,' 32
FairPensions, UK, 102, 168, 172–3, 276–7
Federal Reserve System, Board of Governors, 193
Fidelity (mutual funds group, US), 71, 207, 212
fiduciary, defined, 23–4, 112
fiduciary accountability, 106, 281, 282
fiduciary finance, for wealth of planet, 1–12
fiduciary finance law, 2, 5, 101–52; and bank governance, 190–200; care and prudence duty, 130–40; common law systems, 101–2, 140; concept, 101; evolution of fiduciary law and trusts, 105–10; financial actors' fiduciary

responsibilities, 110–14; governing documents, obeying, 114–16; impartiality duty, 126–30; legal framework, 24; liability and remedies, 140–3; loyalty, duty of, 23, 109, 116–26; reform requirement, 1, 6–9, 9–11; and responsible investment, 104–5, 150–1; retail and institutional finance *see* retail and institutional finance; whether social responsibility or fiduciary folly, 101–5

fiduciary law: and bank governance, 190–200; boundaries, jurisdictional differences, 106; evolution, 41, 105–10; fiduciary responsibility versus social and environmental considerations, 101–5; function, 105–6; proscriptive versus prescriptive duties, 107; reform, 269; in retail and institutional finance, 153–225; in retail funds, 209–11; roots, 107–8; and social responsibility, 103–4; terminology, 41, 109; *see also* fiduciary finance law

fiduciary relationships, 24; ascertaining, 110–12; factual circumstances, arising from, 111; governance frameworks for ethical deliberation, 301; trust as quintessential example of, 110–11, 120

fiduciary responsibilities: *ad hoc* fiduciary obligations, 111–12; ascertaining, 110–12; civil law systems, fiduciary-like responsibilities in, 24, 143–6; court rulings, 24; and enlightened shareholder value, 185–6; and environmental law, 23, 24; fiduciary finance, 110–14; financial institutions, 2, 36, 194–7, 199–200; in institutional contexts, 112–14; insurance companies, 203–4; legal doctrine, 2; loyalty, duty of, 116–26; pension funds, 165–9; remedies for breach, 140–3; state, 11–12, 311; United Nations Principles for Responsible Investment, 93

finance: altering cost of, 56–63; as 'grease to the economy,' 43

finance capitalism, and environmental unsustainability, 1

financial advisers, 220–4; suitability standard, 222, 223

financial corporations, 142, 184–90; reform requirement, 10–11

financial institutions, 5, 20; fiduciary responsibilities, 2, 36, 194–7, 199–200; *see also* banks; public financial institutions, RI by

Financial Market Authority, France, 146

Financial Reporting Council (FRC), UK, 76

Financial Services and Markets Act (2000), UK, 96, 206, 212, 218, 305

Financial Services Authority (FSA), UK, 96, 305; rules on shareholder control, 74–5

Financial Services Commission, Ontario, 149

Finn, Paul, 306

Fisch, Jill, 68

Flannery, Tim, 104

Flannigan, Robert, 105–6, 140, 141

Foley v. Hill, 194, 195

Fondaction, Canada, 63

foreseeability standard, 288–9, 291

Forest Monitor (UK group), 64

Fortune 1000 companies, 155

Forum for Sustainable and Responsible Investment (US-SIF), 48–9

fossil fuels, investment in, 55, 79

France: environmental law, 215; Financial Market Authority, 146; pension funds, 170–1

free riders, 65

French Pension Reserve Funds (FRR), 255–62, 263, 265; establishment and legal framework, 255–8; Responsible Investment Committee of Supervisory Board, 260; RI policies and practices, 258–62; Supervisory Board, 256–7, 258, 259, 260

Freshfields Bruckhaus Deringer (UK law firm), 90

Freshfields report (2005), 33, 40, 96, 103, 118, 122, 150; pension funds, 168

Friedman, Milton, 4

Fuller vs. Kendon Eco Estate Ltd and Others, 292

Fund Votes, US, 72

fungible and cosmetic standards, responsible investment, 57, 205–9

Future Fund Act (2006), Australia, 235

Future Fund Board of Guardians, Australia, 235

Index 325

Future Fund Ethical Investment Guidelines, Australia, 236

Garnaut Review, Australia, 95
Gay, George, 59
Gemeinschaftsbank, Germany, 62
General Agreement on Trade in Services (GATS) (1997), 25
German Council for Sustainable Development (GCSD), 277, 314
Germany: as bank-based economy, 191–2; civil law system, 145; co-determination, labour, 44–5; impact financing, 62; institutional equity funds, 155–6; *Mittelstand* (small and medium-sized German companies), 49, 192; pension funds, 170; small RI sector, 44, 49, 50, 145, 192; Sustainability Code (2012), 277; *see also specific institutions, legislation and organizations*
GES Investment Services, 234
Getzler, Joshua, 163
GFC *see* global financial crisis (GFC)
Gifford, J., 122
Glass Lewis, 71
Global Alliance on Banking for Values, 63
Global Canopy Programme, 304
Global Compact, UN, 84, 86, 230, 242, 253, 260; preamble, 283
global financial crisis (GFC), 1, 3, 7, 11, 99; and ecological crises, 12–18; and environmental law, 20, 21, 25–6; market risks, systemic, 162, 163–4, 165; and public fiduciary, 269, 305
Global Impact Investing Network, 62
Global Reporting Initiative (GRI), 72, 303–4
globalization, 25, 87; anti-globalization movement, 35
GmbHs (limited liability companies), Germany, 49
Goldcorp's Marlin mine, Guatemala, 303
good faith standard, 186, 204–5
governing documents, obeying, 114–16
Government Pension Fund Norway, 239
Graaf, Frank Jan de, 285
Graver, Hans Peter/Graver Committee, 240, 241
Green Bonds, World Bank, 243
"green" companies, 136

Green Party, Australia, 236
Green Party, New Zealand, 254–5
Green Project Directive, 193–4
Green Project Initiative, Netherlands, 275
Greenfield, Kent, 291
greenhouse gas (GHC) emissions, 7, 314
'Grenelle I' Act (2009), France, 215
'Grenelle II' Act' (2010), France, 257
gross domestic product (GDP), 14, 15, 17, 159
Guardians of New Zealand Superannuation, 250, 262, 264; Board, 250–1; ethical investment policies and practices, 252–5
Guidelines for Multinational Enterprises (OECD), 85
Guidelines for Norges Bank's Work on Responsible Management and Active Ownership (Guidelines II), Norway, 243, 244–5, 251
Guidelines for Observation and Exclusion from the Government Pension Fund Global's Investment Universe (Guidelines I), Norway, 243, 244

Habermas, Jurgen, 37
Haldane, Andrew, 286
Halvorssen, Anita, 264–5
Hardin, Garrett, 80
Harvard College v. Amory, 131–2
Hausbank phenomenon, Germany, 77
Hawken, Paul, 14
Hawley, James, 79, 109, 159, 162
Heal, Geoffrey, 14
Healthy Food Financing Initiative, US, 275
Hebb, Tessa, 18, 177
Heinkel, R., 59
Henderson Global Investors, 300
'herding' behaviour, 109, 285
Hermes (institutional investor), 67
historical evolution of RI, 26–9
Hodgkinson v. Simms, 5
Howell, Robert, 255
human rights/human rights abuses, 30, 233, 281
hydrologic cycle, 3

Illinois Central Railroad Co. v. Illinois (*Illinois Central*), 307

326 *Index*

impact investing, 62–3
impartiality duty, 126–30
incommensurability issue, 8
index tracking funds, 58, 109
India, corporate governance reform, 189–90
influence of RI, 43–100; altering cost of finance, 56–63; business drivers, 55–6; codes of conduct, 83–8; concepts, 46; corporate engagement, 63–78; financial rationale of RI, 50–6; impact on corporate behaviour, evaluating, 46–7; measurement difficulties, 47; private corporate governance influence, 68; shareholder activism and dialogue, 63–6, 69–70, 72, 73; size of market, 48–50; and social investors, 57, 58, 59; ways of exerting, 46; *see also* codes of conduct; responsible investment (RI)
Innovest Strategic Value Advisors, New Zealand, 252
institutional investors: and collective action barriers to RI, 81–2; current engagement patterns, 67; examples, 154; fiduciary responsibility versus social and environmental considerations, 103; growing presence, 18, 65; MPT principles, adherence to, 66; Myners Report, UK, 161; planning, 158–9; rise of, 154–7
Insurance Commission, 200
insurance companies, 200–5; failures, implications, 17; fiduciary responsibilities, 203–4
Insurance Companies Act (1991), Canada, 202
Interfaith Center for Corporate Responsibility (ICCR), US, 30, 47, 64, 298
inter-generational equity, 313
Internal Revenue Code, US, 180
International Accounting Standards Board (IASB), 164, 219
International Cooperative and Mutual Insurance Federation (ICMIF), 201–2
International Corporate Governance Network, 68, 72
International Finance Corporation (IFC), 89
International Financial Reporting Standards, 219
International Labor Organization, Worst Forms of Child Labor Convention (1999), 122
International Organization for Standardization (ISO): 14001 standard, 85; 26000 standard, 84, 283
International Organization of Securities Commissions, 25
International Round-Table Meetings on Finance (UNEP), 303
intra-generational equity, 36
Investment Advisors Act (1940), US, 162, 221
Investment Company Act (1940), US, 206, 212
Investment Industry Regulatory Organization of Canada (IIROC), 223–4
Investment Management Association, UK, 161
Investment Modernization Act (2003), Germany, 145, 206
Investor Group on Climate Change, 254
Investors Environmental Health Network, 97
Irish Law Reform Commission, 148
Islamic law, 107
ISS, 71
Italy, pension funds, 171

Jantzi, Michael, 38; Michael Jantzi Research Associates, 96
Janus Capital Group v. First Derivative Traders, 223
Japan, 49
Jemel-Fornetty, Hager, 268
Johannesburg Stock Exchange (JSE) Listings Requirements Relating to Corporate Governance, 59, 189
John Hancock Mutual Life Insurance Co. v Harris Trust and Savings Bank, 204
Johnston, Keith, 285
Joly, Carlos, 270
Joy, Martin, 293
J.P. Morgan, 62
JP Morgan Chase, 99–100
JP Morgan Chase Bank v. Springwell Navigation Corporation, 197
'jurdification' process, 21
Justinian, Emperor, 306

Kanner, Allan, 308
Kant, Immanuel, 29–30

Kay Review (2012), UK, 58, 158, 220, 294
Kinder, Peter, 214
King Code III, 59, 189
King Committee on Corporate Governance, South Africa, 189
King v. Talbot, 132
KiwiSaver Act (2006), New Zealand, 171
Klassen, Johann, 59
Klein v. First Edina National Bank, 195
Knight, Eric, 66, 163, 187
Kurt, Christopher, 31
Kyoto Protocol, 313

labour economics, 120
laissez-faire approach, 207
Langbein, John, 106
Law Commission, UK, 102
Law of Trusts, The (Scott), 122
Law on the Implementation of the Directive of Shareholder Rights (ARUG), Germany (2009), 75–6
legal accountability of investor, redefining parameters, 277–85
legal standing, 143
legal structures, for RI values, 37–9
liability and remedies, 140–3; breach of trust versus breach of fiduciary duty, 141, 142
liberalization, market, 20, 24
life insurance, 201
Lloyd's Bank v. Cobb, 199
Local Government Pension Scheme (Management and Investment of Funds) (Amendment) Regulations (1999), UK, 170
Logsdon, Jeanne, 47
London Principles of Sustainable Finance, 88
Long-Term Investors Club, 159
long-term perspective, need for, 2, 4, 10, 285–8, 314; *see also* short-termism
loyalty, duty of, 23, 109, 116–26
Luhmann, Niklas, 279

MacBride Principles, US, 233
Macleod, Michael, 97
Malthus, Thomas, 13
Managed Investments Act (1998), Australia, 212
Manitoba Law Reform Commission, Canada, 148
Maple Leaf Foods Inc. v Schneider Corp, 188
Marathon Club, UK, 159
market economy, 13–14
market risks, systemic, 17, 162–5, 286
Maroochy Shire Council v. Barns, 292
Martin v. Edinburgh District Council, 134–5, 138
Massachusetts v. EPa, 287
Maxwell scandal (1991), 113
McConvill, James, 293
McMurtry, John, 13
Means, Gardiner, 65
Megarry, Robert, 118, 125, 127, 178
Mercer Investment Consulting, 137
Mibanco (Peru), 56
Michael Jantzi Research Associates, 96
microfinance, 62
MicroFinance Network, 63
Miles, Kate, 83
Mill, John Stuart, 30
Millennium Ecosystem Assessment (MEA) (UN, 2005), 6
Minister of Water Affairs and Forestry v. Stilfontein Gold Mining Company Ltd, 189
Ministry of Finance, Norway, 243, 246, 247
misrepresentation, controlling, 216–20
Mission Investors Exchange, 63
mission-based investors, 114, 181–90
misunderstanding of financial risks, 163–4
Mittelstand (small and medium-sized German companies), 49, 192
modern portfolio theory (MPT), 16; influence of RI, 52, 66; market risks, systemic, 138, 162, 163
Modernisation Directive, EU, 187
Monbiot, George, 104
Monk, Ashby, 229, 314
Monks, Robert, 18, 79
Monsanto, 246
Montreal Protocol on Substances That Deplete the Ozone Layer (1989), 19
moral relativism, 32, 33
morality, 29–30; *see also* ethics
mortgages, sub-prime, 17
MPT *see* modern portfolio theory (MPT)
Mulligan (Deceased), Re, 133, 269
multinational focus, 40

multi-stakeholder approaches, 12, 37, 88, 91, 181; public fiduciary, 314, 315, 317; and UNEP-FI, 93–5
mutual fund governance: and investor passivity, 211–13; in United States, 71, 72, 99
mutual funds (retail funds), 205–20
mutual insurers, 201
Myners Report on institutional investment, UK, 161

Nader, Ralph, 64
National Association of Pension Funds, UK, 72, 161
National Employment Savings Trust (NEST), UK, Ethical Fund, 237–8
National Environmental Management Act (NEMA) (1998), South Africa, 289, 292
national measures, 10
National Pension Insurance Funds (AP Funds) Act (2000), Sweden, 234
National Pensions Reserve Fund Act (2000), Ireland, 232
National Pensions Reserve Fund (NPRF), Ireland, 296
National Roundtable on Environment and the Economy (NRTEE), 164; Task Force on Capital Markets and Sustainability, 96
National Trust, UK, 183
Natural Capital Declaration (2012), 304, 310
Natural Capital Institute, 209
natural capital/resources, 2, 13, 14, 16, 55, 310; non-renewable resources, depletion, 3, 34, 314, 316
natural law theory, 30
nature conservation, 34
'nature's trust' concept, 2, 39, 311, 317; see also public fiduciary; trusts
Nebraska Investment Council, 147
negligence law, 222
NEI Investments, 67
Netherlands, 62, 144; Dutch Association of Investors for Sustainable Development, 193; Green Project Initiative, 275
Network for Sustainable Financial Markets, 3
New Markets Tax Credit Program (2000), US, 275
New South Wales (NSW) Trustee Act (1925), Australia, 114, 115

New York Stock Exchange, 160
New Zealand Superannuation Fund (NZSF), 73, 138, 227, 228, 250–5, 263, 264, 265; Guardians' ethical investment policies and practices, 252–5; legislative and institutional framework, 250–2
NGOs (non-governmental organizations), 52, 64, 77, 87, 234; Amnesty International, 64, 303; BankTrack, 90, 94, 303; EarthRights International, 246; environmental, 36, 58, 219; Rainforest Action Network, 303
NGPF-G see Norwegian Government Pension Fund - Global (NGPF-G)
Nicholls, D. (Lord), 117
non-maleficence, ethical norm of, 288
non-renewable resources, depletion, 3, 34, 314, 316
Norges Bank Investment Management (NBIM), 239, 247, 249
Norges Bank (Norway's central bank), 239, 246, 248, 249, 251
Northern Ireland, religious discrimination in, 233
Northern Rock, collapse of (UK), 162
Norwegian Government Pension Fund - Global (NGPF-G), 138, 227, 228–9, 238–49, 263, 265, 266; ethical investment mission, 240–2, 281; Ethics Council, 12; France compared, 260, 262; institutional and legal structure, 238–40; New Zealand compared, 252, 253; revised ethical guidelines, 242–5; RI practices, 245–9
nutrient cycle, 3
NZ Council for Socially Responsible Investment (NZCSRI), 255

Obama, Barack, 21, 305
obedience, fiduciary duty of, 106
occupational pension funds, 175, 202
Occupational Pension Schemes (Investment, and Assignment, Forfeiture, Bankruptcy etc) Amendment Regulations (1999), UK, 148, 167
Occupational Pensions Directive, EU, 117, 144
Occupy Movement, 26, 35–6, 298, 299, 315

OECD (Organization of Economic Cooperation and Development): Guidelines for Multinational Enterprises, 85; Principles of Corporate Governance, 84–5
Office of the High Commissioner for Human Rights, 96
Olson, Mancur, 80
Omarova, Saule, 315
Ontario Law Reform Commission, Canada, 118
Ontario Securities Commission, 99
Ontario South African Investment Act, 128
Ontario Teachers Pension Plan, 73–4
OPCVMs (French investment companies), 146
Oposa v. Factoran, 312
Orts, Eric, 23
Ottawa Convention on Anti-Personnel Mines, 240
outsourcing, investment management, 66
Oxford University SWF Project, 229
ozone-depleting chemicals, phasing out, 19

parens patriae, state acting as, 20, 308–9
Park, Jacob, 97
Parsons, Talcott, 279
passive capital, 275
passive investors, 15, 211–13
Pax World Management Corporation (PWMC), 217
Pembina Institute, 98, 219–20
Penner, J. E., 140, 141
Pension Benefits Standards Act (1985), Canada, 121, 167
pension fund governance: beneficiaries' involvement in, 154, 174–81; Canada versus United Kingdom, 113; legal reforms to democratize, 178–81; policy considerations, 174–8
pension funds, 40, 61, 65; beneficiaries, involvement in fund governance, 154, 174–81; Canadian versus UK governance, 113; as 'civic investors,' 80; defined benefit schemes, 175; defined contribution schemes, 175, 180; definition/background, 165–6; fiduciary types, 112; governance *see* pension fund governance; institutional characteristics and fiduciary responsibilities, 165–9; investment disclosure rules, 154, 169–74; transparency-based regulation, 169–70, 172, 216; and trusts, 105–6, 166–7; in United Kingdom, 54, 113
Pensions Act (1995), UK, 112, 148, 169, 170, 178
Pensions Act (2004), UK, 178–9
People & Planet v. HM Treasury, 186
Peoples Department Stores v. Wise, 188
Permanent Building Society (in liq.) v Wheeler, 106
permissive legislation, 286–7
PetroChina, 246
Pharma Futures project, 83
Pharmaceutical Shareowners Group, 83
philosophical approaches to RI, 29–33
phronesis (practical wisdom), 32
Pioneer Fund, 205
planetary trust concept, 307, 311, 312–13
policies and practices (RI), disclosure, 154, 213–20
'polluter pays' principle, 34
pollution control, 20, 21
population growth, 13
portfolio management, 81; *see also* modern portfolio theory (MPT)
postmodernism, 32
post-structuralism, 32
precautionary principle, 34
principal–agent relationship, 24, 110, 111, 112
Principles for Sustainable Insurance, 200
private corporate governance influence, 68
privatization strategy, 20
process standards, 84
Product Disclosure Statements (PDS), 171, 214–15
profitability, versus environmental costs, 8, 15–16, 20, 55
project financing banks, Action Plan requirement, 89–90
prospectus, the, 214
Prospectus Directive, EU, 215
proxy advisory providers, 71
prudence duty, 5, 10, 116, 130–40; consequences for RI, 133–40; duty of prudent investing for long term, 285–8; evolution of prudent investment standard, 130–3; fiduciary law, 105, 138; and short-termism, 109

330 *Index*

public fiduciary, 267–317;
  democratization of fund governance and RI industry, 294–304; duty of prudent investing for long term, 285–8; environmental care, duty of, 288–94; existing legal reforms for RI, 273–7; investor legal accountability, redefining parameters, 277–85; state as nature's trustee, 304–15; sustainable investing for, 285–94
Public Finance Management Act (1999), South Africa, 189
public financial institutions, RI by, 232–8; Australian Future Fund, 235–6; Canada Pension Plan, 237; Swedish AP funds, 229–30, 234–5, 263; US state and municipal funds, 232–4
public interest, acting in, 7–8
public policy and legal reforms, 95–100
public responsibility, notion of, 5
Public Sector Pension Plan Act (1999), British Columbia, 179
public stock corporations, Germany, 49
public trust doctrine, 2, 11, 304–9

Quakers, 27
quasi-fiduciaries, 227–8

Rainforest Action Network, 303
Rajan, Raghuram, 109
Ransome, W., 295–6
Rees, William, 14
reflexive law, 22–3, 37, 280
reform of fiduciary finance law, 9–11
Regents of the University of Michigan v. State of Michigan, 126
Regulation Fair Disclosure (Regulation FD), US, 75
relationship investing, 73–4
relativism, 32–3
remedies, and liability, 140–3
Responsible Care, 85
responsible finance, obstacles to, 157–65; short-termism, 16, 55, 109, 157–62, 288; systemic market risks, 17, 162–5
Responsible Investment Committee, New Zealand, 252
responsible investment (RI), 1–42; altering cost of finance, 56–63; business case style, 27–8, 295; in Canada, 49; causes and issues, 27; codes of conduct, 83–8; collective action barriers to, 79–83; definition issues, 1–2, 26–39; democratization of RI industry, 294–304; disclosure of policies and practices, 154, 213–20; duty of care, consequences for, 133–40; environmental law and conflicted state, 18–26; ethical foundations, 297–300; ethical miasma, negotiating, 294–7; existing legal reforms for, 273–7; and fiduciary finance law, 104–5, 150–1; financial rationale, 50–6; fungible and cosmetic standards, 57, 205–9; Germany, weak in, 44, 49, 50, 145, 192; historical evolution, 26–9; industry definitions, *208*; influence, 43–100; legal structures, for RI values, 37–9; mutual fund governance and investor passivity, 211–13; Norwegian practices, 245–9; philosophical approaches to, 29–33; by public financial institutions, 232–8; public policy and legal reforms, 95–100; RI 'industry'/'movement,' 2, 28; size of market, 48–50; social returns, desire to generate, 45–6; and sovereign wealth funds, 231; statutory reform of relevance to, 146–9; sustainability, 34–7; underlying rationale, 45–6; *see also* socially responsible investment (SRI)
retail and institutional finance, 9, 153–225; charitable 'mission-based' investors, 114, 181–90; and collective action barriers to RI, 82; competition, 71; disclosure of RI policies and practices, 154, 213–20; fiduciary law and bank governance, 190–200; financial advisers, 220–4; financial corporations *see* financial corporations; good faith standard, 186, 204–5; insurance companies, 200–5; misrepresentation, controlling, 216–20; mutual fund governance, 71, 211–13; obstacles to responsible finance, 157–65; pension funds *see* pension funds; retail funds, 205–20; rise of institutional investors, 154–7; *see also* banks; financial institutions
retail funds, 205–20; fiduciary law in, 209–11

Index 331

Rio+20 conference, 316
Risk Limitation Act (2008), Germany, 75
risk-adjusted returns, 118
Riskmetrics, 68
risks: climate, 62; fiduciary finance law, 109–10; systemic, 17, 162–5, 286
Rivoli, Pietra, 58
Rogers Communication v. Buschau, 121
Roman law, 107, 306
Ruggie, John, 281, 283
Ruggie Guiding Principles on business and human rights, 96

S&P 500 Index, 70
Safeguard Policies for social and environmental impact assessment (SEIA), 89
Sakhalin II oil and gas project, 91
Salic law, 107
Sampford, C., 295–6
Santiago Principles (2008), 230, 264–5
Saunders v. Vauthier, 121
Sax, Joseph, 11, 306–7
'science wars,' 32–3
Scott, A. W., 122
Scott v. National Trust, 183
Securities Act (1933), US, 165
Securities and Exchange Commission (SEC), US, 96, 98, 219
Securities Commission, Ontario, 218
securities regulation, 217–18
Selangor United Rubber Estates v. Cradock, 197
self-interest, financial, 2, 4, 27, 32, 53, 150, 205, 272, 316
self-reflection, 37
separate legal personality (separation of ownership from management), 15
Shanghai Stock Exchange, 59
shareholder activism, 10, 139; and dialogue, 63–6; resolutions, 69–70, 72, 73
Shareholder Association for Research and Education (SHARE), Vancouver, 71, 95–6, 98
Shepheard, Mark, 293–4
Shorebank, US, 62, 63
short-termism, 16, 55, 157–62, 288; *see also* long-term perspective, need for
Siemens, 246
Simpson, Anne, 268–9
'sin stocks,' 50, 55

Singapore Technologies Engineering, 240
Singer, Peter, 31
SMEs (small and medium-sized companies), Germany, 49
Social Investment Organization (SIO), Canada, 49, 95
social investors, 3, 4, 7, 23; and influence of RI, 57, 58, 59, 63; legal structures, for RI values, 38–9; philosophical approaches to RI, 30, 31; shareholder activism and dialogue, 63
social justice, principles of, 35
social responsibility, terminology, 103
Social Responsibility 26000 standard, ISO, 84
Social Sciences and Humanities Research Council, Canada, 41
socially responsible investment (SRI), 41, 45, 57, 215
Soederberg, Susanne, 277
'sophisticated investors' (SI), 165
South Africa: divestment campaign against apartheid (1970s), 27, 50, 53, 60, 102, 233; fiduciary responsibility versus social and environmental considerations, 103; Johannesburg Stock Exchange (JSE) Listings Requirements Relating to Corporate Governance, 59, 189; King Committee on Corporate Governance, 189; pension fund law, 168
South African Broadcasting Corporation Ltd and Another v. Mpofu, 189
South African Trust Investments Act (1988), Ontario, 149, 180
South Sea Company, collapse (1700s), 131
Southern Counties Fresh Foods Ltd, Re, 186
Sovereign Wealth Fund Institute (SWFI), 228, 229
sovereign wealth funds (SWFs), 227–66, 305, 314; ethical and financial mandates, 227–32; French Pension Reserve Funds, 255–66; New Zealand Superannuation Fund *see* New Zealand Superannuation Fund (NZSF); Norwegian Government Pension Fund - Global *see* Norwegian Government Pension Fund - Global (NGPF-G); as political fiduciaries, 231; as proponents of sustainability, 262–6; public financial institutions,

RI by, 232–8; and responsible investment, 231
Spain, 45
Sparkes, Russell, 169
species, disappearance of, 19
speculation, 16
sphere of influence concept, 283
sponsors, financial, 20
Stakeholder Relationship Committee, India, 190
standard finance theory, 58
state: and environmental law, 18–26; fiduciary responsibilities of, 11–12; as nature's trustee, 304–15; as *parens patriae*, 20, 308–9
Statement by Banks on Environment and Sustainable Development (1992) (UNEP-FI), 93
Statement by Financial Institutions on the Environment and Sustainable Development (1997) (UNEP-FI), 93, 94
Statman, Meir, 220
Stern Report (2007), UK, 286
Stewardship Code, UK, 76
Stewart, James, 282
Stewart v. Phoenix National Bank, 195
Stock Corporations Act (1965), Germany, 69
strict liability, breach of fiduciary duty, 140, 141
Stromberg, Glorianne, 213
subjectivism, moral, 32
subprime lending, US housing market, 17, 110
Sudan, human rights abuses in, 233
Sudan Accountability and Divestment Act (2007), US, 211, 233, 286
Sudan Divestment Task Force Highest Offenders List, 53
Sullivan, Leon/Sullivan Principles, 83, 84
Superannuation and Retirement Income Act (2001), New Zealand, 250, 251
superannuation funds, 167
Superannuation Industry (Supervision) Act (1993), Australia, 167, 179
Superannuation Legislation Amendment (Choice of Superannuation Funds) Act (2004), Australia, 179
Suriya and Douglas v. Midland Bank, 198
sustainability: concept, 33, 34–7; EC Treaty, 34; and environmental law, 23; financial implications, 54; goal of, 3, 8, 9, 10, 11, 18, 35; indicators, 35; public fiduciary, sustainable investing for, 285–94; sustainable development, active financing, 190–1; SWFs as proponents of, 262–6; *see also* unsustainability
Sustainability Code (2012), Germany, 277
Sustainalytics, 96
Swedish AP funds, 229–30, 234–5, 263
SWFs *see* sovereign wealth funds (SWFs)
systemic market risks, 17, 162–5, 286
systems theory, 279

Takeover Code, UK, 74–5
Takeover Panel, UK, 75
Talisman Energy, 60
Taskforce on the Churches and Corporate Social Responsibility, Canada, 64
Teck Corporation Ltd v. Millar, 188
teleological theories, 30, 31, 242
Teubner, Gunther, 22–3, 37, 280, 292
Thornton, R., 136
TIAA-CREF, shareholder activism by, 70
Tinto, Rio, 73
'toxic debt,' 17
transnational firms, 24
transparency-based regulation, 169–70, 172, 216
Triodos, Netherlands, 62
trust deeds, 114–15, 312
Trustee Act (1995), Manitoba, 287
trustee–beneficiary relationship, 141
trustees: accountability of, 106; versus corporations, 108–9; duties of, 5; state as nature's trustee, 304–15; *see also* fiduciary responsibilities; trusts
trusts, 5, 6, 41; accountability of trustees, 106; breach of obligations, 141, 142; and evolution of fiduciary law, 41, 105–10, 119; Middle Ages, 107–8; and pension funds, 105–6, 166–7; public trust and financial economy, 309–15; public trust doctrine, 2, 11, 304–9; state, as nature's trustee, 304–15; trust as quintessential example of fiduciary relationship, 110–11, 120; *see also* beneficiaries

Index 333

Trusts of Land and Appointment of Trustees Act (UK), 1996, 180
TSC Industries Inc. v. Northway Inc, 217
Tung, Frederick, 77

UEB Industries Ltd Pension Plan, Re, 120
ultra vires doctrine, 290–1
Uniform Prudent Investor Act, US, 133, 182
Uniform Trust Code (UTC), US, 108, 116, 146–7
United Kingdom (UK): pension funds, 54, 113; stock markets, 58; Takeover Code, 74–5; *see also specific institutions, legislation and organizations*
United Nations Environment Programme (UNEP), 6; International Round-Table Meetings on Finance, 303
United Nations Environment Programme-Finance Initiative (UNEP-FI), 12, 28, 51, 303; Climate Principles: A Framework for the Financial Sector (2008), 94, 95; codes of conduct and collaboration, 80, 88, 93–5; Declaration on Climate Change by the Financial Services Sector (2007), 93–4; Freshfields report (2005) *see* Freshfields report (2005); Insurance Working Group established by, 200; Statement by Banks on Environment and Sustainable Development (1992), 93; Statement by Financial Institutions on the Environment and Sustainable Development (1997), 93, 94
United Nations Principles for Responsible Investment (UNPRI), 5, 12, 28, 72, 230; Advisory Council, 91; codes of conduct and collaboration, 80, 84, 86, 88, 91–3; and fiduciary finance law, 102; fiduciary responsibilities, 93; limitations, 92; Secretariat, 92–3, 159
United Nations (UN): climate change conference (Cancun, 2010), 7; Economic and Social Council, 297; Global Compact, 84, 86, 230, 242, 253, 260, 283; Millennium Ecosystem Assessment (2005), 6; *see also* United Nations Environment Programme-Finance Initiative (UNEP-FI); United Nations Principles for Responsible Investment (UNPRI)
United States (US): American Bald Eagle, saving of, 19; corporate engagement, 75; impact financing, 62, 63; mutual fund industry, 71, 72, 99, 212; shareholder advocacy, 69; state and municipal funds, 232–4; subprime lending, housing market, 17, 110; *see also specific institutions, legislation and organizations*
United States v. State Water Resources Control Board, 307
universal owner thesis, 79, 80, 81, 159, 267–8
Universities Superannuation Scheme (USS), UK, 67–8, 82–3, 166
UNPRI *see* United Nations Principles for Responsible Investment (UNPRI)
unsustainability, 1, 5, 6, 23
urban smog pollution, scrapping of limits (US), 21
Uruguayan pulp mills project, 91
utilitarianism, 30, 31

values, 9; legal structures, for RI values, 37–9; World Values Survey, 14
VanCity Credit Union, Canada, 63
Vanguard (mutual funds group, US), 71, 207, 212
Verity and Spindler v. Lloyds Bank, 199
Vickers report, UK, 99
virtue ethics, 31–2
Vogel, David, 95

Walker Report, UK (2009), 69, 76
Waring, Peter, 45
Water Disclosure Project, 261
Water Use Permit Applications for the Waiahole Ditch, Re, 307
Watson Wyatt Worldwide Thinking Ahead Group, 181
Weinrib, E.J., 110
welfare state, norms and institutions, 21
well-being, and economic growth, 14–15
Westpac, 61, 77
Wiggen, Oddny, 282
Williams, Andrew, 79, 159
Williams, Cynthia, 88, 186
Winslow Green Funds, 207

Withers v. Teachers' Retirement System, 129–30
Wójcik, Dariusz, 17
Wood, Mary, 11, 306–7, 310
Wood, Stepan, 282–3
Woods, C., 136–7
Woods v. Martins Bank, 195

World Bank, 89, 243
World Economic Forum (WEF), 157–8
World Values Survey, 14, 32
Worst Forms of Child Labor Convention (1999), ILO, 122

Yaron, Gil, 137, 150